In the Words of Wellington's Fighting Cocks

In the Words of Wellington's Fighting Cocks

The After-action Reports of the Portuguese Army during the Peninsular War 1812–1814

Moisés Gaudêncio and Robert Burnham

Foreword by
Rory Muir

Pen & Sword
MILITARY

First published in Great Britain in 2021 by
Pen & Sword Military
An imprint of
Pen & Sword Books Ltd
Yorkshire – Philadelphia

ISBN 978 1 52676 168 2

Typeset by Mac Style
Printed and bound in Great Britain by
CPI Group (UK) Ltd, Croydon, CR0 4YY

MIX
Paper from
responsible sources
FSC
www.fsc.org   FSC® C013604

Pen & Sword Books Limited incorporates the imprints of Atlas, Archaeology,
Aviation, Discovery, Family History, Fiction, History, Maritime, Military,
Military Classics, Politics, Select, Transport, True Crime, Air World,
Frontline Publishing, Leo Cooper, Remember When, Seaforth Publishing,
The Praetorian Press, Wharncliffe Local History, Wharncliffe Transport,
Wharncliffe True Crime and White Owl.

For a complete list of Pen & Sword titles please contact

PEN & SWORD BOOKS LIMITED
47 Church Street, Barnsley, South Yorkshire, S70 2AS, England
E-mail: enquiries@pen-and-sword.co.uk
Website: www.pen-and-sword.co.uk

Or

PEN AND SWORD BOOKS
1950 Lawrence Rd, Havertown, PA 19083, USA
E-mail: Uspen-and-sword@casematepublishers.com
Website: www.penandswordbooks.com

Contents

Foreword

Every serious historian who has written about Wellington's campaigns in the Peninsula has acknowledged the vital role played by the Portuguese Army which, from 1810 onwards, made up a crucial part – generally about one third – of his forces. But it has been difficult to go much beyond this, and to provide detail about the Portuguese role in particular operations. There are abundant sources for the British army, ranging from Wellington's own voluminous *Dispatches* to the letters, diaries and memoirs of hundreds of officers and men who served under him. However, there is no comparable wealth of material for the Portuguese side of the story: a few memoirs by British officers serving in the Portuguese Army; three doctoral theses written in the 1970s; and, more recently, an excellent biography of Marshal Beresford, the British commander of the Portuguese Army; but not much else. This makes it almost impossible to give due credit to the Portuguese for their contribution to Wellington's victories, even when a historian is actively trying to do so. It is as if two actors dominated a film, but one had all the good lines and the other barely spoke.

It is therefore with immense pleasure that I welcome the publication of this volume of official reports made by Portuguese and British officers serving in the Portuguese Army, written soon after each action and describing the role their unit had played, together with the return of the casualties it suffered. This is a primary source of great importance which is a major contribution to increasing our knowledge of the role played by the Portuguese Army and giving a voice to its officers. Like all primary sources, these reports need to be read with care: officers' reputations were at stake and they naturally tried to present events in the best possible light, although as they were reporting to senior officers who had often been on the spot and had themselves seen what had happened, their scope for creatively rewriting the course of events was limited, and the alert reader can deduce much that is only implied.

The reports begin in the middle of 1812 with the Salamanca campaign, and, while it is unfortunate that the reports on the earlier campaigns are not available, this does at least have the advantage of drawing attention to the Portuguese role in the final three years of the war, which has previously received even less attention than their role in the campaigns of 1810 and 1811. Yet it was in these campaigns that the Portuguese Army reached its highest state of efficiency. After the battle of Vitoria, Sir Thomas Picton, who had been extremely sceptical about the Portuguese troops when he first arrived in the Peninsula, wrote home that 'The Portuguese attached to the Division fully equalled the English during the whole day, and showed an Example of Steadiness and gallantry that equals them to any Troops in the World.' He then underlined the sentence to give it greater emphasis. A couple of months later the army's Judge-Advocate wrote that, 'Nothing can look in a higher order than the Portuguese troops. They are cleaner than our men; or look so, at least. They are better clothed now by far, as they have taken the best care of their clothes: they are much gayer, and have an air, and a je ne sais quoi, particularly in the Caçadores both the officers and the private men, quite new in a Portuguese.' And Wellington himself, in the midst of the difficult fighting in the Pyrenees, famously described his Portuguese troops as 'the fighting cocks of the army'.[1]

In publishing these reports Moisés Gaudêncio and Robert Burnham have helped to fill one of the most grievous gaps in the sources for the Peninsular War and have taken an important step to ensuring that Wellington's 'fighting cocks' receive the credit that they deserve.

Rory Muir

Acknowledgements

Moisés Gaudêncio. For almost two decades, in an extraordinary work, the Arquivo Histórico Militar scanned and made available digitally to the public thousands of documents related to Portuguese military history. Without it, this book would not be possible, so I would like to thank the successive directors and all the staff of the archive.

I also wish to thank everyone who helped me to develop my enthusiasm for the study of Portuguese military history at the time of the Napoleonic Wars. Among them, I would like to mention João Torres Centeno, Jorge Quinta Nova, Anthony Gray, and my fellow co-author, Robert Burnham, who for many years managed the Napoleon Series site and its discussion forum, where I fed myself with the immense knowledge available there.

Last but not least I want to thank my wife Glória for the help she gave me but specially for her patience and understanding.

Robert Burnham. Once again, I would like to thank my friends who are always willing to answer questions on the British Army: Rory Muir, Ron McGuigan, Michael Crumplin, and Steve Brown. Rory was one of the earliest supporters of this book and graciously agreed to write its Foreword. In the twenty-five years that I have worked with Ron, I have only ever stumped him once with one of my queries. I thought I might challenge him this time with some of the obscure British officers who served in the Portuguese Army, but once again he quickly answered my questions. Michael, who is my go-to source on the British medical system of the Napoleonic Wars, provided most of the information on the British medical personnel who served in the Portuguese Army. I can always count on Steve to point me in the right direction when I am stuck. This book also saw two new members added to the team: Marcus de la Poer Beresford, who freely shared his extensive knowledge of Marshal Beresford and the British officers in the Portuguese Army, and Lucy Bamford, whose knowledge of art held by different museums was instrumental in tracking down portraits. I also would like to thank the various individuals, libraries, and museums that provided portraits: Mark Thompson, Nick Haynes, Nick Lipscombe, Garry Willis, Suzie Pack-Beresford, Heritage Mississauga, Anne S.K. Brown Collection, State Library of Victoria, Australia, the Royal Military Academy Sandhurst, and the Regimental Museum of The Royal Welsh. Finally, there is my wife Denah, who, as always, has patiently listened to my anecdotes about men who have been lost to history and gave me wordsmithing advice when needed. I know she is ready to have the dining room table back!

Introduction

Sir Charles Oman published his seven volume *History of the Peninsular War* in the early twentieth century. It has become the premier history of the Napoleonic conflict in the Iberian Peninsula and has been reprinted many times. It was a ground-breaking work that used numerous official reports, memoirs, diaries, and letters to bring to life the campaigns and battles of the seven-year-long war. Although he did use French and Spanish primary sources and their military archives, the same cannot be said about Portuguese sources. In the Preface to Volume II, he stated that he compared English and Portuguese documents,[2] while he wrote in the Preface of Volume IV that he was in debt to Rafael Reynolds who 'obtained for me in Lisbon a number of rare Portuguese volumes, most especially a complete set of Marshal Beresford's *Ordens do Dia* for the whole Peninsula War',[3] yet he never mentions going to the Portuguese Military Archives and accessing the documents there. Why he did not do so is unknown, because a large amount of information about the Portuguese, especially for the years 1812–1814, was available.

Professor Oman's *History of the Peninsular War* tells the story of Wellington's campaigns mostly through the accounts left by British soldiers. At times, the reader is left with the distinct impression that it was Wellington and his British Army that won the war. Yet what about the Portuguese? By 1812, 40 per cent of Wellington's Army were Portuguese soldiers. Is Oman's portrayal of them accurate? Did he downplay their efforts and contributions by either ignoring them or by using mostly British sources to tell their story? Either way, when you compare the battles and actions that are described in the reports below to the descriptions in his *History* you will often be left with a vastly different picture of the Portuguese Army, especially in the latter years of the war.

Portuguese Reports and Returns

In 2017 Moisés Gaudêncio was doing research in the Portuguese Arquivo Histórico Militar[4] when he discovered a series of reports written by commanders on several battles of the Peninsular War. He spent the next three years searching the archives and discovered 273 of these reports, including 158 after-action reports and 115 casualty returns. These documents cover thirty-seven different engagements, including 7 major battles,[5] 3 sieges,[6] and 27 smaller actions.[7]

More than half of the reports were made at the division and brigade level, but infantry regiments and caçadores battalions are well represented also (see Table 0.1).

Table 0.1: Reports and Returns

Type of Unit	# of Reports	# of Returns
Portuguese Division	12	10
Infantry Brigades	68	61
Cavalry Brigades	2	1
Infantry Regiments	22	18
Cavalry Regiments	2	1
Caçadores Battalions	41	17
Infantry Battalions	3	1
Artillery Commanders	8	6
Total	158	115

Marshal William Beresford, the commander-in-chief of the Portuguese Army, issued an order on 31 July 1810 that required commanders to write a report any time their unit was in combat. According to that order, if the units were grouped in independent brigades, they were to send the reports and casualty returns to the brigade headquarters (HQ). The commander should write his own report on the action and compile the brigade's casualty returns. These would be sent to the Adjutant General (AG) Department at the Portuguese HQ. If the brigades were in a Portuguese division, the commanders should send their reports to the division HQ and the division commander should add his own report and send everything to the AG Department. This clearly meant that Beresford wanted the reports to follow the chain of command.

An analysis of the documents shows that this process varied according to circumstances, particularly if the brigade commanders were present commanding and watching the unit's actions. In this case they often sent only their own report and the brigade's casualty return. If they were not eyewitnesses, they normally included the reports of the subordinated units' commanders, attached to their report.

Beresford's order did not mention what was to be done when a Portuguese brigade was assigned to an army division, since in July 1810 this practice had just begun. However, analysis of the reports shows that those brigade commanders wrote two reports. One report, together with a casualty return, was sent to the division commander. The division commander probably used the information to write his own report to Wellington. We found that sometimes the division commanders attached the brigade reports to their own report and sent them to Wellington's HQ.

The second report, along with any reports written by subordinate commanders, and the casualty return were sent to the Adjutant General of the Portuguese Army, Brigadier General Manuel de Brito Mozinho.[8] The AG always accompanied Beresford's HQ on campaign, so Beresford certainly read them. The reports published in this book are the ones sent to the Portuguese AG.

The reports had no specific format, but they were to describe what the unit did, identify the officers and soldiers who distinguished themselves, and include casualty returns for the unit, with the names of the officers who were killed, wounded, or missing. The officers who were required to submit the reports were the commander of the Portuguese Division, brigade and regimental commanders, caçadores battalion commanders, and artillery commanders. Infantry battalion commanders only wrote one if they were detached from the regiment.

Although at times 80 per cent of the brigade commanders were British, 230 (85 per cent) of the reports were in Portuguese, while 40 were in English. Surprisingly, two of the reports were in French.[9] Of the reports in English, 42 per cent were from three officers: Generals Thomas Bradford and Manley Power each produced seven reports, while Colonel James Douglas had three.

An examination of the vocabulary and phrasing of sentences, etc., strongly suggests that almost all the reports in Portuguese that were signed by British officers were dictated by the officer to a Portuguese aide who wrote it down. Supporting this is the fact that the signature on the report was in a different handwriting from the text of the reports. It is likely that the British officers were not comfortable enough with the language to write a detailed official report. Their ability to speak Portuguese was probably good, but it is likely they had not mastered the formal writing that the report required. For that reason, and to be certain of what was written, and to have some confidentiality, some like Bradford and Power chose to write in English. These reports in English were written by the commanders themselves and were translated later into Portuguese by someone in the Portuguese AG Department.[10] A few wrote in French because they could, and they knew that most of the Portuguese senior officers, such as AG Mozinho, understood French.

All the reports in the book were originally in Portuguese, unless noted otherwise. The reports written in Portuguese were translated by Moisés Gaudêncio. The reports in English are transcribed verbatim. Moisés also translated the two reports in French.

Organization of the Book

In the Words of Wellington's Fighting Cocks is the story of the Portuguese Army in the final years of the Peninsular War, as told by its commanders. Although we do provide an overview of the campaigns and battles of 1812 to 1814, it is only from the perspective of officers in the Portuguese Army. It does not cover political and military events that they did not participate in. When we discuss the battles and sieges, the focus is on what the Portuguese did, and we only mention British units in relationship to the Portuguese.[11] We recommend that if you have questions about what the British brigades and regiments were doing, you consult Professor Oman's *History of the Peninsular War* or a book on a specific battle, such as Rory Muir's *Salamanca 1812*.[12]

The book is organized in four parts. The first section consists of two chapters. Chapter 1 is a short history of the Portuguese Army up to 1811. It discusses the major events that shaped it from 1793 to 1812. It also examines its organization and the formation of its brigades, and provides tables of organization for infantry and cavalry regiments, caçadores battalions, artillery brigades, and its engineers. Chapter 2 explains why so many of the brigades and regiments were commanded by British officers. We recommend you read both chapters before you start reading the reports.

Three sections are devoted to the reports and are organized in the same way. Each section covers a specific year and begins with a chapter that discusses the events, campaigns, battles, and sieges in which the Portuguese Army participated in that year. This chapter also looks at the organization of the army at the beginning of the campaign and the changes that occurred among the commanders during that campaign. The section is chronologically organized with a chapter for each battle or siege, or in the case of the minor actions, several that occurred in the same month. For example, the section on 1812 has a chapter each on Salamanca, the siege of Burgos, and the retreat to the Portuguese border. This last chapter has reports on the defence of Valladolid's bridge, the retreat from Madrid, combats at Alba de Tormes and at the fords of the Tormes river, Aldea Lengua, and Villa Muriel.

The reports are arranged in each chapter starting with one flank (usually with whichever flank was in action first) and working across to the units on the other flank. Then they are organized by unit and its subordinate units. For example, the Portuguese Division has its reports, and these are followed by those of its 2nd Brigade. Reports from the 2nd Brigade's two regiments, the 2nd and 14th Infantry, would come next. Then would follow reports from the 4th Brigade and its regiments.

Many commanders also included casualty returns for their units. These returns' tables are collected at the end of each chapter.

We also include two appendices that provide short biographies of the officers who wrote the reports. Appendix A contains biographies of the Portuguese officers, while Appendix B is about the British officers.

Due to the many battles covered by the reports, providing a map to show the actions of the units is not feasible. We recommend you check the Napoleon Series Map Archives at www.napoleon-series.org/military-information/maps/. It has many British and Portuguese maps. Furthermore, we were not able to include all the supplementary material we found in our research, that will be of value to the reader. This material includes listings of the commanders of the brigades, regiments, and battalions, and detailed biographies of the writers of the reports. These data are now available on the Napoleon Series website.

Spelling of Names

In the early nineteenth century there was no formal rule on family names. The nobles and *fidalgos* would often add to their first names a combination of names derived from both their father's and mother's family names. This led to confusion. Because an individual could have so many names, he was usually only known by two or three. For example, before he became Count de Amarante, Francisco da Silveira Pinto da Fonseca Teixeira was commonly known as Francisco da Silveira. Likewise, Francisco Homem de Magalhães Quevedo Pizarro was called Francisco Pizarro. The British were often confused by the different names used for the same officer and when writing journals or memoirs they used a variety of names and spellings. This makes it difficult sometimes to determine who they were writing about.

In the translations and transcriptions of the reports and returns the spellings of names are presented verbatim. However, in our narrative we use the modern spelling of the name.

The same goes for the spelling of the names of British officers. The names in the reports in this book are as they were spelt or used in the original reports. The modern spelling or form of the name is noted. The first time a British officer is mentioned, his full name and British regiment will be shown in the note.

Spelling of Locations

The spelling of the names of cities, towns, villages, and rivers mentioned in the reports was often phonetic and, except for major cities, highly creative. Furthermore, even if there was an acceptable way of spelling the location, its name may have changed over the past 200 years. We kept the original spelling in the report, but if it was different from the modern spelling or if the name of the location had changed, we gave the modern spelling or name in the note.

Names of Portuguese Units

Through much of the war, Portuguese brigades were known by their commanders' names, such as Pack's Brigade. In August 1813 each of the infantry brigades received a number. The Portuguese cavalry brigades continued to be named after their commanders. Furthermore, only the Portuguese numbered their brigades. British and French brigades were named after their commanders. If it is a numbered brigade, such as the 3rd Brigade, it is always referring to a Portuguese infantry brigade.

Portuguese infantry regiments are referred to by their regimental number and the word infantry, for example the 17th Infantry. British infantry regiments are called by their regimental number and the word Foot, such as the 5th Foot. Portuguese cavalry regiments are called by their regimental numbers and the word cavalry, for example the 4th Cavalry. British cavalry regiments are called by their regimental number and the type of cavalry they were, such as the British 7th Hussars. French infantry and cavalry always have the word French in front of the regiment's name, such as the French 3rd Hussars.

List of Abbreviations

AAG	Assistant Adjutant General
ADC	Aide-de-Camp
AG	Adjutant General
AGC	British Army Gold Cross
AGM	British Army Gold Medal
AQMG	Assistant Quartermaster General
CB	Companion of the Most Honourable Order of the Bath (from 1815)
cm	centimetre
DAG	Deputy Adjutant General
DAQMG	Deputy Assistant Quartermaster General
DQMG	Deputy Quartermaster General
EOPS	Employed on Particular Service
Hon.	Honourable
HQ	Headquarters
KB	Knight of the Most Honourable Order of the Bath
KCB	Knight Commander of the Most Honourable Order of the Bath (from 1815)
KCTS	Portuguese Knight Commander of the Tower and Sword
KGA	King's German Artillery
KGCB	Knight Grand Cross of the Most Honourable Order of the Bath
KGL	King's German Legion
km	kilometre(s)
Kt	Knight
KTS	Portuguese Knight of the Tower and Sword
LLL	Loyal Lusitania Legion
OD	Portuguese *Ordens do Dia* (Orders of the Day)
QMG	Quartermaster General
Regt	Regiment

Chapter 1

The Portuguese Army from 1793 to 1812

It would be almost impossible to understand the Portuguese Army in the latter years of the Napoleonic Wars without some historical background on how it became such an integral part of Wellington's Army. This chapter briefly examines Portugal's involvement in the Wars of the French Revolution, the Peninsular War, and the Civil War that divided Portugal in the 1820s and 1830s. We then continue with an overview of the Portuguese military system at the time of the Peninsular War. There is not room to explain in detail the changes, reforms, and reorganizations that the army underwent in this period for that is a book in itself, but we will provide enough information to help the reader's understanding of the events referred to in the reports and biographies.

Years of Turmoil

Despite being isolated from the upheaval of the early years of the French Revolution, Portugal, at the request of Spain, and supported by Britain, joined the 1st Coalition's war against the French Republic in 1792. In 1793 a Portuguese fleet of eighteen ships carried a Portuguese division to Catalonia. This division, of 5,500 men and 22 artillery pieces, was under the command of General John Skelater. It took part in the campaign in Rossillon, southern France, and in the eastern Pyrenees, and Catalonia, and remained there until peace was declared in 1795.

From that date on, France and Spain, now allies, put continuous pressure on Portugal to quit its traditional alliance with Britain. Portugal resisted both diplomatic pressure and military threats until 1801, when it was forced to defend itself against a Spanish invasion, supported by France, the so-called War of the Oranges. Between February and June it engaged in a disastrous campaign and was forced to sign the Treaty of Badajoz on 6 June 1801. In accordance with the treaty, among other harsh conditions, Portugal agreed to close its ports to British shipping and to hand over the town of Olivença to Spain.

Taking advantage of the Peace of Amiens, the Franco-Spanish defeat at Trafalgar, and Napoleon's engagements in central Europe, Portugal delayed complying with the treaty on the closing of its ports to the British for fear of British reprisals against its overseas possessions. Napoleon's Berlin Decree of 21 November 1806 establishing the continental blockade left Portugal in a difficult position, being one of the last European countries open to British commerce. The evasive behaviour of the Portuguese government was no longer to be tolerated, and Napoleon ordered the occupation of Portugal.

In November 1807 a French army under General Andoche Junot, supported by several Spanish divisions, invaded Portugal. The Portuguese Queen Maria and her court fled to Rio de Janeiro, Brazil. Prior to leaving, João, the Prince Regent, ordered that no resistance to the French was to be made. The Prince also appointed a government council in Lisbon to rule the kingdom and deal with the French. In February 1808 Napoleon declared that the Portuguese royal house of Bragança was no longer the legitimate rulers of Portugal. The government council was deposed, the Portuguese military system dismantled, and a corps of Portuguese troops was sent to France. They were organized there as the *Legion Portugaise*.

In the spring of 1808 Spain revolted against the French, who had begun to occupy the country. In June an insurrection against French rule erupted in the northernmost and southernmost provinces of Portugal. Local *juntas* were formed to organize the rebellion. The following month the French sent forces into Beira and Alentejo provinces to suppress the insurrection but had little success. About this time the *Junta Suprema* at Oporto took political control of the northern provinces. In August the British sent a small army under Wellington to assist the Portuguese. A small force hastily raised in the northern provinces by the Oporto *Junta* marched south to join Wellington and their combined army defeated the French at Roliça and Vimeiro. Another small force raised in the southern provinces also marched on Lisbon. The defeat of the French Army resulted in the Convention of Cintra, where it was agreed that the French would evacuate Portugal. The British reinstated the Portuguese government council, known as the Regency, which started regaining political control of the kingdom and organizing an army.

The Regency realized that they needed to modernize their army and looked for an outsider to do it. They asked the British government for an officer to take command of the new army. In March 1809 Lieutenant General William Beresford was appointed commander-in-chief of the Portuguese Army with the rank of marshal. With the support of a group of British officers who were commissioned into the Portuguese Army, he began to organize the Portuguese Army in accordance with British standards. Later that month Wellington, who had been recalled to Britain in October to testify at an inquiry about the Convention of Cintra, arrived back in Portugal to take command of the British Army in Portugal. He also took command of the Portuguese Army with the rank of marshal general. Over the next five years he led the combined Anglo-Portuguese Army in the Peninsular War.

After the war ended in April 1814 Wellington's Army was disbanded and the Portuguese troops marched back to Portugal. The royal court, which had been in Brazil since 1807, decided not to return to Portugal. In 1815 the Prince Regent ordered the raising of the *Divisão dos Voluntários Reais do Príncipe*[13] from the Portuguese Army, under the command of General Carlos Frederico Lecor. The division was shipped to southern Brazil with the objective of invading the *Banda Oriental,* part of the Spanish territories of La Plata, which would become modern Uruguay. From July 1816 to 1820 the division's Peninsular veterans and Brazilian forces fought and defeated the Uruguayan resistance. In the year following *Banda Oriental* was annexed with the name of *Cisplatina* province, whose capital was the city of Montevideo.

In August 1820 a liberal rebellion broke out in Portugal and by September it had brought down the Regency in Lisbon. It installed a parliament known as the Cortes, which wrote and implemented a written constitution for the country. The following year the former Prince Regent, now King João VI, returned to Lisbon and assumed his new role as a constitutional king.

In 1822 Brazil declared its independence from Portugal. Prince Pedro, King João's eldest son, was named Emperor of Brazil. Several army garrisons remained loyal to Portugal, namely those at Bahia, Montevideo, and Maranhão. Fighting broke out, but the Brazilians prevailed and the last Portuguese troops in South America left Montevideo in 1824.

In 1823 Prince Miguel, the king's youngest son, with the support of the army, led a coup-d'état against the Cortes that ended the liberal experience. Portugal returned to an absolutist regime and Prince Miguel was appointed commander-in-chief of the army.

In the next eleven years Portugal was torn apart by the conflict between two parties with irreconcilable visions for the future of the country. The conservative Absolutist Party headed by Prince Miguel fought the liberal Constitutional Party, supporting Princess Maria's claim to the throne, and led by her father, the former Emperor of Brazil, Prince Pedro, leading to an all-out civil war that lasted from 1828 to 1834. The Portuguese Civil War – also known as the Liberal Wars, the Miguelite War, and the War of the Two Brothers – ended with a liberal victory and the establishment of a constitutional monarchy in Portugal.

The Portuguese Military System

The Role of the Sovereign

From 1777 the sovereign of Portugal was Queen Maria but due to her mental illness her son, Prince João, governed in her name from 1792. In 1799 he took the title of Prince Regent and became King João VI in 1816 when his mother died. The sovereign ruled through his ministers and several councils. These ministers were called secretaries of state and they formed the government. Since the seventeenth century the most important ruling body in the army's chain of command was the *Conselho de Guerra* or War Council, which managed the daily administration of the army, the appointment of its officers, and reviewed sentences of courts-martial. Another council, the *Junta dos Três Estados*, was responsible for the finances and supply of the army. The post of Secretary of State for Foreign Affairs and War was created in 1736 to increase the king's control over military matters and to coordinate the action of the different administrative bodies of the army. Over time, the modernization of the military led to an increase in the influence of the secretary at the expense of the War Council. Beginning in 1801 several departments were set up as part of the *Real Erário*[14] to manage supplies, transport, and finances of the army, leaving the *Junta dos Três Estados* with no military responsibilities.

In November 1807, when the Queen and the Prince Regent left for Brazil to escape the French invasion of the country, they appointed a government council to run the kingdom and deal with the French. The council was assisted by secretaries for several administrative branches of the government. The French disbanded this council, which the British would call the Regency. When it was reinstated in September 1808 after the expulsion of the French from Portugal, Brigadier General Miguel Pereira Forjaz was appointed its Secretary for War and later also the Secretary for Foreign Affairs. He was the Regency's executive official for military matters throughout the Peninsular War and until 1820. From 1809 both the British Ambassador in Lisbon and Wellington, as marshal general, were part of the Regency, and could vote on military and finance matters.

The Regency in Portugal was part of the Prince's government, which was in Rio de Janeiro. On paper the Regency had limited powers and its decisions were subject to approval by the government in Brazil. However, because it took so long to get a decision from Brazil, the Regency's autonomy on military matters was extensive, but the government in Brazil always had the last word.

The Army's Commanders

The military forces of the kingdom had at their head a commander-in-chief who reported directly to the sovereign and had the rank of *marechal general* or marshal general. Below him was the *marechal dos exércitos*, the marshal of the forces,[15] whose duty was to command the army in the field. In the eighteenth century these positions were often held by foreign officers. This command structure was not always in place and there were long periods in which the positions were not filled, especially in peace time. The primary reason was that the foreign holders took long leaves of absence and were out of the country. Although the two positions were separate and had different responsibilities, at one time at least the two jobs were held by the same person.[16]

The position of marshal general was held by the Count of Schaumburg-Lippe from 1762 to his death in 1777, but he was absent for many years; by the Duke de Lafões from 1791 to 1801; by the Duke of Wellington from 1809 to 1814; and by William Carr Beresford from 1816 to 1820.

The position of marshal was held by Christian von Waldeck from 1797 until his death in 1798; by Karl von Goltz from 1800 to 1806, but he was absent from 1802; Count Vioménil served in his place but he too was only in Portugal briefly; and by William Carr Beresford from 1809 to 1816.

Military Provinces
In the late eighteenth century Portugal was divided into seven military provinces (or *Governos de Armas*), which coincided with the administrative provinces except for *Partido do Porto*, which included roughly the coastal region north of the Mondego river to the region around Oporto. The seven *Governos de Armas* were, from north to south, Minho, Trás-os-Montes, Partido do Porto, Beira, Estremadura, Alentejo, and Algarve. The position of *Governador de Armas* or military governor was always held by a general. His duty was to supervise the military forces in his province and implement the government's orders relating to military matters. At a lower level, the administration of troops was the responsibility of the regiment. The regimental colonel not only managed their training, equipping, uniforming, and disciplining, but was also their commander in the field.

Inspector Generals
Each branch of the army had an inspector general, who was responsible for inspecting their respective army units and presenting reports and recommendations to the commander-in-chief and the government. This post was held by a general who had served in the respective branch. During the Peninsular War the following officers held the posts:

Infantry Inspector: Lieutenant General John Hamilton
Cavalry Inspector: Brigadier General Count de Sampaio
Artillery Inspector: Brigadier General José António da Rosa

The Officer Corps
Since 1757 the starting point for a military career was admission as a cadet into a regiment. This was almost automatic for the aristocracy and sons of military officers higher than major in the regular army or colonel of the militia. The individual applying to be admitted as a cadet presented to an army board documents proving that he came from a respectable family, and had to be in good health, etc. Once admitted, he joined a unit and was drilled like a soldier. He remained with the unit until he was recommended for a commission as an ensign when a vacancy opened in that or any unit. If the cadet was a noble this was a mere formality, but for others it could take a few years to be commissioned. During peace time the army restricted the number of cadets admitted. Beresford altered this regulation by adding the need for cadets to have an allowance to help with subsistence and limiting candidates to those aged between 15 and 20 years old.

The regulation of 1763 for the Portuguese Army ordered by Marshal General Count Schaumburg-Lippe established that officers would be promoted to the next higher rank as vacancies occurred. This was done by seniority, but the regimental colonel had to justify it with a report on the general conduct of the officer. In 1791 it was established that for ranks above colonel the choice for promotion was the exclusive prerogative of the sovereign, seniority not being mandatory. From 1779 for artillery officers and from 1790 for engineer officers, the promotions depended on the results of technical exams and not only seniority. Progression through the ranks in peace time was slow and officers remained in the same rank for long periods until a vacancy opened for promotion. This promotion system remained in place throughout the Peninsular War.

There were several ways of circumventing the regulations, and these were used mostly by the aristocracy to obtain faster promotions. An example was a decree of 1806 allowing state councillors' sons who wish to enter the army to be commissioned as captains.

In general, only officers from the high nobility reached the higher ranks of the army. The regimental officers came from the provincial gentry, the *fidalgos*, often under the patronage of the nobility, or were the sons of military officers. There were also a few individuals with either a commercial or industrial background who had patrons in the high nobility. Besides these, a small number were volunteers or soldiers who rose through the ranks and reached the lower commissioned ranks.

Traditionally another source of military officers was foreign mercenaries, to whom the Portuguese government offered double pay in relation to the Portuguese. When Count Schaumburg-Lippe arrived in Portugal in 1762, he brought with him many officers of German, British, or Swiss origin. Many of them remained in the Portuguese Army throughout the eighteenth century. Others arrived after the French Revolution, when a great number of aristocratic French officers were appointed to posts in the higher ranks of the army. The presence of foreign officers in the army was naturally always a source of discontent and intrigue among the Portuguese officers.

In 1808 the transfer of the Portuguese royal court to Brazil, the disbandment of the army by the French, and the removal from the country of many officers, along with the uprising against French rule, caused changes in the social background, quality, and recruitment of the new officer corps when the army was re-established by the Regency after the expulsion of the French. Two of the issues facing the Regency were a scarcity of able officers among those discharged from the old army but also what to do with those officers commissioned by the *juntas* during the insurrection. The *juntas* had tried to reorganize the local army units and supported the raising of several volunteers corps. In this process they promoted many patriotic volunteers, sergeants, or militia and *ordenanças* officers to the regular units. Many of these had little or no previous military experience. The Portuguese officers with whom Beresford had to work when he started to organize the army in March 1809 were a mix of officers from the old army and others newly promoted. Most were enthusiastic, but many lacked basic military skills.

To partially address this problem, British officers were appointed to the Portuguese Army, first with the mission to organize and train the units in accordance with the British model and later to command many of them in the field. By the end of the war more than 375 had served in the Portuguese Army. Beresford realized that bringing in British officers would not solve the problem. He had to improve the quality of the Portuguese officers. To do this he ordered the retirement of the oldest and the most inefficient officers, and progressively promoted deserving captains and subalterns while bringing in young aristocrats. In the latter years of the war, when weariness and casualties were taking a toll on the British officers, Beresford had a strong cadre of experienced and able Portuguese officers, and increasingly appointed them to command the units in the field. For more information on the role of the British officers, see Chapter 2.

Beresford, before accepting the role of commander-in-chief, negotiated with the Regency to have full control over officers' promotions in accordance with the traditionally established procedures. Beresford cleverly used the promotion system to raise the efficiency of the officer corps. For instance, it allowed him to attach extra officers to the regiments, who were called *agregados* or attached. These officers served in the regiments but only received half-pay and the allowances of an officer *efetivo*, or effective officer. They could not be promoted before they were appointed *efetivo* in a unit and were always junior in their rank. Beresford used the role of officer *agregados* to bring British officers into the Portuguese Army. They soon became effective as vacancies opened, mostly through the retirement or removal of older and inefficient officers.

Beresford also used this role to discipline his officers. Those who were punished lost their effective position in the unit and were put into an *agregado* situation. This was detrimental for the officer, for he lost half of his pay and had no chance of promotion, but he continued to serve in the unit. One of the rewards that Beresford offered when a unit performed well in battle was the return of the *agregado* officer to *efetivo*. Another award given by Beresford to those officers who distinguished themselves in combat was to promote them immediately afterwards, usually by brevet, until a vacancy opened in the army.

Civil Departments of the Army

Supply and Transport

In 1809 the departments in charge of the supply of provisions and transportation for the army were (since 1801) the *Junta dos Provimentos de Boca para o Exército* or *Junta dos Viveres* and the *Intendência Geral dos Transportes do Exército*, respectively. From the very beginning of the Peninsular War, Wellington and Beresford constantly complained about the inefficiency of these departments, which put at risk the Portuguese Army's ability to operate. In November 1811, after much pressure and based on their recommendations, both departments were replaced by the *Comissariado de Viveres e Transportes*, with new regulations that followed the British model. This somewhat improved the efficiency of the department. Domingos José Cardoso, a magistrate, was appointed the chief commissary officer and head of the department.

Paymaster

The *Tesourarias Gerais das Tropas* were established in 1763 to pay the officers and the troops. In 1811 a *Tesouraria Geral do Exército*, or military chest, under the secretary for war, was provisionally created, on Wellington's recommendation, to pay the expenses of the regular army. The military chest included Portuguese funds and the British subsidy. The head of this department during the Peninsular War was the *Inspector Geral das Tesourarias*, the magistrate Joaquim da Costa e Silva. The *Pagadoria Volante do Exército* accompanied the army and was responsible for paying the army's personnel on campaign.

Military Courts

A reform of the military justice system was carried out based on the recommendation of Count Schaumburg-Lippe in 1763. Regimental courts-martial were created as the lowest form of trying cases under the new Articles of War. Each regiment had a magistrate known as the regimental auditor, who managed the courts-martial. His duties corresponded to the British judge advocates. The courts-martial sentences were reviewed by a council of justice, which approved or changed them if needed according to the laws.

Minor offences committed by soldiers were punished by imprisonment or corporal punishment. The latter was applied by striking the men high on their back with the broad side of a sword a number of times that could not exceed fifty.[17] When he was appointed commander-in-chief, Beresford was authorized by the Portuguese government to revise the court-martial procedures and approve or disapprove their sentences. The results of court-martials were sent to the Army Headquarters where the *Auditor Geral do Exército*, a post corresponding to the British Army's judge advocate, would review them and send a report to the marshal for a decision. Beresford was discontented with the long duration of the procedures and made efforts to shorten it. In consequence, court-martial procedures were changed in 1811. At the same time, a magistrate, called the brigade's auditor, was attached to each brigade to accompany the army on campaign. He had the same duties as the regimental auditors who were provisionally suspended. From 1809, and throughout the war, magistrate José António de Oliveira Leite was the *Auditor Geral do Exército*. He was also the inspector of all the civil departments of the army.

Military Medical Department

The medical department was managed by a board composed of the physician general of the army and the surgeon general of the army, who supervised medical matters, and the *Contador-Fiscal*, who was the head of the department responsible for the finance, accounts, and purchases of military hospitals.

The unit's establishments determined a certain number of surgeons and assistant surgeons to attend the men and there were several military hospitals dispersed throughout the country. In each there was a staff of physicians, surgeons, and auxiliary personnel. When necessary, the sick were also treated in civil hospitals.

The department was undergoing a thorough reform when the French invasion and the disbandment of the army brought the process to a standstill. When Beresford took command of the Portuguese Army, the medical department was in great disarray, though the need for an efficient medical staff was pressing to keep the Portuguese Army in the field.

Beresford applied pressure and after some discussion the Regency appealed to the British government for help. Britain sent much-needed medical instruments and supplies, as well as twelve staff surgeons. William Fergusson, a British deputy inspector of military hospitals, was appointed inspector general of the hospitals in early 1810. In late 1811 the number of British surgeons was increased to twenty. They were attached to the army brigades and to the military hospitals. The intervention of the British medical officers, strongly supported by Beresford, allowed for great improvements in the department. A medical board was established to examine and certify the candidates to fill vacant positions in the units. The surgeons were ranked as captains and the assistant surgeons as lieutenants; both had their pay raised. The measures proposed and implemented by Fergusson in the management of the military hospitals led to a general improvement in their effectiveness. He held the position until November 1813.

A convalescents depot was established in the barracks of Vale do Pereiro, in Lisbon. It was commanded by Major John Carrol from 1811.

From 1812 onwards the Allied Army campaigned in Spain and France, and campaign hospitals followed the army to assist the sick and wounded. After the Battle of Vitoria in 1813 the Allied Army faced the French in the Pyrenees for the rest of the year. During this period of intense fighting, a large Portuguese military hospital was established in Vitoria, as was a convalescents depot.

The Royal Arsenal

The *Arsenal Real do Exército* was located in Lisbon. Here it had workshops, foundries, and warehouses where items needed by the army were produced and stored before being distributed to the army. These included not only uniforms, shoes, accoutrements, tents, and tools, but also artillery pieces, ammunition, and small arms. During the Peninsular War finished materials, such as Brown Bess muskets, imported from Britain, were also stored in the arsenal. In Oporto was a similar but smaller arsenal. Other smaller facilities called *Trem* were located in several other towns and fortresses to meet local requirements. These arsenals and facilities were under the direction of the *Junta da Real Fazenda do Arsenal Real do Exército*, but their management throughout the war was headed by José Botelho Moniz da Silva as *Intendente Geral dos Arsenais Reais do Exército*.

Ordenanças and Recruitment

The *Ordenanças* was the local base for military recruitment. It was not an operational military organization. An extract from a document sent by a government official in October 1785 to the military governor of Alentejo explains this point:

> ... actually the *Ordenanças* are not military corps and had to be considered as a 'nursery' from where civilians are recruited to serve in the regular and militia corps and to where they return when incapable ... the officers of the *Ordenanças* are honoured with that title only to manage their districts for us to have a better knowledge of the men available and dispose of them in an orderly manner.[18]

Each military province was divided into several *Ordenanças* districts called *capitanias-mor de ordenanças*, which were subdivided into *companhias de ordenança or* companies of *ordenanças*. These companies were formed in the municipalities, cities, villages, or lands administered by the aristocracy or the different church institutions. The officer responsible for a *capitania-mor* was called the *capitão-mor* and was assisted by a *sargento-mor*. Each company of *ordenanças* was under the supervision of a *capitão de ordenanças* or captain of *ordenanças*. The *capitão-mor* supervised and controlled the companies in his district.

The primary duty of the company's captain was to keep a record of every man in his district capable of military service. The men were sorted by age, civil status, profession, privileges, etc., from which some were eligible to be conscripted into the regular army, others went to the militia, or were exempted from serving. The procedures were regulated by law but left some discretion to the *Ordenanças* officers, giving them considerable influence, which often led to patronage and abuses.

During the Peninsular War the *Ordenanças* officers were commissioned by the sovereign from a list of local men suggested by the local authorities. This meant that the positions were occupied by the wealthy and influential people of the province, often the provincial aristocracy, the *fidalgos*, or by those they trusted.

When Portugal was invaded by foreign armies, such as the French in 1807, 1809, and 1810, the *Ordenanças* were the footing around which popular resistance could be locally organized. In fact, local men formed groups, armed with what weapons they could find, sometimes led by *Ordenanças* officers but for the most part by other active men in the communities. These groups harassed the enemy by operating along the lines of communications and attacking small enemy detachments or foraging parties, capturing couriers, etc. They always remained in or close to their districts, as their primary aim was to defend their property and families, and, when that was not possible, to avenge their losses. When the enemy threat ceased, these groups normally dissolved themselves and the men returned to their everyday life, if possible. This reaction could be centrally instigated but usually depended very much on the circumstances in the different regions, such as the perception of the enemy's threat or behaviour towards the population.

One exception was the formation of the *Ordenanças* artillery companies by a decree of 10 September 1810. The duties of these sixty companies were to man the artillery in forts and fortresses, including the forts on the Lines of Torres Vedras.

Bringing the army up to authorized strength was always difficult in Portugal, for several reasons, but resistance to conscription and desertion were two important ones. On 24 February 1764 a new regulation for the recruitment of the army, based on Count Schaumburg-Lippe's recommendations, was published, and the *capitanias-mor de ordenanças* were grouped into large districts. The men drawn from each of these districts were sent to one specific unit of the army. The regulations also established exemptions to conscription. The men were chosen by lottery among those eligible to be conscripted and sent to the respective unit.[19]

From 1764 many changes occurred in the established strength of the army, which varied during the period, normally in proportion to the level of threat from Spain. When a threat to the kingdom was perceived, the army numbers were augmented and the pressure on recruitment raised. When needed, the sovereign issued emergency orders overriding the 1764 regulations to enlarge the pool of those eligible for recruitment and to speed up the process. This was not well received by the population, who saw it as a violation of their rights. When the level of threat diminished, the establishment was also reduced and the pressure to recruit diminished accordingly.

From 1797 the duration of military service was fixed at ten years for a conscript and six years for a volunteer. After that, former conscripts could be called to serve only in war time and former volunteers could never be called up again. Often, more favourable conditions and limits were offered for volunteer service when there was an urgent need of men.

The disbandment of the military system by the French in 1807–1808 and the lack of resources caused many difficulties for the Regency in its goal of reconstructing the Portuguese Army. Recruitment was one of the problems that had to be addressed. Initially the call-up of previously discharged men and the absorption of volunteers brought good numbers into the regiments, but it was not enough. The old system of conscription was reinstituted to bring the regiments up to strength, but the difficulty in recruiting enough men continued throughout the war.

On 15 December 1809[20] a decree was published to improve the recruitment system, establishing that all single men from 18 to 35 years in age and taller than 149cm (4ft 10in) were liable for service in the regular army. The decree also defined more clearly the exemptions to military service and established severe penalties for those who avoided serving, and those who hid or assisted them, and also for the officers of the *Ordenanças* who were found to be corrupt or relaxed in their duty. These regulations established that beyond the numbers needed to complete the army establishment, the *Ordenanças* officers also had to provide men equivalent to another 10 per cent of the establishment. This additional tenth was to be maintained throughout the war and those men were to be collected in depots, one in each military province, where they underwent initial training, and could be sent to the units when needed. The decree also stated that recruits had to be taken from their provincial *Ordenanças* lists and sent to the units that recruited there. The process was under the supervision of the provincial military governors (see Table 1.1).

Table 1.1: Recruitment Areas, December 1809–1814

Military Province	Infantry Regiments	Cavalry Regiments	Light Infantry[21]	Artillery Regiments
Estremadura	1st, 4th, 7th, 13th, 16th, 19th, 22nd	1st, 4th, 7th, 10th		1st
Alentejo	5th, 17th	2nd, 5th		3rd
Algarve	2nd, 14th			2nd
Beira	8th, 11th, 20th, 23rd	8th, 11th	1st, 2nd, 4th, 7th, 8th, 9th Caçadores (the last three after 1811); two LLL battalions until 1811	
Trás-os-Montes	12th, 24th	9th, 12th	3rd, 5th	
Minho	9th, 15th, 21st	6th	6th, 12th (this last after 1811)	4th
Partido do Porto	3rd, 6th, 10th, 18th	3rd	10th, 11th (only after 1811)	

The recruit depots established in each province were of two types, one for the infantry and artillery and another for the cavalry. In the latter, besides the training of the men, the depots also received the horses acquired in the province.[22] They were under the supervision of the military governor of the province.

On 24 June 1810 Beresford ordered the transfer of the provincial depots of infantry and artillery to a general depot in the fortress of Peniche. The depot was supervised by Brigadier General Richard Blunt, who was appointed the governor of the fortress and inspector general of recruitment to the infantry, caçadores and artillery on 7 July 1810. The conscripts raised in the various provinces were sent to this depot for basic training before they were sent on to their units. Also sent there were officers and non-commissioned officers from the different branches to train the recruits. In July 1811 this depot was transferred to Mafra and remained there throughout the rest of the war.

At the same time, a centralized depot for the cavalry was established in Queluz, Lisbon, under the supervision of Brigadier General Count de Sampaio, the inspector general of the cavalry.[23] In

March 1812 this depot, which had been under the command of Colonel John Brown since the beginning of that year, was transferred to Salvaterra, near Santarém.

The effectiveness of the recruitment regulations depended much on the zeal and honesty of the *Ordenanças* officers, the magistrates, and the military governors in enforcing them. To improve the system, on 22 August 1812 a decree was published detailing the recruitment procedures and the officials' responsibilities. It also raised the penalties for officials who failed to do their duty, for men who evaded conscription, and for those who helped or covered such evasions.[24] One year later another decree was published, this time clarifying the nature of the exemptions to conscription.[25] The problem of the shortage of men to fill the ranks led to many discussions between the Regency and Beresford throughout the war, and despite all their efforts it was never completely solved. However, this system of conscription, with all its flaws, kept an effective Portuguese Army in the field.

The Militia
During the Peninsular War, since the publication of the new regulations on 20 December 1808, the militia was organized into forty-eight infantry regiments, which were recruited in their respective districts. Each regiment was designated by the name of the main town in its district. The regiments had the establishment shown in Table 1.2.[26]

Table 1.2: Establishment for a Militia Regiment

Regimental Staff		Grenadier or Fusilier Company	
Colonel	1	Captain	1
Lieutenant Colonel	2	Lieutenant	1
Majors	1	Ensigns	2
Adjutants	2	1st Sergeant	1
Quartermaster	1	2nd Sergeants	2
Flag Bearers	2	*Furriel*[27]	1
Drum Major	1	Corporals	8
Fifers	2	*Anspeçadas*[28]	8
Total	12	Drummer	1
		Privates	96
		Total	121

Staff	12
Grenadier Company	121
1st Battalion of four companies	484
2nd Battalion of four companies	484
Regiment Total	1101

In 1796 an important reform transformed the old *Terços de Auxiliares* into the militia regiments, which were to be organized and disciplined as the regular regiments. This was an attempt to make the militia an effective part of the army. In consequence the posts of major and adjutant had to be occupied by officers of the regular army. These two officers could be serving in the regular army or retired. Under the 1808 regulations the other officers had to be chosen from the provincial gentry, or the richest men in the respective militia districts, who were capable of military service.

The men were recruited among those between 18 and 40 years old who were exempted from service in the regular army, either because they were married, or exceeded 30 years of age, or for some other exemption. The men had to purchase their own uniforms and equipment. In peace time the companies and the regiments met during the year for training and exercises. In January 1808 the French disarmed and disbanded the militia, but when the uprising against the French began, ex-militia men and officers joined the uprising and many tried to reform their regiments.

Many were actively involved in the fight. The re-established Regency felt the need to reform and reorganize the militia and in October 1808 issued new regulations, but for most of the war the regiments could not muster the numbers needed and their operational capabilities were limited.

The militia, even with all its flaws, was widely used by Wellington to complement the Allied Army, particularly from 1809 to 1811. Militia units were employed on a variety of missions, from fighting the French in the field to the construction and garrison of the Lines of Torres Vedras.

In Lisbon in 1810 some specialized units were organized outside the militia establishment but were given the same status as the militia. These units were two battalions of light troops, the *Caçadores Nacionais de Lisboa Oriental e Ocidental*,[29] and two artillery battalions, the *Artilheiros Nacionais de Lisboa Oriental e Ocidental*.[30] Their establishment comprised almost 2,500 men, and they were detached to garrison and man artillery positions in the Lines of Torres Vedras.[31] Other units included infantry and cavalry regiments from the *Voluntários Reais do Comércio*[32] and the *Corpo dos Voluntários Reais do Porto*[33], which served as garrisons in the cities of Lisbon and Oporto, respectively.

The Regular Army

The Infantry
In 1812 the Portuguese infantry was organized in line infantry regiments and in light infantry battalions, called caçadores.[34]

The Line Infantry
The line infantry consisted of twenty-four regiments, numbered from 1 to 24. In 1763, at the recommendation of Marshal General Count Schaumburg-Lippe, the commander-in-chief of the Portuguese Army at the time of the Seven Years War, the number of regiments was increased to twenty-six. Some years later three of the regiments were sent to Brazil and remained there. In 1801 the Lisbon Regiment was raised with the personnel of disbanded marine battalions, bringing the number of regiments back up to twenty-four.[35]

The numbering of the regiments was established in May 1806. Previously they were named after the town where they were quartered or after one of their past or present colonels, such as the Lippe, Freire, and Vieira Teles Regiments. This connection between the regiments and the provinces where they were traditionally quartered and recruited was strong (see Table 1.3). The numbering of the regiments and the recruitment regulations published on 15 November 1809, which changed the recruitment province of some regiments to align with the population numbers, did not cut these ties entirely. An example is the unofficial names given to certain brigades composed of regiments raised in the same province. The most notable was the so-called Algarve Brigade, composed of the 2nd and 14th Infantry Regiments, which were raised in that province.

Table 1.3: Recruitment Provinces for Infantry Regiments, pre-1807 to 1814[36]

Number	Pre-1806 Name	Pre-1807	From November 1809
1st	Lippe	Estremadura	Estremadura
2nd	Lagos	Algarve	Algarve
3rd	First Olivença	Alentejo	*Partido do Porto*
4th	Freire	Estremadura	Estremadura
5th	First Elvas	Alentejo	Alentejo
6th	First Oporto	*Partido do Porto*	*Partido do Porto*
7th	Setúbal	Estremadura	Estremadura
8th	Castelo de Vide	Alentejo	Beira
9th	Viana	Minho	Minho

Number	Pre-1806 Name	Pre-1807	From November 1809
10th	Lisbon	Unknown	*Partido do Porto*
11th	Penamacor	Beira	Beira
12th	Chaves	Trás-os-Montes	Trás-os-Montes
13th	Peniche	Estremadura	Estremadura
14th	Tavira	Algarve	Algarve
15th	Second Olivença	Alentejo	Minho
16th	Vieira Teles	Estremadura	Estremadura
17th	Second Elvas	Alentejo	Alentejo
18th	Second Oporto	*Partido do Porto*	*Partido do Porto*
19th	Cascais	Estremadura	Estremadura
20th	Campo Maior	Alentejo	Beira
21st	Valença	Minho	Minho
22nd	Serpa	Alentejo	Estremadura
23rd	Almeida	Beira	Beira
24th	Bragança	Trás-os-Montes	Trás-os-Montes

During the uprising against the French some of the *juntas* tried to bolster their capacity to resist the French reaction by reorganizing the old army regiments traditionally stationed in their provinces or districts. The Oporto *Junta* even issued a short-lived establishment for those in the northern provinces.[37] In this process some infantry regiments were raised again, such as those of Algarve (the 2nd and 14th Infantry), Oporto (6th and 18th Infantry), and Trás-os-Montes (12th Infantry) provinces. The enthusiastic support of the population for the uprising brought many volunteers but the difficulties of arming, clothing, and equipping them, combined with the lack of officers, limited their effectiveness. After the French were expelled from Portugal, the newly reinstated Regency started rebuilding the Portuguese Army using the pre-1807 regimental structure. The Regency quickly realized the scarcity of material and human resources available for the task at hand, but General Forjaz, the secretary for war, immediately began the process with the issue of several decrees, which included the organization of the infantry regiments.

The Decree of 14 October 1808 laid out the establishment of the regiments as shown in Table 1.4.

Table 1.4: Authorized Strength of an Infantry Regiment of Two Battalions, each with One Company of Grenadiers and Four Companies of Fusiliers, from October 1808[38]

Regimental Staff		Grenadier or Fusilier Company	
Colonel	1	Captain	1
Lieutenant Colonel	1	Lieutenant	1
Majors	2	Ensigns	2
Adjutants[39]	2	1st Sergeant	1
Quartermaster	1	2nd Sergeants	2
Flag Bearers[40]	2	*Furriel*	1
Chaplain	1	Corporals	8
Surgeon	1	*Anspeçadas*	8
Assistant Surgeons	4	Drummers	2
Coronheiro[41]	1	Privates	126
Espingardeiro[42]	1		
Bandmaster	1		
Musicians	8		
Drum Major	1		
Drum Corporal	1		

Regimental Staff		Grenadier or Fusilier Company	
Fifers	2		
Total	30	Total	152

Staff	30
1st Battalion	760
2nd Battalion	760
Regiment Total	1,550

The regimental establishment was slightly changed twice in 1809 by Beresford. The first change was published on 29 July 1809 and determined that in each company the number of 2nd sergeants should be increased to four (two more) and of privates to 128 (two more). This rise was compensated by the reduction from eight to six corporals and from eight to six *anspeçadas* per company. The total numbers remained the same.[43] The second change, published on 20 November 1809, determined changes in the regimental staff, adding a quartermaster, a paymaster, two adjutant sergeants, and two quartermaster sergeants. The paymaster was chosen from among the quartermasters, with preference for the most able and honest. His duty was to receive the money to pay all the ranks in the regiment. The adjutant sergeants were to be chosen from the sergeants, regardless of seniority, with preference for the most active and zealous, who could perform the duties of the adjutant, whom they would assist. They were considered senior to all other sergeants. The quartermaster sergeants were chosen in the same way and had to be capable of assisting the quartermaster of their battalion, under whose orders they served. These were minor changes in terms of numbers but were important for improving the management of the regiment. The resulting establishment, shown in Table 1.5, remained unchanged throughout the rest of the war, but the regiments never achieved the numbers established, due especially to the high rate of desertion and the difficulties in recruiting.[44]

Table 1.5: Infantry Regiment Establishment, November 1809–1814

Regimental Staff		Grenadier or Fusilier Company	
Colonel	1	Captain	1
Lieutenant Colonel	1	Lieutenant	1
Majors	2 (one for each battalion)	Ensigns	2
Adjutants	2 (one for each battalion)	1st Sergeant	1
Paymaster	1	2nd Sergeants	4
Quartermaster	2 (one for each battalion)	*Furriel*	1
Adjutant Sergeants	2 (one for each battalion)	Corporals	6
Quartermaster Sergeants	2 (one for each battalion)	*Anspeçadas*	6
Flag Bearers	2	Drummers	2
Chaplain	1	Privates	128
Surgeon	1		
Assistant Surgeons	4		
Coronheiro	1		
Espingardeiro	1		
Bandmaster	1		
Musicians	8		
Drum Major	1		
Corporal Drummer	1		
Fifers	2		
Total	36	Total	152

Staff	36
1st Battalion	760
2nd Battalion	760
Regiment Total	1,556

In the regimental establishment the majors, adjutants, quartermasters, adjutant sergeants, and quartermaster sergeants were on the rolls of the regimental staff but were appointed to the individual battalions by the regiment's commanding officer (see Table 1.6).

Table 1.6: Company Designations in Each Battalion[45]

1st Battalion	2nd Battalion
1st Grenadier Company	2nd Grenadier Company
1st Fusilier Company	2nd Fusilier Company
3rd Fusilier Company	4th Fusilier Company
5th Fusilier Company	6th Fusilier Company
7th Fusilier Company	8th Fusilier Company

In 1809 Beresford introduced the British system of training and fighting to the Portuguese Army. The British officers who entered the Portuguese Army were instrumental in the process. This included the translation into Portuguese of British drill manuals, which was done by Beresford's ADC, Major William Warre, a British officer born and raised in Portugal,[46] and the adaptation of British regulations. The first edition, produced in 1809, was the *Instrucções para a formatura, exercicio, e movimentos dos Regimentos de Infantaria (...)*. These manuals were printed and distributed to the infantry regiments and the Portuguese officers had to study and apply them. They were supported and supervised in this by the British officers assigned to the regiments.

One of the major problems Beresford faced from the very beginning was finding qualified officers to command the regiments. Many of the Portuguese commanders were too old or infirm, or were deemed not suitable for a field command. In September 1809 seven British officers were appointed regimental commanders.[47] By June 1810 eleven of the twenty-four regiments had a British commander and in the next year the number was up to fifteen. In January 1812 eighteen of the commanders were British, but by April 1814 Portuguese officers commanded thirteen of the twenty-four regiments.

The Portuguese regiments carried two flags, of different patterns, with the colours and arms of the kingdom and the regiment's designations. Those that participated in the Campaign of Roussillon and Catalonia were awarded with a battle honour and were authorized to use on their flags the inscription '*Ao Valor do Regimento...*'[48] followed by the regiment's number. These were the 3rd, 4th, 6th, 13th, 18th, and 19th Regiments. Following the Battle of Vitoria, Beresford requested from the Prince Regent a mark of his favour to Stubbs' and Power's Brigades for their exceptional conduct in the battle. In consequence, in a decree of 13 November 1813 (but only published on 13 March 1814), the Prince awarded the infantry regiments of those brigades (the 9th, 11th, 12th, and 23rd Regiments), permission for them to use around the coat of arms on their flags the inscription *Julgareis qual é mais excelente/Se ser do mundo rei, ou se de tal gente.*[49] These were lines from the epic poem *Lusíadas*, by the national poet Luís de Camões.

The Caçadores
In 1812 the Portuguese Army had twelve battalions of caçadores, which performed the duties of light infantry. They were numbered from 1 to 12. The origin of these units can be traced to the short-lived Regiment of Royal Volunteers, raised in 1762 during the conflict with Spain, which was part of the Seven Years War. It was a mixed unit composed of infantry and cavalry, and performed the duties of light troops. It was disbanded probably in 1769 or 1772.[50] The first contact of the Portuguese Army with the combat methods of the French Republican Army in Roussillon and Catalonia brought to light the deficiencies of the Portuguese Army. One was the need for troops capable of performing light infantry missions.[51] On 1 August 1796 a general reorganization of the army's establishment addressed that need by creating a caçadores company in each infantry

regiment, which was to be composed of ten companies: eight of fusiliers, one of grenadiers and one of caçadores.[52]

On the same day was also created the *Legião de Tropas Ligeiras*, an independent legion of light troops, composed of a staff, one infantry battalion, three cavalry squadrons, and one horse artillery battery, in all 1,379 men. General Marquis de Alorna was appointed to command this unit, which was known as Alorna's Legion or the Experimental Legion.

Some commanders saw a need for units that were able not only to perform the traditional duties of light infantry, but also to engage in irregular warfare. This led to the creation in 1801 of several volunteer companies called *Caçadores do Monte*, from men of the mountainous regions of the northern provinces, in preparation for the conflict with Spain. They were deployed with the regular army but saw little action, and were dissolved after the war ended. This was the seed that in 1808 led to the creation of the caçadores battalions.

In the wake of the Portuguese insurrection against the French, the *Junta Suprema* in Oporto obtained political control over the rebellious northern provinces. In July 1808 it began to reorganize the regular army units of those provinces and ordered the raising of four caçadores battalions, one for each province.[53] Between July and September 1808 these caçadores battalions were formed with volunteers from the provinces of Minho (at Braga), Trás-os-Montes (at Vila Real), Beira (at Viseu) and the *Partido do Porto* (at Oporto). Their establishment was of 846 men, with a staff and six companies. They were named Minho's Caçadores Battalion, Trás-os-Montes' Caçadores Battalion, Beira's Caçadores Battalion, and Oporto's Caçadores Battalion.[54]

In August 1808 the Oporto *Junta* assembled a corps of about 8,000 men under the command of General Bernardim Freire de Andrade. Wellington furnished 5,000 muskets to this poorly armed corps.[55] From that force about 2,000 men were detached under the command of Lieutenant Colonel Nicholas Trant to join Wellington. This force had some artillery, about 300 cavalry, and the rest infantry. Among the infantry was the Oporto's Caçadores Battalion, comprising about 400 men under the command of Major Manuel Velho da Cunha. It was deployed alongside the light companies of General Rowland Hill's Brigade in the fighting at Roliça. This battalion was the first Portuguese unit to fight alongside the British.[56]

On 14 October 1808 the Regency issued several decrees on the establishments of the units of the new Portuguese Army. In one of them was ordered the creation of six caçadores battalions (see Table 1.7).

Table 1.7: Authorized Strength for a Caçadores Battalion in 1808[57]

Staff		Caçadores and *Atiradores* Companies	
Lieutenant Colonel	1	Captain	1
Major	1	Lieutenant	1
Adjutant	1	Ensigns	2
Quartermaster	1	1st Sergeant	1
Chaplain	1	2nd Sergeants	2
Surgeon	1	*Furriel*	1
Assistant Surgeons	2	Corporals	8
Coronheiro	1	*Anspeçadas*	8
Espingardeiro	1	Drummers	2
Drum Major	1	Bugler	1
Fifers	2	Privates	96
Total	13	Total	123

Staff	13
4 Caçadores Companies	492
1 *Atiradores* Company[58]	123
Battalion Total	628

General Forjaz, the secretary for war, had been the adjutant general under the Oporto *Junta*, and was probably the man behind the creation of the northern caçadores battalions. He decided to rename those battalions and to incorporate some volunteer units that were raised outside the framework of the regular army by the *juntas* in Alentejo province, as shown in Table 1.8.

Table 1.8: Origins of the Caçadores Battalions

Battalion	Original Corps
1st	Portalegre Volunteers Regiment
2nd	Transtagana Legion or Beja Volunteers
3rd	Trás-os-Montes' Caçadores
4th	Beira's Caçadores
5th	Transtagana Legion or Beja Volunteers
6th	Oporto's Caçadores

This process was regulated by a decree of 11 November 1808, which also included the design of the well-known brown uniform, as well as the arms and accoutrements for use by the caçadores.[59] He had great difficulty in finding capable officers to organize and command the caçadores battalions[60] but on 21 January 1809 he finally appointed the commanders of the new battalions.

The men of Minho's Caçadores Battalion formed in Braga had been incorporated into the Loyal Lusitanian Legion in Oporto since October 1808.[61] The LLL was assembled in Oporto in August 1808 under the command of Sir Robert Wilson, with a few officers from Britain and mainly comprised volunteers from Oporto, strengthened by the incorporation of Minho's Caçadores Battalion into its ranks. On 24 June 1809 Beresford ordered its reorganization as a light infantry regiment composed of a staff and two battalions, of ten companies each (see Table 1.9). This reorganization marked the full integration of the LLL into the Portuguese Army. The Legion ceased to be a volunteer corps and recruitment followed the Portuguese conscription system.

Table 1.9: Organization of the Loyal Lusitanian Legion from 24 June 1809[62]

Regimental Staff		Grenadier or Fusilier Company	
Colonel	1	Captain	1
Lieutenant Colonels	2	Lieutenant	1
Majors	2	Ensigns	2
Adjutants	2	1st Sergeant	1
Quartermasters	2	2nd Sergeants	3
Flag Bearers	2	*Furriel*	1
Chaplain	2	Corporals	6
Surgeons	2	*Anspeçadas*	6
Assistant Surgeons	4	Drummers	2
Coronheiro	2	Privates	88
Espingardeiro	2		
Bandmaster	2		
Musicians	16		
Drum Major	2		
Fifers	4		
Total	47	Total	111

Staff	47
1st Battalion	1,110
2nd Battalion	1,110
Regiment Total	2,267

Beresford proposed some changes to the establishment of the caçadores battalions, which were published by the government on 29 July and 23 November 1809. As for the infantry regiments, these changes were made to the staff, with the addition of a paymaster, an adjutant sergeant, and a quartermaster sergeant. A band was added, and the drummers were replaced by buglers. The companies kept the same number of men, but the number of sergeants was raised and the numbers of corporals and *anspeçadas* reduced. The total of men was increased from 628 to 638.[63]

Beresford considered five companies an insufficient number for the battalion's tactical deployment and wanted to have an even number of companies. On 20 February 1810 a new establishment for the caçadores battalion was authorized (see Table 1.10).

Table 1.10: Authorized Strength of a Caçadores Battalion from 1810[64]

Staff		Company	
Lieutenant Colonel	1	Captain	1
Major	1	Lieutenant	1
Adjutant	1	Ensigns	2
Paymaster	1	1st Sergeant	1
Quartermaster	1	2nd Sergeants	4
Adjutant Sergeant	1	*Furriel*	1
Quartermaster Sergeant	1	Corporals	6
Chaplain	1	*Anspeçadas*	6
Surgeon	1	Buglers	2
Assistant Surgeons	2	Privates	88
Coronheiro	1	Total	112
Espingardeiro	1		
Band Master	1		
Musicians	8		
Bugle Major	1		
Total	23		

Staff	23
6 Caçadores Companies	672
Battalion Total	695

During 1809 and 1810 Beresford appointed several British officers, most of them with experience in the light infantry, to command and train the caçadores. Their primary mission was to direct the training in accordance with British light troops practices and regulations. For this purpose Beresford published in 1810 a regulation called *Systema de Instrucção e Disciplina para os Movimentos e Deveres dos Caçadores (...)* which was an adaptation of the British regulations for light infantry. It was also translated by Major Warre.

The campaigns of 1809 and 1810 revealed to Wellington and Beresford the value of the caçadores and the need for more light troops in the Allied Army. This reasoning led to the attachment of the 1st and 3rd Caçadores to the Light Division in the spring of 1810, and of one caçadores battalion to each of the Portuguese infantry brigades. From 1810, when the task of training and organizing the different units of the Portuguese Army was achieving results, Beresford started to organize infantry brigades in a more systematic way. The model for each was two infantry regiments and a caçadores battalion.

Another consequence was the decision to raise the number of caçadores battalions to twelve, in theory allowing one for each Portuguese infantry brigade. After some discussion, the decision was made to transform the LLL's two battalions into three caçadores battalions and to raise three new battalions. In consequence the Regency published the decree of 20 April 1811 regulating this new arrangement.[65] The 1st LLL became the 7th Caçadores and the 2nd LLL the 8th Caçadores.

The men and officers from the LLL's battalions that were not needed for these two battalions were joined by new recruits and officers to form the 9th Caçadores. These three battalions would continue to recruit in Beira province, as the Legion had been doing since 1809.[66] The 10th and 11th Caçadores were to be recruited in the *Partido do Porto*, and the 12th in Minho province. British officers were appointed to command these new six battalions, and the last four were recruited and organized between June 1811 and February 1812.[67]

Initially some of the men in the caçadores battalions were equipped with carbines, but there was a shortage of these and eventually all had muskets. By August 1810 at least 800 Baker rifles had been distributed among the caçadores, but which units had them is unknown. It is likely that one company in each battalion was equipped with them. The caçadores battalions did not have flags, but, as mentioned before for the infantry regiments, the caçadores of Stubbs' and Power's Brigades, the 7th and 11th Battalions, were awarded with one ceremonial flag each. The flags, besides the colours and arms of the kingdom, bore the inscription '*Distintos vós sereis na Lusa História/Com os louros que colhestes na vitória*',[68] also from Camões' *Lusíadas*. The flags were not carried in combat but only in ceremonies and the distinction was to last only until the last men present at the Battle of Vitoria died.[69]

The Cavalry

In 1812 the cavalry was composed of twelve regiments, numbered from 1 to 12. Like the infantry, the number of cavalry regiments was established by the reforms of Count Schaumburg-Lippe in 1764. Before 1806 they were named after the place where they were quartered, normally in the province where they recruited. Table 1.11 shows the provinces where the regiments drew their recruits.

Table 1.11: Recruitment Provinces for Cavalry Regiments: pre-1807 to 1814[70]

Number	Pre-1806 Name	Pre-1807	From November 1809
1st	Alcântara	Estremadura	Estremadura
2nd	Moura	Alentejo	Alentejo
3rd	Olivença	Alentejo	*Partido do Porto*
4th	Mecklemburgo	Estremadura	Estremadura
5th	Évora	Alentejo	Alentejo
6th	Bragança	Trás-os-Montes	Minho
7th	Cais	Estremadura	Estremadura
8th	Elvas	Alentejo	Beira
9th	Chaves	Trás-os-Montes	Trás-os-Montes
10th	Santarém	Beira	Estremadura
11th	Almeida	Beira	Beira
12th	Miranda	Trás-os-Montes	Trás-os-Montes

On 14 October 1808 the Regency issued a decree on the establishments of the cavalry regiments of the new Portuguese Army (see Table 1.12).

Table 1.12: Authorized Strength of a Cavalry Regiment, October 1808[71]

Staff		Company	
Ranks	Men	Ranks	Men
Colonel	1	Captain	1
Lieutenant Colonel	1	Lieutenant	1
Major	1	Cornet[72]	1
Adjutant	1	Sergeants	1

Staff		Company	
Ranks	Men	Ranks	Men
Quartermaster	1	*Furriel*	1
Chaplain	1	Corporals	4
Surgeon	1	*Anspeçadas*	4
Assistant Surgeons	2	Trumpeter	1
Picador[73]	1	Farrier	1
Trumpet Major	1	Privates	57
Seleiro[74]	1	Total	72
Coronheiro	1		
Espingardeiro	1		
Total	14		
Each regiment had four squadrons of two companies.		The first four companies each had a standard bearer.	
Staff	14		
8 Companies	576		
Standard Bearers	4		
Regiment Total	594		

Beresford also proposed some changes in the staff and established the number of horses allowed for each rank. The new establishment was published in a decree of 20 November 1809 and remained the theoretical establishment until the end of the war (see Table 1.13).

Table 1.13: Authorized Strength of a Cavalry Regiment, November 1809–1814[75]

Staff			Company or Troop		
Ranks	Men	Horses	Ranks	Men	Horses
Colonel	1	3	Captain	1	1
Lieutenant Colonel	1	2	Lieutenant	1	1
Major	1	2	Cornet	1	1
Adjutant	1	1	Sergeants	2	2
Quartermaster	1	1	*Furriel*	1	1
Paymaster	1	1	Corporals	4	4
Adjutant Sergeant	1	1	*Anspeçadas*	4	4
Quartermaster Sergeant	1	1	Trumpeter	1	1
Standard Bearers[76]	4	4	Farrier	1	1
Chaplain	1	1	Mounted Privates	48	48
Surgeon	1	1	Dismounted Privates	8	-
Assistant Surgeons	2	-	Total	72	64
Picador	1	1			
Trumpeter Major	1	1			
Seleiro	1	-			
Coronheiro	1	-			
Espingardeiro	1	-			
Total	21	20			
Staff	Men 21; Horses 20				
8 Companies	Men 576; Horses 512				
Regiment Total	Men 597; Horses 532				

The cavalry was the weakest part of the Portuguese Army, largely due to the lack of suitable horses in the country. The breeding of horses in Portugal was limited and insufficient to meet the needs of the army. The typical horse was small and sturdy but did not have the ideal characteristics needed to perform the duties of light or heavy cavalry. For this reason the Portuguese cavalry was not tactically specialized, and all their regiments were equipped and trained in the same manner.

Thanks to memoirs written by some of the cavalry commanders in the Peninsular War, such as Generals Madden and D'Urban, we understand that the cavalry efficiently performed outpost duties, surveillance, and reconnaissance missions in the front and on the flanks of the enemy. However, in combat it was no match for the experienced French cavalry, which was better mounted and trained. Even though they were not formally trained as light cavalry, they generally performed the duties allotted to that branch in the operations in which they took part.

Fulfilling the manpower and horse requirements for twelve cavalry regiments was extremely difficult, so only a few mounted squadrons were raised and fielded in 1808. After Beresford took command, great efforts were made to mount and train the cavalry. As for the infantry, he appointed a few British officers to the regiments with the mission to train and organize them. One of those officers was George Madden, who in September 1809 was appointed a brigadier general in the Portuguese Army. He left some impressions of the Portuguese cavalry and his task:

> The Portuguese cavalry regiments, as then constituted, were wholly unacquainted with the English system, or indeed any other rational mode of discipline, were without experienced officers, required an entirely new organization, and were totally unfit for any kind of service. These defects were to be remedied under the disadvantage of conveying instruction to them in a foreign language, and without any assistance from other English officers for a long time, which advantage the Portuguese regiments of infantry already possessed.[77]

Beresford ordered the publication of regulations for the training of the cavalry, the *Instruções Provisorias para Cavallaria (...)*, which was compiled and translated by Major Warre and Lieutenant Colonel John Brown, following British manuals.[78] In consequence of these efforts, at the beginning of 1810 some regiments were considered fit for service and took the field under Madden's command. These regiments fought hard in 1810 and 1811 in Spanish Extremadura and around Badajoz while attached to the Spanish Army.

After some discussion, Beresford and the government decided to dismount some of the regiments and drafted their horses into the others. This process began in 1810, culminating with a decree on 14 April 1812 in which it was announced that only six regiments would be mounted. These were the 1st, 3rd, 4th, 6th, 11th, and 12th Cavalry. The timing for this new arrangement coincided with the preparation for the 1812 Allied offensive into the plains of central Spain, where cavalry would be much needed by Wellington's Army. Another provision in this decree was a temporary change to the number of regimental officers determined by the 1809 establishment. The mounted regiments were to have 1 colonel, 2 lieutenant colonels (instead of one), 2 majors (instead of 1), 8 captains, 16 lieutenants (instead of 8), and 8 ensigns. These changes raised the number of officers in each regiment from 27 to 37. To meet these requirements, Beresford made major changes to the personnel of the cavalry regiments. The older officers and those not fit for active duty were retired or transferred to the dismounted regiments. At the same time, he promoted and transferred the ablest officers to the mounted regiments. He also appointed some British officers to the mounted regiments and placed them in command positions. These dispositions permitted the Portuguese Army to put in the field a few brigades of cavalry in the campaigns of 1812, 1813 and 1814. Besides the squadrons in active service in the brigades, one reserve squadron from each regiment was left behind to receive new recruits and horses.

The cavalry regiments carried four standards, one for each squadron. They all had the same design, with the royal arms and regiment designation, but each squadron's standard was of a different colour.

The Artillery

The artillery had been organized into four foot artillery regiments since 1766. In 1806 they were numbered 1 to 4. They had no horse artillery. The role of the artillery regiments was essentially a defensive one, garrisoning the coastal and frontier fortresses, but on the rare occasions on which the Portuguese Army mobilized for active duty, such as in the Catalonia and Rossillon Campaigns or during the War of the Oranges, the artillery regiments furnished the supporting field artillery.

Table 1.14: Recruitment Provinces for Artillery Regiments

Number	Pre-1806 Name	Pre-1807	From November 1809
1st	Corte	Estremadura	Estremadura
2nd	Algarve	Algarve	Algarve
3rd	Estremoz	Alentejo	Alentejo
4th	Oporto	*Partido do Porto*	Minho

To be commissioned as an artillery officer, an individual had to graduate from the *Academia Real de Fortificação, Artilharia e Desenho*, which was founded in 1790. His promotion was not dependent only on seniority but also on the results of a technical exam.

On 14 October 1808 the Regency decided to maintain the establishment in use before the French invasion, which dated from 1 August 1796 (see Table 1.15).

Table 1.15: Authorized Strength of an Artillery Regiment, 1808[79]

Staff		Company	1st	2nd to 5th	6th & 7th	Bombardiers [80]	Miners	Pontoniers
Colonel	1	Captain	1	1	1	1	1	1
Lieutenant Colonel	1	1st Lieutenant	1	1	1	1	1	1
Major	1	2nd Lieutenant	1	1	1	1	1	1
Adjutant	1	Sergeants	2	2	2	2	2	2
Quartermaster	1	*Furriel*	1	1	1	1	1	1
Chaplain	1	Fire Artificers[81]	-	-	-	6	-	-
Secretary	1	Drummers	2	2	2	2	2	2
Surgeon	1	Fifers	2	-	-	-	-	-
Assistant Surgeons	6	Privates	108	110	109	110	110	110
Drummer Major	1	Total	118	118	117	124	118	118
Provost	1							
Total	16							
Staff	16							
10 Companies	1,184							
Regiment Total	1,200							

The reorganization of the artillery regiments benefited from the fact that few artillery officers and men were sent to France after the disbandment of the Portuguese Army in 1807. On 21 May 1809 Beresford appointed Brigadier General José António da Rosa, an artillery officer and the artillery inspector general, to be general commander of the artillery, a position he held throughout the war. General Rosa managed all business related to the artillery and coordinated with both Beresford and the secretary for war.

Beresford proposed a new establishment for the four artillery regiments which was published in a decree on 20 October 1809 (see Table 1.16).

Table 1.16: Authorized Strength of an Artillery Regiment, October 1809–1811[82]

Staff		Company	1st to 7th	Bombardiers	Miners	Pontoniers
Colonel	1	Captain	1	1	1	1
Lieutenant Colonel	1	1st Lieutenant	1	1	1	1
Major	1	2nd Lieutenants	2	2	2	2
Adjutant	1	1st Sergeant	1	1	1	1
Quartermaster	1	2nd Sergeants	4	4	4	4
Chaplain	1	*Furriel*	1	1	1	1
Surgeon	1	Corporals	8	8	8	8
Assistant Surgeons	3	Fire Artificers	-	6	-	-
Band Master	1	Drummers	2	2	2	2
Musicians	8	Privates	92	92	92	92
Drummer Major	1	Total	112	118	112	112
Fifers	2					
Total	22					
Staff	22					
10 Companies	1,126					
Regiment Total	1,148					

By a decree of 12 October 1812 the establishment was considerably changed, with the transformation of the Bombardiers, Miners, and Pontoniers companies into artillery companies.[83] The duties of the Miners and Pontoniers companies, as well as most of the men, were transferred to the newly formed *Batalhão de Artífices Engenheiros*,[84] which was attached to the Royal Corps of Engineers.

From 1813, after these major changes, the artillery regiments had a new establishment of a staff and ten artillery companies, with no change in the total numbers (see Table 1.17).

1.17: Authorized Strength of an Artillery Regiment from October 1813

Staff		Company	
Colonel	1	Captain	1
Lieutenant Colonel	1	1st Lieutenant	1
Major	1	2nd Lieutenants	2
Adjutant	1	1st Sergeant	1
Quartermaster	1	2nd Sergeants	4
Chaplain	1	*Furriel*	1
Surgeon	1	Corporals	8
Assistant Surgeons	3	Drummers	2
Band Master	1	Privates	92
Musicians	8	Total	112
Drummer Major	1		
Fifers	2		
Total	22		
Staff	22		
10 Companies	1,120		
Regiment Total	1,142		

Although a small number of artillery pieces were used in the insurrection against the French in 1808, it was not until 1809 that artillery was assigned to the army for field operations. At this point Beresford, following the British practice, ordered the formation of field brigades.[85] During the Peninsular War the Portuguese artillery continued to garrison the fortresses and the Lines of Torres Vedras, and was engaged in the defence of Almeida, Campo Maior, and Badajoz, and in all the siege operations undertaken by Wellington's Army. In 1812 a company from the 2nd Artillery was detached to Alicante to join the Allied Army on the east coast of Spain fighting at the Battle of Castala and the siege of Tarragona.

Artillery Brigades
During the war the artillery brigades that were fielded were temporary formations. When one was needed, the regiment that was tasked to provide it did not assign an already existing company but took the best qualified officers and men from the regiment, regardless of which company they belonged to. This new formation was initially trained and organized under the supervision of a few British artillery officers appointed to the Portuguese regiments, such as Alexander Dickson and Victor von Arenstchild. When considered fit for service, these brigades were assigned to the field army. The number of artillery brigades on campaign varied throughout the war according to the number of draught animals available. On several occasions the Portuguese artillery was unable to field the planned number of brigades due to the shortage of animals.

The Artillery Drivers
In view of the need for a military organization to service the transports in the artillery brigades, Beresford recommended the formation of a battalion of artillery drivers or *Artilheiros Conductores*. Their duties were probably equivalent to those of the British Army's Corps of Artillery Drivers. Its men and horses were employed in transporting the guns and conveying ammunition and stores.

The establishment for the battalion was published in a decree of 8 October 1812 (see Table 1.18). It was composed of a staff and the number of companies needed to assist the artillery brigades fielded, which were at the time one brigade of 5½-inch howitzers, five 9-pounder brigades and four 6-pounder brigades.

Table 1.18: Authorized Strength of the Artillery Drivers Battalion, October 1812–1814[86]

Staff		Company for Service with a Howitzer Brigade		Company for Service with a 9-Pounder Brigade		Company for Service with a 6-Pounder Brigade		Company for Service with a 3-Pounder Brigade	
Lieutenant Colonel or Major Commandant	1	1st Lieutenant	1	1st Lieutenant	1	1st Lieutenant	1	1st Lieutenant	1
Adjutant	1	2nd Lieutenant	1	2nd Lieutenants	1	2nd Lieutenants	1	2nd Lieutenants	1
Quartermaster	1	1st Sergeant	1	1st Sergeant	1	1st Sergeant	1	1st Sergeant	1
Picador[87]	1	2nd Sergeants	5	2nd Sergeants	5	2nd Sergeants	4	2nd Sergeants	4
Adjutant Sergeant	1	Corporals	8	Corporals	8	Corporals	6	Corporals	6
Quartermaster Sergeant	1	*Alveitar*	1	*Alveitar*	1	*Alveitar*	1	*Alveitar*	1
Alveitar[88]	1	Farriers	4	Farriers	4	Farriers	3	Farriers	3
Farriers	3	Buglers	2	Buglers	2	Buglers	2	Buglers	2
Buglers	2	Drivers	118	Drivers	107	Drivers	76	Drivers	76
Total	12	Total	141	Total	130	Total	95	Total	95

Staff	12
For a howitzer brigade	141
For the five 9-pounder brigades	650
For the four 6 pounder brigades	380
Battalion total at this point	1,183

The establishment given in Table 1.18 was only theoretical. The number of companies mobilized varied according to the number and type of artillery brigades in the field. For the 1813 and 1814 campaigns only four companies accompanied the four brigades fielded by the Portuguese artillery.

The officers appointed to the battalion were mainly retired officers and former sergeants from the cavalry, such as the battalion commander, a retired major from the 7th Cavalry, Agostinho Pereira Velho Sarmento.

The Engineers
The Corps of Engineers was created in 1787 and was named the Royal Corps of Engineers in 1792. It was composed only of engineer officers. Their duties included the planning, construction and repairing of forts, barracks or depots, campaign fortifications, siege warfare, terrain reconnaissance and cartography. At the beginning of the Peninsular War the Royal Engineers were commanded by Major General José de Morais Antas Machado. After he retired in 1810, Beresford appointed on 16 December 1810 Major General Matias José Dias Azedo, an engineer officer, to be the corps' commandant. General Azedo held the position throughout the war. The commandant managed the corps and coordinated its duties with both Beresford and the secretary for war. To be commissioned as an engineer officer, the individual had to graduate from the *Academia Real de Fortificação, Artilharia e Desenho*. His promotion was not dependent only on seniority but also on the results of a technical exam.

On the recommendation of Beresford, the 'Provisional Regulations for the Royal Corps of Engineers' was published on 12 February 1812. The corps was reorganized, and its duties were described in detail. One important change was the creation of one battalion of *Artífices Engenheiros* or Artificers Engineers to be included in the corps and officered by engineer officers. This battalion resulted from the disbanding of the Miners and Pontoniers companies in the artillery regiments and the transfer of their men and duties to the battalion. The new organization and establishment of the Royal Corps of Engineers is shown in Tables 1.19 and 1.20.[89]

Table 1.19: Authorized Number of Royal Engineers

Staff		Officers	
General Officer Commandant	1	Brigadiers	2
Adjutants	2	Colonels	4
Secretary (1st Lieutenant)	1	Lieutenant Colonels	4
Total	4	Majors	8
		Captains	12
		1st Lieutenants	12
		2nd Lieutenants	24
		Total	66
Total 70			

Table 1.20: Establishment of the Artificers Engineer Battalion

Staff		Artificers Company[90]		Pontoniers Company[91]	
Major Commandant	1	Captain	1	Captain	1
Adjutant	1	1st Lieutenant	1	1st Lieutenant	1
Quartermaster Paymaster	1	2nd Lieutenants	2	2nd Lieutenant	1
Quartermaster Paymaster Sergeant	1	1st Sergeants	4	1st Sergeants	4
Total	4	2nd Sergeants	5	2nd Sergeants	5
		Furriel	1	*Furriel*	1
		Corporals	10	Corporals	10
		Anspeçadas	10	*Anspeçadas*	10
		Privates	100	Privates	40
		Drummer	1	Drummer	1
		Total	135	Total	74
Staff 4					
2 Companies of Artificers 270					
1 Company of Pontoniers 74					
Battalion Total 348					

The establishment shown in Table 1.19 was published in the Provisional Regulations of 12 February 1812 and was expanded by a decree of 18 October 1813. The expansion of the Artificers Companies was the result of their good service at the siege of San Sebastian.[92]

During the Peninsular War the Portuguese Engineers were extensively employed in the planning and construction of the Lines of Torres Vedras, as well as participating in some of the siege operations conducted by Wellington's Army.

Formation of the Portuguese Army's Division and Brigades

The Infantry Brigades

Beresford took command of the Portuguese Army in March 1809 when Soult was already campaigning in northern Portugal. The French invasion culminated in the fall of Oporto, the country's second largest city, on 28 March 1809. Wellington's offensive against Soult at the beginning of May prompted the need to field Portuguese units for the campaign. With no time to lose, Beresford ordered the formation of several provisional brigades from the few regiments that he found capable of taking the field.

When Wellington advanced into Spain to join the Spanish army in the Talavera campaign, Beresford was again under pressure to get the Portuguese Army to support the allies. He gathered the units that were fit for service around Ciudad Rodrigo, and grouped the regiments and battalions into provisional brigades to march south in support of Wellington'. In his first six months in command Beresford had to have his army on the move, with little time to even clothe, arm, or train his units properly, much less to organize them in some definitive form.

After the campaign of 1809, Beresford, by an order of 29 September 1809, organized the army into twelve infantry brigades and appointed the commanders of some of them (see Table 1.21). With very few changes, Beresford re-established the arrangement already ordered by a decree of 19 May 1807 but never implemented because of the French invasion of November 1807.

Table 1.21: Infantry Brigade Organization, 29 September 1809

Brigades	Commanders
1st and 16th Regiments	Not appointed
2nd and 14th	Brigadier General Agostinho Luís da Fonseca
3rd and 15th	Brigadier General Charles Miller
4th and 10th	Temporarily by the senior officer of the regiments who was Colonel Archibald Campbell of the 4th
5th and 17th	Brigadier General António Marcelino da Vitória
6th and 18th	Brigadier General William Howe Campbell, who was also the commander of the troops collected at Coimbra
7th and 19th	Brigadier General Richard Blunt
8th and 22nd	Not appointed
9th and 21st	Not appointed
11th and 23rd	Brigadier General Francis John Colman, who was also commander of the troops collected at Leiria
12th and 24th	Temporarily by the senior officer of the regiments who was Colonel William Cox of the 24th
13th and 20th	Not appointed

By the end of September 1809 the infantry regiments and the caçadores battalions were dispersed in cantonments around the country to begin in earnest their refitting and training. Only the brigades to which a commander had been appointed were activated, since their regiments were cantoned in the same town. This allowed the regiments to begin training to act together as a brigade.

In essence, this brigade scheme remained in place until the end of the war, although some changes occurred. Some of these brigades were never organized, or were organized with different regiments, according to their readiness and other circumstances. Beginning in August 1810 a caçadores battalion was assigned to each brigade, except for what would become the 2nd Brigade.

Eventually ten brigades were organized and were usually referred to by their commanders' names until 13 August 1813, when the brigades were numbered (see Table 1.22).

Table 1.22: Brigade Numbering and Composition

Number	Composition
1st	1st and 16th Infantry and 4th Caçadores
2nd	2nd and 14th Infantry
3rd	3rd and 15th Infantry and 8th Caçadores
4th	4th and 10th Infantry and 10th Caçadores
5th	6th and 18th Infantry and 6th Caçadores
6th	7th and 19th Infantry and 2nd Caçadores
7th	8th and 12th Infantry and 9th Caçadores
8th	9th and 21st Infantry and 11th Caçadores
9th	11th and 23rd Infantry and 7th Caçadores
10th	13th and 24th Infantry and 5th Caçadores

From April 1810 some of the Portuguese brigades started to be assigned to the Allied divisions. Eventually only the 1st and 10th Brigades remained independent throughout the war. The 2nd and 4th formed the Portuguese Division early in 1810[93] and Beresford appointed Major General John Hamilton as its commander.

The Cavalry Brigades

On 24 September 1809 Beresford ordered the formation of three cavalry brigades and appointed their commanders, as shown in Table 1.23. With some changes in both composition and commanding officers, these three brigades were active during the next two years, particularly Madden's Brigade.

Table 1.23: The Cavalry Brigades in September 1809

Brigade Composition	Commander
1st and 7th Cavalry	Daniel Seddon
2nd and 5th Cavalry[94]	George Madden
4th and 10th Cavalry	Count de Sampaio

While Beresford had a problem finding qualified officers to command the infantry and cavalry regiments, he had even greater problems finding suitable officers to command his division and brigades.[95] This shortage of competent senior officers continued throughout much of the war. Beresford replaced those brigade commanders whose performance was lacking or who became casualties, or, in the case of the British, resigned their commissions in the Portuguese Army.

After Beresford was appointed commander-in-chief in 1809, his goal over the next two years was to organize and train the Portuguese Army so that it could stand in open combat against the French and win. As units were deemed combat ready, they were assigned to Wellington's Army and fought alongside their British counterparts. By early 1811 ten brigades had been formed and were considered an integral part of Wellington's Army. The Portuguese soldiers proved themselves at the river Coa, Bussaco, Fuentes D'Oñoro, Albuera, the first and second sieges of Badajoz, Arroyo Molinos, and many smaller combats through 1811. By 1812 they were fully integrated into Wellington's Army and would participate in almost every combat, battle, and siege fought by it over the next three years. By the end of the war in 1814, 40 per cent of Wellington's Army was Portuguese. The following is their story, as told by their leaders during the last three years of the Peninsular War.

Chapter 2

British Officers in the Portuguese Army, 1808–1826

The evacuation of the French Army from Portugal in September 1808 did not put Portugal out of danger. The large French forces remaining in Spain were a constant threat, so the re-established Portuguese government needed to rebuild its army, most of which had been disbanded at the beginning of 1808. It was not an easy task. One of the problems was that its best troops had been sent to France to form the *Legion Portugaise* and what was left were locally formed groups, hastily raised during the uprising, that were poorly armed, badly equipped, and had little training. The Portuguese government realized that they needed a general who could not only command the army but oversee its organization and training. On 26 December 1808 it asked the British government to provide such an officer. In February 1809 Major General William Beresford was ordered to take up the position.[96] He was a good fit for the job. He was an experienced commander and an excellent administrator, with the reputation of being a strict disciplinarian. It also helped that he spoke Portuguese and had more experience than any other British general in dealing with the Portuguese authorities and society in general. He was in command during the British occupation of Madeira between 1807 and 1808 and was virtually the administrator of the island. He was also one of the British delegates to the joint commission that settled the disputes over French compliance with the terms of the Cintra Convention. Furthermore, he was junior to Wellington, who was being groomed to return to Portugal to take command of the British forces there. Upon arriving in Lisbon, Beresford was promoted to theatre rank of lieutenant general in the British Army and on 7 March 1809 to marshal and commander-in-chief of the Portuguese Army.[97]

The government's plan for the new Portuguese Army was for an establishment of 24 infantry regiments, 6 caçadores battalions, 12 cavalry regiments, and 4 artillery regiments, which was the same as the pre-1808 army except for the caçadores battalions. The British government had a long history of providing their allies with money, weapons, equipment, and uniforms, and were willing to do so for the Portuguese. They also knew that, in addition to an able general, they would also need to provide trainers and leaders to implement at unit level a new system based on the British way of fighting. Twenty-one officers were selected for service in the Portuguese Army and Wellington was told that no more would be authorized.[98] However, it quickly became apparent that more officers were needed. Beresford's plan was for British officer to be in command, or to be second-in-command where the Portuguese commander was capable, of every regiment and cacadores battalion. Each infantry regiment would have five British officers, while the caçadores battalions and cavalry regiments would have three each.[99] As an inducement to volunteer, the officer would be promoted one step in rank in the Portuguese Army. Additionally, the officer would continue to be paid by the British Army while he also was paid by the Portuguese. There would also be opportunities to be promoted in brevet rank, which was army rank and not regimental rank.

Initially twenty-four officers were selected for service with the Portuguese and Spanish armies.[100] They were known as Employed on Particular Service (EOPS) officers. In becoming EOPS officers, they agreed to give up their regimental commission and be appointed one rank higher in British Army rank. For example, a regimental major would become a lieutenant colonel and a regimental captain would become a major. Their promotions within the British Army would be by brevets and most were promoted to the next higher rank by 1813. No longer having a regimental commission did not prevent the officers from exchanging their new rank for regimental rank. However, if they did so, they would no longer be EOPS officers and would have to leave the Portuguese Army and join their new regiment. One disadvantage for the EOPS officers was that when they left the Portuguese Army, they were not guaranteed a new position in the British Army and their future employment was dependent on finding a job. If no positions were available, they would be placed on half-pay. This did not prevent them from being promoted or exchanging into a regiment. Another major advantage of being EOPS officers was that when they were appointed into the Portuguese Army, it was at a rank higher than their current army rank. For the EOPS officers this meant two steps in promotion over those who were not. The number of EOPS officers was increased to twenty-five in March 1811 and by the end of the war twenty-eight EOPS officers had served in the Portuguese Army. Of the original twenty-four, three were designated for Spanish service, while one officer's selection was revoked due to him not meeting seniority requirements.[101] The twenty officers who went to Portugal in March and April 1809 were:

- Majors promoted to lieutenant colonel with their new date-of-rank in the British Army:
    Archibald Campbell, 71st Foot, 16 February 1809
    William Cox, 61st Foot, 16 February 1809
    Thomas McMahon, 2nd West India Regiment, 4 May 1809
- Captains promoted to major with their new date-of-rank in the British Army:
    John Brown, 27th Foot, 16 February 1809
    James Oliver, 4th Foot, 16 February 1809
    Robert Patrick, 57th Foot, 16 February 1809
    James Douglas, 45th Foot, 16 February 1809
    Richard Bushe, 7th Foot, 16 February 1809
    John Doyle, 87th Foot, 16 February 1809
    John Waters, 1st Foot, 16 February 1809
    William MacBean, 6th Foot, 16 February 1809
    Thomas Hill, 53rd Foot, 16 February 1809
    John Campbell, 10th Foot, 16 February 1809
    Robert Arbuthnot, Chasseurs Britannique, 13 April 1809
    Henry Hardinge, 57th Foot, 13 April 1809
    Havilland Le Mesurier, 21st Foot, 13 April 1809
    George Elder, 95th Foot, 13 April 1809
    Michael McCreagh, 1st Foot, 27 April 1809
    Henry Pynn, 82nd Foot, 15 November 1809
    Henry Watson, 48th Foot, 18 January 1810

It soon became apparent that more officers were needed, and a call went out for volunteers, which was quickly answered. Most of them came from the regular infantry and cavalry regiments, as well as the artillery. The duty was opened to all officer volunteers, with two caveats. Army regulations prohibited more than two captains and two subalterns from a regiment from serving in a staff position outside the regiment. Whether service with the Portuguese Army was considered a staff position is not known, but this guidance was generally followed. The second caveat was that Army regulations also prohibited an officer from serving on the staff before he had at least four years of service.[102] This restriction was also generally followed. Should more than four officers wish to serve, the regimental colonel would have to give his permission. This rarely happened, but there were a few regiments that over the course of the war had multiple officers serving with the Portuguese Army. The 3rd and 11th Foot had ten officers each who served, but not simultaneously (although at one time each had six officers serving with the Portuguese). The 39th Foot had eight officers in the Portuguese Army and six of them were serving simultaneously. The 71st Foot had seven volunteers, the most prominent being Denis Pack, and six of them were with the Portuguese at the same time. There were many volunteers and the officers who were selected came from eighty-four different infantry regiments and fourteen cavalry regiments, as well as six from the Royal Artillery. No officers came from the King's German Legion, but four were from its artillery component, the King's German Artillery.

Medical personnel were also needed and by March 1810 fourteen of them were serving in a variety of positions. By the end of the war twenty-nine surgeons, assistant surgeons, and hospital inspectors had been seconded to the Portuguese Army. The first fourteen were considered EOPS officers and received a step-in rank in the British Army.

It was also recognized that there was a need for officers to help with the administration of the army. A call went out for senior NCOs to take commissions, usually to serve as adjutants at various levels. The exact number is unknown, but there were at least eleven of them. Only one joined in 1809, the rest in the following years. The most successful was Sergeant Johann Schwalbach of the 60th Foot. He stayed in the Portuguese Army and eventually retired as a major general. For his service he was created the Visconde de Setúbal.[103] The last group of volunteers were British gentlemen who could not obtain a commission in the British Army initially and joined the Portuguese Army instead. While in the Portuguese Army, they were commissioned a few months later into the British Army. Their number was small.

By the end of 1809 there were 111 British officers and one sergeant serving as officers in the Portuguese Army. They included one general officer,[104] 20 EOPS officers, 74 regimental officers, 3 Royal Artillery officers, 13 medical personnel, and 1 sergeant. These numbers would continue to expand for the rest of the war. By April 1814 at least 376 had served, of whom 195 were still in the Portuguese Army at the end of the war (see Table 2.1).

Table 2.1: Rank of British Soldiers Commissioned in the Portuguese Army in 1809–1814

Rank[105]	Number
Lieutenant General	1
Brigadier General	1
Colonel	6
Lieutenant Colonel	22
Major	33
Captain	72
2nd Captain	1
Lieutenant	168
1st Lieutenant	4
Ensign	23
Staff Surgeon	22
Assistant Surgeon	6
Inspector of Hospitals	2
Sergeant Major	4
Quartermaster Sergeant	1
Sergeant	6
Former or Retired Officer	3

The officers came from every branch of the army except for the Royal Engineers. Not surprisingly, since the greatest need was for infantry officers, 80 per cent of the officers were infantry. By volunteering, an officer was immediately promoted to the next higher grade in the Portuguese

Army and of those who stayed long enough, many had been promoted two or three ranks by the end of the war. The lieutenants who volunteered usually served as company commanders, often of the grenadier companies. The captains, upon being promoted to major, were either battalion commanders in the infantry regiments, or in the caçadores battalions were either second-in-command or, in a few cases, the commander. When a British major was commissioned as a lieutenant colonel in the Portuguese Army, he was usually assigned to an infantry regiment. In the early days of the war he would often be appointed a regimental commander or, if second-in-command, he would be the de facto commander, because his regimental colonel was either too old or infirm for field command. This created some problems administratively at first. A regiment was only authorized to have a certain number of officers at each rank and most of these positions were already filled by Portuguese officers. The solution was to appoint the British officers in *agregado* rank. This meant they were excess to the authorized number and technically could not be on the regiment's books. The officers served in the regiment and performed the duties of the rank they held. When the senior Portuguese officer left a regiment, the officer *agregado* would take his place on the regimental rolls and would become known as an officer *efetivo*. Regardless of their status, the officer was always called by his rank. Those who came in as colonels usually started as regimental commanders, but most ended their service as brigade commanders and general officers.

Table 2.2: Specialty of British Officers who Served in the Portuguese Army from 1809 to 1814

Artillery	9
Cavalry	24
Infantry	310
Medical	30
Royal Marines	1
Staff	3

British Officers Holding Senior Commands

Infantry Brigade Commanders
One of the biggest issues Beresford faced was finding senior officers who had experience in commanding brigades. Most of the senior Portuguese officers were too old for field service and he had no choice but to select qualified British officers instead. Initially there were not many suitable candidates.[106] Over the years he replaced brigade commanders whose performance was lacking, which included the five original Portuguese and two of the British officers. In January 1812, 70 per cent of the brigades were commanded by British officers, which was a decrease from the year before. In January 1813 the number rose to 80 per cent. However, in 1814 the number dropped to 70 per cent.

Table 2.3 shows the nationality of the brigade commanders. Until 1813 the brigades were usually referred to by their commanders' names, but from 13 August 1813 the brigades were numbered. For the sake of clarity, the following tables use their numbers, regardless of the year.

Table 2.3: Nationality of Infantry Brigade Commanders, 1810–1814

Brigade	1810	January 1811	January 1812	January 1813	January 1814	12 April 1814
1st	British	British	British	British	British	British
2nd	Portuguese	Portuguese	Portuguese	Portuguese	Portuguese	Portuguese
3rd	British	British	British	British	Portuguese	Portuguese
4th	British	British	British	British	British	British
5th	British	British	British	British	British	British
6th	British	British	British	Portuguese	British	British
7th	British[107]	British	Portuguese	British	British	British

Brigade	1810	January 1811	January 1812	January 1813	January 1814	12 April 1814
8th	Portuguese	Portuguese	Portuguese	British	British	British
9th	British	British	British	British	Portuguese	Portuguese
10th		British[108]	British	British	British	British

Cavalry Brigade Commanders

On 24 September 1809 Beresford authorized the creation of three cavalry brigades. British officers commanded these brigades on campaign through most of the war. In 1813 the brigades were commanded by British officers, but in 1814 a Portuguese officer commanded the one brigade on campaign that was still in existence.[109]

Infantry Regimental Commanders

Beresford also had to replace regimental commanders. It was not just that many were old; his plan was to retrain the regiments to use British drill and tactics, such as a two-deep line instead of a three-deep line. Finding replacements was not easy. One of the EOPS officers was a brigade commander. Of the remaining nineteen officers, seven were given command of an infantry regiment, three were assigned to cavalry regiments, and the rest served either as the second-in-command of a regiment or on the army staff.[110] By June 1810 eleven of the twenty-four regiments had a British commander and in the next year the number was up to twelve. In January 1812 thirteen of the commanders were British, and sixteen in January 1813. The number of British commanders dropped back to thirteen in January 1814, and by the end of the war, the number was down to twelve. Between 1809 and 1814 thirty-eight different British officers commanded a regiment (see Table 2.4).

Table 2.4: Nationality of Infantry Regimental Commanders, 1809–April 1814

Regiment	January 1809	January 1810	January 1811	January 1812	January 1813	January 1814	12 April 1814
1st	Portuguese	British	British	British	British	British	British
2nd	Portuguese	Portuguese	Portuguese	Portuguese	Portuguese	Portuguese	Portuguese
3rd	Portuguese	Portuguese	Portuguese	Portuguese	Portuguese	Portuguese	Portuguese
4th	Portuguese	Portuguese	British	British	British	British	British
5th	Portuguese	Portuguese	Portuguese	British	British	British	British
6th	Portuguese	British	British	British	British	British	British
7th	Portuguese	Portuguese	Portuguese	Portuguese	British	Portuguese	British
8th	Portuguese	British	British	British	British	British	British
9th	Portuguese	British	British	British	British	British	British
10th	Portuguese	Portuguese	Portuguese	Portuguese	Portuguese	Portuguese	Portuguese
11th	Portuguese	British	British	British	British	British	British
12th	Portuguese	Portuguese	Portuguese	Portuguese	British	British	British
13th	Portuguese	Portuguese	Portuguese	Portuguese	Portuguese	Portuguese	Portuguese
14th	Portuguese	British	British	British	British	Portuguese	Portuguese
15th	Portuguese	British	British	Portuguese	Portuguese	British	Portuguese
16th	Portuguese	British	British	British	Portuguese	Portuguese	Portuguese
17th	Portuguese	Portuguese	Portuguese	Portuguese	British	British	British
18th	Portuguese	Portuguese	Portuguese	Portuguese	Portuguese	British	British
19th	Portuguese	Portuguese	Portuguese	British	British	Portuguese	Portuguese
20th	Portuguese	British	British	British	British	British	British
21st	Portuguese	Portuguese	Portuguese	Portuguese	British	Portuguese	Portuguese
22nd	Portuguese	Portuguese	Portuguese	British	British	Portuguese	Portuguese
23rd	Portuguese	British	British	Portuguese	British	British	Portuguese
24th	Portuguese	British	British	British	Portuguese	Portuguese	Portuguese

Cavalry Regimental Commanders

Three of the original EOPS officers were assigned to cavalry regiments. Lieutenant Colonel John Campbell was first assigned to the 15th Infantry, but within a month was transferred to command the 4th Cavalry. Lieutenant Colonel John Brown was assigned to the 13th Infantry but in January 1811 was given command of the 8th Cavalry. Lieutenant Colonel Henry Watson was assigned to the 4th Cavalry and on 24 March 1812 was appointed the commander of the 1st Cavalry. Lieutenant Colonel Richard Diggens was assigned to the 5th Cavalry and appointed the commander of the 6th Cavalry on 19 November 1812. A fifth officer, Major Edward Knight, assumed command of the 11th Cavalry when its commander was wounded at Majadahonda on 11 August 1812. Major Knight was still in command at Vitoria, but in July 1813 a Portuguese officer had taken command.

Caçadores Battalion Commanders

In 1809 there were six caçadores battalions. This number was raised to twelve in 1811, two of the new units deriving from the battalions of the LLL which were transformed into caçadores battalions. Lieutenant Colonel George Elder, an EOPS officer, was given command of the 3rd Caçadores on 14 June 1809. In 1810 three more British officers were appointed commanders of caçadores battalions. Over the next two years, as the number of battalions increased, so did the number of British commanders. By 1812 eleven of the twelve battalions had British commanders, although by the end of the war only half were commanded by British officers (see Table 2.5).

Table 2.5: Nationality of Caçadores Battalion Commanders, 1809–April 1814

Battalion	January 1809	January 1810	June 1811	January 1812	January 1813	January 1814	12 April 1814
1st	Portuguese	Portuguese	Portuguese	British	British	Portuguese	Portuguese
2nd	Portuguese	British	British	British	British	British	British
3rd	Portuguese	British	British	Portuguese	Portuguese	Portuguese	Portuguese
4th	Portuguese	Portuguese	Portuguese	British	British	British	British
5th	Portuguese	Portuguese	British	British	British	British	British
6th	Portuguese	Portuguese	Portuguese	British	British	British	British
1st LLL/7th		British	British	British	British	British	British
2nd LLL/8th		British	British	British	Portuguese	British	British
9th			British	British	Portuguese	Portuguese	Portuguese
10th			British	British	Portuguese	Portuguese	Portuguese
11th			British	British	British	Portuguese	Portuguese
12th			British	British	Portuguese	Portuguese	Portuguese

Service from April 1814 to 1829

After the war ended, British officers continued to be promoted, especially at the general officer and field grade officer[111] levels. In 1815 there were two British major generals and seven brigadier generals – or 20 per cent of all generals – in the Portuguese Army. Of the seventy-six British officers who chose to stay at the regimental and battalion level, four were colonels commanding infantry regiments and one commanded a cavalry regiment. Eight of the twelve caçadores battalions were commanded by British lieutenant colonels. Five infantry regiments and one cavalry regiment were commanded by a British lieutenant colonel. Of the fifteen infantry regiments commanded by Portuguese officers, only nine were commanded by colonels, the other six were commanded by lieutenant colonels. Of the nine cavalry regiments not commanded by British officers, two were commanded by Portuguese colonels, the other seven were commanded by lieutenant colonels. By

1818 the number of British generals had increased to one lieutenant general, seven major generals, and six brigadier generals – or 21 per cent of all generals – in the Portuguese Army. There were still fifty-eight British officers at the unit level and most had been promoted. Twenty-four were commanders. Ten were colonels commanding infantry regiments, four were colonels commanding cavalry regiments, and six were lieutenant colonels commanding caçadores battalions. There were also British officers serving on the army staff, and commanding fortresses and military districts. In theory there were many command positions left for deserving Portuguese officers. However, of the fourteen infantry regiments that were not commanded by British officers, only seven were commanded by Portuguese colonels. The other seven were commanded by Portuguese lieutenant colonels. In the cavalry four regiments were commanded by British colonels, seven by Portuguese colonels, and the twelfth by a Portuguese lieutenant colonel. In the caçadores battalions it was evenly split. Six battalions were commanded by British lieutenant colonels and six by Portuguese lieutenant colonels.[112]

The war had now been over for four years and this perceived preference for British commanders over Portuguese commanders created resentment in the Portuguese officer corps. This was the primary reason for the support given by much of the Portuguese Army to the Liberal Revolt of 26 August 1820, which led to the establishment of a new government and a parliament. One of the things the Liberal government did was to dismiss all British officers still serving in the Portuguese Army. However, on 5 March 1821 the government passed a decree regulating the dismissal of these officers. All were still discharged, but they received the thanks of the Portuguese nation and most continued to be paid by Portugal for a period equal to the time they served in the Portuguese Army between 1808 and 1814. Others could retire with a pension that was equal to one-third of their pay.

Many of the British officers returned to Britain in very reduced circumstances. By not returning to the British Army at the end of the war, those who were not EOPS officers were forced to exchange their regimental commissions for equivalent army rank and had been placed on half-pay on 25 December 1816. They received half-pay in addition to their Portuguese Army pay, but since they were no longer in the Portuguese Army, all they received was their British half-pay. They could exchange their army rank for an equivalent rank in a regiment, but this was often at a considerably lower rank and lesser responsibilities than they had enjoyed in the Portuguese Army. For example, Bryan O'Toole was a colonel and regimental commander in the Portuguese Army, but when he returned home in 1820 he reverted to his army rank of major and went on half-pay. Alexander Dickson was a colonel in the Portuguese Army and a brevet lieutenant colonel in the British Army. By the time the war was over in 1814, he was serving as Wellington's chief of artillery. When he resigned from the Portuguese Army in October 1814 he reverted to his Royal Artillery rank of captain. Despite his experience in the Peninsula, he was not considered senior enough to command an artillery brigade of six guns. He ended up taking staff positions and served as Wellington's chief of siege artillery in the Waterloo campaign. He was not promoted to major in the Royal Artillery until 1823.

Awards and Decorations

Deserving senior British officers serving in the Portuguese Army were recognized with sovereign awards. Beresford was created a Peer of the Realm on 3 May 1814 when he became Baron Beresford of Albuera and Dungarvon. Twelve officers were created a KB in 1814 and 1815.[113] Many were inducted into the Order of the Bath. Beresford was created a KB on 16 October 1810 and a KGCB on 2 January 1815. Two days later twelve others were created KCBs.[114] On 4 June 1815 twenty were created a CB.[115] On 22 June 1815 John Campbell and John Gomersall were also created a CB.

Beginning in 1808, the British Army awarded a gold medal to officers who commanded an infantry battalion or cavalry regiment (or higher) in battle and had been brought under musket fire. Staff officers, artillery officers commanding artillery brigades and troops, as well as officers commanding ad hoc light infantry formations were also eligible to receive the medal. By 1815 medals for twenty-seven different battles were awarded, twenty of which were from the Peninsular War. Recipients were often awarded multiple medals, but they could only receive one medal. Additional awards were made in the form of clasps bearing the name of the battle that would be placed on the medal's ribbon. If the individual received four or more awards, the medal and clasps would be replaced with an Army Gold Cross with four arms, each arm with the name of a battle on it. Additional awards would be of a clasp to go on the ribbon of the AGC. British officers in the Portuguese Army also were awarded the medals; the first were for Bussaco, when they were awarded sixteen of the fifty-eight medals.

The Portuguese government also recognized the service of the senior British officers by inducting them into the Order of the Tower and Sword. Beresford and Hamilton were created KCTS. Nineteen were created CTS,[116] and thirty-three were created KTS.[117] They were also awarded the Portuguese Cross of Distinction of the Peninsular War and the Portuguese Command Medal for the Peninsular War.

Casualties

Although much can be said in praise of the awards and recognition these officers received for their service, many of them paid a steep price for them. Of the 376 officers that we have identified, 169 (45 per cent) had become casualties, and 44 (12 per cent) were killed in action or died of their wounds. Another 17 (4 per cent) died of illness, disease, or exhaustion. No fewer than 104 were wounded (28 per cent), 34 (9 per cent) of whom had been wounded more than once. Of the wounded, 74 (20 per cent) were seriously wounded. Another five had been captured, three of whom had been wounded at the time. An untold number returned home broken in health and would die within ten years of the war's end.

To put this in perspective, a British officer in the Peninsula not serving with the Portuguese had a 40 per cent chance of becoming a casualty, a 6.1 per cent chance of being killed or dying from his wounds, a 29 per cent chance of being wounded, and a 4 per cent chance of dying from disease or illness (see Table 2.6).

Table 2.6: Chances of a British Officer Becoming a Casualty between 1811 and 1814[118]

	Serving with the Portuguese Army	Serving in Wellington's Army	Serving in the British Army Worldwide
Chance of Becoming a Casualty (%)	44	40	6
Killed or Died of Wounds (%)	12	7	1
Died of Disease or Sickness (%)	4	4	?
Wounded (%)	28	29	5

Chapter 3

An Overview of the Campaign of 1812

At the beginning of 1812 Napoleon had occupied every major city and fortress in Spain except for Cadiz. Control of the cities did not bring peace and Napoleon had to keep a force of over 350,000 men[119] in the country. These troops were divided into six major commands: the Army of Aragon, the Army of Catalonia, the Army of the Centre, the Army of the North, the Army of Portugal, and the Army of the South. The Armies of Aragon and Catalonia were operating in eastern Spain, while the Army of the North protected the lines of communication from southern France. The Army of the Centre was deployed mostly in garrisons in the vicinity of Madrid. The two armies that concerned Wellington most were the Armies of Portugal and the South. These were the two largest armies, with the Army of the South having almost 80,000 men[120] and the Army of Portugal 75,000 men.[121]

At the beginning of 1812 Wellington could field an army of 68,000 men, including 59,000 infantry and 7,900 cavalry. The Portuguese portion of his army numbered more than 30,000 men, or 45 per cent of his total strength.

Wellington was determined to go on the offensive, but there were two things he had to do before he could march into Spain. The first was to capture the fortified cities of Ciudad Rodrigo and Badajoz. Both had fallen to the French in 1810 and sat on the main invasion routes into Portugal. If he did not capture these two cities, the French could use them to conduct operations in Portugal, while Wellington was elsewhere with his army. Additionally, Wellington had to ensure that the Armies of Portugal and the South could not unite. He knew his army was strong enough to defeat them individually, but if they combined their forces he would have no option but to retreat to Portugal.

Moving an army in Spain was not easy due to the terrain. The biggest obstacle was the 1,000km-long Tagus river. There were only five bridges across the Tagus in Spain between Toledo and the Portuguese border. Further restricting movement by the armies was the lack of major roads running east–west. Most roads ran generally north–south. This was due to the need to avoid the mountain ranges in central Spain, which typically run east–west. The mountains south of the Tagus river in the vicinity of the bridges at Arzobispo and Talavera are so rugged and the east–west road so poor they were virtually impassable. The destruction of the bridges at Almaraz and Alcantara would force an army moving north or south to make a detour of 6–700km to the bridge at Toledo.

The bridges at Almaraz and Alcantara were destroyed in 1809. The French built a pontoon bridge 2km downstream of the bridge at Almaraz and this became their main crossing point across the Tagus. This bridge allowed the French to move forces northwards faster than Wellington could move his. Wellington knew that if he destroyed this bridge, and at the same time repaired the bridge at Alcantara, he could reduce the length of time it would take for the two wings of his army to unite by five days. It would also add several weeks onto the length of time it would take for the two French armies to join up.

Once the border cities were captured and the bridge at Almaraz was destroyed, Wellington would decide whether to attack the Army of Portugal in central Spain or the Army of the South in southern Spain.

The Siege of Ciudad Rodrigo

On 8 January Wellington's Army began besieging Ciudad Rodrigo. He had the 1st, 3rd, 4th, and Light Divisions, as well as Brigadier General Denis Pack's Independent Brigade, to conduct the siege. By 19 January two breaches in the wall were deemed practical and Wellington ordered the city to be assaulted that night. Portuguese troops took part in the assault, the most heavily engaged units being the 1st and 3rd Caçadores. Pack's Brigade made a feint against the Santiago Gate, while the 2nd Caçadores made a diversionary attack against the Castle Gate. The city fell on the morning of 20 January. Portuguese casualties were 47 dead and 68 wounded.[122]

The Siege of Badajoz

On 19 February Wellington began moving his forces to Badajoz. Three weeks later the army was in the vicinity of the Portuguese fortress of Elvas, 20km to the west of Badajoz. The siege began on 16 March and the army was divided into three parts. Lieutenant General Thomas Graham, with the 1st, 6th, and 7th Divisions, would screen the besiegers to the southeast towards Seville, while Lieutenant General Rowland Hill, with the 2nd and Portuguese Divisions, would screen north and east towards Merida. The 3rd, 4th, 5th, and Light Divisions would conduct the actual siege operations. The Portuguese troops included:

Champalimaud's Brigade, 3rd Division
Harvey's Brigade, 4th Division
Spry's Brigade, 5th Division
1st and 3rd Caçadores, Light Division

By 6 April three breaches in the walls were deemed practical and Wellington ordered the attack to be made that night. After a night of fighting, Wellington's troops had captured most of the city and the garrison surrendered at dawn. Unlike the assault on Ciudad Rodrigo two months before, where the Portuguese troops were mostly in a supporting role, here they were actively involved in the assault and took heavy casualties: 394 officers and men were killed or died from wounds, 471 were wounded, and 2 were missing.[123]

The Raid on Almaraz

During the siege of Badajoz, the Army of Portugal moved from Salamanca to threaten Ciudad Rodrigo. Its mission was not to retake the fortress but to force Wellington to send back some of his troops besieging Badajoz to prevent the capture of Ciudad Rodrigo. However, Wellington kept his focus on Badajoz and refused to send any troops north. After the fall of Badajoz, Wellington decided to move against the Army of Portugal. Before he could do this, he needed to destroy the bridge at Almaraz. In mid-April Wellington ordered General Hill to do so. He also ordered the bridge at Alcantara be repaired.

On 7 May Hill began the raid. His force consisted of approximately 7,000 troops. Among them were Ashworth's Brigade and Campbell's Cavalry Brigade. The bridge at Almaraz was destroyed on 21 May and Alcantara bridge was repaired by late May. Wellington began moving his forces from the south to the north, leaving Hill with the 2nd and Portuguese Divisions near Badajoz to protect the southern approaches into Portugal.

The March into Spain

By early June Wellington had successfully moved the bulk of his Army to cantonments near Ciudad Rodrigo. With his army were 18,000 Portuguese troops, organized into one cavalry and seven infantry brigades. Additionally, the Light Division had the 1st and 3rd Caçadores assigned to it. On 13 June the army moved; the French were caught by surprise and abandoned Salamanca. Wellington entered the city on 17 June, but instead of pursuing the retreating French, he decided to capture the three forts in the city and wait for the French to attack him. The forts surrendered on 27 June. By mid-July Marshal Marmont, the commander of the Army of Portugal, had gathered enough troops to go on the offensive and engaged Wellington at Salamanca on 22 July.

The Battle of Salamanca

Wellington had no intention of fighting a battle unless he could inflict a significant loss on the enemy. He deployed his army south of Salamanca behind a series of ridges that prevented the French commander from seeing all his forces. Marmont was prepared to give battle, but his primary objective was to force Wellington to retreat to the border. He deployed his army to attack Wellington's right flank and force him back towards Salamanca. This in turn would expose the centre of the army and make its position untenable, leaving Wellington no choice but to retreat.

The three French divisions making the attack on Wellington's right and centre were to attack together to provide mutual support. However, the length of the march caused them to spread out and their attack went in piecemeal. Wellington, seeing this, ordered his two divisions on the right to attack. The French were again caught by surprise, and the infantry fire combined with a well-timed charge by Portuguese and British cavalry broke the French attack.

During this attack Marmont was seriously wounded, and General Jean Bonnet assumed command. Within an hour he too was wounded, and General Bertrand Clausel took over. He saw the collapse of his army's left flank but believed he could still salvage the situation by attacking the centre with three divisions. The initial attack went well, with the Allies falling back, but Wellington brought up his reserves and halted the French advance. Wellington ordered his counter-attack to continue. The attack by three Allied divisions and a charge by British heavy cavalry broke the three French divisions. Clausel had no option but to order his army to retreat. The rearguard slowed Wellington's advance long enough for the shattered French to withdraw, but it too was hit hard, especially by Resende's Brigade of the 6th Division.

Portuguese troops were involved in the fighting from the very beginning and took heavy casualties, including 506 dead, 1,035 wounded, and 86 missing. Among the wounded was Beresford, who was shot in the chest.

The Liberation of Madrid and the Siege of Burgos

Wellington liberated Madrid on 12 August. By late August he knew that the French were moving against him. The Army of the South was marching north, while the French Armies of Aragon and Valencia had marched west and joined the Army of the Centre, and the Army of Portugal was nearing Valladolid, threatening his lines of communication.

Wellington was faced with a dilemma. Once all the French armies were together, he would be greatly outnumbered. The logical thing would be to abandon Madrid and retreat to Portugal. Wellington estimated that he had at least a month before the French armies united, so he split his forces; leaving the 3rd, 4th, and Light Divisions to protect Madrid, he marched northwest with the 1st, 5th, 6th, and 7th Divisions, and Pack's and Bradford's Brigades to eliminate the threat to his rear.

Clausel's movement south was a bluff and he withdrew northwards when Wellington came within a few days' march. Wellington followed him and by mid-September had reached Burgos, the logistical hub for the French in Spain. He decided to besiege the city with the 5th and 7th Divisions, plus two Portuguese brigades. Portuguese troops were heavily involved in the siege. By mid-October Wellington's greatest concern was realised. The French armies were uniting, and he had no option but to retreat to Portugal.

The Retreat to Portugal

Wellington's Army had been reduced to fewer than 50,000 men and the approaching French numbered over 150,000 infantry and cavalry. Madrid was abandoned and Wellington moved back to Salamanca. The French pursuit caught up with the rearguard at Villa Muriel, where Spry's Brigade was engaged. The French maintained relentless pressure on the retreating army and on 28 October Collins' Brigade fought at Valladolid. Wellington set up positions on the Douro river to delay the French, but on 5 November they were across the river and he pulled back to Salamanca. At the same time that Wellington was retreating, Hill marched north with 15,000 men. He linked up with the three divisions left in the vicinity of Madrid so that he now had under his command the 2nd, 3rd, 4th, and Light Divisions, plus the Portuguese Division. These troops included six Portuguese brigades and the two caçadores battalions assigned to the Light Division. Hill joined Wellington at Alba de Tormes. On 15 November Wellington began to withdraw to the border, which they reached by 19 November. Collins' Brigade was part of the rearguard and on 17 November fought at San Muñoz.

The Portuguese Army

By the summer of 1812 the Portuguese regular army had almost 30,000 men and had already three years of campaign experience. Some of the battalions and regiments were battle-hardened units. Beresford accompanied Lord Wellington on the campaign and with him were the Portuguese Headquarters staff, whose principal officers were:

> Portuguese Military Secretary: Major General António de Lemos Pereira de Lacerda
> British Military Secretary: Colonel Robert Arbuthnot
> Adjutant General: Brigadier General Manuel de Brito Mozinho
> Acting Quartermaster General: Deputy Quartermaster General Lieutenant Colonel Henry Hardinge

The Infantry

By the summer of 1812 the Portuguese Army was able to field all twenty-four infantry regiments and twelve caçadores battalions. Almost all were assigned to brigades, which were, for the most part, assigned to the infantry divisions. Under the direct command of Lord Wellington were seven brigades plus two caçadores battalions:

- Brigadier General Denis Pack's Independent Brigade, about 2,600 men:
  1st Infantry commanded by Colonel Thomas Hill
  16th Infantry commanded by Colonel Neil Campbell[124]
  4th Caçadores commanded by Lieutenant Colonel Edmund Williams

This brigade was one of the most experienced in the Portuguese Army. It was part of the force that covered the Allied retreat to Bussaco in 1810 and was heavily engaged there. The brigade was part of the advance in the pursuit of Marshal Massena's forces during his retreat to Spain in 1811, fighting at Pombal, Redinha, and Condeixa. Pack had commanded it since 7 July 1810.

- Brigadier General Thomas Bradford's Independent Brigade, about 1,900 men:
  13th Infantry commanded by Lieutenant Colonel Joaquim da Câmara
  24th Infantry commanded by Colonel William MacBean[125]
  5th Caçadores commanded by Lieutenant Colonel Michael McCreagh

This brigade was new and inexperienced. It was formed in August 1811 when the 24th Infantry joined the 13th Infantry and the 5th Caçadores. The latter was the only unit with combat experience, having been at Albuera. Bradford assumed command on 20 January 1812.

- Brigadier General Manley Power's Brigade, 3rd Division, about 2,200 men:
  9th Infantry commanded by Lieutenant Colonel Charles Sutton
  21st Infantry commanded by Brevet Lieutenant Colonel John Gomersall[126]
  12th Caçadores commanded by Lieutenant Colonel Arthur Crookshank

This brigade, composed of units recruiting in Minho province, was a seasoned unit. It joined the 3rd Division in April 1810 and fought at Bussaco, Fuentes D'Oñoro, and El Bodon. It distinguished itself in the assault on Badajoz. The 12th Caçadores joined the brigade in April 1812. Power took command of the brigade in July 1812.

- Colonel Thomas Stubbs' Brigade, 4th Division, about 2,500 men:
  11th Infantry commanded by Lieutenant Colonel Alexander Anderson
  23rd Infantry commanded by Lieutenant Colonel James Miller[127]
  7th Caçadores commanded by Major John Ward[128]

This brigade was one of the most experienced units in the army. It was assigned to the 4th Division on 22 February 1810 and was at Bussaco. The 1st LLL Battalion joined it in March 1811 and in May became the 7th Caçadores. The brigade distinguished itself at Albuera, was at Ciudad Rodrigo and enhanced its reputation at Badajoz, where its commander, Colonel William Harvey, was severely wounded. In June 1812 Stubbs, 23rd Infantry, being the senior colonel, took command.

- Brigadier General William Spry's Brigade, 5th Division, about 2,300 men:
  3rd Infantry commanded by Colonel João António Tavares
  15th Infantry commanded by Colonel Luís do Rego Barreto
  8th Caçadores commanded by Major Dudley Hill

This brigade was one of the least experienced in the army. It was assigned to the 5th Division on 6 October 1810, and was present at Bussaco and Fuentes D'Oñoro. The 2nd LLL Battalion joined it in March 1811 and in May became the 8th Caçadores. During the assault on Badajoz, it effectively supported the division's other brigades. Spry commanded it from 16 August 1810.

- Brigadier General Count de Resende's[129] Brigade, 6th Division, about 2,600 men:
  8th Infantry commanded by Colonel James Douglas[130]
  12th Infantry commanded by Colonel António Lacerda Pinto da Silveira[131]
  9th Caçadores commanded by Lieutenant Colonel Gustavus Brown

The brigade's regiments had already had some combat experience, particularly the 8th Infantry, which was heavily engaged at Bussaco. The brigade was formed on 4 October 1810 and assigned to the 6th Division two days later. At the time it was composed of the 8th Infantry and the LLL. In March 1811 the LLL left and was replaced by the 12th Infantry. The 9th Caçadores joined in April 1812. Count de Resende took command on 30 April 1812.

- Colonel Richard Collins' Brigade, 7th Division, about 2,200 men:
  7th Infantry commanded by Lieutenant Colonel Francisco Xavier Calheiros
  19th Infantry commanded by Lieutenant Colonel Francisco da Costa Amaral[132]
  2nd Caçadores commanded by Lieutenant Colonel Bryan O'Toole[133]

This brigade was formed in September 1809, with the 2nd Caçadores joining in September 1810. It joined the 7th Division on 5 March 1811. It was temporarily attached to the 3rd Division during the siege of Ciudad Rodrigo but returned to the 7th Division in February 1812. On 27 February 1812 Collins was appointed its commander. The brigade fought at Bussaco and was present at Fuentes D'Oñoro, where the 2nd Caçadores was heavily engaged. The infantry regiments took part in the assaults on the San Cristobal Fort at Badajoz in June 1811. The brigade took part in the siege of Ciudad Rodrigo, and the 2nd Caçadores was part of the assault.

- 1st and 3rd Caçadores, the Light Division, about 1,100 men:
  1st Caçadores commanded by Lieutenant Colonel John Algeo
  3rd Caçadores commanded by Brevet Major Manuel Caetano Teixeira Pinto[134]

By June 1812 the record of the 1st and 3rd Caçadores was already long, having fought with distinction in almost every action of the Light Division since the spring of 1810. They were heavily engaged at Bussaco and the storming of Badajoz. Their first commanders were Lieutenant Colonel Jorge de Avilez and Lieutenant Colonel George Elder, respectively. Algeo took command of the 1st Caçadores in February 1812 when Avilez was promoted to colonel of the 2nd Infantry. Brevet Major Pinto temporarily commanded the 3rd Caçadores after its senior officers, Lieutenant Colonel Elder and Major Manuel Pinto da Silveira, were severely wounded at Badajoz on 6 April 1812.

Three brigades, two of which were in the Portuguese Division, were with Hill in the vicinity of Badajoz:

- Lieutenant General John Hamilton's Portuguese Division:
  Brigadier General António Hipólito da Costa's Brigade, about 2,800 men:
  2nd Infantry commanded by Colonel Jorge de Avilez
  14th Infantry commanded by Lieutenant Colonel John McDonald
  Brigadier General Archibald Campbell's Brigade, about 2,600 men:
  4th Infantry commanded by Lieutenant Colonel Allan Campbell
  10th Infantry commanded by Colonel Luís Maria de Sousa Vahia
  10th Caçadores commanded by Lieutenant Colonel Richard Armstrong

Since its formation, the Portuguese Division always acted with the 2nd Division, under the command of Hill. Campbell commanded his brigade since its formation in September 1809, with the 10th Caçadores joining in April 1812. Costa took command in January 1812. His brigade was sometimes called the Algarve Brigade, because its regiments were recruited there. The division was present at Bussaco, fought at Albuera, and took part in the first siege of Badajoz.

- Colonel Charles Ashworth's Brigade, 2nd Division, about 2,800 men:
  6th Infantry commanded by Lieutenant Colonel Maxwell Grant
  18th Infantry commanded by Colonel Manuel Pamplona Carneiro Rangel
  6th Caçadores commanded by Lieutenant Colonel Sebastião Pinto de Araújo Correia

This brigade was formed in September 1809 with the 6th Caçadores joining in December 1810. It was assigned to the 2nd Division on 8 June 1811. Ashworth, 6th Infantry, took command of the brigade on 14 March 1811. It was present at Bussaco, and fought at both Fuentes D'Oñoro and Arroyo de Molinos, but was never significantly engaged.

Hill also had at his disposal the regiments garrisoning Elvas and Badajoz:

The 5th Infantry, commanded by Lieutenant Colonel Henry Muller, saw action at Albuera and took part in the sieges of Badajoz in 1811 and 1812

The 17th Infantry, commanded by Lieutenant Colonel John Rolt, saw action in the sieges of Badajoz

The 22nd Infantry, commanded by Colonel John Buchan, was a garrison regiment

The 11th Caçadores, commanded by Lieutenant Colonel Thomas Dursbach, was at the sieges of Badajoz

At the beginning of July all these units joined Hill near Albuera to face the French advance in Extremadura. Hill had about 12,000 Portuguese with him. When he marched north to join Wellington at the beginning of September the three infantry regiments were left behind in Merida and Trujillo, under the command of Buchan. They return to Elvas, except the 22nd, which remained in Merida until the end of the year. The 11th Caçadores remained in Elvas after Hill marched to join Wellington.

The 20th Infantry, under the command of Lieutenant Colonel John Prior, was part of the Cadiz garrison from 1810. It accompanied Colonel John Skerrett's force that moved from Cadiz to join Wellington after the French evacuated Andalusia. On 17 October 1812 it was attached to the Light Division. The 20th Regiment had seen action at Barossa.

The Cavalry

The Portuguese cavalry was able to field two brigades for the 1812 campaign. At the beginning of June a cavalry brigade was assembled in the northern province of Trás-os-Montes under the command of Brigadier General Benjamin D'Urban. It comprised the 1st, 11th, and 12th Cavalry. The 1st Cavalry mustered about 550 horses, close to its full establishment. The 11th Cavalry mustered only two weak squadrons, about 250 horses, and the 12th Cavalry three weak squadrons, about 320 horses. In mid-July D'Urban sent a squadron of the 12th Cavalry, about 100 horses, to join General Silveira's militia division in Trás-os-Montes.

D'Urban wrote to Beresford on 2 July expressing his opinion of the 1st Cavalry: 'I think the 1st Regt. has reached in every respect a pitch of perfection that I have never seen or expected to see in any Portuguese Cavalry.'[135]

In D'Urban's own words, his mission was initially 'to act from that side [north of the Douro] against the rear and communications of the enemy as occasion may serve'.[136] This was done until 15 July, when the brigade was ordered to join the main army. The conduct of the 1st and 11th Regiments at Salamanca was generally praised but two weeks later, at Majadahonda, the brigade disgraced itself against the French.

The brigade's regiments had the following commanders at the beginning of the campaign:

1st Cavalry commanded by Lieutenant Colonel Henry Watson[137]
11th Cavalry commanded by Lieutenant Colonel Domingos Bernardino Ferreira de Sousa[138]
12th Cavalry commanded by Lieutenant Colonel Viscount de Barbacena[139]

In the south with Hill was a second brigade composed of the 3rd Cavalry, about 400 horse, the 4th Cavalry, about 250 horse, and the 6th Cavalry, with three squadrons, about 360 horse. The brigade was commanded by Colonel John Campbell, 4th Cavalry. When Hill advanced north to Madrid he took with him the 4th and 6th Regiments and left the 3rd Cavalry in Extremadura. These cavalry regiments performed well alongside the British cavalry in the multiple skirmishes fought in Extremadura, around Madrid, and during the retreat to Portugal.

The regimental commanders at the beginning of the campaign were:

3rd Regiment commanded by Lieutenant Colonel João da Silveira de Lacerda
4th Regiment commanded by Colonel John Campbell
6th Regiment commanded by Lieutenant Colonel Richard Diggens

The Artillery

The Portuguese artillery fielded four brigades for the upcoming campaign:

- The 1st Artillery fielded a brigade under Brevet Major Sebastião José de Arriaga, composed of six 24-inch howitzers. It was attached to Wellington's Reserve Artillery, which was commanded by Lieutenant Colonel Alexander Dickson, 4th Portuguese Artillery Regiment, and was employed primarily in the reduction of the Salamanca forts and at the siege of Burgos.
- Two brigades were attached to the Portuguese Division at the beginning of the campaign, both under the overall command of Lieutenant Colonel Alexander Tulloh, 3rd Artillery:
  The 1st Artillery fielded a brigade of 6-pounder guns under Captain João da Cunha Preto
  The 2nd Artillery fielded a brigade of 9-pounder guns under Captain William Braun, an officer from the 4th Artillery
- The 4th Artillery fielded a brigade under Captain Duarte Guilherme Ferreri, which was attached to Silveira's militia division in Trás-os-Montes province. In August 1812 Silveira advanced to Zamora, blockading the French garrison there.

Chapter 4

The Battle of Salamanca

On 22 July, after manoeuvring over the previous week, Wellington's Army and Marmont's French Army of Portugal met in battle about 5km south of the city of Salamanca. Wellington had with him about 50,000 men, of whom 18,000 were Portuguese. Opposing them were about 50,000 French. Wellington deployed his army in the morning, with the 7th Division on the left, and the 1st Division behind them in reserve. To the right of them was Pack's Brigade near the Lesser Arapile. The 6th and 5th Divisions were in the centre, while the 4th Division was to their right, with Bradford's Brigade to its right. Anchoring the right of the line was the 3rd Division. On the far-right flank was D'Urban's Cavalry Brigade, as well as a British light cavalry brigade. The Light Division was still moving forward and would be on the far left.

The French were deployed about a kilometre away, with two divisions on their right, two in reserve, two in the centre, and two on the left. Marmont's plan was to force Wellington to retreat to Portugal by turning the Allied Army's right flank. The morning began with skirmishing between light troops from the 7th Division and Pack's Brigade and those of General Maximilien Foy's Division. Included in this affair were the 2nd and 4th Caçadores. Wellington was convinced that the French would attack his right flank and ordered the 5th Division to move so it was to the right of the 4th Division. The 7th Division was shifted to the centre of the line, where it sat in reserve behind the 5th Division.

In mid-afternoon Wellington noticed several French divisions moving to the right. These were spread out and not in mutual support of each other. Wellington ordered the 3rd Division to attack the French division on the Monte da Azan. Part of the 3rd Division was Power's Brigade, and supporting it was D'Urban's Cavalry. The 3rd Division was unstoppable. It forced the French off the ridge and knocked the French division out of the battle. D'Urban's Cavalry broke a battalion and the 12th Caçadores captured a French Eagle.

Wellington, seeing the French falling back, ordered the 5th Division to attack. It caught a division deploying and forced it back onto the division behind it. A timely charge by a British heavy cavalry brigade completed the destruction of the three French divisions. About the time the 5th Division attacked, the 4th Division moved forward with Stubbs' Brigade on its left flank. They successfully pushed the French brigade off the ridge to their front, but the troops quickly rallied and with another brigade counter-attacked with support from a dragoon division. The 4th Division's attack collapsed, and its troops ran for the rear, pursued by infantry and cavalry. The French commander decided to continue the attack and ordered the division on the right to go with them. Wellington, seeing his centre in danger, sent the 6th Division forward to stabilize the line. It was at this critical moment that Spry's Brigade, the rear brigade of the 5th Division, made a bayonet charge on the French flank, helping to break their attack.

While the 4th Division was making its failed assault, Pack decided to clear the French from the Greater Arapile. The assault was well planned, but a combination of difficult terrain and heavy artillery fire badly disordered the troops. As they neared the top, they were surprised by the French infantry, which broke them and chased them back down the hill.

About this time the French commander decided that the battle was lost and ordered a retreat. He left a division as a rearguard and hurried his troops off the battlefield. Wellington ordered the 6th Division, which included Resende's Brigade, to attack the rearguard. The first attack was made with the Portuguese in the second line, but the French artillery fire was so heavy the attack was stopped before they got within 400m of the French. Additional units were moved up in support. The second attack went in with the Portuguese in the first line. They made it to the top of the ridge and engaged the French in a firefight until the French withdrew.

Salamanca is often considered one of Wellington's finest victories. His Portuguese troops were involved in some of the heaviest fighting and lost more than 2,000 men killed, wounded, or missing. Among them was Beresford, two brigade commanders, four regimental commanders, and five lieutenant colonels and majors.

D'Urban's Cavalry Brigade (1st, 7th, and 11th Cavalry)
D'Urban's Cavalry Brigade was deployed on the far right. Around 3 p.m. Wellington ordered the 3rd Division to march to the far right and attack the French left flank on the Heights of Pico de Miranda. D'Urban was ordered to protect the division's right flank. As the Allies neared the heights, D'Urban spotted a French infantry battalion[140] in a column of companies and ordered the 1st Cavalry to charge it. The leading French company fired and caused some casualties, but the 2nd Squadron hit the flank of the infantry, breaking their formation. The brigade continued to support the 3rd Division's attack. When the 5th Foot was charged and broken by French cavalry, D'Urban ordered his brigade to counter-charge, which prevented the French cavalry from destroying the fleeing British soldiers. Considering that the brigade participated in two charges, its losses in men and horses were relatively light, losing less than 10 per cent of both regiments.

Letter[141] from General D'Urban to AG Mozinho

Sir,
I think I cannot answer your letter of 29th last month in a more satisfactory manner than forward to you a faithful extract of the reports[142] I sent to His Excellency the Marshal Commander-in-Chief of the Army.[143] I believed that was enough to meet the purpose.
God save you, Sir
Camp Puerto de Guadarrama 8 August 1812
Manoel de Brito Mozinho

Your most obedient servant
B D'Urban

P.S. Only yesterday I received your letter of 29th last month.

See Table 4.1.

3rd Division

Power's Brigade (9th and 21st Infantry, 12th Caçadores)
Power's Brigade was the 3rd Division's reserve during the battle and saw little action. The division took the 12th Caçadores and the light companies from each of the British battalions and formed an ad hoc light battalion under the command of Lieutenant Colonel Crookshank[144] of the 12th Caçadores. They screened the advance of the division as it attacked the French on the Heights of Pico de Miranda. The attack was successful, and the division continued along the heights and assaulted the Monte de Azan, where it hit General Eloi Taupin's division in the flank. The first regiment they encountered was the French 22nd Line, which in addition to having to fight the 3rd Division was attacked by British heavy cavalry. The 12th Caçadores captured the eagle of the French 22nd Line Regiment.[145] The brigade lost 29 killed or died of wounds, 32 wounded, and 14 missing, of whom the 12th Caçadores lost 25 killed or died of wounds, 24 wounded, and 14 missing.

Report[146] from General Power to AG Mozinho

Camp St. Ildefonso
August 8th 1812
Sir,
I was not honoured with your letter of the 26th ultimo until late yesterday in answer to which however I have now to acquaint you for the information of Marshal Sir William Beresford that although I very much regret the Brigade under my command had not an opportunity of particularly distinguishing itself in the action of the 22nd ultimo, nothing could exceed the gallantry, good conduct and anxiety to be more actively employed, than was shown by the officers and men. Our most positive and particular orders were to support the right[147] and left[148] English Brigades, which was done I trust to the satisfaction of Major General Packenham commanding the Division,[149] but in the course of which service it did not fall to our lot to be particularly engaged with the enemy. I beg leave to recommend Lieutenant Colonel Sutton[150] and Lieutenant Colonel Gomersall,[151] of the 9th and 21st Regiments, for their great zeal upon the occasion and I am also particularly indebted to my Aide-de-Camp Captain Johnston[152] for his activity in conveying my orders and carrying on the different services entrusted to him, much to my satisfaction.

The 12th Caçadores under the command of Lieutenant Colonel Crookshank were detached from the Brigade upon the above day, but I believe his conduct as well as that of the Battalion was extremely satisfactory to Major General Packenham. I have already reported for His Excellency's[153] information that it was Captain Jeronimo Pereira de Vasconcellos of that battalion who took the Eagle which the Major General mentions to have been taken by the 3rd Division, and which Lieutenant Colonel Crookshank presented the next day to Major General Packenham to be forwarded to the Commander of the Forces.
I have the honour to be Sir,
your most obedient and humble servant

M. Power
Brigade General

To the Adjutant General

5th Division

Spry's Brigade (3rd and 15th Infantry, 8th Caçadores)
About 2 p.m. the 5th Division moved to the right in preparation for an attack on the Monte de Azan. Upon arriving there, it deployed in a valley with its left flank anchored on the village of Los Arapiles. To its left was the 4th Division and to its right the 3rd Division. It formed into two lines, with Spry's Brigade in the second line on the left and three British battalions to their right. The brigade had the 15th Infantry on the left and the 3rd Infantry on the right. To the front were the 8th Caçadores and the division's ten British light companies. Their orders were to attack only after the 3rd Division had begun its attack. The division stayed in the position for over two hours waiting for the order to assault the Monte de Azan about 700m to their front. During that time they were exposed to heavy artillery fire. When they were finally ordered to move against the French, the first line advanced more quickly than the second line. Beresford noticed this and ordered the brigade to halt so they could swing to the left of the first line. The 15th Infantry did so faster than the 3rd Infantry and marched up the ridge at an angle. There they caught General Jean Bonet's division in the flank after it had counter-attacked the Allied 4th Division and pushed it back. The 15th Infantry fired a volley and charged. Captain Edward Brackenbury, commander of the 1st Grenadier Company of the 1st Battalion 15th Infantry, was credited with capturing a French gun. He wrote to his parents two days later that 'I fought with my Portuguese Regt. Who behaved well and bayonetted [sic] a Column of the French, you will scarcely believe how I

could have Escaped, when I assure you I was cutting away in a Solid Column with my Common regulation Sword: but Providence protected me as it did at Badajos [sic] when I mounted the Ladder at the Head of my Regt.'[154] An anonymous officer[155] in the 15th Infantry left a description of the charge in a letter two days later:

> The French feeling the blow on their flank turned around and fled, but short of strength due to the day's fatigue, they were overrun by the regiment. At this point, with Colonel Luís do Rego Barreto and his officers in front, the regiment consummated a horrible carnage. Every bayonet and sword found a French and these ones, dispirited, let themselves be killed almost without resistance, leaving in the hands of the regiment artillery and colours. The few that escaped brought terror and disorder to their comrades that continued to fiercely resist the furious attacks of the other troops of our army.[156]

The 3rd Infantry followed the 15th Infantry and engaged the French in a firefight. Once the Monte de Azan was taken, the division pursued the retreating French. The brigade lost 237 men or 10 per cent of its strength in the battle.

Report[157] from General Spry to AG Mozinho

Sir,
I have the honour to enclose a return of the dead, wounded and missing of the 3rd and 15th Infantry and the 8th Caçadores.

In the attack on the enemy's army on 22nd ultimo, the Brigade was ordered to advance in second line, following the two British brigades of the 5th Division, which it did in very good order, though it was not possible to preserve the distance when the British fixed bayonets and passed the heights in our front.

The Brigadier received orders from Marshal Count de Trancozo[158] to turn [the Brigade] to the left and to move forward the First Battalion of the 3rd Regiment; to execute this the regiment halted, but the 15th Regiment continued its movement until it arrived in the flank of an enemy corps formed and firing on the British. At that time, the Brigadier tried to deploy the 15th Regiment to the left in view of taking the advancing enemy by his exposed flank and rear, but he was not able to do it in time. However, the enemy returned by the same direction and then the 15th Regiment fired and charged with the bayonet on his flank causing many casualties.

Considering that this Regiment had many new soldiers who never before had been exposed to the fire, it is no wonder if some confusion occurred, but they showed every disposition to attack and none to avoid the enemy.

Colonel Rego[159] showed his usual spirit leading his men against the unbroken enemy columns,[160] and Captain Brackenbury[161] from the 15th Regiment's 1st Grenadier Company alone took one of the enemy's guns pulled by two mules and defended by five men, among the enemy columns.

The 3rd Regiment did not advance in time to help in that critical moment but remained in a steady line.

The 8th Caçadores Battalion behaved in its usual and excellent manner in several skirmishes during the day with some loss, being deprived of its brave commander Major Hill[162] who was wounded by a bullet through his arm and entering the body.
God save you, Sir
25 July 1812
Manoel de Brito Mozinho
Brigadier Adjutant General

W. Fred. Spry
Brigadier

Return[163] of the Dead, Wounded and Missing in the 3rd Brigade of the 5th Division,[164] in the Battle of Salamanca, 22 July 1812

Killed
3rd Regiment: 17 Corporals and Privates
15th Regiment: 1 Lieutenant; 1 Ensign; 12 Corporals and Privates
Total killed: 1 Lieutenant; 1 Ensign; 29 Corporals and Privates

Wounded
3rd Regiment: 1 Ensign, 3 Sergeants, 49 Corporals and Privates
15th Regiment: 1 Lieutenant; 1 Ensign; 99 Corporals and Privates
8th Caçadores: 1 Major; 1 Captain; 1 Ensign; 2 Sergeants; 21 Corporals and Privates

Total wounded: 1 Major; 1 Captain; 1 Lieutenant; 3 Ensigns; 5 Sergeants; 169 Corporals and Privates

Bruised
3rd Regiment: 1 Brevet Colonel; 2 Ensigns

Missing
3rd Regiment: 20 Corporals and Privates
8th Caçadores: 3 Corporals and Privates

Total missing: 23 Corporals and Privates

Names of the officers killed, wounded, and bruised

Killed
15th Regiment: Lieutenant Jose Maria Leite; Ensign Miguel da Cunha Alcoforado

Wounded
3rd Regiment: Ensign Joaquim de Souza Pinto Cardozo, slightly
15th Regiment: Lieutenant Bento Gonsalves, severely;[165] Ensign João de Matos Maio, slightly
8th Caçadores: Major Hill,[166] severely; Captain Dubry,[167] severely; Ensign Pereira,[168] slightly

Bruised
3rd Regiment: Brevet Colonel João Antonio Bilstein, Ensign João Teotonio da Fonseca Quintanilha, Ensign Gerardo Brancamp

W. Fred. Spry
Brigadier

4th Division

Stubbs' Brigade (11th and 23rd Infantry, 7th Caçadores)
Cole's 4th Division was deployed in the centre of the Allied line, with the 5th Division to its right and the 6th Division to its left rear. The division consisted of two British brigades and Stubbs' Brigade. One brigade was defending the Lesser Arapiles, leaving the Portuguese and British Fusilier Brigades to attack when the order came. They were deployed in a line with Stubbs on the left. The 7th Caçadores were part of the light infantry screen that preceded the division. The 11th Infantry were on the right and the 23rd Infantry on the left. Prior to the attack, the men were ordered to put an additional ball in their barrel of their muskets. At 5:45 p.m. they advanced against Clausel's Division on the ridge about a kilometre to their front. The senior officers in the 11th Infantry were on horseback as they advanced.[169] Before they moved out, the 23rd Infantry

fell 'on their knees, offer a short prayer, and with greatest firmness continue their advance'.[170] As they advanced, Cole was concerned about the threat to his left flank and sent the 7th Caçadores to screen it. The two brigades were brought under heavy artillery fire as they crested the ridge. There they engaged in a short firefight that forced General Marie-Etienne Barbot's Brigade to retreat. The Allied regiments on the ridge stopped to re-form their lines. Clausel rallied the retreating French soldiers and led his division back up the hill, where the Allies were still trying to organize themselves. As they marched, General Bonet, who was on the right of Clausel's Division, attacked the 7th Caçadores, forcing them to fall back. This exposed the left flank of the 23rd Regiment, which was brought under heavy fire. The Portuguese and British, seeing their flank threatened, fired two volleys at Clausel's Division and ran back down the hill. Three regiments of French dragoons took the opportunity to charge the fleeing infantry. Fortunately for the Portuguese soldiers, their officers were able to get most of their men into squares. Rather than charging the squares, the enemy cavalry veered to the right and attacked the 6th Division. Stubbs reorganized his brigade, and it was part of the attack on the French rearguard later in the evening. They took heavy casualties with 180 men killed, 285 wounded, and 11 missing.

Report[171] from Colonel Stubbs[172] to AG Mozinho

Sir,

Today I received your letter of 26th ultimo where you request information, by order of His Excellency Marshal Beresford, Count de Trancozo, about the conduct of the corps of the Brigade under my command at the battle of 22 July. I have the satisfaction to tell you that the 11th and 23rd Regiments showed great bravery facing the superior force to which they were exposed.[173] The 11th Regiment attacked with the bayonet a strong enemy position in a very gallant manner.[174] The 23rd Regiment, forming the left flank of the line, was flanked by the enemy extending his line, and nearly surrounded, sustained with the utmost steadiness a heavy fire,[175] and advancing attacked two enemy columns in front, forcing them to retreat and abandoning their position in the heights.[176]

Lieutenant Colonel Anderson,[177] commander of the 11th Regiment, and Captain King[178] of the 23rd Regiment are the officers, I believe, most distinguished. The first, not only for the state of discipline attained by his regiment, but also by the gallantry with which he led them in the bayonet attack, and the example he gave. Captain King was the senior officer present and the regiment having only one superior officer I appointed him to do the duties of a Major, which he performed with zeal and activity, and I believe, concurred, with his intrepidity, to the good conduct of the regiment.[179]

I must add that all the other officers of the two regiments behaved very well, to the general good fortune of the Brigade.

The 7th Caçadores Battalion was detached at the beginning of the battle by Lieutenant General Cole; they formed in extended order, and engaged the enemy with intrepidity. They did not re-join the Brigade that day and remained detached through the night.

God save you, Sir

Camp of Segovia 9 August 1812

Brigadier Manoel de Brito Mozinho

Thomas William Stubbs
Colonel commander of the Brigade

6th Division

Resende's Brigade (8th and 12th Infantry, 9th Caçadores)
The 6th Division spent much of the day in reserve. It was deployed in two lines on a ridge due west of the Greater Arapiles and east of the 1st Division. The first line had the two British brigades,

while Resende's Brigade was the second line. After seeing the 4th Division's attack on the ridge fail, Wellington ordered the 6th Division to advance. As it was doing so, the two French divisions that stopped the 4th Division continued to advance. The 6th Division was able to restore order and helped stop the French counter-attack. Clausel, who was now commanding the French Army, decided to break off and retreat. General Claude Ferey's Division formed the rearguard and his nine battalions deployed on the forward slopes of a ridge called El Sierro. The 6th Division was ordered to attack with two brigades in the first line and Resende's Brigade in reserve. The French artillery with the rearguard disrupted the division badly enough that it had to halt and reform. While it was doing so, reinforcements from the 1st and 4th Divisions were brought up in support. Resende's Brigade moved to the left of the first line and with the other brigades now formed a continuous line, with the 8th Infantry on the right and the 12th Infantry on the left. The 9th Caçadores formed a skirmish line. As they advanced the caçadores angled to the right and were able to get on the French flank. Captain Jean-Baptiste Lemonnier-Delafosse of the French 31st Light Regiment witnessed their approach:

> we saw the enemy marching up against us in two lines, the first of which was composed of Portuguese. Our position was critical, but we waited for the shock: the two lines moved up towards us; their order was so regular that in the Portuguese regiment in front of us we could see the company intervals, and note the officers behind keeping the men in accurate line, by blows with the flat of their swords or their canes. We fired first, the moment that they got within our range; and the volleys which we delivered from our two first ranks were so heavy and so continuous that, though they tried to give us back fire for fire, the whole melted away.[180]

The French captain was incorrect about the Portuguese melting away. In fact, they stood and exchanged fire with the French for about 20 minutes, before the French retired. Resende's Portuguese lost just under 500 men killed, wounded, or missing. Among the wounded was Resende. The brigade had more casualties than any other Portuguese brigade.

Report[181] from General Count de Resende[182] to AG Mozinho, enclosing several reports from the commanding officers of the several corps in his brigade

Sir,

I have the honour to enclose the report from the 9th Battalion Caçadores' commander for the information of His Excellency the Marshal Count de Trancozo Commander-in-Chief of the Portuguese Army. It is my duty to notice the noble and gallant conduct of Lieutenant Colonel Count de Ficalho[183] from the 8th Regiment until he was severely wounded. The conduct of Major Arnot[184] from the 12th Regiment was also very gallant and praiseworthy. The conduct of the Brigade Major[185] was very meritorious until he was severely wounded. The conduct of Ensign Lemos,[186] serving as my Aide-de-Camp, was magnificent, aside from conveying my orders, he asked my permission, to which I consented, to go with one of the battalions in a charge made against the enemy. I think this officer deserves the attention of His Excellency.

God save you, Sir.

S. Vicente 28 July 1812

Manoel de Brito Mozinho

Conde de Rezende D. Luis
Brigadier commanding the 8th, 12th and 9th Caçadores

See Table 4.2.

12th Infantry

Report[187] from Colonel Silveira to AG Mozinho

Sir

I have the honour to enclose the reports that I just received from Lieutenant Colonel Pizarro[188] and Major Arnot for information of His Excellency the Marshal Count de Trancozo. On 22 last month, those officers commanded under my orders the Regiment's battalions. I have only to add that I am extremely pleased with the conduct of both and also of Ensign Lemos[189], who was serving as Aide-de-Camp to the Brigade commander,[190] and performed the duties of that post very efficiently.

God save you, Sir

Villa de Canellas 15 August 1812

Manoel de Brito Mozinho

António de Lacerda[191]

Colonel 12th Regiment

1st Battalion, 12th Infantry

Report[192] from Lieutenant Colonel Pizarro to Colonel Silveira

Sir

In consequence of your order to inform about those officers and men of the 1st Battalion of the Regiment, which I had the honour to command, who have distinguished themselves in the action, I have the pleasure to ensure you that they all did their duty, honouring the Portuguese nation and deserving the notice of His Royal Highness.

In addition to the names listed in the enclosed, to which I join the report from the 2nd Battalion, it is my duty to recognize my obligation to the captain of the 5th Company João Antonio de Sampaio, not just for his assistance in keeping the battalion in good order, until we took possession of the last height, but also by his reasonable advice. I beg leave to ask you to bring the attention of the Marshal Commander of the Army to the conduct of this officer who deserves every commendation. The same I beg to all those listed because they are worthy of the attention and benevolence of His Royal Highness, particularly the sergeants which I think can fill the vacancies open by the killed and injured officers in the platoons. All this I ask to feel myself rewarded.

God save you, Sir

Camp of Ornillas

29 July 1812

Antonio de Lacerda Pinto da Silveira

Colonel 12th Regiment

Francisco Homem de Magalhães

Quevedo Pizarro

Lieutenant Colonel

Return of the Officers and Inferior Officers who Distinguished Themselves in the Action of 22 instant

Captains João Antonio Sampaio and Guilherme [sic] White[193]

Lieutenants Antonio Jozé Carneiro and João Maria da Fonseca

Ensigns Alexandre de Lacerda Pinto da Silveira,[194] Antonio Maria Tudella, Antonio Bernardo de Abreu

1st Sergeants Jozé da Silva Vieira and Antonio Manoel Varejão

2nd Battalion, 12th Infantry

Report[195] from Major Arnot to Lieutenant Colonel Pizarro

Sir

In consequence of your order I have the honour to inform you that in the action on 22 of this month I had the honour to command the 2nd Battalion 12th Infantry Regiment. The Battalion deserves every compliment for the general conduct of the officers, inferior officers and men who had the glory to serve under its flag on that day. I have every reason to be satisfied with the conduct of the Captain of the 2nd Company of Fusiliers, Francisco da Silva Teixeira, but I must do justice and recommend particularly, begging you to notice to His Excellency the Marshal Commander in Chief, the conduct of the 8th Company's Captain Ignacio Luiz Madeira, Lieutenant Green,[196] commanding the 2nd Grenadier's Company, Ensign Donovan,[197] 4th Company, Ensign Duarte Cardozo de Sá, 8th Company, Adjutant Sergeant Manoel Józé Correia, who being wounded, refused to go to the rearguard and remained with the battalion, and First Sergeant Luis Antonio Doutel, 8th Company. This is all I have to report.
Camp 31 July 1812
Lieutenant Colonel Francisco Homem de Magalhães Quevedo Pizarro

Lawrence Arnot
Major 12th Infantry

9th Caçadores

Report[198] from Lieutenant Colonel Brown to Count de Resende

Sir,
Being detached from the Brigade under Your Excellency's command, on 22, at the battle near Salamanca, it is my duty to send a detailed report of the circumstances related to the battalion under my command. Operating detached, its action could not be noticed by Your Excellency to whom I beg to have the goodness to lay it before His Excellency the Marshal Count de Trancozo.

During all day I complied with the orders of Major General Clinton,[199] and nothing particular happened until, advancing the battalion under my command in line on the right of the Division to the attack on the last enemy's position on a great height,[200] I was ordered to advance a company in extended order, to oppose the great number of skirmishers that the enemy sent to the plain. I immediately moved forward the 1st Company under the command of its Captain Antonio Luis de Moraes Sarmento and continued to advance with the battalion in line about one hundred paces, when I received a new order to advance in quick time without further detail. Then seeing that by an oblique movement by the right I could flank the enemy's left,[201] I advanced in this manner, closing on the enemy that had a howitzer and a gun posted on the slope of the mountain supported by an infantry battalion at the top. To support this movement, I formed a reserve on my right under the command of Major Luiz Maria Cerqueira, which I ordered to engage the flank of the enemy when the rest of the battalion charged with the bayonet. I had the good fortune of seizing the howitzer with its wagons, and in the pursuit, I forced the enemy to abandon the gun on the other side of the mountain.[202]

I had the opportunity to notice that all the officers and men did their duty in these actions; Major Luiz Maria Cerqueira lost his horse, and with a broken hand kept advancing on foot with his party, in the best order. The Adjutant Sergeant,[203] with a few men, whom I could not recognize because of the dark, killed the artillery men who defended the guns to conclude the happy event of taking the howitzer.
God save you, Sir
Camp 27 July 1813
His Excellency Count de Rezende

G. Brown
Lieutenant Colonel commander 9th Caçadores

See Table 4.3.

Pack's Independent Brigade (1st and 16th Infantry, 4th Caçadores)

Pack's Independent Brigade was in the vicinity of the Lesser Arapiles and to the left of the 4th Division. His orders were discretionary: 'He was to watch and mark the Arapiles, and not to let any of the enemy come down from it to molest the flank or rear of our left Division (Cole's).[204] He was to exercise his own judgment, and if he saw a favourable opportunity, he was authorised to try and carry the Hill of the Arapiles [the Greater Arapile].'[205] To do so Pack deployed his brigade in a position from where he could assault the Greater Arapile, which was occupied by the French 120th Line Regiment of about 1,800 men and a battery of artillery. The brigade was arranged with its four grenadier companies under the command of Colonel Neil Campbell deployed in line in the centre. Behind them on the right was the 1st Infantry in two columns of companies, all under the command of Colonel Hill. On the left was Lieutenant Colonel Vidigal with the 16th Infantry in two columns of companies. Screening the formation to the front were two companies of the 4th Caçadores under the command of Major Fearon of the 1st Infantry. These two companies were to be the storming party. On both flanks were two companies of the 4th Caçadores. Pack ordered the men to lie down to reduce their exposure to enemy fire. They waited for several hours until they were ordered to move to support the 4th Division. This order was soon cancelled and only the 4th Caçadores went forward. They fought to stem the attack on its left. To relieve the pressure on the 4th Division from the French counter-attack, Pack decided to assault the Greater Arapiles. He no longer had the 4th Caçadores to screen the assault, so he used two companies from each of the regiments. The brigade moved smartly up the hill, but soon the enemy artillery fire and the steep terrain caused the attack to stall. They were almost at the top when the French fired a massive volley and charged down the hill scattering the brigade before them. Pack's brigade was spent and saw no further action that day. By the end of the day, it had lost almost 500 officers and men, mostly in the assault on the Greater Arapiles.

Report[206] from General Pack to AG Mozinho

At dawn, observing some of our cavalry falling back from the enemy's cavalry (supported by skirmishers), I sent two companies (one from the 1st Regiment, the other from the 16th) to support them. This service was beautifully executed under the command of Captain Zagalo.[207] The enemy, being considerably reinforced with cavalry and infantry, advanced again. At this time General Cole[208] requested that I send down the 4th Caçadores under the command of Lieutenant Colonel Williams[209] and Major Adamson.[210] A sharp skirmish immediately began, during which the Caçadores behaved singularly well, deserving Lieutenant General Cole's approbation. The enemy was forced to retreat, and immediately after I was ordered to move with my brigade opposite to the height in front of the centre of our army,[211] which was taken by the enemy and I received instructions from the Commander-in-Chief to attack it. However, this attack was for the time deferred.

In the afternoon, my Brigade was ordered to move to the right to support the cavalry; the line regiments were countermanded, but the Caçadores proceeded and almost immediately engaged. They came under very heavy musketry and cannon fire for the next two hours; no troops could have behaved better and Lieutenant Colonel Williams, who was wounded, speaks highly of Ensigns Sebastião de Elvas Montaes[212] and Domingos da Costa Ferraz,[213] both severely wounded, the former three times before he was forced to leave the field.

In the afternoon, when it was decided to begin the general action against the enemy, I returned to the line regiments of my brigade to put in execution the Commander-in-Chief's initial plan to attack the height mentioned before. The Caçadores' ammunition was expended and they could not return in time to re-join us. So we advanced with two companies of each regiment extended as skirmishers to our front, under the command of Major Fearon;[214] while the 1st Regiment's fusilier companies, under Colonel Hill,[215] moved in column by the right, those of the 16th, under Lieutenant Colonel Vidigal[216] by the left, and the grenadiers of both regiments in line as the reserve,[217] under Colonel Campbell.[218] It's impossible that troops advancing with such apparent steadiness did not inspire their commander with confidence in their success. The advanced companies started to fire too soon but had almost gained the height, with the immediate support of the 1st Regiment's column, when an almost inconceivable sudden alarm led the

troops to flee and, suffering excessively from the enemy's fire, nothing could rally them. I am satisfied with the diligence of the superior officers and the others in rallying the troops. I beg leave to mention the zeal and courage of my Aide-de-Camp Captain Synge[219] (who was severely wounded), most conspicuous, particularly in this attack. I only want to remark that the attack was at the unfortunate moment that the Division[220] on our left retreated, which naturally inspired confidence in the troops[221] on the height (1,700 men and two guns) causing them to oppose us with more resolution than I believe they would; in spite of all this, they seemed to me ready to leave, which they did briefly later.
Camp on the River Cega, 2 August 1812

D. Pack
Brigadier

See Table 4.4.

7th Division

Collins' Brigade (7th and 19th Infantry, 2nd Caçadores)
The 7th Division was deployed on the far left of the Allied Army, near Calvarisa de Ariba and opposite the heights of Nuestra Señora de la Peña, which were occupied by a screen of light troops from the division. Opposing them was Foy's Division, which was ordered to take the heights and did so with Foy's own light troops. Wellington was in the vicinity at the time and ordered General Hope to retake the ridge. Among those that went forward was Captain Amado's Company from the 2nd Caçadores. By mid-day the sector was quiet, and the 7th Division moved towards the centre. It was stationed behind the village of Los Arapiles and to the right of the 6th Division. It remained there for the rest of the day. Although it was in reserve, it was subjected to intermittent artillery fire. It had only 22 casualties; among them was its commander, who was slightly wounded.

Report[222] from Colonel Collins to AG Mozinho

Sir,
Today I was honoured with your letter of 26 July. On 4 of this month I had the honour of writing to you in duplicate, sending the return of the killed, wounded, and missing of this Brigade on 22 July. The Caçadores' Company, which I mentioned,[223] under the orders of Captain Amado,[224] who had under his command Ensigns Antonio do Prado Fragozo and Joaquim de Salazar Pinheiro, both meritorious officers, was the only one in the brigade that fought on the occasion. Every corps was exposed to heavy artillery fire during the battle, when advancing to the enemy, and when formed in the last position.
    I am in great debt to Lieutenant Colonels Calheiros,[225] O'Toole,[226] and Amaral,[227] commanders of the different corps, and to all other superior officers, for their help on that important occasion. Every officer in the brigade did his best to honour the Portuguese Army; it's my duty to mention the zeal, activity and intelligence of the officers whose duty was to transmit my orders, Captain Brigade Major Colthurst,[228] Captain Carlos [sic] Turner,[229] and Adjutant Joze Manuel Vannes, the latter two from the Caçadores' battalion.
    I beg leave to remind His Excellency the Marshal Commander in Chief that Captain Colthurst served also on my staff at the battle of Albuhera. The wound that I received there was of a nature that prevented me to mention his conduct on that glorious day so I take this opportunity to do him justice and ensure His Excellency, in the strongest manner, of his praiseworthy conduct.
God save you, Sir
10 August 1812
Manoel de Brito Mozinho
Brigadier Adjutant General

R. Collins
Colonel

See Table 4.5.

Bradford's Independent Brigade (13th and 24th Infantry, 5th Caçadores)
Bradford's Brigade was to the right of the 5th Division. When that division advanced to attack the French, the brigade was supposed to advance to protect the division's flanks and prevent any French force getting between the 5th and the 3rd Division, which was about 2km to the right. The 5th Division started its attack before Bradford was in position to move and the brigade was not part of the attack. It was in reserve for the rest of the battle and had only six casualties.

Report[230] from General Bradford to AG Mozinho

Sir,
In answer to your letter, I have the honour to inform His Excellency Marshal Count de Trancozo that I have every reason to be satisfied with the conduct of all officers and men of my Brigade in the action of 22 July, but on this occasion none of them had the opportunity to distinguish more than another.
God save you, Sir
Becerril de la Sierra 10 August 1812
Manoel de Brito Mozinho
Adjutant General

T Bradford
Brigadier

See Table 4.6.

Light Division

During the battle the Light Division was deployed on the far-left flank, with its 1st Brigade on the right and the 2nd Brigade on the left. It saw little action until late in the day. About 7 p.m. the division advanced against the retreating French of Foy's Division. The Light Division moved forward in two columns, with four companies of the 3rd Caçadores covering the 1st Brigade and at least one company of the 1st Caçadores covering the 2nd Brigade. These companies were deployed in extended order in the front. As dusk began to fall, they reached a ravine that was covered by the rearguard. The two brigades deployed into line but before they could assault, the French retreated. They followed them until about midnight. Casualties in the two caçadores battalions were light, with fewer than 20 men killed or wounded.

1st Caçadores

Report[231] of Lieutenant Colonel Algeo to AG Mozinho

Sir
Today I received your letter of 26 July in answer to which I must state that all the individuals in the Battalion under my command conducted themselves magnificently in the Light Division's charge against the French's right flank in the action of 22nd of that month. Captain Manoel Jorge Rodrigues, Lieutenant Joze de Andrade e Souza and Ensign Domingos Marques Coelho particularly distinguished themselves advancing with their company in extended order; they showed their bravery, charging the enemy with intrepidity and properly directing their men. Also, Ensign Adjutant Manoel Baptista Lisboa distinguished himself, showing his zeal and activity in conveying my orders everywhere.
God save you, Sir
Camp Portillo de Baros
11 August 1812
M. de Brito Mozinho
Brigadier Adjutant General

J H Algeo
Lieutenant Colonel commander 1st Caçadores Battalion

See Table 4.7.

3rd Caçadores

Report[232] from Major Pinto to AG Mozinho

Sir

In answer to your letter of 26 July regarding the conduct of the battalion under my command in the action of 22, I have the honour to report that all the officers and men did their duty. The four companies, that attacked in extended order covering the Division's line, advanced with so much courage and gallantry that in a short time they evicted an enemy's column posted in the heights. On this occasion Ensign Joze Teixeira Pinto, commanding the 6th Company, conducted himself with extraordinary bravery, encouraging his men by advancing about 30 paces in front of them. Lieutenant João Chrisostomo Guedes Correia de Andrade, acting Adjutant, directed the men in the best order and conveyed my orders with readiness, being in this occasion an example to the men.

God save you, Sir

Camp near Escorial 11 August 1812

Manoel de Brito Mozinho

Manoel Caetano Teixeira Pinto
Major commander 3rd Caçadores

See Table 4.8.

Table 4.1: Durban's Brigade. Return[233] of the Killed, Wounded and Missing in the 1st and 11th Cavalry Regiments on 22 July 1812

	Men				Horses			
	Present	Killed	Wounded	Missing	Present	Killed	Wounded	Missing
1st Cavalry Regiment	210	4	13	6	218	10	13	4
11th Cavalry Regiment	181	1	5	4	195	8	-	3
Total	391	5	18	10	413	18	13	7

N.B. In the number of the wounded are included Lieutenant Colonel Henrique [sic] Watson,[234] 1st Regiment, and Captain Dom Antonio Maria de Menezes;[235] in that of the killed are included Lieutenant Antonio Thomas Dias Pereira[236] and Cadet Joze Ferraz

B D'Urban
Brigadier General

Table 4.2: Resende's Brigade. Infantry Brigade composed of the 8th and 12th Infantry Regiments and the 9th Caçadores Battalion. Return of the killed, wounded, prisoners and missing in the action of 22 July 1812[237]

Killed

Camp 2 August 1812	Colonel	Lieutenant Colonel	Majors	Captains	Subalterns	Flag Bearers	Sergeants and Furriéis	Musicians and Drummers	Corporals and Privates
9th Caçadores Battalion	-	-	-	-	-	-	1	-	15
8th Regiment	-	-	-	1	-	-	-	-	33
12th Regiment	-	-	-	2	-	-	-	-	35
Total	-	-	-	3	-	-	1	-	83

Ranks and names of the officers killed

Captain Antonio Raimundo da Silva 8th Regiment; Captain Joze Luis da Fonseca 12th Regiment; Captain Antonio Bernardo Cabral 12th Regiment

Wounded

Camp 2 August 1812	Colonel	Lieutenant Colonel	Majors	Captains	Subalterns	Flag Bearers	Sergeants and Furriéis	Musicians and Drummers	Corporals and Privates
9th Caçadores Battalion	-	-	-	-	-	-	1	-	24
8th Regiment	-	1	2	1	7	-	4	-	115
12th Regiment	1	-	-	1	5	-	6	1	253
Total	1	1	2	2	12	-	11	1	392

Ranks and names of the officers wounded

8th Regiment:
Lieutenant Colonel Count de Ficalho, severely[238]; Major Francisco Euzebio Roxo, severely; Captain Marlay,[239] severely; Ensign Mariano de Lemos, severely[240]; Ensign Joaquim Antonio Franco, severely[241]; Major Wylde,[242] slightly; Lieutenant Joze Pereira Carneiro, slightly; Lieutenant Francisco Xavier Abelho, slightly; Adjutant Luis Ignacio de Gouveia, slightly; Ensign João Antonio do Carmo, slightly; Ensign Joze Alves da Silva, slightly
12th Regiment:
Colonel Antonio de Lacerda Pinto da Silveira, slightly; Captain João Joze Souza Machado, severely; Adjutant Antonio de Magalhães Peixoto, severely[243]; Ensign Antonio Bernardo de Abreu, severely; Ensign Paullo Maurity, severely; Ensign Alexandre de Lacerda Pinto da Silveira, severely*; Ensign Antonio Maria de Macedo Tudella Forjaz, severely

Missing and Prisoners

Camp 2 August 1812	Colonel	Lieutenant Colonel	Majors	Captains	Subalterns	Flag Bearers	Sergeants and Furriéis	Musicians and Drummers	Corporals and Privates
9th Caçadores Battalion	-	-	-	-	-	-	-	-	23
8th Regiment	-	-	-	-	-	-	-	-	-
12th Regiment	-	-	-	-	-	-	-	-	-
Total	-	-	-	-	-	-	-	-	23

Ranks and names of the officers missing and prisoners

Total

Camp 2 August 1812	Colonel	Lieutenant Colonel	Majors	Captains	Subalterns	Flag Bearers	Sergeants and Furriéis	Musicians and Drummers	Corporals and Privates
9th Caçadores Battalion	-	-	-	-	-	-	2	-	62
8th Regiment	-	1	2	2	7	-	4	-	148
12th Regiment	1	-	-	3	5	-	6	1	288
Total	1	1	2	5	12	-	12	1	498

Observations

Two horses belonging to the 8th Regiment were killed in the action: one belonged to the Colonel and the other to the first Major.
Two horses of the same regiment were severely wounded: one belonged to the second Major and the other to the first Adjutant.
The horse of the second Adjutant of the same regiment was slightly wounded.
The Major of the 9th Caçadores Battalion had his horse severely wounded; the horse was left in the field because could not carry on.
In the number of the 9th Caçadores Battalion's corporals and privates wounded are included two Cadets.

Count de Rezende, D. Luis
Brigadier

* this officer died due to the wound a few days after the action.

Table 4.3: Return[244] of the Killed, Wounded and Missing in the 9th Caçadores Battalion

Alba de Tormes 23 July 1812	Sergeants	*Furriéis*	Corporals and Privates	Total
Killed	1	-	15	16
Wounded	-	1	24	25
Missing	-	-	23	23
Total	1	1	62	64

N.B. Did not include two cadets wounded

G. Brown
Lieutenant Colonel commander

Table 4.4: Pack's Brigade. Return[245] of the dead, wounded and prisoners in the infantry brigade, 1st, 16th, 4th Caçadores Battalion. Camp near Salamanca, 22 July 1812

Corps	Killed									Wounded									Missing and Prisoners									Total								
	Colonels	Lieutenant Colonels	Majors	Captains	Subalterns	Flag Bearers	Sergeants and *Furriéis*	Musicians and Drummers	Corporals and Privates	Colonels	Lieutenant Colonels	Majors	Captains	Subalterns	Flag Bearers	Sergeants and *Furriéis*	Musicians and Drummers	Corporals and Privates	Colonels	Lieutenant Colonels	Majors	Captains	Subalterns	Flag Bearers	Sergeants and *Furriéis*	Musicians and Drummers	Corporals and Privates	Colonels	Lieutenant Colonels	Majors	Captains	Subalterns	Flag Bearers	Sergeants and *Furriéis*	Musicians and Drummers	Corporals and Privates
1st	-	-	-	-	-	-	1	-	34	-	-	-	-	3	-	5	-	93	-	-	-	-	-	-	-	-	10	-	-	-	-	3	-	6	-	137
16th	-	-	-	1	-	-	1	-	52	-	-	-	4	6	-	4	-	138	-	-	-	-	-	-	-	-	34	-	-	-	5	6	-	5	-	224
4th Caç.	-	-	-	1	-	-	-	-	7	-	1	-	1	3	-	2	-	80	-	-	-	-	-	-	-	1	48	-	1	-	2	3	-	2	1	135
Total	-	-	-	2	-	-	2	-	93	-	1	-	5	12	-	11	-	311	-	-	-	-	-	-	-	1	92	-	1	-	7	12	-	13	1	496

Killed — Ranks and names of the officers killed:
16th Captain Antonio Pedro Nolasco Pinto
4th Caç. João [sic] Wardlaw[246]

Wounded — Ranks and names of the officers wounded:
4th Caç. Lieutenant Colonel Williams[247]; 16th Captain Francisco de Salles da Costa; 16th Captain Ignacio Pedro Quintela, severely; 16th Captain Francisco de Alpoim 16th Captain Webb[248], 4th Caç. Captain McGregor,[249] severely; 1st Lieutenant João Augusto Belles, severely; 16th Lieutenant Germano Antonio Pereira; 16th Lieutenant João Correa Manoel de Aboim, severely; 16th Lieutenant Francisco Baptista Martins[250], 16th Lieutenant Antonio Pereira Rangel; 4th Caç. Lieutenant Francisco de Paula; 1st Ensign João Chrisostomo; 1st Ensign João [sic] Horan; 16th Ensign Jozé António Rangel; 16th Jozé Mascarenhas de Sande, severely[251]; 4th Caç. Ensign Sebastião de Elvas Montaes, wounded three times before he conceded to leave the field; 4th Caç. Ensign Domingos de Almeida da Costa, nothing could exceed his bravery.

Missing and Prisoners — Ranks and names of the officers missing and prisoners

Observations: Captain Carlos [sic] Synge, Aide de Camp, severely wounded

D. Pack
Brigadier

Table 4.5: Collins' Brigade. Return[252] of the Casualties in the 7th Division's Brigade in the action of 22 July 1812 near Salamanca

Regiments and Corps	Killed	Wounded			Missing
	Corporals and Privates	Colonel	Ensign	Corporals and Privates	Corporals and Privates
Staff	-	1	-	-	-
2nd Caçadores	2	-	1	10	-
7th Regiment	1	-	-	3	-
19th Regiment	1	-	-	1	2
Total	4	1	1	14	2

N.B. Officers wounded:
Staff: Colonel Collins, the brigade's commander, slightly
2nd Caçadores Battalion: Ensign Antonio Joze Pereira, severely

N Colthurst
Brigade Major

Table 4.6: Bradford's Brigade, 13th, 24th Regiments and 5th Caçadores. Return[253] of the Killed, Wounded and Missing on 22 July 1812

Regiments	Killed									Wounded									Missing and Prisoners									Total								
	Colonels	Lieutenant Colonels	Majors	Captains	Lieutenants and Ensigns	Flag Bearers	Sergeants and *Furriés*	Musicians and Drummers	Corporals and Privates	Colonels	Lieutenant Colonels	Majors	Captains	Lieutenants and Ensigns	Flag Bearers	Sergeants and *Furriés*	Musicians and Drummers	Corporals and Privates	Colonels	Lieutenant Colonels	Majors	Captains	Lieutenants and Ensigns	Flag Bearers	Sergeants and *Furriés*	Musicians and Drummers	Corporals and Privates	Colonels	Lieutenant Colonels	Majors	Captains	Lieutenants and Ensigns	Flag Bearers	Sergeants and *Furriés*	Musicians and Drummers	Corporals and Privates
5th Caçadores	-	-	-	-	-	-	-	-	2	-	-	-	-	-	-	-	-	1	-	-	-	-	-	-	-	-	-	-	-	-	-	-	-	-	-	3
13th Regiment	-	-	-	-	-	-	-	-	1	-	-	-	-	-	-	-	-	2	-	-	-	-	-	-	-	-	-	-	-	-	-	-	-	-	-	3
Total	-	-	-	-	-	-	-	-	3	-	-	-	-	-	-	-	-	3	-	-	-	-	-	-	-	-	-	-	-	-	-	-	-	-	-	6
	Ranks and names of the officers killed									Ranks and names of the officers wounded									Ranks and names of the officers missing and prisoners									Observations								

Camp 23 July 1812

G Lenon[254] [sic]
Brigade Major

Table 4.7: Return[255] of the Killed, Wounded in the 1st Caçadores Battalion on the Action of 22 instant

Quarters at Villa de Olmedo, 28 July 1812	Corporals and Privates	Total
Killed	2	2
Wounded	4	4
Total	6	6

J H Algeo
Lieutenant Colonel commander

Table 4.8: 3rd Caçadores. Return[256] of the Killed and Wounded in the Action of 22 instant

Quarters at Flores de Avila 24 July 1812	Killed						Killed			Wounded						Wounded		
	Lieutenant Colonel	Major	Captains	Lieutenants	Ensigns	Total	Sergeants and *Furriés*	Corporals and Privates	Total	Lieutenant Colonel	Major	Captains	Lieutenants	Ensigns	Total	Sergeants and *Furriés*	Corporals and Privates	Total
Total	-	-	-	-	-	-	-	-	-	-	-	-	-	-	-	1	13	14

Manoel Caetano Teixeira Pinto
Major commander 3rd Caçadores

Chapter 5

The Siege of Burgos Castle

After defeating the French at Salamanca, Wellington liberated Madrid on 12 August. Meanwhile, Clausel, the new commander of the French Army of Portugal, was busy reorganizing his army. By late August Clausel had moved towards Valladolid and was in a position to cut Wellington's 300km-long lines of communication to the border. Furthermore, Wellington had received intelligence that Soult's Army of the South was marching north, and that Suchet and the French Army of Aragon and Valencia had linked up with King Joseph and his Army of the Centre.

Wellington was faced with a dilemma. If he defended Madrid, there was a chance he could be surrounded by a vastly numerically superior army. If he ignored Clausel, there was a very real possibility that his lines of communication to Portugal would be cut. Wellington decided to split his army. He left the 3rd, 4th, and Light Divisions to protect Madrid and marched with the 1st, 5th, 6th, and 7th Divisions, as well as Pack's and Bradford's Brigades, to eliminate the threat to his rear posed by Clausel.

Clausel had no intention of fighting and as Wellington drew closer, he began to retreat north. By mid-September Wellington was close to Burgos. The city was the logistical hub for the French armies in Spain. All reinforcements, replacements, and supplies went through the city. Its defences were formidable and were centred around an old castle sitting on a hill 75m above the city. There were three lines of walls and entrenchments, with the highest having a large battery called the Napoleon Battery. On a large hill about 200m to the east was a hornwork 'of large dimensions; the front scarp of which, hard and slippery, 25 feet in height, stood at an angle of about 60°, and was covered by a counterscarp 10 feet in depth'.[257]

The siege began on 19 September when the 5th and 7th Divisions, plus the two Portuguese Brigades, surrounded the city. Portuguese troops were in the lines during most of the siege. They helped capture the hornwork on 19 September and were part of the assault made on the outer walls on 22 September. Parties from the 13th Infantry and the 5th Caçadores were working on the breach in the second wall on the night of 8 October when the garrison sortied from the castle. Their attack was repulsed, but the Portuguese troops took heavy casualties.

By mid-October the strategic situation was deteriorating. The Army of Portugal was moving towards Burgos. It was supported by the Army of the North, while Soult and the Army of the South were approaching Madrid. Wellington abandoned the siege on 21 October. Pack's Brigade had the mission of covering the withdrawal from Burgos.

The French Sally, 8 October 1812

Bradford's Independent Brigade (13th and 24th Infantry, 5th Caçadores)

Report[258] from General Bradford to AG Mozinho

I have the honour to forward to you the enclosed reports to be laid before His Excellency the Marshal Count of Trancozo and at the same time informing that after an examination of the circumstances it appears that the reports from both officers, Jeronimo Soares Barboza and Francisco Alexandre Lobo,[259] are correct.

Sergeant Gaspar, particularly recommended by Lieutenant Colonel McCreagh[260], besides the present notice in his favour, had previously given proof of deserving promotion; his youth and excellent appearance give me hope that His Excellency will favourably answer to the request of Lieutenant Colonel McCreagh, promoting him in his battalion. I think that this act of benignity will be a beneficial stimulus to the service.

I take the liberty to state to His Excellency that Ensign Jeronimo Soares Barboza is a good officer, trusted by his commanding officer Dom Joaquim da Camara.[261]

Ensign Francisco Alexandre Lobo, 5th Battalion [Caçadores], being a first sergeant in the battalion, was promoted by His Excellency to Ensign for his brave conduct in the first siege of Badajoz.[262]

God save you, Sir

Ibeas 17 October 1812

Manoel de Brito Mozinho

Brigadier Adjutant General

T Bradford
Brigadier General

5th Caçadores

Report[263] from Lieutenant Colonel McCreagh to General Bradford

Camp before Burgos 13th October 1812

Sir,

His Excellency the Marshal Count of Trancozo having been pleased in some instances when Sergeants have distinguished themselves to prove his approbation of their conduct by the honourable recompense of promoting them to Ensigncies [sic], I am [illegible word] to solicit through you that mark of his favour for Sergeant Gaspar de Brito of this battalion in consideration of his very gallant and exemplary behaviour when engaged in repulsing the sortie from the castle of Burgos on the night of the 7th of this month.[264]

The particulars of his distinguishing himself so highly in instantly collecting that portion of the working parties of the 5th Caçadores consisting of fifty men which were under his immediate command after Captain Perry[265] fell, his twice charging up the glacis and establishing himself in spite of the superior numbers of the French assisted by a destructive fire from their ramparts, have been reported to you by officers who were witnesses of his conduct, and if their assertions required further confirmation the testimony of the soldiers engaged may be deemed worthy of attention, who all with one accord declare his inspiring words and behaviour, with his personal example of bravery, to have animated all around him.

Sergeant Gaspar de Brito is I understand of respectable parents in Serpa.[266] He is nineteen years of age, has served in this battalion four years with the best character and is highly respected by his comrades. In full confidence that he will do credit to my recommendation and approve himself every way worthy so distinguished a mark of His Excellency's approbation I beg leave to recommend him for an Ensigncy [sic] in this battalion in which there are at present five vacancies.

I have the honour to be Sir your very obedient servant

M. McCreagh
Lieutenant Colonel 5th Caçadores

Brigadier General Bradford

13th Regiment

Report[267] from Lieutenant Colonel Câmara to General Bradford

Sir,

I have the honour to present to you a report from Ensign Jeronimo Soares Barboza of the 13th Infantry Regiment, under my command.

God save you, Sir

Camp of Ibeas 17 October 1812

Brigadier Bradford

D. Jm da Camara
Lieutenant Colonel 13th Regiment commander

Report[268] from Ensign Barbosa to Lieutenant Colonel Câmara

Sir,

I report to Your Excellency that in the 7th instant about midnight I was ordered to go with the working party for the Burgos's castle. The party was composed of 4 subalterns, 3 sergeants and 110 men, all under the command of Captain Henry Perry, 5th Caçadores, who according to orders, sent 44 men, 1 sergeant, and 1 subaltern to work on the trench. Of those a sentry was placed in front being both sides covered by the fire of the German troops of the British army from the parapet; the rest of the party remained in the esplanade in front of the breach;[269] from those 12 men and 1 sergeant were ordered to bring the working tools. In the moment that the men joined, the sentry in front of the trench shouted to arms and to which followed a great outcry all around the parapet. The enemy, taking advantage of the darkness of the night, attacked us in great numbers and immediately took some of the workers. Our brave Captain Perry and the other officers on the esplanade directed our people against the enemy at the breach and suddenly face-to-face with the enemy, under its illuminating fire, our captain ordered to fix bayonet and fire. In this instant he received a musket ball in the chest and then was bayoneted, the same fate had befallen Major Cocks[270] who was the senior officer of the day.

At this time the Germans who occupied the breach's parapet and fired from it, seeing the enemy moving through the parapet turned around and showing their bayonets pushed my men (under my command after the captain's death) aside and ran away through the esplanade. By this the enemy became master of the breach and all our people in great confusion. In this moment I received two blows from a musket and fell surrounded by the enemy. I recovered and escaped to our side where, with Ensign Francisco Alexandre Lobo, 5th Caçadores, shouting to the men, we were able to regroup most of them and charge the breach two times but we were repulsed by a continuous fire of grape and hand grenades. We tried a third time and were joined by a captain from General Pack's Brigade and some soldiers from the 1st and 16th Regiments (the captain's regiment) and successfully expelled the enemy from the breach. Our loss was 43 or 44 dead and wounded. We continued to defend the breach keeping a steady fire. By 5 o'clock in the morning some British officers appeared and one of them asked for the senior officer. I told him that he was dead, and my men were tired, and the parapet needed reinforcements. The British officer told me that in the village below was the 12th British Regiment[271] and sent me to call them. I found a British sergeant and conveyed the order. After about 20 minutes a British reinforcement arrived. I finally was relieved and gave the orders for the dead to be buried and the wounded collected.

Camp of Ibeas 17 October 1812

Jeronimo Soares Barboza
Ensign

Artillery

Report[272] from Lieutenant Colonel Dickson, Commander of the Reserve Artillery, to AG Mozinho

Sir,

I must inform you that three of the howitzers belonging to the artillery brigade[273] under my command have been destroyed at the siege of the Salamanca's Forts and of Burgos Castle, and also that all the Brigade's carriages are ruined and the ammunition expended. His Excellency Marshal General Lord Wellington observing that those howitzers did not perform as he had hoped, as battering pieces, gave orders to the remaining three with their equipment to be handed over to Almeida's governor, to be employed in the service of that place. He also ordered the artillery companies, drivers and beasts of the 1st and 2nd Brigades, under the command of Major Arriaga[274] and Captain Rozierres,[275] to cantonments in São João da Pesqueira and Marialva, to rest and for the convenience and treatment of the oxen. Captain Rozierres'

Brigade should deposit their guns in Almeida's arsenal, as all the wagons and forges of both brigades are to be repaired and put in an effective state, ready to be employed on campaign. However, it is His Excellency Marshal General Lord Wellington's intention to annex both companies with their beasts and wagons to a heavy park to be established, but this is not yet determined. In consequence both brigades' wagons are now at Almeida's arsenal to be repaired without changes to their interior compartments until a decision is made about the calibre of the ammunition that they will carry in the future. All this to the information of His Excellency Marshal Beresford.

I enclose a return of the killed, wounded in the Reserve Artillery Brigade, under my command, during the siege of Burgos' Castle. I state to you, for His Excellency Marshal Beresford's information, that, in this arduous employment, the military conduct of all officers, inferior officers and artillerymen, was very good.

I take the liberty on this occasion to ask His Excellency the Marshal Count de Trancozo's clemency in favour of 2nd Lieutenant Ignacio Xavier da Costa Judice, who is *agregado* by one of His Excellency's orders of the day, since last June.[276] His conduct was very good in the siege batteries and during the commission to which he was appointed. He was ordered to go to Reinosa with twenty pairs of beasts from the artillery park to bring some heavy artillery,[277] but with the sudden lifting of the siege, this officer saw his communication with the army almost completely cut. With intelligence and activity, he managed by forced marches to bring his detachment to Puente de Toro and reunite with me at Rueda. This he did without losing any of the animals and to my complete satisfaction.[278]

God save you, Sir

Salamanca, 13 November 1812

A. Dickson
Lieutenant Colonel Commander of the Reserve Artillery

See Table 5.1.

Pack's Independent Brigade (1st and 16th Infantry, 4th Caçadores)

See Tables 5.2, 5.3, and 5.4.

6th Division

Douglas' Brigade (8th and 12th Infantry, 9th Caçadores)

See Table 5.5.

Table 5.1: Return[279] of the Killed and Wounded in the Reserve Artillery Brigade during the Siege of Burgos

Rueda 4 November 1812	Killed								Wounded							
	Major	Captain	1st Lieutenant	2nd Lieutenants	Sergeants and *Furriéis*	Drummers	Corporals and Privates	Total	Major	Captain	1st Lieutenant	2nd Lieutenants	Sergeants and *Furriéis*	Drummers	Corporals and Privates	Total
1st Brigade	-	-	-	1	-	-	2	3	-	-	-	-	-	-	5	5
2nd Brigade	-	-	-	-	-	-	1	1	-	-	-	-	-	-	-	-
Total	-	-	-	1	-	-	3	4	-	-	-	-	-	-	5	5

Officer killed: 2nd Lieutenant Felizardo Xavier Pereira[280]

A. Dickson[281]
Lieutenant Colonel commander of the Reserve Artillery

Table 5.2: Pack's Brigade. Return[282] of the Killed, Wounded, Prisoners and Missing in the Infantry Brigade's 1st and 16th Infantry, 4th Caçadores Battalion before Burgos from the 20 to the 28 September 1812

Corps	Killed									Wounded									Missing and Prisoners									Total								
	Colonels	Lieutenant Colonels	Majors	Captains	Subalterns	Flag Bearers	Sergeants and *Furriéis*	Musicians and Drummers	Corporals and Privates	Colonels	Lieutenant Colonels	Majors	Captains	Subalterns	Flag Bearers	Sergeants and *Furriéis*	Musicians and Drummers	Corporals and Privates	Colonels	Lieutenant Colonels	Majors	Captains	Subalterns	Flag Bearers	Sergeants and *Furriéis*	Musicians and Drummers	Corporals and Privates	Colonels	Lieutenant Colonels	Majors	Captains	Subalterns	Flag Bearers	Sergeants and *Furriéis*	Musicians and Drummers	Corporals and Privates
1st	-	-	-	-	-	-	-	-	1	-	-	-	-	-	-	1	-	5	-	-	-	-	-	-	-	-	-	-	-	-	-	-	-	1	-	6
16th	-	-	-	-	-	-	-	-	-	-	-	-	-	1	-	-	-	2	-	-	-	-	-	-	-	-	-	-	-	-	-	1	-	-	-	2
4th Caçadores	-	-	-	-	-	-	-	-	-	-	-	-	-	-	-	-	-	3	-	-	-	-	-	-	-	-	-	-	-	-	-	-	-	-	-	3
Total	-	-	-	-	-	-	-	-	1	-	-	-	-	1	-	1	-	10	-	-	-	-	-	-	-	-	-	-	-	-	-	1	-	1	-	11
	Rank and names of the officers killed									Rank and names of the officers wounded									Rank and names of the officers missing and prisoners									Observations								
										Lieutenant Luis Jose Pimentel Maldonado, 16th Regiment, severely																										

D. Pack
Brigadier

Table 5.3: Pack's Brigade. Return[283] of the Killed, Wounded, Prisoners and Missing in the Infantry Brigade's 1st and 16th Infantry, 4th Caçadores Battalion in the Operations before Burgos since 28 September 1812

Corps	Killed									Wounded									Missing and Prisoners									Total								
	Colonels	Lieutenant Colonels	Majors	Captains	Subalterns	Flag Bearers	Sergeants and *Furriés*	Musicians and Drummers	Corporals and Privates	Colonels	Lieutenant Colonels	Majors	Captains	Subalterns	Flag Bearers	Sergeants and *Furriés*	Musicians and Drummers	Corporals and Privates	Colonels	Lieutenant Colonels	Majors	Captains	Subalterns	Flag Bearers	Sergeants and *Furriés*	Musicians and Drummers	Corporals and Privates	Colonels	Lieutenant Colonels	Majors	Captains	Subalterns	Flag Bearers	Sergeants and *Furriés*	Musicians and Drummers	Corporals and Privates
1st	-	-	-	-	-	-	-	-	-	-	-	-	-	-	-	-	-	6	-	-	-	-	-	-	-	-	1	-	-	-	-	-	-	-	-	7
16th	-	-	-	-	-	-	-	-	-	-	-	-	-	-	-	-	-	2	-	-	-	-	-	-	-	-	-	-	-	-	-	-	-	-	-	2
4th Caçadores	-	-	-	-	-	-	-	-	-	-	-	-	-	-	-	-	-	4	-	-	-	-	-	-	-	-	-	-	-	-	-	-	-	-	-	4
Total	-	-	-	-	-	-	-	-	-	-	-	-	-	-	-	-	-	12	-	-	-	-	-	-	-	-	1	-	-	-	-	-	-	-	-	13
	Rank and names of the officers killed									Rank and names of the officers wounded									Rank and names of the officers missing and prisoners									Observations								
																												After the return was made the private missing fell in								

Camp before Burgos 5 October 1812

D. Pack
Brigadier

Table 5.4: Pack's Brigade. Return[284] of the Killed, Wounded, Prisoners and Missing in the Infantry Brigade's 1st and 16th Infantry, 4th Caçadores Battalion in the Operations before Burgos since 5 October 1812

Corps	Killed									Wounded									Missing and Prisoners									Total									Observations
	Colonels	Lieutenant Colonels	Majors	Captains	Subalterns	Flag Bearers	Sergeants and *Furriés*	Musicians and Drummers	Corporals and Privates	Colonels	Lieutenant Colonels	Majors	Captains	Subalterns	Flag Bearers	Sergeants and *Furriés*	Musicians and Drummers	Corporals and Privates	Colonels	Lieutenant Colonels	Majors	Captains	Subalterns	Flag Bearers	Sergeants and *Furriés*	Musicians and Drummers	Corporals and Privates	Colonels	Lieutenant Colonels	Majors	Captains	Subalterns	Flag Bearers	Sergeants and *Furriés*	Musicians and Drummers	Corporals and Privates	
1st	-	-	-	-	-	-	-	-	1	-	-	-	-	-	-	-	-	14	-	-	-	-	-	-	-	-	-	-	-	-	-	-	-	-	-	15	
16th	-	-	-	-	-	-	-	-	3	-	-	-	-	-	-	-	-	4	-	-	-	-	-	-	-	-	-	-	-	-	-	-	-	-	-	7	
4th Caçadores	-	-	-	-	-	-	-	-	1	-	-	-	-	-	-	-	-	2	-	-	-	-	-	-	-	-	-	-	-	-	-	-	-	-	-	3	
Total	-	-	-	-	-	-	-	-	5	-	-	-	-	-	-	-	-	20	-	-	-	-	-	-	-	-	-	-	-	-	-	-	-	-	-	25	
	Rank and names of the officers killed									Rank and names of the officers wounded									Rank and names of the officers missing and prisoners																		Observations

Camp before Burgos 12 October 1812

D. Pack
Brigadier

Table 5.5: Return[285] of the Killed, Wounded, and Missing during the Siege of the Castle of Burgos: 8th Infantry Regiment

Camp 23 October 1812	Killed									Wounded									Missing and Prisoners									Total									Observations
	Colonels	Lieutenant Colonels	Majors	Captains	Subalterns	Flag Bearers	Sergeants and *Furriés*	Musicians and Drummers	Corporals and Privates	Colonels	Lieutenant Colonels	Majors	Captains	Subalterns	Flag Bearers	Sergeants and *Furriés*	Musicians and Drummers	Corporals and Privates	Colonels	Lieutenant Colonels	Majors	Captains	Subalterns	Flag Bearers	Sergeants and *Furriés*	Musicians and Drummers	Corporals and Privates	Colonels	Lieutenant Colonels	Majors	Captains	Subalterns	Flag Bearers	Sergeants and *Furriés*	Musicians and Drummers	Corporals and Privates	
Total	-	-	-	-	-	-	1	-	16	-	-	-	-	-	-	-	-	32	-	-	-	-	-	-	-	-	1	-	-	-	-	-	-	1	-	49	
	Names of the officers killed									Names of the officers wounded									Names of the officers missing and prisoners									Observations									

José de Vasconcellos[286]
Colonel commander

Chapter 6

The Retreat to Portugal, October–November

By mid-October the French armies in Spain had finally begun to move against Wellington. The united French forces numbered over 150,000 men, while Wellington had fewer than 50,000. Wellington ordered Madrid to be abandoned and the army to begin retreating to the Portuguese border.

Wellington slowly fell back towards Salamanca and took up positions along the Pisuerga river. The French pursuit was slow over the first few days, but soon they were engaged daily. By 25 October part of the army was at Villa Muriel,[287] where Spry's Brigade formed part of the rearguard. Three days later Collins' Brigade was engaged at Valladolid. Wellington's plan was to hold the Douro river line to cover Hill, who was coming up from the south. The French crossed the river on 5 November and Wellington retreated to Salamanca.

While Wellington retreated from the north, Hill, who was covering the southern approaches to Madrid, retreated towards Salamanca. By 30 October Hill had linked up with the three divisions left in the vicinity of Madrid and his force now consisted of the 2nd, 3rd, 4th, and Light Divisions, plus the Portuguese Division. Under Hill there was a total of six Portuguese brigades and two caçadores battalions assigned to the Light Division. Hill marched towards Salamanca and on 8 November was at Alba de Tormes, 25km south of Salamanca, where he joined the rest of the army.

Wellington remained near Salamanca until French troops began probing the Tormes river line. The Portuguese Division fought in a series of combats along the river from 11 to 14 November. The next day Wellington ordered the retreat to the Portuguese border. Most of the army arrived there by 19 November. Collins' Brigade was part of the rearguard on 17 November and fought at San Muñoz. Soon the men began to straggle due to exhaustion brought on by exposure to bad weather and hunger. Many Portuguese soldiers, unable to go on, were left alongside the road and were either captured by the French or died.

Defence of Valladolid's Bridge, 28 October 1812

On the morning of 28 October Collins' Brigade was ordered to defend the bridge across the Pisuerga river at Valladolid. The 2nd Caçadores were placed in the suburbs on the far side of the river. The 19th Infantry was part of the force that defended the city. The 2nd Caçadores were forced back across the river, but the Portuguese and British held the bridge. Collins withdrew from Valladolid early the next morning.

7th Division

Collins' Brigade (7th and 19th Infantry, 2nd Caçadores)

> Report[288] from Colonel Collins to AG Mozinho
>
> Sir,
> I have the honour to send you the return of the killed and wounded of the detachments of this brigade employed in the defence of Valladolid's bridge on the day and night of 28th instant. The distinguished conduct of these troops is sufficiently proved by the division order, of which a copy is enclosed, to be

laid before His Excellency the Marshal. The general conduct of the officers mentioned by His Excellency Lord Dalhousie,[289] has been, since I have known them, good on every occasion. In consequence of the representation made by his commander I take the liberty to mention the zeal and steadiness showed on this occasion by Captain Jorge Firmino Pereira Amado, from the Caçadores Battalion,[290] who distinguished himself also at the battle of Salamanca, as I had already informed you.

God save you, Sir

Villa Nueva del Duero

29 October 1812

Manoel de Brito Mozinho

R Collins

Colonel Brigade commander

P.S.: It would be an injustice to omit the gallantry of Sergeant Francisco Luis Pacheco,[291] 2nd Grenadier Company of the 19th Regiment. To this brave man, with a small party, was entrusted the defence of a street, which he did with great success against superior numbers of the enemy. His general conduct is exemplary in all aspects and he deserves His Excellency's favour. Captain Ross[292] testified to the good example given by his subalterns in the attack.

Division Order 7th Division[293]

Villa Nueva 29th October 1812

D.O.

Lieutenant General Lord Dalhousie desires to express his perfect satisfaction, at the conduct of the Caçadores,[294] and the other Portuguese Troops, engaged yesterday and last night at the Bridge of Valladolid.

    They merit the highest praise.

    The Lieutenant General requests Lieutenant Colonel O'Toole and Major Zuliche [sic],[295] and also Captain Ross, of the Grenadiers of the 19th Portuguese Regiment, to accept his thanks, and he will not fail to report to the Marquis of Wellington the gallantry of Captain Ross's company in repelling two attacks of Bayonets made by superior numbers of the enemy.

Fr Doyly[296]

Assistant Adjutant General

See Table 6.1.

The Retreat from Madrid

Portuguese Division

See Table 6.2.

Combats at Alba de Tormes and at the Fords of the Tormes River, 10-12 and 14 November 1812

Hamilton had the mission of defending the Tormes river near Alba de Tormes. Screening the approaches to the river was General Long's Light Cavalry Brigade.[297] Supporting the cavalry in the suburbs on the right bank of the Tormes was the 10th Caçadores. On the left bank of the river were the Portuguese Division and General Kenneth Howard's Brigade of the 2nd Division. On 10 November the French advanced and the troops on the right bank withdrew across the river. They defended the river line until 15 November, when Wellington ordered the army to retreat.

Portuguese Division

Report[298] from General Hamilton to General Hill dated 11 November 1812

Alba de Tormes

Sir,

I have the honor [sic] to report the steps I have taken to carry into effect your instructions for the defence of this place, which, I am happy to say, have obliged the enemy to withdraw the greatest part of the force opposed to us; and I feel almost confident we shall be able to retain our position as long as you may deem expedient.

I yesterday garrisoned and provisioned the castle, and by the exertions of Captain Goldfinch[299] of the engineers, it is put into as good a state as circumstances will admit; he is continuing strengthening it. Captain Goldfinch has been of great assistance to me.[300]

I have appropriated to each regiment a district of this town, and the commanding officer has barricaded the streets and buildings in a very judicious manner. Brigadier [sic] Da Costa[301] and Campbell's[302] brigades are in our positions on the left bank of the Tormes. Brigadier [sic] Campbell reports his having caused the enemy some loss, in their attempt to pass a ford near his position.

Lieutenant Colonel Tulloch [sic][303] has made so good an arrangement of his two brigades of guns, that, united with the position of the two brigades of infantry on the left bank of the Tormes, I consider my flanks secure.

Early yesterday morning Major General Long, commanding the cavalry in front, reported that the enemy were advancing in great force; I was therefore induced to retire the cavalry.

About ten o'clock the enemy appeared on the heights in considerable force of cavalry, and a few infantry, covering as I conceived, a reconnaissance of several officers of rank.[304] About two o'clock the enemy's force was increased to fifteen squadrons and six thousand infantry, and twenty guns, including six six-inch howitzers, which immediately commenced firing, and continued until it was dark. The enemy's light troops advanced close to the walls we had hastily thrown up; but from the cool and steady conduct of the 50th regt., Col. Stewart;[305] 71st regt., Col. The Hon. H. Cadogan;[306] the 92nd, Col. Cameron[307] (General Howard's brigade), the enemy dared not attempt the town.

About eight o'clock in the evening, I was repeatedly informed that the enemy's infantry was considerably increasing, which induced me to order three battalions of Brigadier [sic] Da Costa's brigade into the town, leaving his other battalion for the protection of the fords. The enemy during the night withdrew their artillery, and I have left a small force of cavalry and infantry, who kept up a smart fire. I have to regret the loss of a considerable number of men, but which I trust you will not deem great, when you consider the heavy and incessant fire of artillery for so many hours. The loss of the Portuguese was while on duty this morning, and I have real pleasure in reporting their steady and animated conduct.

I feel much indebted to Major General Howard who rendered me every possible assistance, as also to every officer and soldier of his excellent brigade, for their steady, zealous, and soldier-like conduct.

To Captain Pinto Saavedra, my Assistant Adjutant General; to Captain Watson,[308] Royal dragoons, Assistant Quarter Master General; and to Captain Bunbury,[309] my aid de camp [sic], I consider myself obliged, for their prompt execution of my orders.

I enclose a return of the killed and wounded and trust we shall not have many more casualties.

I have the honor [sic] to be, &c.

John Hamilton, Lieut. General.
Lieut. General Sir Rowland Hill, K.B.

See Tables 6.3 and 6.4.

2nd Infantry

Report[310] from Captain Savedra, AAG Attached to the Portuguese Division to AG Mozinho

Sir,
Lieutenant General Hamilton sent to you a copy of a report from Lieutenant Colonel João Telles,[311] 2nd Regiment, about the picquets taken by the enemy at the fords of the Tormes on the morning of 14, when a large part of the enemy's army crossed the river and the allied army retreated to the heights of Calvarrasa de Arriba. If we believe one of the three men who had escaped, the pickets formed a square and resisted but were surrounded by such superior numbers and some were killed, and the others captured.

Lieutenant Pinto, 2nd Regiment, who distinguished himself so much in the combats at Alba de Tormes, died of his wounds yesterday.

God save you, Sir
Arapiles 16 November 1812
Manoel de Brito Mozinho

J Pinto
Captain Adjutant

Report[312] on the Defence of the Fords from Alba de Tormes to above Siete Iglesias by Four Companies of the 2nd Infantry under the Command of Lieutenant Colonel João Telles

The posts were reinforced yesterday with the available men; this morning seeing the French columns approaching I immediately gave warning and a little time later the posts on the right also gave notice of the enemy. The lieutenant commanding at the ford at Encinas de Arriba fell back with his people. The ford above that village, near a mill, was commanded by a sergeant under the eye of the lieutenant. From the people at this ford only three men escaped, who say that after hearing the beat of a drum in the woods across the river, columns of cavalry immediately appeared galloping and crossed the river.

The ensign commanding the people defending the ford of Siete Iglesias is also missing. From that post nobody came back; in total we have an ensign, two sergeants, and fifty-four men missing.

João Telles de Menezes e Mello
Lieutenant Colonel

Combat of Aldea Lengua[313] on the Tormes River, 11 November 1812

Pack's Brigade was deployed on the left flank of the army along the Tormes river near Aldea Lengua. Its mission was to screen the river from the French divisions bivouacked in Huerta. On 11 November a French division conducted a reconnaissance in force to investigate the state of the river crossings. The French retreated after several hours of skirmishing.

Pack's Independent Brigade (Infantry Brigade 1st and 16th Regiments and 4th Caçadores Battalion)

See Table 6.5.

Combat of San Muñoz, 17 November 1812

On 17 November the cavalry covering the rear of the 7th and Light Divisions marched before the two infantry divisions were ready to move. Two dragoon divisions attacked the British picquets and French cavalry got between the two divisions. The 7th Division's baggage was plundered and General Paget, Wellington's second-in-command, was captured. The 7th Division formed on the far side of the Huebra river, with Collin's Brigade in the centre. It covered the withdrawal of the Light Division across the river and stood in columns for several hours under heavy artillery fire. The next morning the division withdrew and arrived in Ciudad Rodrigo the following day.

7th Division

Collins' Brigade (7th and 19th Infantry, 2nd Caçadores)

Report[314] from Colonel Collins to AG Mozinho

Aldeia da Ponte 21 November 1812
Sir,
I have the honour to send you the return of the killed and wounded in the brigade under my command on 17 of this month, in a rearguard action near San Muñoz on the River Huebra. On this occasion the 7th Division, supporting the Light Division, was formed in contiguous columns of battalions for several hours under the fire of the enemy's artillery. Of the five Portuguese battalions, formed in the centre of the division, there was not a single one that wasn't hit by a shot or a shell but they all showed great steadiness and discipline and deserve that their conduct be known to His Excellency the Count de Trancozo.

Some were severely wounded, but I have the pleasure of informing you that notwithstanding the difficulties caused by the circumstances, the amputations and other surgical procedures were carried out with regularity; the wounded were conducted safely to Almeida's hospital.
I have the honour to be, Sir, your most humble and obedient servant
R Collins

Brigadier General Mozinho
Adjutant General

See Table 6.6.

Light Division

3rd Caçadores

See Table 6.7.

The Retreat of Other Portuguese Units

Some of the Portuguese units were only lightly engaged by the enemy during the retreat but still took significant losses. Spry's Brigade was extremely hard hit. Despite his exculpatory report, Beresford rebuked the brigade's officers in the Order of the Day of 17 January 1813, since it was the most reduced. Beresford made it an example to the army, accusing the officers that by neglecting their duties they were responsible for the loss of the men. Eleven company officers from the 3rd and 15th Regiments were punished by putting them in the state of *agregados*.

5th Division

General William Pringle temporarily commanded the division on 25 October. It was the rearguard and was ordered to defend the Carrion river at Villa Muriel. On 27 October he wrote to General John Oswald, the new commander of the 5th Division, about the combat at Villa Muriel. He went into detail about the performance of Spry's Brigade, especially the 8th Caçadores:

I had detached the cacadores [sic] from the Portuguese brigade to defend the ford near the hill, these troops continued to defend the different posts allotted to them for above four hours. About 2 o'clock I was informed that the cacadores were obliged to retire from the fords near the hill, by the enemy's cavalry having crossed the river lower down & having come on their flank in force. In consequence of this movement our right flank was left totally unprotected & the enemy had already got in rear of the village before I was made acquainted with the circumstance of the cacadores having retired.[315]

Spry's Brigade (3rd and 15th Infantry, 8th Caçadores)

Report[316] from General Spry to AG Mozinho

Sir,

Transmitting to you for the information of His Excellency the Marshal the returns of the killed, wounded, prisoners and missing, I beg leave to express my deepest regret on the great loss suffered by the brigade under my command and at the same time to explain some of the unfortunate circumstances which were the cause of that loss.

On 21 of October the 5th Division started from its position in front of Burgos at 8 P.M. beginning a march of six leagues using small paths over a country with very few roads. On 22 and 23 the division kept its march across the country, many beasts carrying the baggage became useless and the baggage lost, some men were taken by the enemy. On these days, after dark, the Division entered a thick wood and the men, tired of marching all day, laid down scattered in the wood. The darkness prevented us from finding and warning them but many re-joined in the morning but some that could not march fell into the hands of the enemy.

When we arrived at Dueñas the number of sick in the brigade had increased very much and I ordered that the men unable to march with their companies had to go to the rear to join the baggage guard, the regimental prisoners, and convalescents etc., under an officer and a surgeon. At this time the Division was preparing to attack the enemy in front[317] and so the officer in charge unfortunately thought that to avoid the enemy it was safer to take a path by Palencia, but the enemy having forced the bridge in that place intercepted them and almost everyone was taken.

I was much surprised when on arrival at Salamanca I found that the loss in the brigade was so great, the 3rd Regiment lost 144, the 15th lost 156, a total of 300 officers and men. Of this number many joined later and by reports made to me no more than 75 from both regiments left the ranks on the march and 5 died of hunger, cold and exhaustion; I must observe that the 5th Division's Portuguese Brigade did not have the help of any means of transportation, in consequence 10 men could not be saved from captivity or death and were abandoned along the way being incapable of moving.

The concurrence of all those unhappy circumstances, which I beg you to strongly express to His Excellency the Marshal Count de Trancozo, show that our loss was not the result of negligence or inattention towards their duties by the officers and commanders of the corps. I request that you inform His Excellency that after a careful investigation I am doing justice to them by stating that, which is my opinion.

On 17th instant in the march to Salamanca I was forced to leave the division, having suffered so much from fatigue, poor health, and the bad weather, capable of moving only on horseback. On this day many were taken prisoners with an Adjutant of the 15th Regiment who was trying to get the weak forward. Many other officers had close escapes.

God save you, Sir

Puebla de Azaba 23 November 1812

Manoel de Brito Mozinho

Brigadier Adjutant General

W. Fred. Spry

Brigadier

Commander 3rd, 15th, and 8th Caçadores

See Table 6.8.

Table 6.1: Collins' Brigade. Return[318] of the Killed, Wounded and Missing in the Pickets of 7th Division's Brigade Detached to Defend Valladolid's Bridge on 28 October 1812

Regiments or Corps	Killed			Wounded	Missing
	Corporals and Privates	Officers	Sergeants	Corporals and Privates	Corporals and Privates
Staff	-	-	-	-	-
7th Regiment	-	-	-	-	-
19th Regiment	-	-	-	9	-
2nd Caçadores	-	-	1	3	-
Total	-	-	1	12	-

N Colthurst
Brigade Major

Table 6.2: Return[319] of Sick and Their Escort, belonging to the 2nd Infantry Brigade,[320] sent to Morata[321] on the Night of the Last 27 October, Who by All Probabilities Were Taken Prisoners. Guadarrama 2 November 1812

	Assistant Surgeon	Sergeants	Corporals and Privates	Total
2nd Regiment	-	2	13	15
14th Regiment	1	1	27	29
Total	1	3	40	44

J Pinto Saavedra[322]
Captain Adjutant

Table 6.3: Portuguese Division. Return of Killed and Wounded of the Army under the Command of General the Marquis of Wellington, K.B., in the defence of Alba de Tormes on the 10th and 11th November 1812

	Officers	Serjeants	Rank and File	Horses	Total loss of officers, Non-commissioned officers, and Rank and File
Killed	-	-	21	-	21
Wounded	3	4	85	-	92
Missing	-	-	-	-	-

Table 6.4: Return[323] of the Killed, Wounded and Missing in General Hamilton's Division, on the Actions at Alba de Tormes on 10, 11, and 12 November 1812

Corps	Superior Officers			Captains			Subalterns			Staff			Sergeants			Drummers			Corporals and Privates			Horses			Mules		
	Killed	Wounded	Missing	Killed	Wounded	Missing	Killed	Wounded	Missing	Killed	Wounded	Missing	Killed	Wounded	Missing	Killed	Wounded	Missing	Killed	Wounded	Missing	Killed	Wounded	Missing	Killed	Wounded	Missing
Artillery																											
2nd Regiment					1			1											6	25							
14th Regiment														1					2	6							
4th Regiment																											
10th Regiment																				2							
10th Caçadores Battalion																											
Total					1			1						1					8	33							

2nd Regiment: Captain Rozendo[324] bruised; Lieutenant Pinto[325] dangerously wounded

J Pinto Saavedra
Captain Adjutant

Table 6.5: Pack's Brigade. Return[326] of the Killed, Wounded, Missing and Prisoners on 11 November 1812

	Killed									Wounded									Missing and Prisoners									Total								
	Colonels	Lieutenant Colonels	Majors	Captains	Subalterns	Flag Bearers	Sergeants and *Furriés*	Musicians and Drummers	Corporals and Privates	Colonels	Lieutenant Colonels	Majors	Captains	Subalterns	Flag Bearers	Sergeants and *Furriés*	Musicians and Drummers	Corporals and Privates	Colonels	Lieutenant Colonels	Majors	Captains	Subalterns	Flag Bearers	Sergeants and *Furriés*	Musicians and Drummers	Corporals and Privates	Colonels	Lieutenant Colonels	Majors	Captains	Subalterns	Flag Bearers	Sergeants and *Furriés*	Musicians and Drummers	Corporals and Privates
1st	-	-	-	-	-	-	-	-	-	-	-	-	-	-	-	-	-	1	-	-	-	-	-	-	-	-	-	-	-	-	-	-	-	-	-	1
16th	-	-	-	-	-	-	-	-	-	-	-	-	-	-	-	1	-	3	-	-	-	-	-	-	-	-	1	-	-	-	-	-	-	1	-	3
4th Caçadores	-	-	-	-	-	-	1	-	-	-	-	-	-	1	-	1	-	4	-	-	-	-	-	-	-	-	-	-	-	-	-	1	-	2	-	5
Total	-	-	-	-	-	-	1	-	-	-	-	-	-	1	-	2	-	8	-	-	-	-	-	-	-	-	1	-	-	-	-	1	-	3	-	9

Observations:

Killed — Rank and names of the officers killed

Wounded — Rank and names of the officers wounded: Lieutenant Francisco de Paula da Cunha, 4th Caçadores

Missing and Prisoners — Rank and names of the officers missing and prisoners

D. Pack
Brigadier

Table 6.6: Collins' Brigade. Return[327] of the Casualties in the 7th Division's Brigade on the Action of 17 November, on the Huebra River

Regiments or Corps	Killed — Corporals and Privates	Wounded — Lieutenant	Wounded — Ensign	Wounded — Corporals and Privates	Missing — Corporals and Privates
Staff					
2nd Caçadores		1			
7th Regiment	2			5	
19th Regiment	6		1	9	
Total	8	1	1	14	

Officers Killed and Wounded:
2nd Caçadores: Lieutenant Jose Antonio Gabriel do Carmo Lima slightly wounded
19th Regiment: Ensign Francisco Pinto de A. e Castro slightly wounded

N Colthurst
Brigade Major

Table 6.7: 3rd Caçadores. Return[328] of the Killed, Wounded, and Prisoners in the Action on 17 November 1812

	Killed							Wounded							Prisoners							
	Superior Officers	Captains	Subalterns	Staff	Sergeants and *Furriéis*	Buglers and Musicians	Corporals and Privates	Superior Officers	Captains	Subalterns	Staff	Sergeants and *Furriéis*	Buglers and Musicians	Corporals and Privates	Superior Officers	Captains	Subalterns	Staff	Sergeants and *Furriéis*	Buglers and Musicians	Corporals and Privates	Total
	-	-	-	-	-	-	2	-	-	-	-	-	-	2	-	-	-	-	-	-	3	7
	Name of the officers killed							Name of the officers wounded							Name of the officers taken prisoner							

Camp near Ciudad Rodrigo 18 November 1812

Manuel Pinto da Silveira
Lieutenant Colonel commander

Table 6.8: Spry's Brigade. Return[329] of the Dead, Wounded, Prisoners, and Missing in the Brigade Composed of the 3rd, 15th [Infantry Regiments], and 8th Caçadores from 23 September until the Present Day

Cantonment of Puebla de Azaba 23 November 1812		Missing					Wounded				Prisoners — Staff				Prisoners			Dead				Total
		Assistant Surgeons	Drummer Corporal	Sergeants	Drummers	Corporals and Privates	Officers	Sergeants	Drummers	Corporals and Privates	Adjutant	Chaplain	Assistant Surgeon	Musicians	Sergeants	Drummers	Corporals and Privates	Officers	Sergeants	Drummers	Corporals and Privates	
3rd	In Burgos Castle																				2	2
	In march from Burgos to Salamanca				4	36																40
	25 October — In combat									3								1				4
	25 October — In march											1	1	1	2		108					113
	In march from Salamanca to here					10																10
	17 November																11					11
	Total				4	46				3		1	1	1	2		119	1			2	180
15th	In Burgos Castle						1			1												2
	From Burgos to Salamanca	2	1	2	2	39											110					156
	In 25 October's combat							1		2												3
	From Salamanca to here					28					1						7					36
	17 November														1	2	17					20
	Total	2	1	2	2	67	1	1		3	1				1	2	134					217
8th Caçadores							10	7	1	109					2	1	9		4	2	31	176
Recapitulation																						
3rd Regiment					4	46				3		1	1	1	2		119	1			2	180
15th Regiment		2	1	2	2	67	1	1		3	1				1	2	134					217
8th Caçadores							10	7	1	109					2	1	9		4	2	31	176
Total		2	1	2	6	113	11	8	1	115	1	1	1	1	5	3	262	1	4	2	33	573

Names of the Officers Wounded[330]
Captain Francisco da Gamma Lobbo Botelho, 15th Regiment, severely[331]; Major Dudley St. Leger Hill, 8th Regiment, severely;Captain Carlos [sic] Western,[332] 8th Caçadores, slightly;Captain Manuel Caetano Ferraz, 8th Caçadores, severely; Captain Carlos [sic] Western,[332] 8th Caçadores, slightly; Lieutenant Antonio Carlos Pereira, 8th Caçadores, severely; Lieutenant João Baptista Ferreira, 8th Caçadores, severely[333]; Lieutenant Domingos de Sá Farinha, 8th Caçadores, slightly; Ensigns João Salustiano da Costa e Sá and Jose Fernandes dos Santos, 8th Caçadores, both severely wounded and made prisoners because it was not possible to transport them; Ensign Rodrigo Navarro de Andrade, 8th Caçadores, slightly; Ensign James Lexe [sic],[334] 8th Caçadores, slightly

Names of the Officers Taken Prisoner
Adjutant Joaquim Jose de Figueiredo, 15th Regiment; Chaplain Jose Luis da Silva, 3rd Regiment; Assistant Surgeon Anselmo Jose Marques, 3rd Regiment

Names of the Officers Missing
Assistant Surgeons Antonio Pedro Cardoso and Antonio Joaquim, 15th Regiment

Names of the Officers Killed
Major Eduardo Ovens [sic], 3rd Regiment[335]

W. Fred. Spry
Brigadier
Commander 3rd, 15th, and 8th Caçadores

Chapter 7

An Overview of the Campaigns of 1813

After Wellington and his army reached the border in November 1812, he began to plan for 1813. Despite being forced back to Portugal, the campaign had been a strategic success. The Allies now controlled all the fortresses along the border and all of Spain south of the Tagus river had been liberated.

On paper, the situation for the French in January 1813 could have been worse. Although they had lost the southern half of the country, they had about 200,000 men. This was not to last, because after his defeat in Russia Napoleon needed to rebuild his army in Central Europe and the quickest way to do so was to withdraw troops from Spain. By June Napoleon's forces in Spain had been reduced to fewer than 100,000 men. Of those, about 70,000 men were available to oppose Wellington.

Wellington spent the winter of 1812/1813 rebuilding his army and had more than 100,000 men, including 52,000 British, 30,000 Portuguese, and 25,000 Spanish troops. He had seven Anglo-Portuguese divisions, a British division, a Portuguese division, five Spanish divisions, and two independent Portuguese infantry brigades, as well as 12,000 cavalry, and 102 artillery pieces. They formed three corps. The largest, commanded by Graham, comprised six divisions, two independent Portuguese brigades, and four cavalry brigades, one of which was D'Urban's Brigade. Hill's Corps comprised the 2nd, Light, and Portuguese Divisions, Morillo's Spanish Division, six British cavalry brigades, Campbell's Portuguese cavalry brigade, and Sanchez's Spanish cavalry brigade. The 2nd, Portuguese, and Morillo's Divisions, plus one cavalry brigade, were in the vicinity of Badajoz, while the Light Division and the rest of the cavalry were near Ciudad Rodrigo. Four Spanish infantry divisions and a cavalry brigade were under the command of General Pablo Giron.

Graham's Corps comprised more than 16,000 Portuguese troops in seven infantry brigades, a cavalry brigade, and two artillery brigades. Hill's Corps had 10,350 Portuguese troops in three infantry brigades, two of which formed the Portuguese Division, a cavalry brigade, two caçadores battalions, and two artillery brigades. Beresford and the Portuguese Army HQ were co-located with Wellington's HQ.

A late spring forced Wellington to postpone operations until early May. His plan was not to engage the French south of the Douro river and force them to retreat north by manoeuvring to their rear. Graham's Corps was to march through the mountainous north and debouch onto the plains north of the Douro river. Hill's Corps was to advance via Salamanca and link up with Graham on the other side of the Douro. Graham set out on 26 May and by 3 June he was north of the Douro. Hill had started on 22 May and liberated Salamanca on 26 May. His primary mission was to screen Graham's movements. Hill waited at Salamanca until orders reached him to cross the Douro. The French learned of Wellington's advance and retired, concentrating on the Douro river. By 7 June the French had retreated to Burgos, which they blew up on 13 June. The next day Graham crossed the Ebro river. By 20 June the French commander, Marshal Jourdan, had consolidated his army at Vitoria, where he would make a stand. He had 46,000 men in eight infantry divisions, 9,000 cavalry, and 150 artillery pieces.[336]

The Battle of Vitoria

On 21 June Wellington deployed his 72,000 men in three groups. On the right was Hill with the Portuguese and the 2nd Divisions, as well as Morillo's Spanish Division. His mission was to attack the Heights of Puebla. In the centre were two columns, the one on the right comprising the 4th and Light Divisions plus four cavalry brigades, including D'Urban's, and the left column comprising the 3rd and 7th Divisions. On the far left was Graham with the 1st and 5th Divisions, Longa's Spanish Division, and two independent Portuguese brigades. Graham's mission was to cut the main road to France and attack the French flank and rear.

Hill attacked about 8 a.m. and took the Heights of Puebla, forcing Jourdan to weaken his centre to reinforce his left. About noon the Light Division crossed the river. Wellington ordered the 3rd and 4th Divisions to attack the French centre. On the Allies' left flank Graham began attacking the French right about 2 p.m.

Jourdan, seeing that his centre was about to collapse, ordered the troops there to retire to the Heights of Zuazo. By 4 p.m. the French had occupied the heights and were supported by more than fifty artillery pieces. It was a strong position but Graham outflanked it. When Wellington ordered the 3rd, 4th, 7th, and Light Divisions to attack the heights, Jourdan chose to retreat. The French were pursued by both cavalry and infantry. However, they escaped, and the pursuit ended when the pursuers discovered the French baggage train, which they stopped to loot. The French lost 4,300 men, almost all their artillery, and their baggage train. Wellington lost more than 5,100 men, of whom 950 were Portuguese.

The Pursuit of the French

Wellington ordered Graham to move north in hopes of cutting off the French retreat to France. Graham found Foy's Division at Villafranca on 24 June and at Tolosa on 25 June. After two days of fighting, the French retreated to France. Pack and Bradford's Brigades took part in both actions. By 1 July all French forces had been withdrawn from Spain except for the garrisons in San Sebastian and Pamplona, those on the east coast, and three divisions in the Bastan valley. Hill was ordered to take the Maya Pass, which led to France. The operation began on 5 July and it took three days to evict the French from the Bastan valley. During the fighting, Amarante commanded the advance guard, which included a Portuguese infantry regiment, a British infantry brigade, and a British light cavalry squadron. This was the first time a Portuguese officer had commanded British troops during the Peninsular War.

The Siege of San Sebastian: Part I

Wellington needed to rest his troops and to secure the fortresses of Pamplona and San Sebastian before he could begin further offensive operations. He planned to besiege San Sebastian and to starve Pamplona into surrender. The siege began on 7 July and two assaults were made in mid-July. Both the Portuguese independent brigades and Spry's Brigade were involved. Siege operations were suspended on 25 July when the French Army counter-attacked across the Pyrenees.

The Battles of the Pyrenees

After the Vitoria débâcle, Marshal Soult took command of the French forces. He organized them into a single army, with three corps. He had been ordered to relieve both Pamplona and San Sebastian, and decided to relieve Pamplona first. One corps would move through the Maya

Pass and the other two through the Roncesvalles Pass. The operation began on 25 July and the Allied troops in the Maya Pass were quickly brushed aside. The two corps moving through the Roncesvalles Pass were slowed by the narrow winding roads. The French caught up with part of the Allied Army at Sorauren on 27 July and fought them there the next day. Campbell's Brigade, as well as the Portuguese Brigades of the 3rd, 4th, and 6th Divisions, were involved in the fighting on 28 July. The next day both armies brought up reinforcements, including Lecor's Brigade. On 30 July Soult tried to manoeuvre around the Allies' left flank but Wellington ordered his men to attack the French columns. Soult decided that it would be impossible to relieve Pamplona and ordered his army to withdraw to France. While the 2nd Battle of Sorauren was being fought, Hill, with the 2nd Division and Costa's Brigade, engaged a corps at Beunza, 25km to the northwest.

The Siege of San Sebastian: Part II

After the battles of the Pyrenees, Wellington turned his attention to taking San Sebastian. The siege continued until 31 August, when an assault was made on the two breaches in the walls and the city fell. The Portuguese 3rd and 10th Brigades took part in the attack. On the same day Soult attacked across the Bidassoa river to relieve the pressure on the city. The 9th Brigade was defending the river line in the vicinity of the Heights of Salain and took heavy casualties. Further east, the 3rd Caçadores helped defend the river crossing at Vera, while the 3rd and 7th Brigades fought at Zugarramurdi and Urdax.

The Crossing of the Bidassoa River

Wellington spent September refitting his army while waiting for Pamplona to surrender. He also spent time gathering intelligence about the Bidassoa river. The Portuguese Division was ordered to make a diversionary attack near Banca to draw French attention away from the Bidassoa. The attack across it was made on 7 October. The 1st and 3rd Brigades took part in the assault near the estuary of the river, while the Light Division's 1st and 3rd Caçadores and the 17th Infantry attacked upstream near Vera. To help hide where the main assault was taking place, the 7th Brigade made a feint at Urdax. The attacks succeeded and the last of the French troops in northern Spain were evicted.

The Battle of Nivelle

Wellington was in a good position. Except for the French garrison in Pamplona and the French army on the east coast, all of Spain had been liberated. He now began planning for the invasion of France. Soult had built a line of fortifications based on the Nivelle river from its mouth at San-Jean-de-Luz to Espelette 35km to the east. These positions covered the passes through the Pyrenees and west to the Atlantic Ocean, and were defended by 60,000 men.

Wellington had more than 82,000 men, divided into fifteen divisions (7 Anglo-Portuguese, 1 British, 1 Portuguese, and 6 Spanish). Wellington chose to mass his forces in the centre of the French positions and make feints elsewhere to keep Soult from moving troops against the attack. Hill, with five divisions, was to the east. To the west Hope had four divisions and two brigades. Beresford was responsible for the main attack in the centre and had five divisions, and Bradford's 10th Brigade. The Portuguese forces with Wellington numbered more than 25,000 men and it would be the first time that every Portuguese unit assigned to his army would be involved in the same battle. Additionally, Major General Carlos Lecor commanded the 7th Division. This was another first for the Portuguese, for never had a Portuguese officer commanded a division containing British troops.

The attack began at daybreak on 9 November. The feints in the east and the west pinned the French forces in place. In the centre, the Light Division captured the Lesser Rhune, while the 3rd, 4th, and 7th Divisions assaulted the lines to the east. On Wellington's right flank Hill's troops began their attack late and despite it being only a feint, pushed the French out of their positions. By the end of the day the French had abandoned their defensive lines and withdrawn about 15km to the Nive river. The Portuguese had suffered 403 casualties. The 7th Caçadores Battalion lost the most, and had 19 per cent of all the Portuguese casualties.

The Battles of Nive

Wellington had secured his foothold in France and he was not inclined to continue operations. His troops were tired, and their equipment and uniforms worn out. A long rest was necessary, and plans were made to put the army into winter quarters. However, in early December Wellington decided to push the French back from the Nive river to the Adour river. By doing so, he believed he could move his troops into winter quarters without worrying about the French attacking them. Hill would attack in the east with three divisions, while Beresford attacked in the centre with two divisions. In the west Hope would make a demonstration with three divisions and three brigades.

The attack began at daybreak on 9 December when Hill crossed the river. Heavy rains caused his forces to become bogged down and it was not until late afternoon that they contacted the French at Villefranque. When night fell the French commander took the opportunity to withdraw back to Bayonne, 10km to his rear. In the west Hope moved at first light and by mid-afternoon had reached Bayonne. He left the 1st, 3rd, and 10th Brigades on a height overlooking Bayonne and withdrew the rest of his force 10km towards Saint Jean-de-Luz.

Soult spotted the exposed Portuguese forces in the west and that night moved the four divisions that were defending against Hill to attack them. The assault began about 9 a.m. with eight divisions. The fighting was intense, and the Portuguese took heavy casualties. They were in danger of being pushed back when reinforcements arrived, and Soult called off the attack.

The next day, 11 December, was relatively quiet, with an unofficial ceasefire in place. It was broken by the Allies when Wellington ordered the French outposts in the west to be pushed back. The French retaliated with a two-division attack but stopped and withdrew when reinforcements arrived. The next day Soult shifted six divisions to the east and attacked Hill's force. The 5th Brigade took the brunt of the initial assault. By 11:30 a.m. most of the 2nd Division had been committed. While the attack was being made in the east, French forces also attacked in the west. By noon the attacks had lost their momentum and were called off. The Allies counter-attacked across the whole front. Soult decided there was nothing to gain from holding the ground they had just taken and ordered a withdrawal to Bayonne. Minor skirmishing continued until both armies entered winter quarters. During this final battle of 1813 the Portuguese were heavily involved in the fighting on both flanks. At times they held the line on their own. Their casualties during the four days were almost 2,000 men killed, wounded, or missing.

The Portuguese Army

By the last days of November 1812 the Allied Army was in winter cantonments. The army had lost heavily in both men and material during the retreat. The Portuguese units were severely hit by the hardships of the retreat. To return the Portuguese Army to a state that would enable it to participate in the 1813 campaign, it was necessary both to fill the ranks and to meet its material needs, which would help restore its morale and readiness. This task was attended to by the Portuguese government and Beresford, whose exertions during the winter and spring of 1813 enabled the army to field about 30,000 men for the upcoming campaign, comprising almost one third of the Anglo-Portuguese Army. They were able to field 21 infantry regiments, 11 caçadores battalions, 5 cavalry regiments, and 4 artillery brigades. Among them were many veterans, with several years of campaigning under their belts, but also a significant proportion of new recruits.

Beresford accompanied Wellington during the 1813 campaign. He took with him his personal staff and the staff of the Portuguese HQ, whose heads were the same as in 1812.

The Infantry

The Portuguese brigades' organization was nearly the same as in 1812. Only small changes occurred in the brigades' composition but there were some significant changes among their commanders. There were two minor organizational changes: the 17th Infantry was assigned to the Light Division on 17 October 1812 and the 12th Caçadores was replaced by the 11th Caçadores in Power's Brigade in April 1813.

Two important changes to the command structure were made in March 1813. Lieutenant General the Count de Amarante was appointed commander of the Portuguese Division, while Brigadier General Carlos Frederico Lecor was given command of the Portuguese brigade attached to the 7th Division. A further administrative change was made on 13 August 1813. The brigades were numbered one to ten as shown in brackets below.

The infantry brigades at the beginning of the campaign were organized and commanded as follows:

Lieutenant General Count de Amarante's Portuguese Division:
Brigadier General António Hipólito da Costa's Brigade, about 2,500 men (2nd Brigade)
    2nd Infantry commanded by Colonel Jorge de Avilez[337]
    14th Infantry commanded by Lieutenant Colonel John McDonald[338]
Brigadier General Archibald Campbell's Brigade, about 2,800 men (4th Brigade)
    4th Infantry commanded by Lieutenant Colonel Allan Campbell[339]
    10th Infantry commanded by Colonel Luís Maria de Sousa Vahia[340]
    10th Caçadores commanded by Lieutenant Colonel Richard Armstrong[341]

Colonel Charles Ashworth's Brigade, 2nd Division, about 3,100 men (5th Brigade)
    6th Infantry commanded by Lieutenant Colonel Maxwell Grant
    18th Infantry commanded by Colonel Manuel Pamplona Carneiro Rangel[342]
    6th Caçadores commanded by Major Samuel Mitchell[343]
Brigadier General Manley Power's Brigade, 3rd Division, about 2,500 men (8th Brigade)
    9th Infantry commanded by Lieutenant Colonel Charles Sutton
    21st Infantry commanded by Major Francisco Joaquim Carreti[344]
    11th Caçadores commanded by Lieutenant Colonel Thomas Dursbach[345]
Colonel Thomas Stubbs' Brigade, 4th Division, about 2,850 men (9th Brigade)
    11th Infantry commanded by Lieutenant Colonel Alexander Anderson
    23rd Infantry commanded by Lieutenant Colonel James Miller[346]
    7th Caçadores commanded by Lieutenant Colonel Bryan O'Toole[347]
Brigadier General William Spry's Brigade, 5th Division, about 2,400 men (3rd Brigade)
    3rd Infantry commanded by Major Charles Stewart Campbell[348]
    15th Infantry commanded by Colonel Luís do Rego Barreto[349]
    8th Caçadores commanded by Lieutenant Colonel Dudley Hill[350]
Brigadier General George Madden's Brigade, 6th Division, about 2,500 men (7th Brigade)
    8th Infantry commanded by Colonel James Douglas[351]
    12th Infantry commanded by Lieutenant Colonel Havilland Le Mesurier[352]
    9th Caçadores commanded by Lieutenant Colonel Gustavus Brown

Brigadier General Carlos Frederico Lecor's Brigade, 7th Division, about 2,450 men (6th Brigade)

    7th Infantry commanded by Lieutenant Colonel Francisco Xavier Calheiros[353]

    19th Infantry commanded by Colonel John Doyle[354]

    2nd Caçadores commanded by Major George Zulke

Portuguese Units in the Light Division, about 1,950 men

    1st Caçadores commanded by Lieutenant Colonel John Algeo,[355] in General Vandeleur's Brigade

    3rd Caçadores commanded by Brevet Lieutenant Colonel Manuel Pinto da Silveira, in General Vandeleur's Brigade

    17th Infantry commanded by Lieutenant Colonel John Rolt, in General Kempt's Brigade

Brigadier General Denis Pack's Independent Brigade, about 2,300 men (1st Brigade)

    1st Infantry commanded by Colonel Thomas Hill[356]

    16th Infantry commanded by Colonel Francisco Homem de Magalhães Pizarro

    4th Caçadores commanded by Lieutenant Colonel Edmund Williams

Brigadier General Thomas Bradford's Independent Brigade, about 2,500 men (10th Brigade)

    13th Infantry commanded by Lieutenant Colonel Dom Joaquim da Câmara[357]

    24th Infantry commanded by Lieutenant Colonel Inácio Emídio Aires da Costa[358]

    5th Caçadores commanded by Lieutenant Colonel Michael McCreagh[359]

Many changes in the command of the brigades occurred as a result of wounds, ill-health, or requests to leave the field army during the 1813 campaign.

The most noticeable was the resignation of Amarante as the commander of the Portuguese Division during the first days of September, allegedly due to his failing health but most probably a result of his dissatisfaction with Wellington and Beresford. He was replaced by General Archibald Campbell until the beginning of November, when General Hamilton returned. Hamilton stayed in command until 3 December, when his poor health meant he was replaced by Major General Carlos Lecor, who kept the command until the end of the war. Colonel Doyle replaced Lecor in command of the 6th Brigade.

In the Portuguese Division Costa was severely wounded during the fighting in the Pyrenees, and was temporarily replaced by General John Buchan until 20 November when he returned. General Campbell was replaced in command of the 4th Brigade at the beginning of September by Colonel Vahia, 10th Infantry. In early November Campbell returned to his brigade until 23 November, when he left to command the 1st Brigade. Buchan then took command of the 4th Brigade.

Colonel Stubbs was promoted to brigadier general and left the field army in mid-August. The 9th Brigade was commanded temporarily by several officers, including Brigadier General Manuel Pamplona Rangel, Lieutenant Colonel James Miller, 23rd Infantry, and Colonels Henry Hardinge, and MacBean. At the beginning of October Colonel José de Vasconcelos e Sá joined his regiment, the 23rd Infantry, and being the senior officer, commanded the brigade until the end of the war.

Major General Spry's ill-health forced him to return to Britain on 7 September 1813. Colonel Barreto, 15th Infantry, took command of the 3rd Brigade in September 1813.

General Madden was relieved from his command at the end of August 1813. He was replaced by Colonel Douglas, 8th Infantry.

General Pack left Portuguese service on 1 July and was replaced in mid-July by General John Wilson. Wilson commanded the 1st Brigade until 18 November, when he was severely wounded at Bidart. He was replaced by General Archibald Campbell, who took command on 23 November.

The Cavalry

The cavalry fielded five regiments for the campaign, in two brigades:

Brigadier General Benjamin D'Urban's Brigade, about 890 men
   1st Cavalry commanded by Major António Feliciano Teles Aparicio[360]
   11th Cavalry commanded by Major Edward Knight[361]
   12th Cavalry commanded by Lieutenant Colonel Viscount de Barbacena[362]
Colonel John Campbell's Brigade, about 650 men
   4th Cavalry commanded by Colonel John Campbell
   6th Cavalry commanded by Lieutenant Colonel Richard Diggens

In November General D'Urban was detached from the brigade to resume his duties as QMG when Beresford assumed a corps command. He was replaced by Colonel Viscount de Barbacena.

On 12 July Campbell's Brigade was disbanded. The 6th Cavalry was assigned to D'Urban's Brigade and the 4th Cavalry to General Henry Fane's Cavalry Brigade.

The Artillery

Four artillery brigades were with the army for the campaign. The 1st Artillery fielded three brigades:

Brevet Major Sebastião José de Arriaga's Brigade of 9-pounder guns
Brevet Major João da Cunha Preto's Brigade of 6-pounder guns
Brevet Captain António da Costa e Silva's Mountain Brigade of 3-pounder guns

One artillery company of the 1st Regiment under Captain Pedro de Roziers had no guns but accompanied the army and was used to man the siege guns at San Sebastian.

The 2nd Artillery fielded one brigade:

Captain Charles Michell's Brigade of 9-pounder guns

The artillery attached to the Portuguese Division, Preto's and Michell's Brigades was under the command of Lieutenant Colonel Alexander Tulloh, 3rd Artillery. Arriaga's Brigade was part of the Artillery Reserve, commanded by Lieutenant Colonel Georg Hartmann, KGA.

The Engineers

Two companies of the Artificers Battalion, under the command of Major José Jerónimo Granate, Royal Corps of Engineers, were employed at San Sebastian during the last stages of the siege.

Chapter 8

The Battle of Vitoria, 21 June 1813

'… and the Portuguese troops in the 3rd and 4th divisions, under the command of Brigadier General Power and Colonel Stubbs, led the march with steadiness and gallantry never surpassed on any occasion.'

Wellington, 21 June 1813[363]

'The 4th battalion of caçadores and the 8th Caçadores, particularly distinguished themselves.'

Wellington, 21 June 1813[364]

Vitoria sits in a river basin surrounded by high mountains. The town was a junction for numerous roads, including the main road to Bayonne[365] and one to Pamplona. Marshal Jourdan had to stop the Allies here or withdraw from Spain. The Zadorra river which runs through the basin was about 40m wide and fordable to infantry and cavalry. It was also crossed by many bridges. Jourdan's Army consisted of 46,000 men in eight infantry divisions, plus 9,000 cavalry and 150 artillery pieces. Because the river was easy to cross, he was forced to deploy along a 12km front.[366]

Occupying the Heights of Puebla on the far left of his position was an infantry brigade. In the centre were six divisions, with three divisions on the Heights of Ariñez overlooking the Zadorra river. Directly behind them was a fourth division near the Ariñez. Two more divisions were kept in reserve about a kilometre west of Vitoria. On the far right, protecting the road to France, was General Sarrut's Division, while at Vitoria was a division that served as the army reserve. The cavalry was in the plains covering the river line between the centre and the right.

On 21 June Wellington deployed his 72,000 men[367] in three groups. On the right was Hill with the Portuguese, 2nd, and Morillo's Spanish Divisions. Their mission was to attack the French brigade on the Heights of Puebla. In the centre were two columns, the right one comprising the 4th and Light Divisions and four cavalry brigades, including D'Urban's Portuguese Cavalry Brigade, and the left column comprising the 3rd and 7th Divisions. On the far left, under the command of Graham, were the 1st and 5th Divisions, Longa's Spanish Division, and two independent Portuguese infantry brigades. Graham's mission was to cut the main road to France, while striking the right flank and rear of the French Army.

Wellington wanted to attack simultaneously, but the great distance between Hill and Graham prevented it. Hill began his attack about 8 a.m. It was successful and Jourdan had to take forces from his centre to shore up his left flank. This weakened the French centre and Wellington ordered the Light Division across the river. There it occupied a high hill overlooking the French lines. The 3rd Division, to the left of the Light Division, halted at the river and waited for the 7th Division. Wellington became impatient and ordered it and the 4th Division across the river. On the far left Graham arrived about 2 p.m. and began attacking the right of the French positions.

Jourdan, seeing that his forward lines were in danger of collapsing, ordered them to retreat to the Heights of Zuazo. A rearguard, supported by several artillery batteries, stayed on the Heights of Ariñez. The rearguard delayed the Allies long enough for the retreating French to reach the Heights of Zuazo, and then withdrew. By 4 p.m. the French had occupied their new position, which was supported by fifty artillery pieces. Wellington ordered the 3rd, 4th, 7th, and Light Divisions to attack this final French defensive position. The position was a strong one; however, its flank was threatened by Graham, while the main road to France had been cut by Longa's Spanish

Division. Jourdan ordered his army to retreat. The French on the Heights of Zuazo had brought the 7th Division under fire and had stopped the advance of the 3rd Division when they received word to withdraw. The French were pursued by British cavalry and infantry, but the pursuit halted when the British troops stopped to loot the French baggage train.

The French Army lost 4,300 men killed, wounded, and prisoners, plus its baggage train, and all its artillery, except for two guns. Wellington lost more than 5,100 men, of whom 950 were Portuguese. The most heavily engaged Portuguese units were Power's and Stubbs' Brigades. Two thirds of the Portuguese casualties were in these two brigades. Among the wounded was Stubbs.

The Right Wing

Portuguese Division

The Portuguese Division was in reserve throughout much of the battle. After the Heights of Puebla were taken, it moved there. Amarante was with Costa's Brigade and a brigade of 6-pounders on the right, and they followed Morillo's Division. Campbell's Brigade, with a brigade of 9-pounders, was on the left and followed the 2nd Division. Only two men and two horses were killed.

Report[368] from Count de Amarante to Beresford

Sir,
I have the honour to enclose a return of the killed and wounded of this Division, as that already sent to General Hill. When I was ordered to advance I sent General Campbell's Brigade with the 9 pounder artillery brigade[369] in the direction of Vitoria and I rode, with the 2nd Brigade[370] and the 6 pounder brigade,[371] to the heights on our right to where an enemy column also moved. At the top of this height were General Hill's brigades. The enemy withdrew and we followed until night. At this time, we camped here. General Campbell handled his brigade very well as did Lieutenant Colonel Tulloh commanding the 9-pounder brigade. I know that both brigades seized much baggage and some pieces of artillery. All the division was willing to do their duty if the circumstances allowed.
God save Your Excellency
Camp at Gamiz 22 July 1813
His Excellency the Marquis de Campo Maior

Count de Amarante

See Table 8.1.

Report[372] from Count de Amarante to AG Mozinho

Sir,
I received your letter of the 22nd. On that day I sent to His Excellency the Marquis de Campo Maior the return of the killed and wounded of this Division in the battle of 21st and mentioned his services.

The 2nd and 14th Regiment's Brigade[373] mounted the heights on our right quickly and followed the enemy until 8 o'clock at night. The 4th and 10th Regiment's Brigade[374] moved to Vitoria in very good order and the 9-pounder artillery brigade directed its fire to good effect against the enemy posted in a wood.

The Division carried out its duties very well in the service it was employed. Brigadier Campbell is worthy of praise by the good manner he directed his brigade, as Brigadier Costa by the way his brigade got up the heights. Lieutenant Colonel Tulloh is also worthy of praise for the way he handled the artillery under his command.

Every officer and man showed the desire to face the enemy if the occasion arose, and when they were ordered to advance, they did it with steadiness.

I gave the order that the sick men in the Division and those of the 6th Cavalry Regiment should be removed to the hospital in Vitoria.
God save you, Sir
Camp of Ibarguren 24 June 1813
Manoel de Brito Mozinho

Count de Amarante

2nd Division

'My battalion on that day accompanied the 71st and commenced the Battle by an attack on the Enemy's extreme left posted on the Heights beyond Puebla, and I was near the gallant Colonel Cadogan when he fell. We drove them from that position and held it during the day notwithstanding their repeated attempts to dislodge us.'

Captain Richard Brunton, 6th Caçadores.[375]

Ashworth's Brigade (6th and 18th Infantry, 6th Caçadores)
Ashworth's Brigade was to the left of Cadogan's Brigade in the assault on the Heights of Puebla but was not heavily engaged. It remained on the heights through most of the day. During that time the 6th Caçadores skirmished with the French, and the brigade helped stop the French counter-attack in the afternoon.

Report[376] from Colonel Ashworth to AG Mozinho

Sir,
In consequence of your letter of the 22nd that I just received, I have the honor [sic] to acquaint you, for the information of His Excellency the Marshal Marquis de Campo Maior, with the conduct of the individuals of the brigade under my command in the battle of the 21st of this month. I cannot point out anyone in particular because I had the satisfaction of observing in all, the greatest coolness and promptitude, which convinced me that if such an occasion arises (not ordinary in battle) to distinguish themselves, they will seize the opportunity.
    The wounded in the action (the return of which I already sent to you), by order of the Division, were removed to Puebla under the care of an Assistant Surgeon escorted by an adequate number of men.
God save you, Sir
Camp 23 June 1813
Manoel de Brito Mozinho

Carlos [sic] Ashworth
Colonel commander of the 6th and 18th Regiments' Brigade

See Table 8.2.

The Centre

Light Division (1st and 3rd Caçadores, 17th Infantry)

On the morning of the battle, the Light Division marched towards the Zadorra river and deployed just downstream of Villodas. Kempt's Brigade was on the right and Vandeleur's Brigade was on the left. The 95th Rifles formed a skirmish line along the front of the division. At about 11:30 a.m. word was received that the bridge across the river at Tres Puentes, about 2km away, was unguarded. Wellington ordered Kempt to cross the river and take the high ground on the other side. With his brigade was the 17th Infantry. Vandeleur was sent further downstream to support the advance of the 7th Division. As the latter moved to take the Heights of Ariñez, the Light Division was sent to help, with Kempt on the right and Vandeleur on the left. The 17th Infantry was the division's reserve. In this attack the 1st Caçadores were part of the screen that preceded the advancing troops. During the assault its 1st Company was attacked by French light cavalry, but was able to fall back in good order. Upon reaching the crest of the heights 'a ball struck the close column of the 17th Portuguese not a yard from the place the 43rd colours had just left & about 16 yards from us. It killed a sergeant & took the leg of each of the ensigns[377] with the colours.'[378]

1st Caçadores

Report[379] from Lieutenant Colonel Algeo to AG Mozinho

Sir,
I have the honour to transmit to you, for the information of His Excellency the Marquis de Campo Maior, that the battalion under my command behaved magnificently in the action of the 21st instant, particularly the 1st Company under the command of Captain Manuel Jorge Rodrigues, which when in extended order was attacked by the enemy's cavalry, fell back in the best order firing at the enemy until it was supported by our cavalry.

This company's subalterns, Lieutenant Antonio Vicente Vasconcellos and Ensign Pedro Ozorio, helped the captain, and their conduct was brave as was that of First Sergeant Grigorio Jose dos Santos. For those services all of them deserve the highest commendation.
God save you, Sir
Camp of Pamplona, 25 June 1813
Manoel de Brito Mozinho

JH Algeo
Lieutenant Colonel commander 1st Caçadores Battalion

See Table 8.3.

3rd Caçadores

Report[380] from Lieutenant Colonel Silveira to AG Mozinho

Sir
I have the honour to transmit to you, for the information of His Excellency the Marshal Count of Campo Maior, that the officers, inferior officers and men of the battalion under my command, behaved in the best manner as they always do. I also send the return of the killed and wounded.[381]
God save you, Sir
Camp 27 June 1813
Manoel de Brito Mozinho

Manoel Pinto da Silveira
Lieutenant Colonel commander

17th Infantry

17th Infantry. Return[382] of the killed, wounded and prisoners on 21 June[383]

Killed:
    1 1st Sergeant
    1 Soldier
    1 Drummer
Total: 3

Severely wounded:
    1 Flag Bearer
    1 2nd Sergeant
    10 Privates
Total: 12

Slightly Wounded:
    1 Ensign Jozé Antonio da Silva Araujo
    1 Flag Bearer
    8 Privates
Total: 10

Lieutenant Colonel Rolt's horse was killed.
Camp Vitoria 22 June 1813

John Rolt[384]
Lieutenant Colonel commander 17th Infantry Regiment

4th Division

'The Division behaved as usual very well and my Portuguese Brigade admirable. In fact, nothing could have been more gallant than their conduct.'

General Cole, Commander of the 4th Division[385]

Stubbs' Brigade (11th and 23rd Infantry, 7th Caçadores)
The 4th Division was deployed to the right of the Light Division and to the left of Hill's troops, in the vicinity of Nanclares.[386] In mid-afternoon orders were received to cross the Zadorra river using the bridge near the village. Skerrett's Brigade went first, followed by Anson's Brigade. Stubbs' Brigade was the last to cross. They waited in a field until 3 p.m., when they attacked the Heights of Ariñez.[387] Anson was on the right, Stubbs on the left, and Skerrett in reserve. The Portuguese marched in line with the 11th Infantry on the right, the 23rd Infantry on the left, and the 7th Caçadores in front. The division attacked under fire from the French artillery on the ridge and 'Our Portuguese kept on our left, outside the wood, to clear the road. The enemy retired beyond a ravine which afforded them a good opportunity to pepper at us as we emerged from the wood. The Portuguese, being in compact order, fired a well-directed volley, gave a hearty shout and advanced to the charge.'[388] Stubbs' Brigade broke the French 4th Battalion 100th Line Regiment and in the process captured their battalion fannion,[389] three artillery batteries, and thirty wagons. The French did not stay on the heights long and the division's light troops, including the 7th Caçadores, pursued them to the next ridge a kilometre to the east.[390] Although the quoted matter above makes it appear that the Portuguese had an easy time of it, they lost 66 killed, 178 wounded, and 1 missing. This was twice as many casualties as the two British brigades combined.[391]

Report[392] from Colonel Stubbs to AG Mozinho

Sir

I have the honour to enclose the reports which were sent to me by the unit commanders of the brigade under my command related to the battle of Vitoria. I believe that the individuals mentioned are worthy of the notice of His Excellency the Marshal Marquis de Campo Maior, which I humbly beg in their favour.

It is also my duty to inform you that Lieutenant Colonel O'Toole, with the 7th Caçadores, had distinguished himself in the past days in several skirmishes and in the battle of Vitoria his conduct was most gallant and praiseworthy.

The 11th Regiment under the command of Lieutenant Colonel Anderson[393] and the 23rd under Lieutenant Colonel Miller[394] aroused general admiration by the steadiness with which they advanced, attacking the enemy repeatedly, regardless of the numerous obstacles which they faced. In these attacks the brigade took some artillery brigades with their baggage and the 23rd Regiment took the flag of the 4th Battalion 100th Regiment.

Lieutenant Colonel Miller distinguished himself throughout the action and by his example of firmness and bravery encouraged his regiment. Lieutenant Colonel Anderson directing his regiment with gallantry concurred to his good conduct in the battle. I cannot praise enough the commitment of these two officers in honour of their corps and I believe His Excellency will take this into account.

I had the opportunity to observe, on several occasions, the zeal, activity, and courage with which Major Joze Correa de Mello, 11th Regiment, distinguished himself.

I observed with satisfaction the distinguished conduct of Major Peacock,[395] 23rd Regiment, who commanded the First Battalion. I have known his military capabilities for a long time, having witnessed his noble and brave example, particularly at the battle of Vitoria. He deserves every commendation.

I have the pleasure to have witnessed the gallant conduct of Captain Phiffen,[396] 11th Regiment. This officer showed courage and intrepidity beyond words during the action until he was severely wounded in the head. This officer is extremely zealous and active, and I believe that he deserves some prize from His Excellency.

I should not omit to mention in this occasion the Adjutant Antonio Roque,[397] 23rd Regiment, who served as my Aide-de-Camp and did his duties with great promptitude, repeatedly showing his bravery, for which I am grateful.

I take the opportunity to inform you of the care and attention which this brigade had received from Doctor MacLagan,[398] its *Cirurgião Mor*,[399] who with great ability and promptitude assisted us and deserves from all the greatest gratitude.

It is with the greatest satisfaction that I communicate to you that every officer and man did his duty and it is quite difficult to distinguish one more than the other, but I beg leave to ask you to recommend the officers mentioned above to the favour of His Excellency.

God save you, Sir

Campo before Pamplona, 25 July 1813

Manoel de Brito Mozinho

Thomas Guilherme [sic] Stubbs[400]
Colonel commander of the Brigade

11th Infantry

The 11th Infantry lost 37 killed, 115 wounded, and 1 missing. This was almost half the casualties of the whole brigade.[401]

Report[402] from Lieutenant Colonel Anderson to Colonel Stubbs

Sir,

I have the honour to lay before you for the information of His Excellency the Marshal the names of those individuals who distinguished themselves the most, in the action of the 21st instant. However, it is my duty to state to you that all behaved with honour and in a most praiseworthy manner, deserving the attention of His Excellency the Marshal.

I received the greatest assistance throughout the action from Major Joze Correa de Mello, to whom I entrusted the command of the Second Battalion, and also from Major Daniel Donahoe.[403] Captain Charles Waldron[404] also distinguished himself directing his company as skirmishers in front of the regiment. Adjutant Lieutenant Simão Joze Clemente, Lieutenant Ignacio Pereira de Lacerda, Adjutant Sergeant João Jeronimo, and 1st Grenadier Company's First Sergeant Joze de Mello Cardozo, all showed always an excellent conduct, the latter I already recommended to His Excellency for his conduct at the battle of Salamanca.

Equally I have the honour to lay before you an exact return of the artillery and its wagons, which the 11th Regiment under my command took from the enemy in spite of the efforts he made to save it with a larger force.

God save you, Sir

Camp of Salvatierra

22 June 1813

Thomaz Guilherme [sic] Stubbs

Alex. Anderson
Lieutenant Colonel commander of the 11th Regiment

Return of the artillery park taken by the 11th Regiment in the action of 21 June

5 guns

1 howitzer

30 ammunition wagons

Alex. Anderson
Lieutenant Colonel commander of the 11th Regiment

23rd Infantry

'I recollect on this day seeing a Portuguese regiment … in our division, marching as steadily in line, with their colours flying, and advancing towards the enemy as if they had been moving on a parade … the men were generally looked upon as very good soldiers, having behaved very bravely in many actions.'

Major Charles Steevens, 20th Foot[405]

Report[406] from Lieutenant Colonel Miller to Colonel Stubbs

Sir,

In consequence of your order related to the conduct of the officers and men of the regiment under my command and those who distinguished themselves yesterday at the battle of Vitoria, I have the satisfaction to state to you for the information of His Excellency the Marshal Marquis de Campo Maior that their conduct could not have been better. When everyone did his particular duty in a most brilliant manner it's difficult to choose, however I cannot omit to mention to you that Major Francisco de Paula Azeredo,[407] commanding the Second Battalion, provided me with his assistance in advancing the regiment and followed my orders with zeal until he was wounded, forcing him to leave the field. Major Peacocke, commanding the First Battalion, particularly distinguished himself by his activity directing the regiment and with his example of bravery attracted the admiration of his men.

Among the company officers I noticed those mentioned below by their activity in maintaining their companies in good order when they had to overcome the successive obstacles that hinder the regiment's march. They are Captains G.D. Craufurd,[408] Jeronimo Freiro,[409] Thomaz Roboach,[410] Steiger[411] and Captain *Agregado* Francisco Joze Pereira;[412] Lieutenants Christovao de Abronhozo,[413] Jeronimo Regado,[414] and Pedro Roboach;[415] Ensigns Caetano Joze dos Campos, Joze Maria de Albuquerque, Antonio Luis da Fonseca, Joao Antonio Roboach,[416] and A. de Lemos.[417] It is also my duty to report to you that the *Porta Bandeira*[418] Antonio Felixberto and Joze Freire de Andrade, the Adjutant Sergeants Antonio Cardozo de Menezes[419] and A.R. Medeiros, and the 1st Grenadier Company's First Sergeant Joze Maria Ilharco, behaved with great steadiness and energy. The 2nd Grenadier Company's Second Sergeant took an enemy flag.

It is my great pleasure to inform you that the regiment captured two artillery brigades with their wagons[420] and also a flag from the 100th Battalion which was presented by order of General Cole, the Division's commander, to His Excellency the Marshal General Duke da Vittoria.[421]
God save you, Sir
Quarter of Salvatierra, 22 June 1813
T.W. Stubbs

J. Miller
Lieutenant Colonel commander of the 23rd Regiment

7th Caçadores

Report[422] from Lieutenant Colonel O'Toole to Colonel Stubbs

Sir
I beg leave to ask you to have the goodness to inform His Excellency the Marshal Commander in Chief of the Portuguese Army that the conduct of the 7th Caçadores Battalion on the 18th, 19th, and particularly on the 21st was of great merit. Regarding the recommendation of any individual who distinguished himself in those days I feel that I would do an injustice to all the others because all behaved very well and carried out their duties in an equal manner. So, if His Excellency has the desire to promote some individuals in the battalion, I will be extremely pleased because I can assure that all deserve.
  I have the honour to be, Sir, your servant
Thomas Guilherme [sic] Stubbs

B. O'Toole
Lieutenant Colonel commander of the 7th Caçadores

3rd Division

Wellington's plan called for a two-column attack on the French centre. The right attack would be made by the 4th and Light Divisions, while the 3rd and 7th Divisions were on the left. On the morning of 21 June both divisions were in bivouacs near the town of Anda along the Bayas river. They had a 10km march over a mountainous trail to get to the battlefield. The 3rd and 7th Divisions were supposed to attack together with the 4th and Light Divisions on the right, but the 3rd Division arrived at the Zadorra river near Mendoza several hours before the 7th Division. By the time the 4th Division started its attack, only one brigade of the 7th Division was present. General Picton decided he had waited long enough and ordered the 3rd Division forward.

The first troops to cross the Zadorra were a massive screen of light infantry led by Colonel John Keene, the commander of the 5th Battalion 60th Foot, and including the 11th Caçadores.[423] The bridge was covered by a French artillery battery which was forced to retreat by the screen, but before doing so caused many casualties among the light troops. Brisbane's Brigade crossed the bridge next, followed by Power's Brigade. Colville's Brigade was the last to cross. All three brigades crossed unopposed.

The division, in two columns, with Brisbane on the right, and Power on the left, bypassed the heights and attacked Ariñez in the valley behind the heights.[424] A desperate fight took place around the village and casualties were heavy. After it was taken, Wellington ordered the 3rd, 4th, 7th, and Light Divisions to attack the French on the ridge above them. As they advanced, the French artillery wreaked havoc on the columns and the Portuguese took heavy casualties. The French withdrew and soon the ridge was in the Allies' hands. The advance continued into Vitoria, until the troops stopped to loot the French baggage train. Power's Brigade lost more than 500 men killed, wounded, or missing, which was about 50 per cent of all Portuguese casualties. Losses among the officers were extremely high, with 6 killed and 24 wounded. Particularly hard hit were the company commanders. Of the 25 captains authorized, 3 were killed and 5 wounded.

Power's Brigade (9th and 21st Infantry, 11th Caçadores)

'The Portuguese brigade attached to the division was the admiration of the army: it advanced in line over difficult and broken ground in front of nearly fifty pieces of cannon and a continual volley of musketry, without ever hesitating, and drove the enemy from several commanding positions which they successfully occupied.'

General Picton, Commander 3rd Division[425]

Report[426] from General Power to AG Mozinho

Salvatierra, June 23rd 1813

Sir,

In obedience to the orders of His Excellency Marshal Sir William Carr Beresford, K.B. Marquis of Campo Mayor, which I was honoured with yesterday, I beg leave to transmit for His Excellency's information my report upon the officers of the Brigade, under my command, during the action near Vittoria, on the 21st instant.

When the conduct of the whole, was so conspicuously good, it is difficult to particularize individual merit, however I cannot withhold my recommendation in the first instance of Lieutenant Colonel Sutton commanding [the] 9th and Major Carretti[427] commanding [the] 21st Regiment, whose zeal, gallantry and coolness under a very heavy fire, to which we were exposed, I very particularly noticed, as well as that of Major Paty,[428] a most deserving officer, and Captain Mathias de Souza,[429] each commanding a battalion of the 9th Regiment and whose exertions were highly praiseworthy. I have also to add the names of Captain Antonio Azevedo e Cunha, Captain Graham,[430] and Adjutant Joze Antonio Pereira D'Eça of the 21st Regiment whose conduct during the action, came under my immediate observation, and which has also been particularly mentioned by Major Carretti.

The grenadier companies of these corps, which formed the advance, under the command of Major Ross,[431] merit my warmest commendation, and I beg leave very particularly to recommend that officer to His Excellency's notice. I am sorry to observe, that he was very severely wounded, as were the four captains commanding these companies viz. Cotter,[432] Jermyn,[433] Antonio Joze Soares,[434] and Fernando de Villas Boas.[435] The latter of whom, a very gallant and excellent officer, is I am sorry to learn since dead.

With respect to the 11th Caçadores under the command of Lieutenant Colonel Dursbach, I understand that they behaved remarkably well, but as they were detached, I had no opportunity of observing them. I therefore enclose herewith, for His Excellency's information, the report of Colonel Keane, under whose immediate orders, that corps was placed, as well as the report of Lieutenant Colonel Dursbach.

I am happy to have this opportunity of mentioning my Aide de Camp [sic] Captain Johnston,[436] whose zeal, professional knowledge, activity, and gallantry I have witnessed upon this, as well as upon every other occasion, since I have been in the Portuguese service and for whom, I humbly solicit some mark of His Excellency's favor [sic] and approbation, and in justice to my Brigade Major Joao Leandro de Macedo Valladas I cannot omit acknowledging his services, upon the late occasion.

I have the honor to be, Sir, your most obedient humble servant

M. Power
Brigadier General

Adjutant General

11th Caçadores

Letter[437] from Colonel Keane to General Power

Camp near Bacique [?]
June 23rd 1813
Sir

I have much pleasure in reporting to you that the conduct of the 11th Caçadores forming part of the advanced guard of the Division in the action on the 21st instant, was to a degree creditable. Every individual of the corps did his duty. I have the honour to enclose Lieutenant Colonel Dursbach's report.
I have the honor to be, Sir, your obedient and humble servant

J. Keane
Colonel

To Major General Power

Report[438] from Lieutenant Colonel Dursbach to Colonel Keane

Camp at Salvatierra 23 June 1813 morning
Sir!

I have the honour to inform you, that I have every reason to be perfectly satisfied with the conduct of officers and men of the battalion under my command, who were present on the 21st.

On the right under Major Kilsha, who I hope has been noticed by you, Lieutenant Silva[439] the first passing the rivers [sic] in a gallant style; as did Lieutenant Pinto[440] on the left. The former was wounded soon after the passage but not severely.

I beg leave strongly to recommend to your notice Captain Jose Bento de Magalhens who not only behaved in a gallant manner but was my principal assistance in entering the contested village on the left of Vitoria.

I have also to recommend my Adjutant Teixera de Mesquita for his bravery and zeal. Sergeant Vianna who acted as Sergeant Major;[441] Sergeant Cardozo, whom I had already noticed at the scaling at Badajoz, and Sergeant Simao deserve my praise, the latter was badly wounded.

I must also notice Ensign Vidal,[442] who notwithstanding being wounded, and told by me to go to the rear, persisted in remaining with his section till the end and only had his wound dressed the next morning.

Ensign Manoel Pinto de Souza Magalhens also deserved the good opinion I had formed of him, when I formerly had recommended him for his present [sic].

I can not conclude without assuring you, that every individual has [illegible word] to their utmost.
I have the honour to be your most humble servant

Ths. Dursbach
Lieutenant Colonel commanding 11th Caçadores

To Colonel Keane
Commander Advanced Guard
3rd Division

See Table 8.4.

7th Division

Lecor's Brigade was late in arriving at the battle and missed the attack against the centre of the French line. It was in reserve on the far left during the four-division attack against the French centre and was not engaged.

Lecor's Brigade (7th and 19th Infantry, 2nd Caçadores)

Report[443] from General Lecor to AG Mozinho

Sir,

In consequence of your letter from today, I have the honour to tell you, for the information of His Excellency the Marshal Marquis of Campo Maior, that on the 23th last month I obeyed His Excellency's order of the 22th of that month sending to you my report by way of the 7th Division Head Quarters. In it I informed you that the Brigade under my command did not have any killed, wounded or missing and both officers and inferior officers and men showed the greatest steadiness in the march in line that the Brigade made against the woods occupied by the enemy. The post was abruptly abandoned by the enemy, without resistance. I do not have any recommendations to make to His Excellency, but I can assure you that the men under my command had the best disposition to attack the enemy if he had afforded the occasion.

I enclose a return of the officers *agregados* by punishment present at the action of the 21st of last month. God save you, Sir
Camp Noain 1 July 1813
Manoel de Brito Mozinho

Carlos Frederico Lecor
Brigadier

Return of the Officers *Agregados* by Punishment, belonging to the Brigade under the command of Brigadier Lecor, present at the Action on 21 June

2nd Caçadores Battalion:

Lieutenant Joze Vicente de Vargas
7th Regiment:
Lieutenant Dom Bartolomeu Sallazar
Ensign Marcelino Joze de Souza

Camp of Noain 1 July 1813

Carlos Frederico Lecor
Brigadier

The Left Wing

Graham's mission was to cut the main road to France, while attacking the French positions in the flank. He had the 1st and 5th Divisions, Longa's Spanish Division, plus Pack's and Bradford's Brigades. On 21 June they were bivouacked about 15km from Vitoria. Pack's Brigade led the advance, just behind the light cavalry screen. Following it were the 5th Division, Bradford's Brigade, and the 1st Division. They arrived at Aranguiz about noon and there they found a French force occupying the village and the Montes de Araca. Pack was ordered to take both the village and the hill, with the 5th Division in support. Bradford was sent to the right to link up with the Allied divisions in the centre. Prior to the attack, the 8th Caçadores were detached from Spry's Brigade and attached to Pack's Brigade.

The French pulled out of Aranguiz before they could be pinned in place but stayed on the hill until they were attacked. This left the Allies the choice of three bridges across the river. Graham ordered Longa to take the Durana bridge and cut the main road. The 5th Division was to take the bridge at Gamarra Mayor, while the 1st Division, with Pack's and Bradford's Brigades, would take the Arriaga bridge. By 5 p.m. the 5th Division had taken Gamarra Mayor but not the bridge, while Longa had seized the Durana bridge. Graham did not make a serious effort to take the Arriaga bridge.

5th Division

Spry's Brigade was in reserve until the attack on Gamarra Mayor. During most of the fight the brigade provided a skirmish screen in the outskirts of the village. Because the 8th Caçadores had been detached, the regiments had to send out men to form a skirmish line under Major Archibald Campbell. This line consisted of 500 men, 200 from the 3rd Infantry, 100 men from each of the two grenadier companies and another 100 men from the 15th Infantry. They fought for several hours. Towards the end of the fight, the brigade advanced into the village as the French retreated. The brigade suffered 81 casualties, half of which were in the 8th Caçadores.[444]

Spry's Brigade (3rd and 15th Infantry, 8th Caçadores)

Report[445] from General Spry to AG Mozinho

Sir,

Until now I have not had enough time to collect the information related to the conduct of the officers of the Brigade under my command on the 21st instant.

Concerning the 8th Caçadores Battalion I can only tell you that Lieutenant Colonel Hill[446] and all in the battalion distinguished themselves during the day. I believe that General Pack, under whose orders this battalion was, will praise the corps in his report.

Lieutenant Colonel Hill speaks highly of the conduct of his Adjutant Sergeant Domingos Lopes.

Nothing could exceed the steadiness of the 3rd and 15th Regiments, both when advancing to attack the village[447] under artillery and musketry fire, and when for several hours under a heavy artillery fire, they remained in support of the brigade that was attacking the enemy. Being deprived of the Caçadores battalion, I was therefore forced to deploy men from those regiments in extended order in front. These officers and men, from the 3rd and 15th [Regiments], distinguished themselves under the command of Major A. Campbell, 15th Regiment, to my greatest satisfaction and to the applause from all who observed their conduct throughout the day. Unfortunately, Major A. Campbell was wounded at the beginning of the advance of the skirmishers of both regiments. The command devolved to Captain T. Smith,[448] 3rd Regiment, who, with Captain Bernardo Baptista, 15th Regiment, resisted all enemy attempts in an admirable manner, during the day. I regret to inform you that both were wounded, and I am afraid that Captain Smith received a dangerous wound. These officers distinguished themselves on all occasions and I can only offer my highest recommendation to His Excellency.

I received all the assistance needed from my Brigade Major C. Fitzgerald[449] (who was slightly wounded but remained on the field) and also from the activity of Captain Brackenbury, 15th Regiment, who has shown ability and zeal for the service on all occasions.

It is my duty to name the subalterns from the 3rd and 15th Regiments who volunteered to advance with Major Campbell, 15th Regiment, and behaved very well facing the enemy.

3rd Regiment:
    Ensign Joze Maria de Mello
    Ensign Francisco Cardozo da Gama
15th Regiment:
    Lieutenant Azinheira de Gr.
    Ensign Joze de Magalheis
    Ensign Bernardo de Goveia
God save you, Sir
23 June 1813
Manoel de Brito Mozinho

                                                       W. Fred. Spry
                                                        Brigadier

8th Caçadores

As General Graham's column neared the battlefield, Pack was ordered to attack a large French force with artillery on the Montes de Araca, a hill that towered about 100m over Gamarra Mayor. He was supported by the 8th Caçadores, which with the 4th Caçadores cleared the hill. When Pack moved towards Arriaga, the 8th Caçadores went with him and stayed with Pack's Brigade throughout the day. The 8th Caçadores lost 13 killed and 27 wounded.

Report[450] from Lieutenant Colonel Hill to General Spry

5th Division
June 22nd 1813
Sir

Being detached from your Brigade in the action of yesterday, I have the honor [sic] to report to you for the information of His Excellency Marshall Sir William Carr Beresford that I was ordered by Major General Oswald[451] to place the 8th Caçadores under the immediate direction of Brigadier General Pack and in conjunction with the 4th Caçadores drive the enemy off the heights they occupied in front of the left column of the army. This order was carried into execution with the greatest promptitude and I cannot say sufficient in praise of the gallantry and forwardness of my men and officers. The heights we had to ascend were difficult of [sic] access and the fire of the enemy was very heavy yet did we succeed in driving the enemy from the different hills they successively occupied and obliged them to retire beyond the river.[452]

The conduct of the battalion in pursuing the enemy afterwards on their retreat was no less conspicuous, having advanced in front of the various lines and columns of the army in conjunction with the 4th Caçadores driving before them the enemy's numerous light troops of infantry and cavalry. As General Pack will of course make a report to His Excellency on the conduct of the troops engaged under his command I beg you will refer his Excellency to his report, and that you will have the goodness to mention in yours, your opinion of the conduct of the Battalion in the first part of the engagement which could not have escaped your observation.

The officers of the Battalion behaved with the greatest gallantry and to recommend those who distinguished themselves would be to [illegible word] the whole. I have however to beg you will report to His Excellency the extreme bravery and gallant conduct of the Sergeant Major of the battalion who in all occasions during the day distinguished himself by heading the advance of every company and exhibited the greatest coolness and judicious arrangements in placing those intrusted to his command. The name of the Sergeant Major is Domingos Lopes, who has before been recommended for good conduct.

I have the honour to be, Sir, your obedient servant

Dudley Hill
Lieutenant Colonel 8th Caçadores
Brigadier General Spry

Pack's Independent Brigade (1st and 16th Infantry, 4th Caçadores)
Pack's Brigade was the lead infantry unit during Graham's advance to Vitoria. Pack was ordered to clear Montes de Araca, a large hill about 100m high that was just to the left of Aranguiz and to the north of Gamarra Mayor. He was given the 8th Caçadores to assist in the assault. He deployed his two infantry regiments in line and sent the 4th and 8th Caçadores up the hill. The attack by the caçadores forced the French off the hill and across the Zadorra river. The 16th Infantry, which was deployed on the left of the brigade, also took part in the assault. After the hill was taken, the brigade was sent with the 1st Division to Abechuco. The men were ordered not to cross the river until the French began withdrawing. They pursued the French until nightfall. Total casualties were fewer than 100 men.

Report[453] from General Pack to AG Mozinho

Sir,

I have the greatest satisfaction to report to you, for the information of His Excellency, that the conduct of the brigade under my command in the glorious day of yesterday has my entire approbation, particularly the 4th Caçadores Battalion, to which more occasions were offered to distinguish itself, under the command of Lieutenant Colonel Williams,[454] who showed his bravery and intelligence directing the battalion which behaved in a most gallant manner.

I enclose the return of the casualties on this occasion.

Lieutenant Colonel Williams praises Major Adamson and Captain McGregor, who is wounded for the second time. I recommend him to His Excellency.

The officers commanding the corps did not particularize the conduct of any of his officers because all behaved in a manner that makes it difficult.

I take the opportunity to bring to the memory of His Excellency Lieutenant Colonel Gomersall, 16th Regiment, and Major Fearon, 1st Regiment, both already recommended by me; to those I have to add now Captains William Queade[455] and Victorino Jozé de Almeida, with a view to His Excellency rewarding them.

I have every reason to be pleased with the conduct of the 8th Caçadores Battalion which on this occasion acted in conjunction with the 4th Caçadores.

God save you, Sir
Camp near Vitoria 22 June 1813
Manoel de Brito Mozinho

D. Pack
Brigadier

See Table 8.5.

Bradford's Independent Brigade (13th and 24th Infantry, 5th Caçadores)

Graham ordered Bradford to link up with the 3rd and 7th Divisions. Bradford crossed the river at Yurre and joined the pursuit of the French. The brigade was never seriously engaged during the battle and took only 23 casualties.

Report[456] from General Bradford to AG Mozinho

Andoain July 1st 1813
Sir,

I have the honor [sic] to request you will be pleased to submit to His Excellency the Marshal Commander in Chief the enclosed paper which, as nearly as I can recollect, is agreeable to the report I made to Sir Thomas Graham commanding the left column of the Army on the 23th ultimo of the proceedings of the brigade under my command on the 21st at the battle of Vittoria. I have to beg at the same time that you will be kind enough to request the Marshal will have the goodness to excuse the omission I fear I have been guilty in not sooner sending this report to be laid before His Excellency, which arose from the supposition that the representation I made to Sir Thomas Graham would have been forwarded to the Headquarters. I trust this mistake of mine, which I am extremely sorry should have happened, will not prevent His Excellency expressing any feelings of approbation which he may consider the Brigade entitled to, as in justice to them I must bear testimony of my entire approbation of their good conduct in that day and particularly of the 5th Caçadores and the Grenadier Battalion,[457] the former under the command of Lieutenant Colonel McCreagh and the latter under Major Snodgrass[458] of the 13th Regiment, whose fortune it was to be more engaged than the rest in the pursuit of the enemy.

I have the honor [sic] to be, Sir, your most obedient and humble servant

T. Bradford
Adjutant General

Report[459] from General Bradford to General Graham

June 23rd 1813
Sir,
I have the honor [sic] to report to you that agreeable to your orders, I moved from Vitoriana[460] on the morning of the 21st June to the heights to the left of Guita d'Ariba[461] with a view of communicating between the left column and the 7th Division. Seeing the column of the left halted and the Division on the right making progress towards Vitoria, I descended from the heights and moved upon the bridge below Zurri,[462] crossing to the left bank of the Zadora [sic], and from thence upon the village of Ariazo,[463] at the period that Colonel Halket's brigade was advancing to the attack of the bridge leading to that place; by this movement the enemy's post was taken in flank which I conceive may have facilitated the evacuation of it and the capture of their guns as they retired almost immediately. I then put myself in communication with the cavalry of General Anson and General Ponsonby's Brigades and continued in support of them till the night prevented further pursuit. I cannot avoid mentioning with what zeal and alacrity this movement was performed by the officers and men of the brigade under my command as to derive any advantage from it, it was necessary to advance in double quick time for near two leagues.
I have the honor [sic] to be your most humble servant

T. Bradford

To Lieutenant General Sir Thomas Graham

See Table 8.6.

Artillery
Most of the Portuguese Artillery was kept in reserve until the attack by the four divisions against the centre. The guns were brought up to engage the fifty French guns on the heights behind Ariñez. The artillery duel lasted less than 20 minutes before the French retired. Major Arriaga's 1st Brigade did the most firing, averaging fifteen shots per gun.

Report[464] from Lieutenant Colonel Dickson, Commander of the Portuguese Artillery, to AG Mozinho

Sir,
I enclose the return of the killed and wounded of the Portuguese artillery brigades and the return of the spent ammunition, in the battle of the 21st instant. I have to tell you, for the information of the Marshal the Marquis de Campo Maior, that Lieutenant Colonel Hartman,[465] commander of all the Reserve Artillery, assured me of the good behaviour of the 1st Brigade of Artillery, under the command of Major Arriaga,[466] which made good and accurate fire. About the 3rd and 4th Brigades, under the command of Lieutenant Colonel Tulloh, I can only say that the 3rd did not fire, and the 4th spent only 22 shots but the Count de Amarante was pleased with his fire.
    It is all I have to inform for now.
God save you, Sir
Villa Casseda
29 June 1813
Manoel Brito Mozinho

A. Dickson
Lieutenant Colonel commander of the Artillery

See Table 8.7.

Report[467] from Lieutenant Colonel Tulloh, Commander of the Artillery Brigades, to AG Mozinho

Sir,

In consequence of your letter from June 22, I have the honour to state to you that the 3rd Brigade of 6 pounders did not fire but that of the 9 pounders did. Captain Mitchell [sic],[468] 3rd Artillery Regiment, was present and directed the fire in an excellent manner, despite suffering from a continuous fever since he took command of that brigade. I remind you of the good conduct, zeal and activity of this captain as well as 1st Lieutenant Joze Joaquim Barreiros, 4th Artillery Regiment, 2nd Lieutenant Vicente Antonio Buys, 2nd Artillery Regiment, and also 1st Sergeant Antonio Vicente de Abreu and Corporal Joze Xavier, 2nd Regiment, for the same reasons. I beg leave to recommend those individuals to His Excellency the Marquis de Campo Maior. As the brigade which entered in action did not have any casualties, except a beast wounded, I hope you will excuse me for not sending a return.

God save you, Sir

Camp 24 June 1813

Manoel de Brito Mozinho

Alex. Tulloh
Lieutenant Colonel commander of the Artillery Brigades

D'Urban's Cavalry Brigade (1st, 11th, and 12th Cavalry)

The brigade was in reserve with Hill's forces. It received some artillery fire but took no casualties. 'The Troops behaved splendidly; the Ground was not of a nature to admit of the services of the cavalry … Pursued till dark.' Brigadier General Benjamin D'Urban, Commander.[469]

Report[470] from General D'Urban to AG Mozinho

Ordoñana 26 June 1813

My dear general

I have just received your letter from yesterday. I already wrote to His Excellency the Marshal informing that the Brigade under my command did not have any killed, wounded, or missing, and nobody distinguished himself. But I see that it is required to report to you all the same, I have to inform you that on the 21st my Brigade did all its movements with great precision and regularity; also sustained a cannonade with great coolness, deserving my approbation; fortunately the Brigade didn't lose a man or a horse, did not have an occasion to charge or receive one. In consequence I have every reason to be sure of the goodwill of the officers and men. None of them could distinguish himself.

Your humble servant, Sir

Manoel Brito Mozinho

B. D'Urban

Table 8.1: Return[471] of the Killed, Wounded, Missing and Prisoners in the Portuguese Division under the Command of Lieutenant General Count de Amarante in the Action of 21 June 1813 near Vitoria

Corps			Killed									Wounded									Missing and Prisoners									Total									
			Colonels	Lieutenant Colonels	Majors	Captains	Subalterns	Flag Bearers	Sergeants and *Furriés*	Musicians and Drummers	Corporals and Privates	Colonels	Lieutenant Colonels	Majors	Captains	Subalterns	Flag Bearers	Sergeants and *Furriés*	Musicians and Drummers	Corporals and Privates	Colonels	Lieutenant Colonels	Majors	Captains	Subalterns	Flag Bearers	Sergeants and *Furriés*	Musicians and Drummers	Corporals and Privates	Colonels	Lieutenant Colonels	Majors	Captains	Subalterns	Flag Bearers	Sergeants and *Furriés*	Musicians and Drummers	Corporals and Privates	Killed Horses
Artillery	3rd Brigade[472]																																						1
	4th Brigade[473]																																						
Infantry	2nd Brigade	2nd Regiment																																					
		14th Regiment																																					
	4th Brigade	4th Regiment																																					
		10th Regiment																		2																		2	
		10th Caçadores																																					
Total																				2																		2	
Ranks and names of the officers killed												Ranks and names of the officers wounded									Ranks and names of the officers missing and prisoners																		

Count de Amarante
Lieutenant General commander Portuguese Division

Table 8.2: Ashworth's Brigade. Infantry Brigade 6th, 18th and 6th Caçadores Battalion. Return[474] of the Killed, Wounded, Missing and Prisoners in the Battle of 21 June 1813

Camp 23 June 1813	Killed									Wounded									Missing and Prisoners									Total								
	Colonels	Lieutenant Colonels	Majors	Captains	Subalterns	Flag Bearers	Sergeants and *Furriéis*	Musicians and Drummers	Corporals and Privates	Colonels	Lieutenant Colonels	Majors	Captains	Subalterns	Flag Bearers	Sergeants and *Furriéis*	Musicians and Drummers	Corporals and Privates	Colonels	Lieutenant Colonels	Majors	Captains	Subalterns	Flag Bearers	Sergeants and *Furriéis*	Musicians and Drummers	Corporals and Privates	Colonels	Lieutenant Colonels	Majors	Captains	Subalterns	Flag Bearers	Sergeants and *Furriéis*	Musicians and Drummers	Corporals and Privates
6th Regiment	-	-	-	-	-	-	-	-	2	-	-	-	-	-	-	-	-	16	-	-	-	-	-	-	-	-	-	-	-	-	-	-	-	-	-	18
18th Regiment	-	-	-	-	-	-	-	-	-	-	-	-	-	-	-	-	-	-	-	-	-	-	-	-	-	-	-	-	-	-	-	-	-	-	-	-
6th Caçadores Battalion	-	-	-	-	1	-	-	-	-	-	-	-	-	-	-	-	-	9	-	-	-	-	-	-	-	-	-	-	-	-	-	1	-	-	-	9
Total	-	-	-	-	1	-	-	-	2	-	-	-	-	-	-	-	-	25	-	-	-	-	-	-	-	-	-	-	-	-	-	1	-	-	-	27
Observations	Ranks and names of the officers killed									Ranks and names of the officers wounded									Ranks and names of the officers missing and prisoners																	
	Ensign Antonio Ozorio[475]																																			

Carlos [sic] Ashworth
Colonel commander of the brigade

Table 8.3: 1st Caçadores. Return[476] of the Dead, Wounded, Missing and Prisoners on 19 and 21 July 1813

Killed						Wounded						Missing and Prisoners						Total					
Lieutenant Colonel	Major	Captains	Subalterns	Sergeants	Corporals and Privates	Lieutenant Colonel	Major	Captains	Subalterns	Sergeants	Corporals and Privates	Lieutenant Colonel	Major	Captains	Subalterns	Sergeants	Corporals and Privates	Lieutenant Colonel	Major	Captains	Subalterns	Sergeants	Corporals and Privates
-	-	-	-	-	3	-	-	-	-	-	4	-	-	-	-	-	-	-	-	-	-	-	7
Ranks and names of the officers killed						Ranks and names of the officers wounded						Ranks and names of the officers missing and prisoners						Observations					

JH Algeo
Lieutenant Colonel commander 1st Caçadores Battalion

Table 8.4: Power's Brigade. Return[477] of the Dead, Wounded, Missing and Prisoners in the Battle of 21st instant before the Town of Vitoria

Camp east of Vitoria 22nd June 1813	Killed									Wounded									Missing and Prisoners									Total[478]									Observations
	Colonels	Lieutenant Colonels	Majors	Captains	Subalterns	Flag Bearers	Sergeants and Furriéis	Musicians and Drummers	Corporals and Privates	Colonels	Lieutenant Colonels	Majors	Captains	Subalterns	Flag Bearers	Sergeants and Furriéis	Musicians and Drummers	Corporals and Privates	Colonels	Lieutenant Colonels	Majors	Captains	Subalterns	Flag Bearers	Sergeants and Furriéis	Musicians and Drummers	Corporals and Privates	Colonels	Lieutenant Colonels	Majors	Captains	Subalterns	Flag Bearers	Sergeants and Furriéis	Musicians and Drummers	Corporals and Privates	
11th Caçadores				1	2				2					3		2		10																		16	
9th Infantry				2	1				22			1	2	6	1	8		168									16									23	
21st Infantry							1		23				3	7	1	8		196									23									39	
Total				3	3		1		47			1	5	16	2	18		374									39										

Names and ranks of the officers killed: Captain Fernando de Villas Boas, 9th Regiment; Captain Carlos João de Araujo, 21st Regiment; Captain Manoel Vicente de Sequeira, 21st Regiment; Lieutenant Palmer,[479] 21st Regiment; Ensign Martinho da Cunha, 9th Regiment; Ensign João Malheiro, 9th Regiment

Names and ranks of the officers wounded: Major Ross, 9th Regiment; Captain Mathias Joze de Souza, 9th Regiment; Captain G. Cotter, 9th Regiment; Captain Antonio Joze Soares, 21st Regiment; Captain Diogo Machado, 21st Regiment; Captain Samuel Jermyn, 21st Regiment; Lieutenant Antonio Rodrigues da Silva, 11th Caçadores; Lieutenant Pedro de Magalhães Peixoto, 11th Caçadores; Lieutenant Martinho Quesado, 9th Regiment; Lieutenant Galbraith,[480] 21st Regiment; Lieutenant Fernando de Lima, 21st Regiment

Ensigns:
Antonio Justiniano Vidal, 11th Caçadores; Antonio Pimenta da Gama, 9th Regiment; Thomaz Joze Maciel, 9th Regiment; Caetano Joze Gomes, Ensign Adjutant, 9th Regiment; Ignacio Lopes Barreto, 9th Regiment; Joaquim Nunes de Mattos, 9th Regiment; Tristão de Araujo, 21st Regiment; Joze de Oliveira, 21st Regiment; Joaquim Pereira de Eça, 21st Regiment; João Antonio Pinto, 21st Regiment; Antonio Joze Soares, 21st Regiment; The Caçadores' Lieutenant Colonel reports that the ensign wounded remained in the field until the end of the action.

Names and ranks of the officers missing and prisoners

M. Power
Brigadier

Table 8.5: Pack's Brigade. Return[481] of the Dead, Wounded and Prisoners in the Infantry Brigade 1st, 16th, 4th Caçadores Battalion in the battle before Vitoria on 21 June 1813

Corps	Killed									Wounded									Prisoners									Total									Observations
	Colonels	Lieutenant Colonels	Majors	Captains	Subalterns	Flag Bearers	Sergeants and *Furriéis*	Musicians and Drummers	Corporals and Privates	Colonels	Lieutenant Colonels	Majors	Captains	Subalterns	Flag Bearers	Sergeants and *Furriéis*	Musicians and Drummers	Corporals and Privates	Colonels	Lieutenant Colonels	Majors	Captains	Subalterns	Flag Bearers	Sergeants and *Furriéis*	Musicians and Drummers	Corporals and Privates	Colonels	Lieutenant Colonels	Majors	Captains	Subalterns	Flag Bearers	Sergeants and *Furriéis*	Musicians and Drummers	Corporals and Privates	
1st	-	-	-	-	-	-	-	-	-	-	-	-	-	-	-	-	1	4	-	-	-	-	-	-	-	-	-	-	-	-	-	-	-	-	1	4	
16th	-	-	-	1	-	-	-	-	7	-	-	-	1	1	-	-	-	49	-	-	-	-	-	-	-	-	-	-	-	-	2	1	-	-	-	56	
4th Caç.	-	-	-	-	-	-	1	-	9	-	-	-	1	1	-	3	-	27	-	-	-	-	-	-	-	-	-	-	-	-	1	1	-	4	-	36	R.A.D'Abreu[483] Brigade Major
Total	-	-	-	1	-	-	1	-	16	-	-	-	2	2	-	3	1	80	-	-	-	-	-	-	-	-	-	-	-	-	3	2	-	4	1	96	
	Ranks and names of the officers killed									Ranks and names of the officers wounded									Ranks and names of the officers missing and prisoners									Observations									
	Captain Thomas Lynch, 16th Regiment									Captain Manoel Jozé Xavier, 16th Regiment, slightly Captain MacGregor, 4th Caçadores, severely Ensign Fernando Telles da Silva Penalva, 16th Regiment, slightly Ensign Frazão,[482] 4th Caçadores, slightly																											

Table 8.6: Bradford's Brigade. Return[484] of the Killed, Wounded and Missing in the action of 21 June 1813 in the Brigade 13th, 24th Infantry and 5th Caçadores

Quarters at Ordona 23 June 1813	Killed									Wounded									Prisoners and Missing								
	Lieutenant Colonels	Majors	Captains	Lieutenants	Ensigns	Sergeants	Drummers	Corporals and Privates	Total	Lieutenant Colonels	Majors	Captains	Lieutenants	Ensigns	Sergeants	Drummers	Corporals and Privates	Total	Lieutenant Colonels	Majors	Captains	Lieutenants	Ensigns	Sergeants	Drummers	Corporals and Privates	Total
5th Caçadores Battalion	-	-	-	-	-	-	-	5	5	-	-	-	-	-	-	-	13	13	-	-	-	-	-	-	-	-	-
13th Regiment	-	-	-	-	-	-	-	-	-	-	-	-	-	-	-	-	1	1	-	-	-	-	-	-	-	-	-
24th Regiment	-	-	-	-	-	-	-	-	-	-	-	-	-	-	-	-	4	4	-	-	-	-	-	-	-	-	-
Total	-	-	-	-	-	-	-	5	5	-	-	-	-	-	-	-	18	18	-	-	-	-	-	-	-	-	-

T Bradford

Table 8.7: Return[485] of the Casualties in Personal and Material in the Three Portuguese Artillery Brigades in the Battle of 21 June 1813

Quarters at Arassuri 26 June 1813	Killed									Wounded									Beasts						Spent Ammunition					
---	---	---	---	---	---	---	---	---	---	---	---	---	---	---	---	---	---	---	Killed			Wounded			Howitzer			Gun		
	Major	Captains	1st Lieutenants	2nd Lieutenants	Sergeants and *Furriéis*	Drummers	Corporals and Privates	Artificers	Total	Major	Captains	1st Lieutenants	2nd Lieutenants	Sergeants and *Furriéis*	Drummers	Corporals and Privates	Artificers	Total	Horses	Mules	Total	Horses	Mules	Total	Shells to five and ½ inches howitzers	Case shot	Total	Round shot	Case shot	Total
1st Brigade 9-pounder	-	-	-	-	-	-	1	-	1	-	-	-	-	-	-	1	-	1	-	-	-	-	-	-	8	-	8	90	-	90
3rd Brigade 6-pounder	-	-	-	-	-	-	-	-	-	-	-	-	-	-	-	-	-	-	-	-	-	-	-	-	-	-	-	-	-	-
4th Brigade 9-pounder	-	-	-	-	-	-	-	-	-	-	-	-	-	-	-	-	-	-	-	-	-	-	1	1	-	-	-	22	-	22
Total	-	-	-	-	-	-	1	-	1	-	-	-	-	-	-	1	-	1	-	-	-	-	1	1	8	-	8	112	-	112

A. Dickson
Lieutenant Colonel, commander of the Artillery

Chapter 9

Tolosa, 25 June 1813

On 22 June Wellington ordered Graham to take the 1st Division and Pack's and Bradford's Brigades and head north and then east. He hoped that Graham would be able to get between the retreating French and Pamplona. The route he was to take was the same one that Longa was ordered to take earlier to capture a French convoy under General Maucune.

Unknown to Wellington, Foy was in the area protecting the lines of communications back to France. On 24 June Graham caught up with Foy at Villafranca,[486] where both Portuguese brigades were engaged. Pack's was to the left of the road and Bradford's to the right. Foy delayed them long enough for the convoy to safely continue its retreat. He finally ordered a withdrawal towards Tolosa, where he decided to make a stand. He chose a strong position along the Oria river, supported by the fortified town. He had about 14,000 men to oppose the 16,000 Spanish and 10,000 Anglo-Portuguese.[487]

On 25 June Graham reached Tolosa and reconnoitred the position. Rather than make a frontal assault, he ordered the Spanish to swing wide towards the east to get behind the French. Bradford was ordered to take his brigade and three battalions of KGL infantry to outflank the French to the east. Once they reached the main road[488] to Pamplona they were to turn west and attack Tolosa. Pack was ordered to send one battalion, along with several Spanish light infantry companies, to turn the French western flank.[489]

Bradford engaged the French left flank and evicted them from a hill overlooking Tolosa. They made several unsuccessful attempts to force Bradford off the hill. About 6 p.m. Graham ordered the attack to begin. Progress was slow, with Bradford doing most of the fighting on the eastern flank. Pack was unable to break into the town. Eventually the French withdrew to the border.

Pack's Independent Brigade (1st and 16th Infantry, 4th Caçadores)

Report[490] from General Pack to AG Mozinho

I have the honour to transmit enclosed the return of yesterday's casualties of the brigade under my command, and to which I must add my approbation of the conduct of the three companies from the 4th Caçadores Battalion under the command of Lieutenant Colonel Williams, and the two of grenadiers from the 1st Infantry Regiment under the command of Major Fearon.

Lieutenant Colonel Williams praises very highly the behaviour of the officers and men of the companies mentioned above, and particularly the conduct of Lieutenant Antonio Vicente de Queiroz and Ensign Vasconcellos[491] from the 4th Caçadores; the former advancing ahead of the troops to the town's gates, which were closed and well-guarded with enemy troops; the latter losing an eye in this service.

I conclude stating to you for the information of His Excellency the Marshal Marquis de Campo Maior that nothing could exceed the conduct of these two officers.
God save you, Sir
Quarters in Tolosa 26 June 1813
Manoel de Brito Mozinho

D. Pack
Brigadier General

See Table 9.1.

Bradford's Independent Brigade (13th and 24th Infantry, 5th Caçadores)

Report[492] from Major Snodgrass to General Bradford

Ernani 30th June 1813

Sir

I conceive it my duty to report to you, that during the time I commanded the Grenadiers of the thirteenth and twenty fourth Regiments, I could not help observing the superior status of discipline of the first company of Grenadiers of the Twenty fourth regiment, commanded by Romao Jose Soares, Lieutenant of that company, which I solely attribute to the attention, and judgement of that officer, who likewise when engaged with the enemy at Vittoria and in the affairs of 24th and 25th instant displayed the greatest coolness and gallantry.[493]

I am Sir your most obedient humble servant

K. Snodgrass
Major 13th Regiment

To Major General Bradford

See Tables 9.2 and 9.3.

Table 9.1: Pack's Brigade. Return[194] of the Killed, Wounded and Prisoners in the Brigade's 1st, 16th and 4th Caçadores on 25 June 1813 before Tolosa

Corps	Killed									Wounded									Prisoners									Total								
	Colonels	Lieutenant Colonels	Majors	Captains	Subalterns	Flag Bearers	Sergeants and Furriéis	Musicians and Drummers	Corporals and Privates	Colonels	Lieutenant Colonels	Majors	Captains	Subalterns	Flag Bearers	Sergeants and Furriéis	Musicians and Drummers	Corporals and Privates	Colonels	Lieutenant Colonels	Majors	Captains	Subalterns	Flag Bearers	Sergeants and Furriéis	Musicians and Drummers	Corporals and Privates	Colonels	Lieutenant Colonels	Majors	Captains	Subalterns	Flag Bearers	Sergeants and Furriéis	Musicians and Drummers	Corporals and Privates
1st Infantry	-	-	-	-	-	-	-	-	1	-	-	-	-	-	-	-	-	8	-	-	-	-	-	-	-	-	4	-	-	-	-	-	-	-	-	13
16th Infantry	-	-	-	-	-	-	-	-	-	-	-	-	-	-	-	-	-	-	-	-	-	-	-	-	-	-	-	-	-	-	-	-	-	-	-	-
4th Caçadores	-	-	-	-	-	-	-	-	3	-	-	-	-	2	-	-	-	14	-	-	-	-	-	-	-	-	2	-	-	-	-	2	-	-	-	19
Total	-	-	-	-	-	-	-	-	4	-	-	-	-	2	-	-	-	22	-	-	-	-	-	-	-	-	6	-	-	-	-	2	-	-	-	32
	Ranks and names of the officers killed									Ranks and names of the officers wounded									Ranks and names of the officers prisoners									Observations								
										Ensign Vasconcellos, 4th Caçadores severely Ensign Telles,[495] 4th Caçadores, severely																									

D. Pack
Brigadier General

Table 9.2: Bradford's Brigade. Brigade 13th, 24th and 5th Caçadores. Return[496] of the Killed, Wounded, Prisoners, and Missing on 24 June 1813[497]

	Killed									Wounded									Prisoners and Missing								
	Lieutenant Colonels	Majors	Captains	Lieutenants	Ensigns	Sergeants	Drummers	Corporals and Privates	Total	Lieutenant Colonels	Majors	Captains	Lieutenants	Ensigns	Sergeants	Drummers	Corporals and Privates	Total	Lieutenant Colonels	Majors	Captains	Lieutenants	Ensigns	Sergeants	Drummers	Corporals and Privates	Total
5th Caçadores Battalion	-	-	-	-	-	1	-	11	12	-	-	-	-	-	1	1	17	19	-	-	-	-	-	-	-	-	-
13th Regiment	-	-	-	-	-	-	-	-	-	-	-	1	-	-	-	-	3	4	-	-	-	-	-	-	-	-	-
24th Regiment	-	-	-	-	-	-	-	-	-	-	-	-	-	-	-	-	1	1	-	-	-	-	-	-	-	-	-
Total	-	-	-	-	-	1	-	11	12	-	-	1	-	-	1	1	21	24	-	-	-	-	-	-	-	-	-
	Ranks and names of the officers killed									Ranks and names of the officers wounded									Ranks and names of the officers prisoners and missing								
										Captain Benjamin Jones,[498] 13th Regiment																	

T Bradford

Table 9.3: Bradford's Brigade, 13th, 24th and 5th Caçadores. Return[499] of the Killed, wounded, Missing, and Prisoners in the Brigade on 25 June 1813[500]

	Killed									Wounded									Missing and Prisoners								
	Lieutenant Colonels	Majors	Captains	Lieutenants	Ensigns	Sergeants	Drummers	Corporals and Privates	Total	Lieutenant Colonels	Majors	Captains	Lieutenants	Ensigns	Sergeants	Drummers	Corporals and Privates	Total	Lieutenant Colonels	Majors	Captains	Lieutenants	Ensigns	Sergeants	Drummers	Corporals and Privates	Total
5th Caçadores Battalion	-	-	-	-	-	1	-	8	9	-	-	1	-	-	2	1	19	23	-	-	-	-	-	-	-	-	-
13th Regiment	-	-	-	-	-	-	-	4	4	1	-	-	-	1	3	-	24	29	-	-	-	-	1	-	-	1	2
24th Regiment	-	-	-	1	1	1	-	6	9	-	-	1	1	4	2	-	66	74	-	-	-	-	-	-	-	36	36
Total	-	-	-	1	1	2	-	18	22	1	-	2	1	5	7	1	109	126	-	-	-	-	1	-	-	37	38

Ranks and names of the officers killed

Lieutenant João Baptista Reimão, 24th Regiment
Ensign Luis Jeronimo,[501] 24th Regiment

Ranks and names of the officers wounded

Lieutenant Colonel Dom Joaquim da Camara, 13th Regiment
Ensign Diogo Ignacio de Souza, 13th Regiment
Captain Antonio Xavier da Rocha, 24th Regiment
Lieutenant Luis de Azevedo,[502] 24th Regiment
Ensign Joze Maria, 24th Regiment[503]
Ensign João Baptista,[504] 24th Regiment
Ensign Joaquim Ercullano,[505] 24th Regiment
Ensign Joze Manuel,[506] 24th Regiment
Captain Dom Francisco,[507] 5th Caçadores

Ranks and names of the officers prisoners and missing

Ensign Joze Pais,[508] 13th Regiment

T Bradford

Since this return was made until today, 8 July, 9 of the missing men re-joined.

Chapter 10

Combat in the Bastan Valley, 5–8 July 1813

By 1 July the only French troops in Spain other than on the east coast were the garrisons of San Sebastian and Pamplona, and an infantry division in an area called the Bastan. The Bastan is a high valley on the upper Bidassoa river, and through it runs the road from Pamplona to Bayonne via the Col de Velate[509] and the Maya Pass.[510]

The French in the Bastan valley included General Cassagne's Division, with Colonel Joseph Braun's Brigade defending a series of positions in the valley from the Col de Velate in the south and along the road to Ziga 18km to the north, while General Blondeau's Brigade was at Elizondo 25km further north, close to the French border. Behind them were two divisions, plus General Gruardet's Brigade. All were under the command of General Gazan. The French were short of everything, from food to ammunition to artillery, and their morale was shaky.

Wellington ordered Hill to force the French out of the Bastan valley and back into France. In addition to the 2nd Division,[511] which included Ashworth's Brigade, he had Costa's Brigade from the Portuguese Division. General Amarante, the Portuguese Division commander, was given command of the advance guard, which included Costa's brigade, the 6th Infantry from Ashworth's Brigade, a British brigade, and a squadron from the British 14th Light Dragoons.

The operation began on 5 July. Rather than engaging Hill, the French waited until the approaching Portuguese and British deployed to attack their position and then withdrew up the valley to their next position. There was some skirmishing, but no major engagements. By nightfall Hill was at Ziga, where he found Gazan's two divisions and another infantry brigade, totalling about 13,000 men. When Wellington arrived and saw the strength of the French, he ordered the 7th Division to march on their flank the next day.

That night General Gazan withdrew to the Maya Pass. Wellington ordered an attack on the French position on 7 July, with the British brigade attacking the French left flank, while Costa was to make a demonstration against their centre. The attacks had limited success and the French withdrew the next day.

The significance of this action was that for the first time since the British had arrived in the Peninsula in 1808, a Portuguese officer was entrusted with the command of a large number of British troops. It would not be the last time.

Portuguese Division

Report[512] from Count de Amarante to Beresford

I have the honour to transmit to Your Excellency the return of the wounded of the division under my command in the actions of the 7th and 8th instant.

On the 7th, in Elizondo, I received the order to take command of the 1st British Brigade,[513] the Portuguese 6th Infantry Regiment,[514] and a cavalry squadron of the 14th Regiment;[515] and in conjunction with the Portuguese Brigade, composed of the 2nd and 14th Infantry Regiments, from the division under my command, to march against the enemy posted in Ariscun. The enemy had a strong post in this village, on the road from Elizondo to Maya, and in the rear of Ariscun there is a river which the road crosses by a bridge called La Mearrita. The enemy had some distant columns on his right and then formed a line with some battalions in echelon with the left on a mountain. In the rear, on a mountain in the direction of the village of Maya, the enemy showed a considerable force formed in columns.

All these positions were abandoned the moment our troops advanced and the enemy was closely followed by us until he took position in the Porto de Maya where he posted his right on a lofty knoll and his left on the top of the mountain which rises on the left of the Porto. He posted on the slopes up the mountain small parties of *tirailleurs*.

The British light companies and the grenadier companies of the Portuguese infantry regiments,[516] these acting as light infantry, all under the orders and directed by Lieutenant Colonel Fitzgerald,[517] 60th Regiment, began a furious attack pushing up the enemy's skirmishers; at this time I ordered to come up by the right the 6th Portuguese Regiment and the 71st British Regiment and by the left the 50th and 92nd British Regiments. On the right our troops took the enemy's position on the mountain which opened the way to where the enemy had his main force; the fight lasted until 8 o'clock in the night and the troops remained where they were.

On the 8th all the mountains were covered by a dense fog which hid any movement by the enemy. When the fog lifted and we saw his retreat, General Hill ordered us to pursue; we moved up the mountain without opposition, at the top of which we were joined by a column coming from the left, under the command of General Stewart.[518] All the light infantry, the Portuguese grenadier companies mentioned above, and the 6th Portuguese Regiment followed the enemy down to the foot of the mountain near the village of Urdax. The enemy deployed on the mountains behind the village leaving a strong post defending the bridge on the road to Ainhoué.

Three companies from the 6th Portuguese Regiment moved up the mountain to our right and began attacking the enemy's skirmishers. In the same manner, the companies of the 2nd and 14th Portuguese Regiments moved up by our left and started skirmishing with the enemy. At the same time, the British light companies with some companies from the 6th Caçadores and the 6th Portuguese Regiment dislodged the enemy from the village of Urdax. An order came to stop the fight which caused the enemy to return to the village, which had to be attacked and cleared again, this time with the support of the fire from a gun and a howitzer belonging to a 6 pounder artillery brigade[519] attached to the division under my command.

I beg leave to assure Your Excellency that all the men under my command carry out their duties with dignity but I must particularly mention the conduct of Lieutenant Colonel João Telles,[520] 2nd Infantry, who commanded the grenadier companies with great gallantry. The officers commanding the companies from the 2nd and 4th Regiments also deserve Your Excellency's praise and attention, as well as Brevet Lieutenant Colonel Lourenço Martins,[521] who commanded the 2nd Regiment's 2nd Battalion in the fight, and Major Gil,[522] 6th Regiment, who commanded that regiment's companies which were detached to our right and also Colonel Ashworth, who I saw with the skirmishers firing at the enemy.

I mention these officers because they belong to the Portuguese regiments, however I cannot omit to notice the dignity and merit of Colonel Cameron, commanding the 1st British Brigade and the great gallantry of Lieutenant Colonel Fitzgerald, 60th British Regiment, commanding all the light infantry. Every British officer behaved in an exemplary manner and I had the satisfaction to see the Portuguese equal them.

I cannot report anything to Your Excellency on the brigade composed by the 4th, 10th Infantry Regiments and 10th Caçadores Battalion, from which I have not received any news, since it was detached from my division.[523]

God save Your Excellency

Headquarters in Ariscun 9 July 1813

The Marquis de Campo Maior

Your most obedient servant

Count de Amarante

See Table 10.1.

2nd Division

Ashworth's Brigade (6th and 18th Infantry, 6th Caçadores)

6th Infantry

See Table 10.2.

6th Caçadores

Report[524] from Lieutenant Colonel Correia to AG Mozinho

I have the honour to enclose the return of the killed and wounded in the four companies of the battalion under my command in the action on the 7th instant against the enemy on the heights of Ariscun. By the night of that day, in consequence of my efforts all day and the extreme fatigue, I had a rupture, which will keep me from commanding my battalion for some time. This event took place after I saw with satisfaction the gallant conduct of all the individuals, but particularly those of the four companies mentioned above.

I transmit to you this brief information and soon I will send a more detailed report for the information of His Excellency the Marshal Marquis de Campo Maior.
God save you, Sir
Maya, 8 July 1813
Manoel de Brito Mozinho

Sebastião Pinto de Araujo Corrêa
Lieutenant Colonel

Table 10.1: Return[525] of the Killed, Wounded, and Missing in the Portuguese Division under the Command of Lieutenant General Count de Amarante on 7 and 8 July

Colonels		Killed									Wounded									Prisoners and Missing									Total										Beasts		
		Colonels	Lieutenant Colonels	Majors	Captains	Subalterns	Flag Bearers	Sergeants and *Furriéis*	Musicians and Drummers	Corporals and Privates	Colonels	Lieutenant Colonels	Majors	Captains	Subalterns	Flag Bearers	Sergeants and *Furriéis*	Musicians and Drummers	Corporals and Privates	Colonels	Lieutenant Colonels	Majors	Captains	Subalterns	Flag Bearers	Sergeants and *Furriéis*	Musicians and Drummers	Corporals and Privates	Colonels	Lieutenant Colonels	Majors	Captains	Subalterns	Flag Bearers	Sergeants and *Furriéis*	Musicians and Drummers	Corporals and Privates	Killed	Wounded	Missing
Artillery	3rd Brigade 6 pounder	–	–	–	–	–	–	–	–	–	–	–	–	–	–	–	–	–	–	–	–	–	–	–	–	–	–	–	–	–	–	–	–	–	–	–	–	–	–	–
	4th Brigade 9 pounder	–	–	–	–	–	–	–	–	–	–	–	–	–	–	–	–	–	–	–	–	–	–	–	–	–	–	–	–	–	–	–	–	–	–	–	–	–	–	–
1st Brigade	2nd Regiment	–	–	–	–	–	–	1	–	1	–	–	–	–	–	–	–	–	11	–	–	–	–	–	–	–	–	3	–	–	–	–	–	–	1	–	15	–	–	–
	14th Regiment	–	–	–	–	–	–	–	–	–	–	–	–	–	–	–	–	–	–	–	–	–	–	–	–	–	–	1	–	–	–	–	–	–	–	–	1	–	–	–
2nd Brigade	4th Regiment	–	–	–	–	–	–	–	–	–	–	–	–	–	–	–	–	–	–	–	–	–	–	–	–	–	–	–	–	–	–	–	–	–	–	–	–	–	–	–
	10th Regiment	–	–	–	–	–	–	–	–	–	–	–	–	–	–	–	–	–	–	–	–	–	–	–	–	–	–	–	–	–	–	–	–	–	–	–	–	–	–	–
	10th Caçadores Battalion	–	–	–	–	–	–	–	–	–	–	–	–	–	–	–	–	–	–	–	–	–	–	–	–	–	–	–	–	–	–	–	–	–	–	–	–	–	–	–
Total		–	–	–	–	–	–	1	–	1	–	–	–	–	–	–	–	–	11	–	–	–	–	–	–	–	–	4	–	–	–	–	–	–	1	–	16	–	–	–

Headquarters, Porto de Maya, 8 July 1813

Count de Amarante
Lieutenant General division commander

Table 10.2: Ashworth's Brigade. Return[526] of the Casualties in the Action against the Enemy on 8 July 1813

Casualties	Officers						Sergeants	*Furriéis*	Corporals and Privates	Total	Horses
	Lieutenant Colonel	Majors	Captains	Lieutenants	Ensigns	Staff					
Killed	-	-	-	-	-	-	-	-	1	1	-
Wounded	-	-	-	-	-	-	1	-	22	23	-
Missing	-	-	-	-	-	-	-	-	-	-	-
Total	-	-	-	-	-	-	-	-	23	24	-

In the number of the wounded are 1 corporal and 3 privates of the 18th Infantry Regiment who joined this corps.

Maxwell Grant
Lieutenant Colonel

Chapter 11

The Siege of San Sebastian

After defeating the French at Vitoria, Wellington decided to occupy the Pyrenees to prevent the French moving into Spain, and to capture Pamplona and San Sebastian. He decided to besiege San Sebastian and blockade Pamplona. For the siege, Wellington had ninety artillery pieces, including fourteen 24-pounder and six 18-pounder siege guns, and four 10-inch heavy mortars. Additionally, the Royal Navy provided six short-barrel 24-pounders with crews. In addition to eighteen Royal Engineers, there were the new Royal Sappers and Miners to build the trenches and redoubts needed to protect the besiegers. The infantry would be provided by the 5th Division with Spry's Brigade, as well as General Bradford's and Pack's Brigades.[527]

Lieutenant Colonel Dickson of the Portuguese Army commanded the siege artillery. Included in the artillery forces were Arriaga's 1st Brigade, Roziers' Brigade, and Silva's Mountain Brigade. Initially, 9 officers and 105 artillerymen took part in the siege. In August they were reinforced with 3 officers and 34 men, under the command of 1st Lieutenant José Carlos de Sequeira, all from the 2nd Artillery. In August two companies from the Artificers Battalion of the Portuguese Engineers, commanded by Major José Jerónimo Granate, also joined the siege operations.

In 1813 the city of San Sebastian had about 10,000 inhabitants and a garrison of 3,000 French soldiers. A British officer wrote a description:

> it sat on a low peninsula, running north and south; the defences of the western side being washed by the sea, and those on the eastern side by the Urumea river, which, at high water covers four feet of the masonry scarp.

> The works of land front across the isthmus consist of a single front of fortifications, exceeding 350 yards in length, with a flat bastion and cavalier in the centre, covered by a hornwork, having the usual counterscarp, covered-way, and glacis; but the defences running lengthwise of the peninsula, consist merely of a simple rampart wall, indifferently flanked, without either ditch, counterscarp, glacis, or other obstacle in its front …[528]

Within the walls was La Mota Castle, which sat on a high hill. Protecting the landward approach to the city walls was the Convent of San Bartolomé. The French had fortified the convent, and it would have to be taken before the city could be attacked.

The siege consisted of two parts, often known as the 1st and 2nd Sieges. The first began on 7 July when Portuguese guns opened fire. It took two assaults to take the convent, and a subsequent assault on the town on 25 July was unsuccessful. The siege was suspended on 26 July when French forces attacked through the Pyrenees, but restarted after those attacks were defeated. This was called the 2nd Siege. On 31 August the city was taken. Portuguese troops took part in every phase of the two-month-long siege, from the first to the last bombardment, to the assaults on the outer works, and the two assaults on the city.[529]

First Attack on the Convent of San Bartolomé, 15 July 1813

After a week of building siege works and bombarding the convent, the 4th Caçadores[530] were ordered to take it by surprise. Despite the gallantry of the troops, they failed.

Independent Brigade (1st and 16th Infantry and 4th Caçadores)

4th Caçadores

Report[531] from Lieutenant Colonel Williams to Colonel Hill,[532] the Brigade's Acting Commander

Convent of Antigua
July 15th
Sir
I have the honour to enclose the return of the killed and wounded of the 4th Caçadores in the flank attack of the Convent of St. Bartholome this day, and to express my very great regret on the loss of Captain Joaquim Antonio Alvares who fell gallantly leading his company. Allow me to mention for your notice the good conduct of my junior Lieutenant Jose Texeira de Mello and Lieutenant Queiros,[533] likewise Ensign Cabral.[534]
I have the honour to be your most humble servant

E.K. Williams
Lieutenant Colonel 4th Caçadores

To Colonel Hill

Letter[535] from General Graham to Beresford

Ernani 18th July 1813
My dear Beresford
I have just got the enclosed from Captain Barrallier[536] who was so severely wounded and still suffers I believe severely. You will I am sure do what is in your power to show him some kindness without prejudice to others.

I send you a report creditable to some of the Portuguese officers in a reconnaissance made on the convent on the 15th. And I shall have to report much more to the conduct of those concerned yesterday. One poor fellow an officer of the 4th Caçadores distinguished himself most remarkably and is severely wounded.[537]

I send you a letter sent to me by Geddes about horses. I do not want any. The two [illegible word] are very strong and [illegible word] horses I believe.
Ever faithfully yours

Thomas Graham

Report[538] from Lieutenant Colonel Williams to General Andrew Hay, 5th Division's Brigade commander, to which the Battalion was Temporarily Attached

Camp in front of San Sebastian
15th July 1813
Sir
I have the honour to enclose the report of Major Adamson who was detached with two companies of the 4th Caçadores to feel the right flank of the enemy jointly with the front attack[539] on the convent of St. Bartholeme this day. Allow me to say that officer gained the points he was directed to, and maintained them against superior force of the enemy until I received your orders to withdraw my people. I have thought proper to leave small picquets at these points for the security of our front, and which I hope will meet with your approbation. Herewith I send you the return of killed and wounded.
I have the honour to be, Sir, your most humble servant

E.K. Williams
Lieutenant Colonel
4th Caçadores

Major General Hay

Report[540] from Major Adamson to Lieutenant Colonel Williams

Camp in front of San Sebastian
15th July 1813
Sir
In obedience to your orders I directed the section of Rifles under Lieutenant Jose Teixera de Mello to advance and feel his way towards the ruin near the convent, and supported him with the 2nd and 3rd Companies; but in consequence of the enemy having received considerable reinforcements from the town I was obliged to bring all the men into action. The enemy was beaten back, and the points indicated to me taken and kept till I received your orders to retire. I have to regret the loss of Captain Joaquim Antonio Alves[541], who was killed while gallantly leading on his *atiradores*[542] in drawing back the enemy.

I beg leave to recommend Lieutenants Teixera de Mello and Cairoz[543] for their brave and steady conduct during the affair, the former of which was severely wounded.
I have the honour to be, Sir, Your most obedient servant

P. Adamson
Major 4th Caçadores

To Lieutenant Colonel Williams
4th Caçadores

Storm of the Convent of San Bartolomé and Outer Works, 17 July 1813

On 17 July a second attempt was made, by Bradford's Brigade, supported by fifty men from the 4th Caçadores, the British 9th Foot, and three companies from the 1st Foot. The assault began at 10 a.m. The convent and redoubt were taken with few casualties. However, in their enthusiasm, the troops chased the retreating French to the outer walls of the city, where they came under fire from a French relief column and had to retreat.

Independent Brigade (1st and 16th Infantry and 4th Caçadores)

Report[544] from Colonel Hill, Acting Commander of the Brigade, to AG Mozinho

Sir
I have the honour to transmit enclosed the return of the casualties in the 4th Caçadores Battalion in the 16th and 17th instant in front of San Sebastian and also the report from Lieutenant Colonel Williams on the conduct of Lieutenant António Vicente de Queiróz of that corps on that occasion.[545]

I beg leave to demand that you lay it before His Excellency the Marshal Marquis de Campo Maior, for his favourable consideration.
God save you, Sir
Passages Cantonment, 19 July 1813
Manoel de Brito Mozinho

T. Noel Hill
Colonel
Commander of the Brigade

Report[546] from Lieutenant Colonel Williams, 4th Caçadores, to Colonel Hill, Acting Commander of the Brigade

Sir
I have the honour to forward enclosed the report from Captain Caetano Alberto Canavarro of the battalion under my command, who I ordered, with 25 men from my picquet, to join the advanced force of 30 men under Lieutenant Queirós of the same battalion. The other 50 men of my picquet formed a reserve.

Allow me to declare that General Hay[547] gave me his favourable acknowledgement of the brave conduct of Lieutenant Queirós in the advance and action in the trench near the Convent, where he was wounded, fortunately slightly.
God save you, Sir
Santo Antonio Abbade Convent, 18 July 1813
Colonel Hill
Commander of the Brigade Composed of the 4th Caçadores Battalion and 1st and 16th Regiments

E.K. Williams
Lieutenant Colonel
4th Caçadores

Report[548] from Captain Canavarro, 4th Caçadores, to Lieutenant Colonel Williams

Sir,
In obedience to your orders I directed Lieutenant Queiróz, with thirty men of his picquet, to march to the left of the house located near the wall of the aqueduct and to storm it immediately, while I with my people marched by the right side of the same house and supported him; the enemy was forced to abandon that post and lost some men killed.

Immediately after, we marched, the picquet under Lieutenant Queiróz and half of mine, to gain the heights where the enemy was posted in some force, and the rest of my picquet marched by a road that runs between the mentioned wall and the heights; in the trench we were forced to stop and a heavy exchange of musketry fire begun until men from several corps collected there attacked the enemy post and pursued them until we received Major General Bradford's order to halt. I must mention the gallant and exemplary conduct of Lieutenant Queiróz, just as it was that of all the individuals from the two picquets. I regret to inform you that Lieutenant Queiróz was gravely wounded and that our loss was two men killed and ten wounded. I should add that we were joined by some men from Ensign Calheiros'[549] picquet when we gained the heights.
God save you, Sir
Quarter in the Convent of Saint Anthony in front of San Sebastian
17 July 1813
Edmund Keynton Williams

Caetano Alberto de Sousa Canavarro
Captain 4th Caçadores

Letter[550] from General Graham to Beresford

Ernani 19th July
My dear Beresford
Tho' it will give you some trouble I send you reports to do justice to some of your officers, who deserved to be rewarded.

The Lieutenant's conduct was most exemplary by every account, as was Snodgrass'.[551]
Your letter shall go on board the *Surveillant*.[552]
In haste but ever yours,
Thomas Graham
[P.S.] The 9th [Foot] certainly [illegible word] on to the Portuguese, tho' afterwards I think they led them in to the scrape of the glassis[553] [sic].

Report[554] from General Hay to General John Oswald, 5th Division Commander

Camp in front of St. Sebastian
17th July 1813
Sir

In obedience to the orders I received this morning to take charge of the right attack on the enemy's outworks which I am happy to state was completely carried into execution. I have the honour to make the following report, during yesterday two picquets of the 4th Caçadores consisting of 55 men under the command of Lieutenant de Queiroz had been pushed out in to some ruined houses near the bottom of the ravine and very near a small house where the enemy had their advanced post from the redoubt, but as a detachment of Major General Bradford's brigade were ordered to lead the attack I directed the picquets of the 4th Caçadores to follow closely up and support the detachment of Major General Bradford's, so soon as it should have come down and got in their post by the bottom of the convent garden wall, however that road was found to be impracticable and the detachment came along the walls on the heights where another party of the 4th Caçadores were posted to take down the fire from the redoubts, convent and trenches when the attack should commence, when became necessary to send the detachment down a narrow lane which put them near Lieutenant Queiroz people, under these circumstances it became necessary for Lieutenant Queiroz to attack the enemy's advanced post and to lead the attack which he did in the most gallant and officer like stile [sic] till he got to the edge where he was unfortunately wounded and the service deprived of his further assistance for that day.

The piquects [sic] and detachments after some little delay from the extreme steepness of the ascent succeeded in getting to the bottom of the hedge which you know is backed by a very strong and high [illegible word] wall and which can only be passed at two or three gaps, there, this party under a very heavy fire, waited till a detachment of three companies of His Majesty's 9th Regiment under the command of Lieutenant Colonel Craufurd[555] arrived close up to the rear of the hedge, where he immediately pushed some of the 9th through the gaps led by Lieutenant C. Campbell[556] of that corps who were followed by the other Portuguese and British, the same officer likewise led in to the redoubt.

I was perfectly satisfied with the general conduct of all engaged, but I particularly beg leave to recommend to your notice for the favourable consideration of Marshal Beresford, Lieutenant Antonio Vicente de Queiroz of the 4th Caçadores and also Lieutenant C. Campbell of his Majesty's 9th for their very gallant and exemplary conduct. I am under the greatest obligation to Lieutenant Colonel Craufurd for the very officer like manner in which he brought forward his people in the most perfect order to the attack, and also to Captain Arquimbau[557] Royal Scots[558] who commanded three companies of Royal Scots who moved with Captain Cameron[559] of the same regiment in support.

I should not do justice to Captain Taylor[560] 48th Regiment my Major of Brigade if I did not state my great obligation to them on this and on many former occasions and also to Captain James Stewart Royal Scots who acted as my Aid de Camp [sic] and from his knowledge of the Portuguese language and service of this country was extremely useful to me in conveying my orders to the Portuguese troops. As the rest of the 9th Regiment engaged were under your immediate eye, I forbear any report on their conduct. I however enclose a report from Lieutenant Colonel Williams 4th Caçadores who at present is attached to my brigade.

I regret the loss of Captain Woodham[561] and Lieutenant and Adjutant Thornhill[562] 9th Regiment two very promising officers.

I trust I shall be but a short time deprived of the services of this excellent officer Lieutenant Colonel Cameron,[563] 9th, by the severe concussion he has received.

The return of casualties was sent to Lieutenant Colonel Berkeley.[564]
I have the Honour to be Sir your obedient servant

Andrew Hay
Major General

Major General Oswald
Commander 5th Division

Bradford's Brigade (13th and 24th Infantry, 5th Caçadores)

Report[565] from General Bradford to AG Mozinho

Camp in front of San Sebastian
July 19th 1813
Sir,
I have the honour to transmit to you to be laid before the Marshal Commander in Chief, the enclosed copy of a report I was called upon this morning by Sir Thomas Graham to make of the operations which yesterday gave us possession of the convent and redoubt in front of St. Sebastian. It affords me infinite satisfaction at the same time to represent for His Excellency's information, that every individual of the brigade under my command performed well their duty. I cannot however omit bringing particularly before the Marshal's observation the names of Major Snodgrass and Captain Almeida[566] of the 13th Regiment and Captain Tiago Pedro Martins and Ensign Miguel Correia de Freitas of the 5th Caçadores,[567] and Lieutenant Romao[568] of the First Grenadiers [Company] of the 24th Regiment whose good conduct not only upon this occasion, but invariably in every point of duty merits His Excellency's approbation.
I have the honour to be, Sir, your most obedient and humble servant

T. Bradford
Major General

Report[569] from General Bradford to General Graham

Report made to Sir Thomas Graham KB
Camp near St Sebastian
July 18th 1813
Sir
I have the honour to report to you, that agreeable to your instructions for the attack of the convent and redoubt in front of St Sebastian, 550 men of my Brigade being in readiness at the ground rear the battery, 200 of them under the command of Major Snodgrass of the 13th Regiment, supported by about an equal number under Lieutenant Colonel McCreagh[570] of the 5th Caçadores, moved to the attack of the convent, while 150 under the command of Captain Almeida of the 13th Regiment [Portuguese] supported by 3 companies of British under Lieutenant Colonel Craufurd of the 9th Regiment [British] advanced to the attack of the front face of the redoubt. The remainder of the 9th Regiment under the command of Lieutenant Colonel Cameron remained in reserve and to cover our left flank. The convent was immediately carried by Major Snodgrass in the most gallant and spirited manner at the point of the bayonet, and that column forced its way with great difficulty thro' the ruins and adjacent gardens to attack the redoubt by the breach in the convent garden wall, where they arrived in good time to cooperate with Captain Almeida in his attack of the front face of that work, to which he had advanced in line with the greatest steadiness, under a severe fire of musketry from the enemy. The most determined attack was then made upon the redoubt, in which one company of the 9th Regiment, under the command of Lieutenant Campbell joined, and the work was soon carried by the gallantry of the troops.

In bearing testimony to the good conduct in general of the above detachment of my brigade (inferior in numbers to the enemy they attacked) particularly to those parts of it under the command of Major Snodgrass and Captain Almeida, I cannot avoid expressing how sensible I feel of the advantage we derived from the support of the British troops under the command of Lieutenant Colonels Cameron and Craufurd of the 9th Regiment, whose assistance contributed very much to the success of the enterprise. I beg leave at same time to mention in terms of commendation Lieutenant Antonio de Queiroz of the 4th Caçadores, who with a few men of his picquet joined in the attack of the front face of the redoubt and made himself conspicuous by his gallant conduct.
I have the honour to be, Sir, your most obedient and humble servant

T. Bradford
Major General

The Storm of San Sebastian, 31 August 1813

Bombardment of the walls of the city continued and on 30 August there were two breaches that were considered practicable for an assault. The first was on the wall along the peninsula, the second on the wall along the Urumea river. Bradford was ordered to attack across the river, while Spry was in support of the other brigades in the 5th Division. The assault was led by Major Snodgrass of the 13th Infantry, which was followed by the 24th Infantry, both from Bradford's 10th Brigade. The fighting was intense; although the Portuguese made it over the walls, they had to fight street-by-street before the city was taken.

5th Division

3rd Brigade (3rd and 15th Infantry, 8th Caçadores)

Report[571] from General Spry to AG Mozinho

San Sebastian 1st September 1813
Sir,
I have the honour to transmit for the information of His Excellency Marshal Sir W.C. Beresford, a return of the killed wounded and missing of the Brigade under my command at the successful storm of this place, and to report upon the general conduct of the officers and soldiers of the Regiments composing the Brigade.

This I am happy to say was such as to excite the most unqualified approbation of the General and all other officers, who witnessed the steadiness of the Brigade in taking its station on the Breach and afterwards advancing in to the town, greatly assisting in the expulsion of the Enemy.

It is but just to mention another meritorious part of the conduct of the Brigade that, after having done their duty, opposed to the Enemy, the men continued collected and sober, and all night well prepared to meet any new effort which the Enemy might make.

It is but justice to the officers commanding the Regiments of the Brigade to say that their conduct, generally and particularly was that of officers well qualified to command, they manifested, at every point, firmness and perseverance, intelligence and spirit, and this admirable conduct on the part of these officers, I am persuaded, contributed much to our gaining full possession of the town.

Colonel McCreagh, who was not on duty with the brigade, but on division duty, led the covering party from the Trenches to the Breach, and into the town carrying every thing before him on the right, in consequence of which the Enemy gave way on the left and enabled the British to advance. The Colonel outflanked and took two guns in the street by sending a party on a flank with a Captain Caiola[572] of the 15th Regiment of whose whole conduct the colonel reports very favourably.

Lieutenant Colonel Hill,[573] 8th Caçadores, whose report I have the honour to inclose [sic] took possession of the principal square.

Colonel Luiz do Rego[574] led on his Regiment, in his usual gallant manner, and did every thing which could possibly be required of the Regiment.

It is with considerable regret that I have to report the temporary loss of the services of Major Campbell, 3rd Regiment,[575] in consequence of a severe wound. This officer commanded the Regiment and led it handsomely to the Breach, continuing with it as long as able. I must beg of you to remind His Excellency that Major Stuart Campbell commanded the 3rd Regiment on marching from Lamego, at the Battle of Vittoria and until the commencement of this Siege, with steadiness and ability, and I hope he may be considered as worthy of the particular notice of His Excellency.

I beg leave to transmit also a letter from Colonel Do Rego, mentioning the name of some officers who certainly did their duty most satisfactorily, particularly the Captains Rozado[576] and Caiola.

Lieutenant Colonel Hill has not reported to me any particular officer. I am sure they all behaved well. The 3rd Regiment behaved extremely well, but I cannot particularize many officers, Colonel McCreagh having been absent, and the actual commander, Major Campbell, having been wounded, but the Captains Alexandre[577] and Daniel[578] led on their companies with spirit. After Major Campbell was wounded Captain Jose Valente[579] commanded the Regiment and did his duty with spirit also, until Colonel McCreagh resumed the command of the Regiment in the fort.

I have to add that the conduct of Brigade Major Fitzgerald[580] upon this occasion was highly meritorious, and deserving the favourable notice of His Excellency.

I am also very much indebted to Captain E. Brackenbury,[581] whom I employed as a personal staff officer upon this occasion, for the able assistance he afforded me wherever activity, spirit, and intelligence could contribute to success.

I have the honour to be Sir your obedient humble servant

W. Fred. Spry
Major General

Brigadier General Mozinho
Adjutant General

8th Caçadores

Report[582] from Lieutenant Colonel Hill to General Spry

5th Division
September 1st 1813
Sir,
From the intermixed state of the troops in the attack of yesterday I think it impossible you could have perceived the conduct of all your Brigade and I therefore deem it my duty to report to you that of the Caçadores under my command.

When ordered by Sir James Leith[583] to advance nothing could exceed the eagerness with which the Battalion moved to support the 2nd Brigade[584] already lodged on the Breach and when the town was stormed I had the satisfaction of leading in the Battalion among the foremost. I directed the advance of the Battalion towards the great square which it took in a most gallant manner making some prisoners. Those with a principal officer I have sent to the Head Quarters of the Division. I have only to add that the 8th Caçadores has never distinguished itself more than on this occasion, and their prompt formation when the affair was concluded and alertness during the night merits your notice.

I have the honour to inclose [sic] a return of killed and wounded which is as correct as we can at present collect from the companies.
I have the honour to be Sir your most obedient servant

Dudley Hill
Lieutenant Colonel

Major General Spry
Commander 3rd Brigade
5th Division

15th Infantry

Report[585] from Colonel Barreto to General Spry

Sir,
I have the honour to transmit to you the return of the killed and wounded of my regiment at the breach of this town and at the same time I take this opportunity to state that I'm extremely satisfied with the

conduct of all my officers; however one of them in particular distinguished himself in the fulfilment of his obligations, so I think to be my duty to specially recommend Captain Eduardo [sic] Brackenbury. This officer distinguished himself encouraging the men, calling them to the breach in the most gallant manner.

The conduct of Captain Thomas O'Neill[586] was magnificent, he commanded the Grenadiers, and I saw him, until he was wounded, encouraging, and leading his company in a most handsome manner. Captain Antonio Ignacio Caiola also deserves every compliment; this officer followed me through the breach and afterwards I ordered him to take a piece of artillery that blocked a street. He performed this mission in the best way and was slightly wounded. Captain Antonio Joaquim Rozado was employed in the fascines; seeing a great number of officers wounded thought to be more useful with the regiment; Your Excellency knows this officer very well and the way he presented himself deserves my approbation. I saw Ensigns Antonio Carlos de Magalhaens,[587] Antonio Guedes Seabra,[588] and Jose dos Santos behave in the best possible manner. My Adjutant Theotonio Nobre behaved admirably.[589] I must also mention the good conduct of Adjutant Sergeant Jeronimo Caetano de Almeida Manso[590] and of Adjutant Sergeant Telesfero Joze de Matos.[591]

God save you, Sir

San Sebastian 1 September 1813.

Major General Spry

Luiz do Rego Barretto

10th Brigade (Independent) (13th and 24th Infantry, 5th Caçadores)

Report[592] from General Bradford to AG Mozinho

St Sebastian Calcada

September 2nd 1813

Sir,

I have the honour to transmit to you for the information of His Excellency the Marshal, Commander in Chief and Marquis of Campo Mayor, the report of Colonel McBean [sic][593] and Major Snodgrass; the former moved with 200 men of the 24th Regiment, in support of a Battalion of the 13th Regiment, under Major Snodgrass across the river,[594] but it appeared afterwards for the good of the service those detachments chose to act separately. It was most painful to me, from illness to be compelled to return to my house before the attack commenced, but from what I have seen of the gallant conduct of Major Snodgrass before [on] several other occasions I trust it will in no manner be considered detracting from the high reputation of Colonel McBean [sic] (who has now reached a rank beyond which his promotion may depend upon other circumstances) in hoping that His Excellency may think Major Snodgrass deserving of some mark of His Excellency's approbation. Major Snodgrass will have in October next been 5 years Captain in the 52nd Regiment and a great part of that time serving in the Peninsula. He commanded the Grenadier Battalion of my Brigade at Victoria, and the different affairs the brigade had with the enemy in advancing from thence; and a detachment of the Brigade was led by him in a very distinguished manner at the attack of the redoubt and convent near St. Sebastian.[595]

The good conduct of the other officers named, as having distinguished themselves by Colonel McBean [sic] and Major Snodgrass, I have before witnessed.

I cannot conclude this letter in justice to every individual of the Brigade without stating for the information of His Excellency, that every man volunteered his services to storm, and such is the high spirit which prevailed in every rank that I am convinced their conduct will be equally distinguished upon every future occasion.

I have the honour to be Sir your most obedient servant

T. Bradford

Major General

I beg leave also to enclose a report I have received from Colonel McCreagh of the 3rd Regiment of the good conduct of 200 of the 5th Caçadores that acted under his orders as Colonel of the day. I am happy to have it in my power to send you a more correct return of the killed and wounded than it was before possible to make.

See Table 11.1.

24th Infantry

Report[596] from Colonel MacBean to General Bradford

St Sebastian 1st September 1813
Sir
I have the honour to state to you that I advanced yesterday with a Battalion of the 24th Regiment across the Sands, fording the River and established myself on the Main Breach with some of the troops of the 5th Division. After waiting there for some time in expectation of a general advance, I ordered my Battalion with some of the 5th Caçadores to pass the Breach which they performed in a style the most gallant and praiseworthy, drove the Enemy from the ruins where they were strongly posted, and which were most difficult to pass, and succeeded in getting into the Town. I formed my Battalion near the church now the English Hospital, where I reported to Major General Spry. I can say with satisfaction that my Battalion with some Caçadores were the first who passed the Breach, their noble example induced numbers to follow, nothing could surpass their steadiness and determined bravery.

The following officers and sergeants I beg leave to recommend most strongly as being highly deserving the notice of the Commander in Chief, they particularly distinguished themselves. Captains Gordon[597] and Romão,[598] Lieutenants Joze Azevedo[599] and Padua[600], two very enterprising young officers, the latter I regret to say is severely wounded. Sergeant Major Francisco António[601] by his gallantry attracted the notice of every one, and Sergeant Pinto[602] of the Grenadiers who has on other occasions distinguished himself, was yesterday most conspicuous in the ranks tho' severely wounded. The conduct of all the sergeants was highly praiseworthy, in short I have every reason to praise the gallantry and behaviour of all. My Adjutant[603] was killed, a good and brave soldier.
I have the honour to be Sir your most obedient servant

W. MacBean
Colonel 24th Regiment Infantry

Major General Bradford

5th Caçadores

Report[604] from Colonel McCreagh, Colonel of the Day, to General Bradford

San Sebastian 1st Sept. 1813
Sir
In having been my good fortune yesterday as Colonel of the day in the trenches to conduct the covering parties to the assault and to lead them in over the Breach I think is but justice to report the excellent conduct and gallantry of two hundred men of the 5th Battalion of Caçadores who belonged to the covering party. They formed the head of my Column and their exemplary behaviour was remarked throughout.

The two officers with them (Lieutenant Manoel Joaquim de Menezes and *Alferes*[605] Carrasco[606]) I beg to recommend in the strongest manner for their good conduct and animated behaviour during the whole day.
I have the honour to be Sir your very obedient servant

M. McCreagh
Colonel 3rd Portuguese Infantry

Major General Bradford

13th Infantry

Report[607] from Major Snodgrass to General Bradford

San Sebastian 1st September 1813
Sir
On receiving the orders of Lieutenant General Sir Thomas Graham to advance I moved with a battalion of the 13th Regiment, over the sands, in front of our right battery; and forded the river, near the small breach, and established myself at the bottom, and right side of it, near the top. After remaining some time under heavy fire of musketry and hand grenades, I observed the enemy wavering, and pushed into the breach, when they fled; it was with difficulty that the soldiers entered from the breach, which when effected the enemy were driven before us, followed closely, chiefly on the top of the wall, and thro' the street leading to a large building under the Mirador, thereby getting in rear of nearly all the streets of the town, and obliging the enemy to quit them. No other troops entered the small breach with the 13th Regiment.

I have pleasure in reporting the steadiness, and gallantry shown by every individual in passing the river and lodging on the breach (according to orders) and afterwards in assaulting and carrying it, as well as other works inside the town, and beg particularly to point out to you, for their bravery Captains Severino Joaquim Ferrera da Costa[608] and Joaquim Antonio de Miranda, Lieutenants Jose [sic] Antonio de Castro,[609] Jose Pedro Abreu Sobrinho, Manuel Joaquim,[610] and *Alferes* Lorenzo Justiniano Lima; and as they are the seniors of their different ranks in the Regiment, I will annex their names for promotion, to the vacancies in the Regiment, and beg you will have the goodness to recommend them to His Excellency Marshal the Marquis of Campo Maior, who I hope will be pleased to appoint them soon; as the Regiment is in want of officers, and His Excellency will I trust be pleased to appoint *Alferes* to the different vacancies.
I am Sir your most obedient humble servant

K. Snodgrass
Major Commanding 13th Regiment

To
Major General Bradford

Report[611] from Lieutenant Colonel Dickson, Commanding the Artillery, to AG Mozinho

Sir
I have the pleasure to state to you for the information of His Excellency Marshal Beresford, Marquis de Campo Maior, Commander in Chief of the Army, that the Portuguese artillery's detachments under the orders of Major Arriaga[612] behaved with the greatest activity, zeal and good service during the different operations of the siege against the town and castle of San Sebastian. The accuracy of the fire of our batteries was much praised and I can assure His Excellency that the Portuguese artillery did not work with less willingness than that of their allies.

In the first siege operation Major Arriaga was in charge of directing the fire from a battery of four guns of 24 [pounders] and four mortars; in the second with one of ten mortars. These batteries fired very accurately and to my complete satisfaction. So, it is my duty to do justice to all the officers present at the siege and lay their names before His Excellency.
1st Artillery Regiment:
    Major Sebastião Jozé d'Arriaga served in all siege operations[613]
    Captain Pedro de Rozierres served only in the first one [First siege, July]
    1st Lieutenant João Xavier Costa served only in the last ones [Second siege and castle, August]
    1st Lieutenant Antonio da Costa e Silva served in all siege operations[614]
    1st Lieutenant Jozé da Silva served in all siege operations
    1st Lieutenant Theodoro Jozé Duarte, my Adjutant, served in all siege operations[615]

1st Lieutenant Jozé Maria da Cruz Bureau served in all siege operations

2nd Lieutenant Ignacio Xavier da Costa Judice served in all siege operations[616]

2nd Lieutenant Joaquim Guilherme Rebello Palhares served in all siege operations

2nd Lieutenant Manuel Caetano[617] served in all siege operations

2nd Lieutenant Joaquim Jozé Latino served only in the last ones

2nd Lieutenant Antonio Fortunato da Fonseca served only in the last ones

2nd Artillery Regiment:

1st Lieutenant Jozé Carlos de Siqueira served only in the last ones

I beg leave to recommend particularly to the attention of His Excellency Major Sebastião Jozé de Arriaga, 1st Lieutenant Antonio da Costa e Silva and 2nd Lieutenant Ignacio Xavier da Costa Judice, the seniors in their ranks, who served in all siege operations and to whom I am much obliged by their assistance.

I have also to recommend particularly to His Excellency my Adjutant Theodoro Jozé Duarte, who I put in charge, during the siege, of the ammunition's supply to all the batteries of the main attack,[618] and this he carried out with great precision to the satisfaction of all the battery commanders; this officer has assisted me in all the service for which I have been employed in this last four years; in the sieges of Badajoz, Salamanca and Burgos he served voluntarily at the batteries with the other officers, although, by his post of Adjutant, he was excused of doing so.

God save you, Sir

Passages de La Calçada

17 September 1813

A. Dickson[619]

Lieutenant Colonel commander of the artillery

P.S. I almost forgot to mention to you the excellent conduct and intelligence shown during all the siege operations of 1st Sergeant Pedro Xavier Fragozo and 2nd Sergeant Luiz da Silva Seabra, both from the 1st Artillery Regiment.[620]

A. Dickson

Lieutenant Colonel commander of the artillery

Table 11.1: 10th Brigade. Return[621] of the Killed, Wounded and Prisoners in the Brigade at the Assault of San Sebastian on 31 August 1813

Regiments	Killed										Wounded										Prisoners and Missing									
	Colonels	Lieutenant Colonels	Majors	Captains	Lieutenants	Ensigns	Sergeants	Drummers	Corporals and Privates	Total	Colonels	Lieutenant Colonels	Majors	Captains	Lieutenants	Ensigns	Sergeants	Drummers	Corporals and Privates	Total	Colonels	Lieutenant Colonels	Majors	Captains	Lieutenants	Ensigns	Sergeants	Drummers	Corporals and Privates	Total
5th Caçadores Battalion									21	21					2	1			48	48										
13th Regiment				1		1	2		12	12				1	2	1	5	1	66	66										
24th Regiment							2	1	12	12				1	2	1	1		64	64										
Total				1		1	4	1	45	45				2	6	3	6	1	178	178										

Names and ranks of the officers killed

Captain Neves,[622] 13th Regiment
Ensign Joze Maria,[623] 13th Regiment
Adjutant João Manoel de Abreu, 24th Regiment

Names and ranks of the officers wounded

5th Caçadores:
Lieutenant Miguel Correia Freitas, severely
Lieutenant Manuol Joaquim de Menezes, slightly
Ensign Joze Carrasco Guerra, slightly
13th Regiment:
Captain Joaquim Antonio de Miranda, severely
Lieutenant Joze Pedro,[624] slightly
Lieutenant Manoel Joaquim,[625] slightly
Ensign Lourenço Justiniano,[626] severely
24th Regiment:
Captain Aragão,[627] slightly
Lieutenant Padua, severely
Ensign Joze Manoel,[628] severely
Lieutenant Francisco Xavier,[629] severely

Names and ranks of the officers prisoners and missing

T Bradford

Chapter 12

Battles in the Pyrenees, 23–31 July 1813

In March 1813 Soult was recalled to France. When Napoleon received word of the débâcle at Vitoria, he ordered Soult to take command of all the French armies against Wellington. He was given full authority to reorganize them and do what was necessary to stop Wellington. Soult took command on 12 July and disbanded the various armies and formed them into the Army of Spain. He had 80,000 men in nine divisions. Three corps[630] were organized, each with three divisions, under the command of Reille, Clausel, and D'Erlon.

The French troops' morale had improved dramatically with the change of leadership; however, they were short of food, ammunition, artillery, and vehicles to carry their supplies. Soult intended to go on the offensive to relieve Pamplona. Once this was accomplished, he would then go to the relief of San Sebastian.

Soult's plan was to leave four brigades of reserve infantry along the Bidassoa river while he used two corps to attack over the Roncesvalles Pass and D'Erlon's corps would attack through the Maya Pass. The latter attack would go through the Bastan valley and cut the main route between Wellington's left flank at San Sebastian and his right at Pamplona.

Wellington had ten divisions spread over 80km of mountainous terrain. The 1st Division was near Irun and the Bidassoa estuary. The Light Division was at Vera, on the headwaters of the Bidassoa river. The 5th Division and two Independent Brigades were at San Sebastian. The units nearest to the Maya Pass were the 2nd Division, tasked with guarding it, and the 6th Division and Costa's Brigade in the Bastan valley at San Esteban. The 7th Division was at Echalar, about 20km to the west.

One of the units near the Roncesvalles Pass was the 3rd Division at Olague, 20km north of Pamplona and 45km southwest of the Pass; the 4th Division and Campbell's Brigade were also close to the Pass, as were Byng's Brigade of the 2nd Division, and Morillo's Spanish Division.

On 23 July French National Guards attacked the picquets of the 4th Infantry Regiment of Campbell's Brigade at Aldudes. Two days later, on 25 July, D'Erlon marched undetected to the Maya Pass. The Allied 2nd Division was caught by surprise. Despite its senior leadership being absent, the men held on until late in the day when they were forced to retreat. Except for the 6th Caçadores, Ashworth's Brigade was not involved in the fighting, but a Portuguese artillery brigade was: it lost four guns. While the fighting was going on at the Maya Pass, Costa's Brigade fought at Espegui Pass.

At the same time that the Allied forces in the Maya Pass were being attacked, Soult sent Reille and Clausel to the Roncesvalles Pass. The routes were so narrow that the French advanced on a battalion front throughout much of the battle. By nightfall the French columns had been stopped, but Cole, the commander of the 4th Division, decided to withdraw. No Portuguese troops came under fire during this battle.

The following day, 26 July, the French made little effort to pursue the retreating Allied forces. Hill and his men were able to fall back 16km to Irurita. Cole retreated to Linzoain, about 15km to the southwest and linked up with the 3rd Division. From Roncesvalles Pass Soult sent Reille's Corps towards the Maya Pass to try to cut off Hill's retreat. Clausel pursued cautiously and caught up with the Allies at Linzoain. After some skirmishing the French troops went into bivouac and Allies slipped away in the night.

The Allies' withdrew to the heights just east of Sorauren, 10km north of Pamplona, where the French found them on 27 July. Soult could have bypassed their position and pushed on to Pamplona, but instead he chose to fight. The day was spent skirmishing to capture the Zabaldica Heights but without a major engagement. That night Reille's Corps arrived and was placed on the left of the army. The French continued manoeuvring the next morning and were not in position to attack until 1 p.m.

The Allied forces present on 28 July were the 6th Division on the left flank, the 4th Division in the left centre, and Campbell's Brigade in the right centre. Some 2km to the southeast on the Heights of Huarte[631] was Power with the rest of the 3rd Division. The French assaulted the centre and left flank of the Allied position, but with little success.

The following day both armies waited for reinforcements. D'Erlon was ordered to march south and join the army, but Wellington ordered Hill, with the 2nd Division and Costa's Brigade, to prevent D'Erlon from linking up with the rest of the army. The 7th Division was ordered to Sorauren and arrived there later in the day. Soult decided not to attack the Allies at Sorauren, instead ordering his army to move to his right, link up with D'Erlon, and cut the main road from San Sebastian to Pamplona. Clausel led the march, while Reille followed.

The next morning Wellington saw the French moving across his front to the west in a 6km-long column and ordered his army to attack. The 7th Division hit the front of the column at Olabe,[632] Cole's troops attacked Sorauren, and the 3rd Division attacked the rear of the French column at Zabaldica. The two French corps became separated and there was a possibility that Reille would be cut off from the rest of the army. After fierce fighting, Reille was eventually able to link up with Clausel. However, both corps had been decimated and were in no position to continue offensive operations.

D'Erlon continued to move south and came upon Hill south of Lizaso, 3km to the east of Beunza.[633] He made a flanking attack and by 4 p.m. the Allied troops had been pushed off the ridge towards the west. Allied reinforcements, including Campbell's Brigade, arrived as Hill was consolidating his troops. Since he had been successful in opening the road south to Sorauren D'Erlon called off any further attacks.

The three French corps linked up late on the night of 30 July and retreated to France via the Maya Pass. D'Erlon formed the rearguard. Wellington ordered a pursuit but did not realize that the whole force was retreating along the same route. He sent part of his force towards the Roncesvalles Pass and the rest to the Maya Pass, under Hill's command. The French general Abbé had command of the rearguard and on the morning of 31 July at Venta de Urroz he waited at the mouth of the Donna Maria Passes. His men withstood Allied attacks for six hours to give the rest of the army time to move through the passes. At 4 p.m. they broke contact and continued their retreat.

On 1 August Soult split his army and sent them along different roads to the pass. Clausel formed the rearguard and was caught by the Allied pursuit at Sumbilla, where a minor skirmish took place. At Yanzi Reille ran into Spanish troops who delayed his march and caused many units to scatter. On the morning of 2 August the French rearguard was at Echalar when the 7th Division arrived, and it quickly withdrew. By nightfall the French army was back in France.

Combat of Aldudes, 23 July 1813

The only Allied position in France was in Aldudes, a village 8km to the southeast of Elizondo. There picquets of the 4th Infantry of Campbell's Brigade were attacked by French National Guards and were forced to retreat. Lieutenant Colonel Allan Campbell,[634] the regimental commander, reinforced his picquet line and the French called off their attack.

Portuguese Division

Report[635] from Count de Amarante to Beresford

Sir
I have the honour to enclose a copy of the report from Brigadier General Campbell that I received today at 3 a. m. and the return of the killed and wounded which he had in the action of yesterday.
God save Your Excellency
Headquarters of Erraztu, 24 July 1813
His Excellency the Marquis de Campo Maior

Count de Amarante

Report[636] from General Campbell to Count de Amarante

I have the honour to inform Your Excellency that yesterday afternoon the enemy, 200 to 300 men, attacked a picquet composed of a company of the 4th Regiment. In a first moment his superiority dislodged our picquet, but immediately after, Lieutenant Colonel Campbell arrived with another company of the regiment in support, which forced the enemy to retreat and our posts were again occupied. I enclose a return of the casualties on the occasion. General Hill sent, to be under my orders, a battalion of the 18th Regiment. The French occupied the same positions today.
24 July 1813
I have the honour to be your most humble servant

Arch. Campbell
Brigadier General

See Table 12.1.

Combat of Maya, 25 July 1813

The only Portuguese troops to fight in the Maya Pass were the 6th Caçadores of Ashworth's Brigade and Preto's 6-pounder brigade. Prior to the battle three of the guns and a 5.5-inch howitzer were placed on a rocky knoll on the left. When this position was about to be overrun the guns were spiked and pushed into a ravine. Captain Richard Brunton of the 6th Caçadores was ordered by the division commander to take three companies of caçadores and try to get around the left flank of the French and to delay them as long as possible. Brunton did so but was quickly outnumbered and pushed off his position. During the retreat he was given command of the rearguard, where he was 'occasionally occupying such points as were tenable and urging on the stragglers which were numerous. We were not however molested by the Enemy.'[637]

Costa's Brigade was located at the Espegui Pass[638] overlooking the Baigorrey valley, 10km to the southeast of the Maya Pass. The brigade was attacked in the morning but held its position until the 2nd Division retreated.

Portuguese Division

Report[639] from Count de Amarante to Beresford

Sir
I have the honour to inform Your Excellency that on the 25th instant, at dawn, the enemy occupied the top of the mountain, on my right flank, already behind my advanced posts. I came up by a steep track to the right of my advanced posts and arriving at the Porto de Espegui[640] found out that more than 500 enemy

troops occupied that position. I immediately ordered two battalions to come up and attack the enemy. One was a battalion of the 14th Regiment, commanded by Major Jacinto Alexandre Travaços and the other, from the 2nd Regiment, commanded by Lieutenant Colonel João Telles.[641] They gallantly climbed the mountain and defeated the enemy completely, pursuing for more than a league. To this effect an advanced party that I sent from Porto Espegui, commanded by Colonel Jorge Avillez, [642] contributed very much. I beg leave to state my perfect approbation of the conduct of Colonel Avillez, Major Jacinto and Lieutenant Colonel Telles. To them I am much obliged. In the retreat, on the afternoon of the same day, I did not lose any men or baggage. I do not have any news from the Brigade of the 4th and 10th Regiments.[643] The Division's artillery has been detached for some time. I enclose to Your Excellency information, the return of his losses in the 25th, attached to the 2nd Division, and also from the Brigade of the 2nd and 14th Regiments, the only one I had now under my command and even this one was short of five companies, also detached.
God save Your Excellency
Headquarters of Ziga, 27 June 1813
Marquis de Campo Maior

Count de Amarante

14th Infantry

See Table 12.2.

Artillery

Return[644] of the casualties in the Portuguese Artillery on the Attack at the Maya Post, on 25 July 1813

A howitzer 5 and ½ inches and 3 guns 6 pounders were spiked, and their carriages destroyed in the position because they could not be saved.
   A gun limber and all the ammunition wagons retreated, as well as all the personnel and cattle except for one beast of burden, which was killed.
Camp of Barrueta, 26 July 1813

Alex. Tulloh
Lieutenant Colonel Commander of the Artillery

Sorauren, 27, 28, and 30 July 1813

The Allies' position was on heights near the village of Sorauren, 10km north of Pamplona. There was some skirmishing late in the morning of 27 July when Clausel's troops tried to capture the Zabaldica Heights. However, the French did not press the attack. Reille arrived in the evening and was placed on the left of Clausel. Allied troops also arrived and by nightfall the following were present: the 6th Division, with Madden's Brigade, on the left flank; in the centre the 4th Division on the western part of the Heights of Oricain,[645] with Campbell's Brigade on the eastern part; and directly behind them on the back slope Stubb's Brigade. Some 2km to the southeast on the Heights of Huarte[646] was Power's Brigade.

   The French attack began about 1 p.m. on 28 July with an assault on the centre of the Allied line with two divisions. Campbell's and Ross's Brigades were able to hold most of the ridge, but a French column hit the junction between them and held the hill for about 30 minutes. On the French right flank columns from Taupin's Division advanced up the valley from Sorauren, and found itself surrounded on three sides and had to retreat. The 6th Division counter-attacked up the valley but was unable to take Sorauren. On the French left flank Foy's Division was ordered to make a feint against the 3rd Division on the Heights of Huarte, but not to become seriously engaged. By 4 p.m. the attacks had stopped.

The next day both armies waited for reinforcements. The 7th Division arrived late in the day.

On 30 July Soult ordered his army to move to the right and link up with D'Erlon. Clausel's Corps led the march, while Reille followed. Wellington saw the French moving across his front and ordered his army to attack. The 7th Division attacked the front of the column at Olabe,[647] the 6th Division attacked Sorauren, and the 3rd Division attacked the rear of the column at Zabaldica. The distance between the two French corps grew but, after heavy fighting, Reille was able to catch up with Clausel. Both corps had taken heavy casualties and were incapable of resuming the offensive.

D'Erlon continued to march south and encountered Hill on a high wooded ridge south of Lizaso.[648] D'Erlon made a flanking attack and by 4 p.m. the Allied troops were retreating to the west. Allied reinforcements, including General Campbell's Brigade, arrived as Hill was consolidating his troops. D'Erlon called off any further attacks.

The three French corps met up late that night and began retreating to France via the Maya Pass. D'Erlon formed the rearguard. Wellington ordered a pursuit and sent part of his force to the Roncesvalles Pass, and Hill with the rest to the Maya Pass. Hill caught up with the French rearguard on 31 July at Venta de Urroz and ordered the 2nd Division to attack at 10 a.m. The first two attacks went in piecemeal and failed. The 7th Division came up and was successful in pushing the French rearguard back. However, the French were able to delay the pursuit long enough for the rest of the army to get away.

Portuguese Division

Campbell's Brigade was posted on the north slopes of the Heights of Oricain. It was in line with the 10th Infantry on the left and the 4th Infantry on the right. In front was the skirmish line of the 10th Caçadores. General Vandermaesen's Division of 4,000 men assaulted the 250m-high slope. Despite being fired on by skirmishers the whole way, they soon reached Campbell's line. An intense firefight took place and both sides took heavy casualties. The French were about to force Campbell back when Stubbs was sent in as support. But even these reinforcements could not halt the French. However, to the east of their advance the assault by Maucune's troops was repulsed, leaving Vandermaesen's left flank exposed. Anson's Brigade, after defeating Maucune, moved down the heights and hit Vandermaesen in the flank. This broke the French attack on Campbell's lines and, despite their initial success, the French withdrew down the hill.

Campbell's Brigade (4th and 10th Infantry, 10th Caçadores)

Report[649] from General Campbell, Commander of the Brigade Detached from the Portuguese Division to the 4th Division, to Beresford

Sir

I have the honour to enclose a copy of a report that I sent to Lieutenant General Sir Lowry Cole, under whose immediate orders I have manoeuvred in these last days. I will not annoy Your Excellency with the repetition of the recommendations I made in it, but I beg leave to request Your Excellency's attention to those brave and deserving officers.

As Your Excellency was a spectator of all the actions against the enemy of my Brigade, in these two days, on the heights, I will not dare to enter in any detail on this subject and immediately turn to a more pleasant and satisfactory part of my duties, which is to assure to Your Excellency how much I'm satisfied with the noble spirit of emulation that seemed to excite all men in general, and in particular to beg leave to recommend to Your Excellency, owing to their conspicuous bravery and meritorious conduct, the following officers: Captain Francisco Antonio Pamplona,[650] 10th Caçadores, to whom devolved the command of the battalion, after the removal from the battlefield, severely wounded, of Lieutenant Colonel R. Armstrong[651] and Major J.W. Green;[652] Captain Caetano de Mello Sarria,[653] my Brigade Major and now the senior captain in the 4th Regiment, who thanks to his great zeal and efficiency, helped by my Aide-de-Camp, Lieutenant Jozé Jorge Loureiro and Ensign Jozé Maria de Souza,[654] 10th Caçadores Battalion, enabled me, on the morning of the 27th, to take possession of the Zabaldica Heights, lately the main post on our right. They ran forward with a few men and fired at the head of the enemy column, and at the same time called for more troops, showing that the position was occupied; immediately the enemy column halted and turned to the right, which allowed my Brigade to come up and in a short time occupy the post. These officers continued to distinguish themselves in the following occasions.[655]

The lieutenant colonel commanding the 4th Regiment,[656] mentioned to me the brave and exemplary conduct of Lieutenants Jozé Joaquim Pacheco and Antonio Henriques Lobinho, from the said regiment, in the different charges and attacks made and received by that regiment.

The colonel of the 10th Infantry Regiment[657] recommended particularly the 2nd Grenadier Company's Ensign João Rodarte;[658] Captain Anselmo Jozé Queirós, 10th Caçadores, very conspicuously charged the enemy and was severely wounded; Lieutenant A. Campbell,[659] 4th Regiment, although severely wounded, returned to the field to lead his company until he was completely exhausted.

On account of the small number of officers present with the 4th Regiment and of the great number of them wounded in the actions of these days it happened that their duties devolved to sergeants, and I observed the brave and intelligent conduct of the Adjutant Sergeant *Agregado* of the 4th Regiment, Jozé Antonio de Lemos,[660] and also 3rd Company's First Sergeant Jozé Maria Nogueira, an old and deserving soldier, 2nd Grenadier Company's First Sergeant Bernardino de Sena,[661] who although severely wounded, refused to leave the field, and Second Sergeant Francisco da Silva of the same company.

I enclose also a return of the killed and wounded in my Brigade, which I feel to be so numerous and I have to particularly lament the deaths of two excellent officers, Major Candido Bazilio da Vitoria, 10th Regiment, and Captain Lucas Germano Garcez Palha, 4th Regiment.

My Aide-de-Camp[662] will have the honour to present this report to Your Excellency and I again beg leave to recommend this young and worthy officer.
I have the honour to be Your Excellency's most humble servant
To His Excellency, the Marquis de Campo Maior
Zabaldica Heights 29 July 1813

Arch. Campbell
Brigadier General

Copy of a Report[663] from General Campbell, Commander of the Brigade Detached from the Portuguese Division to the 4th Division, to that Division's Commander, General Cole

Sir,
As Your Excellency witnessed the operations and conduct of my Portuguese Infantry Brigade composed of the 10th Caçadores Battalion and the 4th and 10th Infantry Regiments, after I had the honour to be under the orders of Your Excellency, I deem unnecessary to say anything on the subject. Nevertheless I beg leave to request Your Excellency's favourable recommendation to His Excellency, the Marquis of Wellington, of Lieutenant Colonel Allan William Campbell's well known brave and gallant conduct commanding the 4th Regiment, of Lieutenant Colonel Ricardo [sic] Armstrong, commanding the 10th Caçadores, and of Major J.W. Green, all three were severely wounded.[664]

Captains McDonald[665] and R. Dudgeon[666] commanding the 4th Regiment's Grenadier companies distinguished themselves in the charges and attacks made and received by that regiment; the same I have to add about Lieutenant Colonel Daniel [sic] McNeil.[667]

I will send to His Excellency, the Marquis de Campo Maior, our Commander-in-Chief, a report on the Portuguese officers who more particularly distinguished themselves.

I have the honour to enclose a return of the killed, wounded, and missing of my Brigade on these two days and those of the Spanish Infantry Battalions of the Principe and Pavia, which were under my orders.

I have the honour to be Your Excellency's most humble servant

To Lieutenant General Sir Lowry Cole

Zabaldica Heights 29 July 1813

Arch. Campbell
Brigadier General

See Table 12.3.

3rd Division

Some 2km to the southeast of the centre of the Allies' position was the 3rd Division on the Heights of Huarte. Power's Brigade, except for the 11th Caçadores, was in reserve on the southern slope of the heights. The 11th Caçadores was part of the screen on the northern slopes. The French made a demonstration against the 3rd Division but did not press home the attack.

Power's Brigade (9th and 21st Infantry, 11th Caçadores)

Report[668] from General Power to AG Mozinho

Roncesvales August 3rd 1813

Sir

In consequence of a report which I have received from Colonel Keane (under whose immediate command that corps was serving) of the great gallantry shown by the 11th Caçadores under the command of Lieutenant Colonel Dursbach,[669] on the 30th ultimo, during the enemy's retreat, I have to request that you will lay the same before His Excellency the Marshal Sir W. Carr Beresford, Marquis of Campo Maior.

On this occasion, as well as at the battle of Vittoria, Major Kilsha of that Battalion gave proofs of the most distinguished courage, and animated his men, by a most heroic example. I should have made a particular report of this old[670] and very deserving officer's conduct, at the battle of Vittoria, but I was not made acquainted with the circumstances, until sometime afterwards, however I am happy now to have an opportunity of recommending him most strongly to His Excellency's favor [sic] and protection.

I have the honor to be, Sir, your most obedient humble servant

M. Power
Major General

Adjutant General

11th Caçadores

See Table 12.4.

4th Division

Stubbs' Brigade, except for the 7th Caçadores, was deployed on the reverse slope of the Heights of Oricain. The 7th Caçadores was part of the screen that was in front of Campbell's Brigade on the north side of the heights, near the San Salvador Chapel. From this vantage point they could see Sorauren. The brigade participated in the attack which pushed back the French column that had secured a foothold on top of the heights.

Stubbs' Brigade (11th and 23rd Infantry, 7th Caçadores)

Report[671] from Colonel Stubbs to AG Mozinho

Sir

I have the honour to send to you the enclosed reports to be laid before His Excellency, the Marshal Marquis de Campo Maior. I much regret the wounding of Lieutenant Colonel O'Toole, 7th Caçadores Battalion, whose battalion had a distinguished conduct in yesterday's battle, as they do on all occasions. The Brigade's line Regiments also did their duty, the 23rd Regiment being more actively employed, both sustained the credit they earned in the past. The brigade in whole deserves His Excellency's attention.

It is my duty to mention Major Peacock [sic][672] commanding the 23rd Regiment's 1st Battalion; all those who witnessed his conduct recognized the remarkable professional knowledge of a distinct officer, full of zeal and energy.

Lieutenant Colonel O'Toole was forced to leave his Battalion, and could not report on those who distinguished themselves although I can recommend Captain O'Hara,[673] whose conduct exceeded all that we can expect both in courage and example, and it would be a serious omission on this occasion not to bring it to His Excellency's attention.

God save you, Sir

Camp of Pamplona, 29 July 1813

Manoel de Brito Mozinho

Thomas Guilherme [sic] Stubbs
Colonel,[674] commander of the Brigade

23rd Infantry

Report[675] from Lieutenant Colonel Miller to Colonel Stubbs

Sir

It is with the greatest pleasure that I enclose the report from Major Peacocke who was detached yesterday, with the 1st Battalion of the Regiment under my command, with orders to hold a position. As I remained with the 2nd Battalion, I had the satisfaction to witness the intrepidity and zeal with which it sustained its reputation. The behaviour of everyone was so brilliant that it is impossible to distinguish someone in particular.

God save you, Sir

Camp of Pamplona, 29 July 1813

T.G. Stubbs

J. Miller
Lieutenant Colonel, commander of the 23rd Regiment

Report[676] from Major Peacocke, 1st Battalion, 23rd Infantry, to Lieutenant Colonel Miller

Sir

I have the pleasure to report to you that the battalion under my command, detached to hold a position in the centre, behaved in yesterday's action with its usual gallantry and firmness; each individual did his duty brilliantly. Lieutenant Feliz Joze Ferreira de Corte Real[677] distinguished himself commanding his company in a successful charge with the bayonet against a small enemy column which threatened our left.

God save you, Sir

James Miller

Lieutenant Colonel commander of the 23rd Regiment

T. Peacoke
Major, 23rd Regiment

7th Caçadores

Report[678] from Major Lillie to Colonel Stubbs

Sir,

In consequence of the wounds of Lieutenant Colonels O'Toole and Paes,[679] I judge it my duty to inform you of the gallant conduct of the 7th Caçadores in yesterday's action, which deserves the attention of His Excellency, the Marshal Commander-in-Chief. The Battalion, despite having temporarily lost its commander, in the beginning of the action, continued to conduct itself in a most distinguished manner, preventing me from mentioning any individual. I leave to your goodness to make an individual recommendation so that His Excellency can reward those judged worthy.

God save you, Sir
Camp near Pamplona
29 June 1813
Thomas Guilherme [sic] Stubbs

J.S. Lillie
Major, Commanding the 7th Caçadores Battalion

6th Division

On 27 July Wellington ordered Pack's brigade to march from its bivouacs in Lizaso to Sorauren, a distance of 15km. Leading the march was the 9th Caçadores. As the battalion approached Euce,[680] its commander noticed French soldiers occupying the Heights of Morondo above it. The caçadores cleared the heights and Madden's Brigade took their place. On 28 July the 6th Division, temporarily commanded by Pack, was located on the left flank of the army. Its two British brigades were in the valley directly south of Sorauren and east of the Heights of Oricain. Madden's Brigade, minus the 8th Infantry,[681] was deployed in a line on the Heights of Morondo, 150m above the valley. When the columns from Taupin's Division advanced up the valley from Sorauren, Madden took his brigade down the hill and brought the enemy's flank under fire. The French found themselves surrounded on three sides and retreated to Sorauren. Pack ordered his men to follow the French and to take the town. The attack failed and Pack was seriously wounded.

On 30 July the 6th Division was ordered to support the attack on Sorauren. Madden's Brigade was sent along the Heights of Morondo to attack from the west. The 9th Caçadores did most of the fighting and occupied the western edges of the town. They were unable to prevent the French from leaving the town.

Madden's Brigade (8th and 12th Infantry, 9th Caçadores)

Report[682] from General Madden to Beresford

Roncesvalles 2 August 1813
Sir,

Continued marches and the absence of my baggage have hitherto prevented my laying before Your Excellency the particulars of the conduct of the Brigade under my command during the action with the enemy on the 28 and 30 of July last, on the heights near Pamplona; and although I fancy you personally witnessed its arduous desire to merit Your approbation and maintain its reputation, still I trust I may be indulged in offering to your notice the conduct of many of the individuals to your more particular attention. In claiming this privilege therefore (as biased by favour or affection) I cannot but place Colonel Brown[683] commanding the 9 Caçadores foremost in the list; and guided by such an example I do not worden [sic] at the many daring acts of valour and intrepidity performed by that Corps during both days' actions; the report of Colonel B. himself (which I subjoin) will confirm the homage I am obliged to pay to his eminent services, and his more immediate knowledge of the conduct of the officers of his Corps will best develop the services performed by each; and I can only add that I have every reason to believe that many more officers might have been named as deserving the highest praise, but that the fear of intruding too much on Your Excellency has occasioned Colonel B. to omit them; in short to elucidate the conduct of this Battalion in few words, it was the first of the Division that engaged the enemy, and was the last in contributing to his defeat after fording the river and gallantly repulsing them from the village; such conduct therefore will carry more conviction to Your Excellency's discernment than any encomiums I could offer, for you are well aware of the intensity of the enemy's fire and the obstinacy he displayed until forced by superior valour.

Unfortunately for Colonel Douglas,[684] commanding the 8 Regiment, having been left to occupy the village of Olague, himself and his Corps were absent on the action of the 28, and during that of the 30, it was no otherwise engaged than by a slight cooperation of his advanced sentries of the piquets; however it is but just to say, General Pack whose orders he had obeyed approved highly of his measures for the defence of Olague, and that from his junction with the rest of the Brigade on the 29, Colonel D. and his Corps evinced every desire to try their strength with the enemy and I have no doubt had the opportunity occurred would have emulated the zeal and gallantry displayed by the 12 Regiment; of the behaviour of this latter Corps I can particularly vouch, from having immediately superintended its operations against the enemy on both days' actions, and I feel necessitated to speak more in detail of the conduct of its officers and men, from the inadequate knowledge the present commanding officer of the Regiment (whose letter I annex) could acquire from his situation at the entrance of this Regiment in the action of the 28. This Corps, on that occasion, most nobly advanced under the hottest fire, which in less than a quarter of an hour had struck, killed or wounded all its superior officers (except Major Madeira[685]) and many others, besides 200 upwards of the non commissioned and privates, and notwithstanding unceasingly exposed to the galling effect from a heavy column of the enemy, it maintained its ground and I believe contributed most essentially towards his defeat on the right, at the same time that it caused them an infinitely superior loss in numbers. This was effected by a flank movement of the 12 Regiment on the enemy's column divided in two Battalions, the right column led by Lieutenant Colonel Le Mesurier,[686] whose ardent zeal and undaunted valour prompted him to expose himself to every danger, and to this honourable bias of the mind, he unfortunately fell a victim. He was shot through the head in front of the leading company of his Battalion in almost the first discharge, and died in consequence two days following, universally regretted by us all. In him the Regiment and the Portuguese service have sustained an irreparable loss, as of all the Englishmen in that service I have met, none have exceeded him in real regard for the Portuguese nation, nor with the sincere desire of promoting its welfare; in short, his honourable mind and character is too well known to Your Excellency to need the necessity of eulogium from me. I can only add, I most sincerely esteemed and admired him and shall forever feel for and deplore his loss. In this attack also fell Major Arnot[687] wounded twice, in the arm and thigh, Captains Thornton[688] and Alpoim,[689] both of Grenadier companies, and both shot through the thighs, the second Adjutant Jose Correa[690] struck twice, but who would not quit the field; in fact the animating example of the foregoing and following officers Captains Sampayo,[691] Green,[692] Ensigns Antonio Guedes de Sousa, Cardoso de Sá,[693] and Joao Barracho Correa,[694] is deserving of the highest praise and I trust will merit Your Excellency's consideration.

In the action of the 30 this regiment also furnished a large support to the light troops in the attack on the village[695] and again evinced its gallantry by entering the place at the same time agreeable to the report of Colonel Brown of the 9 Caçadores, proving on all occasions its determined vigour in repulsing the enemy.

I know not if all was done that could be by the troops entrusted to my command, but posted on a hill for its defence solely, without any other orders, I could only venture such aid to the general effect of our attacks, as might serve to ensure the desired end; however as both generals Pack and Pakenham, who commanded the 6 Division on the days of action, have assured me of their satisfaction of the cooperation I did order and afford, I trust the movements judged necessary for the general good and which obtained success against the enemy, may also have met your Excellency's approbation.

I have the honour to be Sir, Your Excellency's obedient and humble servant

George Allan Madden
Brigadier General[696]

To His Excellency Sir W.C. Beresford K.B. Marquis of Campo Maior

9th Caçadores

Report[697] from Lieutenant Colonel Brown, to General Madden

Sir,

I have the honour to acquaint you, for the information of His Excellency, the Marshal Marquis de Campo Maior, Commander-in-Chief of the Army, of the brilliant conduct of the battalion under my command on the 28th and 30th of this month.

On the 28th, the battalion formed the division's advance guard and seeing the enemy occupying a height over the village of Euce[698] that I judged very disadvantageous to our left, I halted the battalion and communicated my observations to General Pack. I requested his permission to attack the enemy which he immediately conceded and I had the satisfaction of expelling them with no loss but inflicting many; the enemy's position and the fatigue of the Caçadores, caused by the excessive steepness of the height, prevented me from making prisoners. The commander of the advance guard in this attack was the 3rd Company's Captain João Mellish Arrison[699] who conducted himself with his usual gallantry.

On the 30th I was ordered (as you know) to support the attack on the enemy's position, especially the village on the river bank.[700] I began ordering the advance of the 1st Company, under the command of Captain Antonio Luiz de Moraes Sarmento,[701] to the village as close as possible. This was perfectly executed by the captain, despite the heavy fire from the houses and trenches, and he kept himself and the company in that situation, flanking the first enemy's position with a very lively fire. At the moment of the attack, the captain led the company across the river and entered the village with the first British troops. I also detached 6th Company's Lieutenant Ignacio Ferreira da Rocha[702] with a party to flank and attack the enemy's position on the mountain on the right bank of the river, which the enemy took during the previous night and morning. The lieutenant executed it at the moment of the 7th Division's attack and by his gallant conduct concurred very much to dislodge the enemy and made fifty prisoners. I judged it necessary to support this attack with another party commanded by Adjutant Andrew Simpson whose conduct was also valiant.

It's my duty to remark to His Excellency that the general conduct of all officers, inferior officers, and men was the best I could hope for, either on the 28th or the 30th; it's also my duty to state that the 6th Company's Lieutenant did his duty in spite of being wounded in the first day, and the 1st Company's Ensign Lourenço Joze de Andrade[703] crossed the river in a most dashing manner, at the beginning of the attack on the village. Adjutant Sergeant Joaquim Manoel da Silva Rocha[704] (that I had the honour to recommend to His Excellency, the Marshal, at the battle of Arapiles) was wounded on the 28th, giving again evidence of his bravery. The 4th Company's Sergeant Estevão Joze Neiva,[705] was the first to close on the village's church and alone attacked and took prisoner the four French soldiers who still resisted inside.

It's also my duty to mention to you that at that moment being the senior officer in the village I directed both the Portuguese and British troops; I also saw the good conduct of Ensign Duarte Cardozo de Sá, 12th Infantry Regiment, commanding the skirmishers of his regiment, who behaved in a manner to rival his comrades.

Much of this was witnessed by you, so I hope that the officers and men under my command met your approbation, and you will not fail to make a well-deserved recommendation to His Excellency the Marshal. God save you, Sir

Camp 31 July 1813

G. Brown

Lieutenant Colonel, commander 9th Caçadores

Brigadier General Madden

P.S. Major Luiz Maria Cerqueira of the battalion under my command was wounded at the beginning of the action and I felt the loss of his services very much.

See Tables 12.5 and 12.6.

7th Division

On 29 July the 7th Division moved from Ollacarrizqueta, 15km northwest of Sorauren, to a position to the left rear of the 6th Division, which occupied the heights northwest of Sorauren. This position overlooked the Ulzama valley, which was the most direct route to the Maya Pass. Lecor's Brigade was on the left near Ollacarrizqueta. On the morning of 30 July Wellington ordered the 7th Division to assault between Olabe and Ostiz. Lecor was ordered to join the fight. Clausel broke off the combat and continued to march up the valley. The 7th Division followed the French and rejoined Hill's force. The next day the three French corps had reunited and marched to the Maya Pass.

The Allied troops under Hill caught up with the French rearguard on the morning of 31 July at Venta de Urroz[706] at the entrance to the passes of Donna Maria. Abbé stood at the mouth of the pass to give the rest of the French Army units time to distance themselves from their pursuers. Hill ordered the 2nd Division to attack at 10 a.m. The first two attacks failed, but when the 7th Division joined in, the French withdrew. The rearguard had delayed the pursuit long enough for the rest of the army to escape. The pursuit continued until 2 August and finally halted when the last of the French troops reached France.

Lecor's Brigade (7th and 19th Infantry, 2nd Caçadores)

Report[707] from General Lecor to AG Mozinho

Sir

I have the honour to enclose a return of the killed, wounded, and missing of the brigade under my command in the actions against the enemy of 29th, 30th, and 31st of last month, for the information of His Excellency, the Marshal Marquis de Campo Maior.

I also beg leave to request you to let His Excellency know that on the 30th I ordered the brigade under my command to cross the river[708] to cut the retreat of several enemy's corps. In this action the brigade made up to 1,500 prisoners including a *chef de batallion* and several other officers. The conduct of the officers, inferior officers, and men that I have the honour to command was, in general, that of the bravest Portuguese. It is my duty to recommend to His Excellency some individuals whom the circumstances afforded the chance to distinguish themselves.

2nd Caçadores Battalion:

Major Jorge [sic] H. Zulchke[709] for the good direction of the battalion on the 30th attack.

Captain Jorge Fermino Pereira Amado[710] for his good behaviour on the same day, being severely wounded, and, by his commanding officer's recommendation, for his gallant conduct in all previous actions in which he was present.

Lieutenant *agregado* by punishment Joze Vicente de Vargas[711] for showing the greatest intrepidity in the crossing of the river under enemy fire, making many prisoners with his company.

Adjutant Sergeant Bartholomeu Nicolau[712] and Cadet Francisco Joze Pereira[713] for their praiseworthy conduct, the former severely wounded and the latter slightly; the Cadet was recognized on the 25th last month and begged his commander to request His Excellency's permission to remain with the battalion until the end of the campaign and only then proceed to Mafra.[714]

19th Infantry Regiment:

Major Forjaz,[715] commanding two companies in support of the Caçadores, showed great bravery and intelligence, as did Captains Mathias de Souza e Castro and João [sic] Ross,[716] Ensigns Francisco Pinto de Araujo, Feliz Joze de Almeida and Antonio Maria Motta, Adjutant Sergeant Francisco Alves de Assis, whom Major Forjaz highly praised for their assistance.

Lieutenant Leslie,[717] commanding the 8th Company, with which he attacked the village[718] in conjunction with the companies from the 7th Regiment, also by the assistance given to the Brunswick battalion, whose commander[719] highly praised him, as also Ensign Francisco Xavier da Cunha and First Sergeant João Felipe Benicio.

7th Regiment:

Major Trapps[720] carried out perfectly the commission which I gave to him, to capture and collect the French stragglers, who hid themselves in the woods.

Captain F. Armstrong,[721] with the 2nd Grenadier Company entered in the attack on the village of Artez[722] and behaved gallantly, as on the next day, in the Lassarra Pass.[723]

Captain T. Shervinton,[724] 7th Company, joined voluntarily the 2nd Grenadier Company, and his conduct was most conspicuous.[725]

First Sergeant Manuel Quaresma da Silva,[726] whose character is an example to the regiment, behaved with great courage in the face of the enemy.

I have the honour of recommending to His Excellency all the mentioned individuals, whose conduct was witnessed by me in general, and in particular by their immediate commanders.

Colonels J. Buchan[727] and J. Doyle[728] directed their respective corps with the greatest coolness and assisted me with zeal and activity.

The Brigade Major, Captain N. Colthurst, assisted me by delivering my orders with the greatest coolness under fire, as did my Aide-de-Camp Lieutenant Joze Ferreira da Cunha, both of whom I take the liberty to recommend to His Excellency, both for their conduct in the three days of action and for their seniority.
God save you, Sir
Campo of Zara 5 August 1813
Manoel de Brito Mozinho

Carlos Frederico Lecor
Major General

See Tables 12.7, 12.8, and 12.9.

Beunza, 30 July 1813

Hill's troops were located on a wooded ridge line that was shaped like a letter L about 600m to the southwest of the village. The ridge towered 200m above the valley. The Allies were deployed in the woods with a strong screen of light troops along the edge of the forest. These troops included the 6th Caçadores. Ashworth was in the centre of the line, while Costa had the 14th Infantry to the left of him and the 2nd Infantry to Ashworth's right. On the far-left flank was Cameron's British Brigade. D'Erlon chose not to make a frontal assault on the ridge. Instead, he ordered Darmagnac's Division to make a feint along the front of the Allied position, while Abbé's Division marched to the far right and climbed the ridge out of sight of the Allies. While Darmagnac made his demonstration, Abbé's Division hit Cameron's Brigade. By 4 p.m. the Allies had been forced off the ridge and had retreated 2km west to the village of Yguaras.[729] Only the 2nd Infantry, which was on the far-right flank, retained its position. Shortly after the Allies had retreated, reinforcements arrived, including Campbell's Brigade. Since he had opened the road to Sorauren, D'Erlon called off any further attacks.

Portuguese Division

Costa's Brigade (2nd and 14th Infantry)

Report[730] from Count de Amarante to Beresford

Sir

I have the honour of transmitting to Your Excellency the return of the casualties of the Brigade under my command, composed of the 2nd and 14th Infantry Regiments, on the actions of the 30th last month. The loss is very considerable but a trifle compared with that the enemy suffered by our repeated bayonet charges. The conduct of Portuguese troops was highly praised by the generals who witnessed their bravery, so all that I could say will be scanty, but I can assure that their conduct meets Your Excellency's best expectations. They showed that his Commander-in-Chief prepared them in advance to present themselves worthily in the battlefield.

It is my duty to recommend to Your Excellency Brigadier General Antonio Hipolito de Costa who distinguished himself at the head of the 2nd Regiment until he was wounded. His Aide-de-Camp Antonio Correa Leote accompanied him gallantly until that point.

The 2nd Regiment's Commander, Colonel Avillez, had the misfortune to break a leg in the beginning of the action, so I have to regret the loss of his services, which I hoped would help us greatly.

The 2nd Regiment's Lieutenant Colonel João Telles, on whom not only the command of the regiment devolved, but sometime after, also of the brigade, behaved with great coolness and bravery, directing his regiment in the charges. He deserves all the praise and attention of Your Excellency.

To Lieutenant Colonel João [sic] MacDonald,[731] 14th Regiment, I am also very obliged by the excellent manner in which he directed the regiment covering the retreat of the left of our line. I assure Your Excellency that this officer assisted me considerably.

Major Lourenço Martins Pegado's,[732] 2nd Regiment, conduct was magnificent until he was killed on the battlefield. I beg leave to call Your Excellency's attention and goodness in favour of the major's numerous family, which by his death will be very distressed.

Major Ray,[733] 2nd Regiment, was wounded but his meritorious services were known to everyone, and I feel that I will lose his assistance for a time. I also regret the loss of Captain McGuibbon [sic],[734] from the 14th Regiment's Grenadier Company, who was mourned by all of us.

I enclose the reports from the corps commanders in which they recommend the individuals who distinguished themselves in the combat. I beg Your Excellency to reward those individuals.

Portuguese Officers

Francisco da Silveira, Count de Amarante. (*Courtesy Quinta do Valdalágea Ltd*)

Luís do Rego Barreto. (*Courtesy Cabral Moncada Leilões/Vasco Cunha Monteiro*)

Carlos Frederico Lecor. (*Museo Histórico Nacional de Uruguay Collection*)

Francisco Homem de Magalhãe Pizarro. (*Biblioteca Brasiliana Guita e José Mindlin Collection*)

British Officers

Colonel Peter Adamson, KTS, *c.* 1864.
(*Courtesy of Heritage Mississauga*)

Sir Alexander Dickson. (*Anne S.K. Brown Collection*)

James Douglas. (*From Regimental Annual Sherwood Foresters, courtesy Steve Brown*)

Major General George Madden. (*Sandhurst Collection*)

John McDonald. (*Authors' collection*)

Sir Denis Pack. (*Provided by kind permission of Suzie Pack-Beresford*)

Kenneth Snodgrass. (*State Library of Victoria, Australia*)

Edmund Keynton Williams. (*Courtesy of The Regimental Museum of The Royal Welsh*)

G. C. BERESFORD, CONDE DE TRANCOZO.

Popular print of a portrait of Marshal William Carr Beresford, commander-in-chief of the Portuguese Army. (*Arquivo Nacional da Torre do Tombo Collection*)

INSTRUCÇÕES
PARA A FORMATURA,
EXERCICIO, E MOVIMENTOS
DOS
REGIMENTOS
DE
INFANTERIA.
POR ORDEM
DO EXCELLENTISSIMO SENHOR
GUILHERME CARR BERESFORD,
MARECHAL E COMMANDANTE EM CHEFE
DOS EXERCITOS
DE SUA ALTEZA REAL
O PRINCIPE REGENTE
DE PORTUGAL.

LISBOA,
NA IMPRESSÃO REGIA.
1809.

Por Ordem de Sua Alteza Real.

Schematic of Manual of Arms from Marshal Beresford's Infantry Instructions. (*Biblioteca Digital do Exército Collection*)

The following sketches were drawn by Lieutenant Manuel Isidro da Paz, ADC to General Bradford during the 1812/Salamanca campaign. It is unknown after which battle the first three were drawn. (*Arquivo Nacional Torre do Tombo Collection*)

Sketch 1: Removal of the wounded from the battlefield.

Sketch 2: Capture of a wounded French officer.

Sketch 3: Assisting wounded French soldiers.

Sketch 4: The army crossing the Agueda on 13 June 1812.

The Lesser Arapiles, Salamanca. Stubbs' Brigade had the Lesser Arapile on its left flank as it attacked in line towards the right of the picture. (*Authors' collection*)

The Greater Arapile, Salamanca: the side of the hill up which Pack's Brigade attacked. (*Authors' collection*)

Villa Muriel: the ford over the Carrion river near Calabazanos that the 8th Caçadores defended. (*Garry Willis Collection*)

Villa Muriel: the row of trees in the middle ground marks the canal in which Spry's Brigade sheltered at the beginning of the action. (*Garry Willis Collection*)

Vitoria: the Tres Puentes bridge across the Zadorra river where the 1st Caçadores moved across to take the high ground on the opposite side. (*Authors' collection*)

Vitoria: the mountains that Power's Brigade marched 10km through to reach the battlefield. (*Authors' collection*)

Vitoria: the fields that Power's Brigade marched across to attack the village of Arinez, which is to the right of the image. The left flank of the brigade was near the church in the centre. (*Authors' collection*)

San Sebastian: view from the fortress of the Urumea river that the 10th Brigade crossed in its attack on the eastern walls of San Sebastian on 31 August 1813. (*Mark Thompson's Collection*)

The river Bidassoa from the Louis XIV Redoubt, looking southwest. The place where the 1st and 3rd Brigades attacked across the river is on the right. (*Nick Lipscombe Collection*)

Nivelle: a view of the Lesser Rhune from the Greater Rhune, looking northwest. The 1st and 3rd Caçadores and the 17th Infantry were part of the assault on the western edge of the position. (*Nick Lipscombe Collection*)

Orthez: the bridge against which the 2nd Brigade made a demonstration. (*Nick Lipscombe Collection*)

The staff of the Division provided me their zealous assistance; Captain Watson,[735] Assistant Deputy Quartermaster General, and Captain Pinto,[736] Assistant Deputy Adjutant General, fulfilled their duties very well. General Hamilton's Aide-de-Camp, Francisco Henriques Teixeira[737] joined the staff and his services deserve Your Excellency's attention, as do those of Luiz de Mendonça e Mello,[738] Brigade Major of the Brigade composed of the 2nd and 14th Regiments, who did his duty with zeal and activity.

The officers from my personal staff: Colonel Manoel da Silveira Pinto,[739] acting Aide-de-Camp, whose conduct pleased me so much, as a general and father; Captain Luiz Manoel de Carvalho, 10th Infantry, who happened to be in the Division's headquarters, joined my staff and from the 25th has accompanied me in all the actions, showing his value and his military knowledge; my Aide-de-Camp Miguel Vaz Pereira Pinto Guedes[740] also did his duty and merits my approbation; both deserve the favour of Your Excellency; Antonio Joaquim Malheiro, serving as my secretary for a long time, deserves a promotion as secretary on the staff of the Trás-os-Montes' province or any other that Your Excellency finds suitable. I must mention Francisco Romão de Goes, former member of the Academic Corps and a clergyman, who accompanied me voluntarily since the beginning of the Restoration,[741] rendering me great services.

Although not under my orders, I cannot omit, for Your Excellency's information, the praiseworthy and gallant conduct of the Brigade composed of the 6th and 18th Infantry Regiments and the 6th Caçadores Battalion;[742] on several occasions I was with the brigade and always had great satisfaction seeing its conduct.

I beg leave, with the highest submission and respect, to represent to Your Excellency my situation as commander of a Division of which I have only commanded a brigade and many times only a part. The Brigade composed of the 4th and 10th Infantry Regiments and the 10th Caçadores Battalion[743] was detached for a long time and joined the Division in the evening of the 30th last month, but on the next day's morning I was informed by its commander that the Brigade was again detached to be under orders of another general. I was again commanding only a brigade and rather less men than that of a brigadier. If this situation was not indecorous to my rank and to all other general officers of the three allied nations, I would not complain. Your Excellency, as Commander-in-Chief of the Portuguese Army, should not permit a Lieutenant General of that army to suffer the indignity of having under his orders less than 1000 men and even these were divided at the time of the action. I believe that I have not given motives to be conceived that I am not able to command troops, so I implore to Your Excellency to order that brigade, or one of the independent ones, to join this Division, as all other Divisions in the army have three brigades and the Portuguese Division only two, it should not have one detached. It is my duty to serve His Royal Highness and to obey Your Excellency's orders, which I do with pleasure, but I'm sure the reasons that forced me to this representation are approved by Your Excellency, because they are founded on the fear of a stain on my reputation.

God save Your Excellency

Headquarters of Espiqueta[744] 2 August 1813

Marquis de Campo Maior

Your most humble servant
Count de Amarante

See Table 12.10.

14th Infantry

Report[745] from Lieutenant Colonel McDonald to Count de Amarante

Sir

I have the honour to inform Your Excellency that I'm entirely satisfied with the conduct of all the individuals in the regiment under my command, and in my opinion everyone behaved well, but Your Excellency and the other generals can judge it better than me, its commander.

I regret infinitely the loss of Adjutant Jozé Maria Cabreira; I lost a good friend and a brave officer, who carried out his duties with great exertions throughout the action; to his family, it will be a consolation to know that he died doing his duty. I beg leave to request that Your Excellency recommend to the Adjutant position the deceased's brother, Lieutenant Thomas Antonio da Guarda Cabreira, who distinguished himself in the action and is a praiseworthy officer. I have also to praise the conduct of Ensign Alberto Magno Rozado and recommend him to a lieutenancy which he deserves both for his conduct and seniority.

I have the honour to recommend in the strongest manner 2nd Grenadier Company's First Sergeant Joaquim Antonio de Freitas,[746] and the same company's Second Sergeant Joze Francisco Coelho,[747] both distinguished themselves and deserve promotion to ensign having the qualities and capability to be good and brave officers; the latter was wounded by a musket ball and twice with a bayonet but is out of danger.

Captain Luiz Fellippe [sic] Pereira de Vasconcellos was severely wounded, and I feel the loss of the services of such a gallant officer, whose conduct on the 30th was so praiseworthy.

I cannot finish without mentioning to Your Excellency that I am much obliged to Captain Antonio Pedro de Brito,[748] 2nd Grenadier Company, from whom I received great assistance; he was the senior captain present in the action and any reward that His Excellency, the Marquis de Campo Maior, can give to this officer and to the officers and sergeants mentioned is well deserved and it is only just.

1 August 1813

His Excellency Count of Amarante

John MacDonald
Lieutenant Colonel, commander of the 14th Regiment

2nd Infantry

Report[749] from Lieutenant Colonel Meneses to Count de Amarante

Sir

I have the honour to enclose the list of the officers present at the action of 30 July, under my orders. I will not recommend particularly the conduct of the companies' officers because all did their duties, but it would be an omission to my own duty not to mention the gallant conduct of Brevet Lieutenant Colonel Lourenço Martins Pegado, who was killed almost at the beginning of the action, leaving a numerous and poor family. I beg leave to ask Your Excellency to recommend this family to the protection of His Royal Highness.

The conduct of Major Roberto [sic] Ray was also praiseworthy for his activity until he was wounded right after the beginning of the action and whose assistance I missed very much.

The regiment felt deeply the loss of Captain Dugald MacGuibbon [sic], who died at the head of his company, full of enthusiasm.

I also take the occasion to recommend Adjutant Sergeant Joze Joaquim Correa, who during the action performed with great zeal the commissions assigned to him and to this he adds a good and civil behaviour.

God save Your Excellency

Camp of Elizondo, 1 August 1813

His Excellency the Count de Amarante

João Telles de Menezes
Lieutenant Colonel, commander

Return from the 2nd Infantry Regiment's Officers Present at the Action on 30 July 1813

Staff:

Lieutenant Colonel João Telles de Menezes
Brevet Lieutenant Colonel Lourenço Martins Pegado
Major Roberto [sic] Ray

Captains:
    1st Grenadier Dugald MacGuibbon [sic]
    2nd Fusiliers Pedro Joze Pereira de Carvalhal
    4th ditto Simão Manoel de Azevedo
    6th ditto Antonio Pereira de Brito
    7th ditto D. MacPherson [sic][750]
    8th ditto Lazaro Soares de Almeida

Lieutenants:
    Ludovico Joze da Roza
    João Nepomuceno de Ataide
    Joze Anacleto Cabrita
    Francisco Rebello de Moura

Ensigns:
    Francisco de Paula Cabrita
    Joaquim Carlos Vianna
    Henrique Luis da Fonseca
    Arcenio Pompeo Correa de Freitas
    Francisco Pedro Furtado
    Gaspar de Villa Lobos
    Joze Fortunato de Azevedo
    Bento Joze Tavares
    Joze Correa de Freitas
    Antonio Silvestre de Sousa
    Manoel Gerardo de Sousa
    Joze Pedro Tavares

João Telles de Menezes
Lieutenant Colonel, commander

2nd Division

Ashworth's Brigade (6th and 18th Infantry, 6th Caçadores)

Report[751] from Colonel Ashworth to AG Mozinho

Sir

I have the honour to enclose the returns of the killed, wounded, and missing from the brigade under my command in the actions against the enemy on the 30th[752] and 31st[753] last month. I have the satisfaction to communicate to you, for His Excellency's, the Marshal Marquis de Campo Maior, information, that the brigade I have the honour to command showed, in those actions, bravery, steadiness, and discipline in a high degree that none other could match, particularly in the afternoon of the 30th when they twice charged the enemy (very superior in number) with the bayonet.

The conduct of the officers was, in general, excellent, but I would not do my duty if I omit to particularly mention Colonel Manoel Pamplona,[754] 18th Regiment, and also Lieutenant Colonel Henrique [sic] Pynn,[755] from the same regiment, both unfortunately wounded shortly after the beginning of the action. Lieutenant Colonel Maxwell Grant, commanding the 6th Regiment, Brevet Lieutenant Colonel Rafael [sic] Ouseley,[756] to whom devolved the command of the 18th Regiment, being wounded the other two superior officers, Major Samuel Mitchell, commanding the 6th Caçadores Battalion, all carried out their duties with the greatest bravery, particularly Lieutenant Colonel Grant who added to his coolness great intelligence.

I should not forget also to recommend to His Excellency's attention Captains Henrique Silva[757] and Hugo [sic] Lumley,[758] both of the 18th Regiment, Ricardo [sic] Brunton,[759] 6th Caçadores, and João [sic] Sutherland,[760] 6th Regiment, and also Lieutenant Antonio da Guerra,[761] 18th Regiment, and the Adjutants, Lieutenants Joze Joaquim Fernandes, 18th Regiment, and Manuel Joaquim Moniz, 6th Regiment.[762] I personally witnessed the good conduct of these officers.

Adjutant Sergeant Antonio Ferreira Borges, 6th Regiment, behaved with great gallantry as did also 1st Grenadier Company's First Sergeant Gonçalo Joze Carneiro, of the same regiment.[763] These two sergeants, not only by their behaviour in the actions of July 30th and 31st, but also by a continued good conduct, deserve to be rewarded by His Excellency, the Marshal Marquis de Campo Maior, and in my humble opinion, they may become very good subaltern officers.

God save you, Sir

Camp in the heights of Maya, 2 August 1813

Manoel de Brito Mozinho

Carlos [sic] Ashworth
Colonel,[764] commander of the Brigade 6-18 [sic]

See Tables 12.11 and 12.12.

Table 12.1: Portuguese Division. Return[665] of the Killed, Wounded, and Missing in the 4th Infantry Regiment in the heights above Aldudes on 23 July 1813

Casualties	Officers						Sergeants	Drummers	Corporals and Soldiers	Total	Horses
	Lieutenant Colonel	Majors	Captains	Lieutenants	Ensigns	Staff					
Killed	-	-	-	-	-	-	-	-	1	1	-
Wounded	-	-	-	-	-	-	-	-	7	7	-
Missing	-	-	-	-	-	-	-	-	2	2	-
Total	-	-	-	-	-	-	-	-	10	10	-

Count de Amarante
Lieutenant General, division commander

Table 12.2: 14th Infantry. Return[766] of the Killed, Wounded and Prisoners in the Action of Loriete on 25 July 1813

Camp of Loriete 25 July 1813	Killed													Wounded												
	Colonel	Lieutenant Colonels	Majors	Adjutants	Adjutant Sergeants	Flag Bearers	Drummer Major	Captains	Lieutenants	Ensigns	Sergeants and *Furriés*	Drummers	Corporals and Privates	Colonel	Lieutenant Colonels	Majors	Adjutants	Adjutant Sergeants	Flag Bearers	Drummer Major	Captains	Lieutenants	Ensigns	Sergeants and *Furriés*	Drummers	Corporals and Privates
Total													1													8

Ranks and names of the officers killed

Ranks and names of the officers wounded

Ranks and names of the officers prisoners

Count de Amarante
Lieutenant General division commander

Table 12.3: Return[767] of the Killed, Wounded, and Missing in the 4th Portuguese Infantry Brigade under the command of Brigadier Archibald Campbell on the Field of Sorauren on 27 and 28 July 1813

Corps	Superior Officers			Captains			Subalterns			Staff			Sergeants			Drummers			Corporals and Privates			Grand Total	Horses			Mules		
	Killed	Wounded	Missing and Prisoners	Killed	Wounded	Missing and Prisoners	Killed	Wounded	Missing and Prisoners	Killed	Wounded	Missing and Prisoners	Killed	Wounded	Missing and Prisoners	Killed	Wounded	Missing and Prisoners	Killed	Wounded	Missing and Prisoners		Killed	Wounded	Missing and Prisoners	Killed	Wounded	Missing and Prisoners
10th Caçadores Battalion	-	2	-	-	2	-	1	1	-	-	-	-	-	3	2	-	-	-	10	19	11	51	-	-	-	-	-	-
4th Infantry Regiment	-	2	-	1	2	-	-	6	-	-	1	-	-	9	-	-	-	-	24	167	36	248	-	-	-	-	-	-
10th Infantry Regiment	1	1	-	1	2	-	-	9	-	-	2	-	1	6	-	-	-	-	66	147	6	242	1	1	-	-	-	-
Total	1	5	-	2	6	-	1	16	-	-	3	-	1	18	2	-	-	-	100	333	53	541	1	1	-	-	-	-

N.B. The men missing, and prisoners are judged dead in the several charges made against the attacking enemy.
10th Caçadores
  Officers Killed:
    Ensign Venceslau Aires Tavares
  Wounded:
    Lieutenant Colonel Ricardo [sic] Armstrong, severely;
    Major Jozua [sic] W. Green, severely;
    Captain Anselmo Joze de Queiros, severely;
    Captain Joze Rodrigues de Lima, severely;
    Lieutenant João Honorato Rolim, slightly;

4th Regiment
Officers Killed:
    Captain Lucas Germano Garcez Palha
Wounded:
    Lieutenant Colonel Allan Guilherme [sic] Campbell, severely;
    Major Antonio Eliseo de Almeida, slightly;
    Captain Luis de Lemos Mello e Vasconcellos, slightly;
    Captain Pedro Joze Frederico, slightly;
    Lieutenant Bernardino Mascarenhas Roza, severely;
    Lieutenant Luis Mascarenhas Roza, severely;
    Lieutenant Archibald Campbell, slightly;
    Ensign Doarte Ferreira Soares de Azevedo, slightly;
    Ensign Doarte Chavier da Silva Araujo, severely;
    Ensign Dom Joze António de Noronha, slightly;
    Adjutant Joze Pedro dos Reis, severely;
10th Regiment
Officers Killed:
    Major Candido Bazilio da Vitoria;
    Captain Antonio Francisco Travaços;
Wounded:
    Major Grigorio Pereira de Faria, slightly;
    Captain Manoel Antonio da Serra, severely;
    Captain Joaquim Manoel da Fonceca, severely;
    Lieutenant Manoel Martiniano Girão, severely;
    Lieutenant Pedro Pinto de Moraes Sarmento, slightly;
    Lieutenant João Gualberto, slightly;
    Lieutenant Antonio de Abreo, severely;
    Ensign João Rodarte, severely;
    Ensign João Maria de Araujo, severely;
    Ensign Anselmo Chavier de Noronha, severely;
    Ensign Antão de Sá Valente, severely;
    Adjutant João dos Santos, slightly;
    Adjutant Joze Nunes de Siqueira, severely;
    Ensign Dom Antonio da Silveira, severely

A Campbell
Brigadier General

Table 12.4: 11th Caçadores. Return[768] of the Killed and Wounded in the Action of 30th July instant

Camp on the Pyrenees in front of the Roncesvalles Pass, 7 August 1813	Bugler	Privates	Observations
Killed		1	
Wounded	1	3	
Missing			
Total	1	4	

M Power
Major General

Table 12.5: 8th Brigade. Return[769] of the Killed, Wounded, Missing and Prisoners in the Infantry Brigade 8th, 12th and 9th Caçadores

	Killed								Wounded								Missing and Prisoners								Total							
	Colonels	Lieutenant Colonels	Majors	Captains	Subalterns	Sergeants	Drummers	Corporals and Privates	Colonels	Lieutenant Colonels	Majors	Captains	Subalterns	Sergeants	Drummers	Corporals and Privates	Colonels	Lieutenant Colonels	Majors	Captains	Subalterns	Sergeants	Drummers	Corporals and Privates	Colonels	Lieutenant Colonels	Majors	Captains	Subalterns	Sergeants	Drummers	Corporals and Privates
9th Caçadores								3						8	1	42														8	1	45
8th Regiment																																
12th Regiment						1		29		1	1	2	1	8	1	218										1	1	2	1	8	1	247
Total						1		32		1	1	2	1	16	2	260										1	1	2	1	16	2	292
	Names and ranks of the officers killed								Names and ranks of the officers wounded								Names and ranks of the officers missing and prisoners								Observations							
									Lieutenant Colonel Havilland Le Mesurier, mortally[770] Major Lawrence Arnot Captain Guilherme Henrique [sic] Thornton,[771] severely Captain João Borges Cerqueira de Alpoim, severely Adjutant Manuel José Correia																							

Camp 29 July 1813

J Maher[772]
Brigade Major

Table 12.6: 8th Brigade. Brigade composed of the 8th, 12th and 9th Caçadores. Return[773] of the Killed, Wounded, Missing, and Prisoners in the Battle of 30 July 1813

	Killed								Wounded								Missing and Prisoners								Total							
	Colonels	Lieutenant Colonels	Majors	Captains	Subalterns	Sergeants	Drummers	Corporals and Privates	Colonels	Lieutenant Colonels	Majors	Captains	Subalterns	Sergeants	Drummers	Corporals and Privates	Colonels	Lieutenant Colonels	Majors	Captains	Subalterns	Sergeants	Drummers	Corporals and Privates	Colonels	Lieutenant Colonels	Majors	Captains	Subalterns	Sergeants	Drummers	Corporals and Privates
9th Caçadores								2		1	1		2	3		42										1	1		2	3		44
8th Regiment																4																4
12th Regiment																4																4
Total								2		1	1		2	3		50										1	1		2	3		52
	Names and ranks of the officers killed								Names and ranks of the officers wounded								Names and ranks of the officers missing and prisoners								Observations							
									Lieutenant Colonel G. Brown, slightly Major Luiz Maria de Cerqueira, severely Lieutenant Ignacio Ferreira da Rocha, slightly Ensign Joaquim Izaquiel da Rocha, slightly																							

J Maher
Brigade Major

Table 12.7: Return[774] of the Killed, Wounded, and Missing of the Brigade under the command of Brigadier General Lecor in action on 30 July 1813 near Pamplona

Camp 31 July 1813	Killed	Wounded						Missing	
	Privates	Captains	Lieutenants	Ensigns	Adjutant Sergeant	Sergeants	Privates	Privates	Total
2nd Caçadores Battalion	7	1	-	-	1	1	35	-	45
7th Infantry Regiment	-	-	-	-	-	-	13	10	23
19th Infantry Regiment	3	-	1	2	-	-	28	-	34
Total	10	1	1	2	1	1	76	10	102

Officers:
Captain Jorge Fermino Pereira Amado, severely;
Lieutenant Lesley, slightly;
Ensign Francisco Xavier da Cunha, slightly;
Ensign Antonio Maria da Motta, slightly

Nicolão [sic] Colthurst
Brigade Major

Table 12.8: Return[775] of the Killed, Wounded, and Missing of the Brigade under the command of Brigadier General Lecor in action on 31 July 1813[776]

Camp 1 August 1813	Killed		Wounded			Missing	Total
	Captain	Privates	Lieutenant	Sergeants	Privates	Privates	
2nd Caçadores Battalion	-	2	-	-	4	2	8
7th Infantry Regiment	-	1	1	2	8	4	16
19th Infantry Regiment	1	1	-	-	3	8	13
Total	1	4	1	2	15	14	37

Officers:
Captain Campbell,[777] killed
Lieutenant Antonio Pereira Heitor, slightly

Nicolão [sic] Colthurst
Brigade Major

Table 12.9: Return[778] of the Killed, Wounded, and Missing of the Brigade under the command of Brigadier General Lecor in action on 2 August 1813[779]

Camp 3 August 1813	Killed	Wounded				
	Privates	Ensign	Sergeant	Bugler	Privates	Total
2nd Caçadores Battalion	1	1	-	1	3	6
7th Infantry Regiment	-	-	-	-	-	-
19th Infantry Regiment	-	-	1	-	2	3
Total	1	1	1	1	5	9

Officers:
Ensign Antonio Maximo Figueira, slightly

Nicolão [sic] Colthurst
Brigade Major

Table 12.10: Portuguese Division. Return[780] of the Killed, Wounded, and Prisoners in the 2nd Infantry Brigade in the Action of 30 July 1813

Camp 31 July 1813	Killed												Wounded												Prisoners and Missing											
	Colonels	Lieutenant Colonels	Majors	Adjutants	Surgeons	Adjutant Surgeons	Captains	Lieutenants	Ensigns	Sergeants and *Furriés*	Drummers	Corporals and Privates	Colonels	Lieutenant Colonels	Majors	Adjutants	Surgeons	Adjutant Surgeons	Captains	Lieutenants	Ensigns	Sergeants and *Furriés*	Drummers	Corporals and Privates	Colonels	Lieutenant Colonels	Majors	Adjutants	Surgeons	Adjutant Surgeons	Captains	Lieutenants	Ensigns	Sergeants and *Furriés*	Drummers	Corporals and Privates
2nd Regiment	-	-	1	-	-	-	1	-	-	1	-	30	1	1	1	-	-	-	-	2	4	9	-	174	-	-	-	-	-	-	-	-	-	-	-	20
14th Regiment	-	-	-	1	-	-	-	-	-	-	-	21	-	1	1	-	-	-	2	1	-	1	-	53	-	-	-	-	-	-	-	-	-	-	-	18
Total	-	-	1	1	-	-	1	-	-	1	-	51	1	2	2	-	-	-	2	3	4	10	-	227	-	-	-	-	-	-	-	-	-	-	-	38

Ranks and names of the officers killed

2nd Regiment:
Brevet Lieutenant Colonel Lourenço Martins Pegado
Captain 1st Grenadier Company Dugald McGibbon

14th Regiment:
Adjutant José Maria Cabreira

Ranks and names of the officers wounded

Brigadier Antonio Hippolito Costa, severely

2nd Regiment:
Colonel Jorge de Avillez, broken leg
Lieutenant Colonel João Telles, bruised
Major Ray,[781] severely
Lieutenant Francisco Rebello de Moira, severely
Lieutenant João Nepomuceno, mortally[782]
Ensign Francisco de Paulla Cabrita, slightly
Ensign Bento Jozé Tavares, severely
Ensign Arcenio Pomppeu,[783] slightly
Ensign Francisco Jozé Furtado, severely

14th Regiment:
Lieutenant Colonel João [sic] McDonald, bruised
Major Francisco de Paulla de Brito, slightly
Captain Luiz Felipe,[784] dangerously
Captain Thomas Potter, slightly
Tenente Bartholomew Casey, slightly

Ranks and names of the officers missing

Observations

The 18 corporals and privates from the 14th Regiment who were made prisoners are from a detached company and it seems likely that they were wounded when taken by the enemy

Count de Amarante
Lieutenant General, Division's Commander

Table 12.11: Ashworth's Brigade. Infantry Brigade 6th, 18th and 6th Caçadores Battalion. Return[785] of the Killed, Wounded, Missing, and Prisoners in the action of 30 July 1813

Corps	Killed									Wounded									Missing and Prisoners									Total								
	Colonels	Lieutenant Colonels	Majors	Captains	Subalterns	Flag Bearers	Sergeants and *Furriés*	Musicians and Drummers	Corporals and Privates	Colonels	Lieutenant Colonels	Majors	Captains	Subalterns	Flag Bearers	Sergeants and *Furriés*	Musicians and Drummers	Corporals and Privates	Colonels	Lieutenant Colonels	Majors	Captains	Subalterns	Flag Bearers	Sergeants and *Furriés*	Musicians and Drummers	Corporals and Privates	Colonels	Lieutenant Colonels	Majors	Captains	Subalterns	Flag Bearers	Sergeants and *Furriés*	Musicians and Drummers	Corporals and Privates
6th Regiment	-	-	-	-	-	-	1	-	11	-	1	1	2	4	-	1	-	83	-	-	-	-	-	-	-	-	27	-	1	-	2	4	-	2	-	121
18th Regiment	-	-	-	-	-	-	2	-	23	1	1	1	-	2	-	4	1	124	-	-	-	-	-	-	-	-	35	1	1	1	-	2	-	6	1	182
6th Caçadores	-	-	-	-	-	-	-	-	7	-	-	1	3	2	-	2	2	50	-	-	-	-	-	-	-	-	19	-	-	1	3	2	-	2	2	76
Total	-	-	-	-	-	-	3	-	41	1	2	2	5	8	-	7	3	257	-	-	-	-	-	-	-	-	81	1	2	2	5	8	-	10	3	379

Killed: Ranks and names of the officers killed

Wounded: Ranks and names of the officers wounded

6th Regiment:
Lieutenant Colonel Maxwell Grant, slightly Captain João Joaquim,[786] slightly; Captain João [sic] Sutherland, severely; Lieutenant João Maria,[787] slightly; Lieutenant Manoel Joze da Cunha, slightly; Ensign Antonio Joaquim de Mendonça, slightly; Ensign Joze de Souza Pinto, severely

18th Regiment:
Colonel Manuel Pamplona,[788] severely; Lieutenant Colonel Henryique [sic] Pynn, dangerously; Major Francisco de Paula Biker, severely; Ensign Victorino Joze da Silva, dangerously; Ensign Antonio Vieira de Vasconcellos, slightly

6th Caçadores:
Major Samuel Mitchell, slightly; Captain W.H. Temple,[789] slightly; Captain Ricardo [sic] Brunton, slightly; Captain João Joze de Moraes, severely; Tenente Pio Manoel de Souza, severely[790], Ensign E.A. Barckhausen,[791] slightly

Missing and Prisoners: Ranks and names of the officers missing and prisoners

Total: Observations

Carlos [sic] Ashworth
Colonel, commander of the Brigade

Table 12.12: Ashworth's Brigade. Infantry Brigade 6th, 18th and 6th Caçadores Battalion. Return[792] of the Killed, Wounded, Missing, and Prisoners in the Action of 31 July 1813

Corps	Killed									Wounded									Missing and Prisoners									Total								
	Colonels	Lieutenant Colonels	Majors	Captains	Subalterns	Flag Bearers	Sergeants and *Furriéis*	Musicians and Drummers	Corporals and Privates	Colonels	Lieutenant Colonels	Majors	Captains	Subalterns	Flag Bearers	Sergeants and *Furriéis*	Musicians and Drummers	Corporals and Privates	Colonels	Lieutenant Colonels	Majors	Captains	Subalterns	Flag Bearers	Sergeants and *Furriéis*	Musicians and Drummers	Corporals and Privates	Colonels	Lieutenant Colonels	Majors	Captains	Subalterns	Flag Bearers	Sergeants and *Furriéis*	Musicians and Drummers	Corporals and Privates
6th Regiment	-	-	-	-	-	-	-	-	6	1	-	1	-	1	-	-	-	16	-	-	-	-	-	-	-	-	2	1	-	1	-	1	-	-	-	24
18th Regiment	-	-	-	-	-	-	-	-	-	-	-	-	-	-	-	-	-	1	-	-	-	-	-	-	-	-	-	-	-	-	-	-	-	-	-	1
6th Caçadores Battalion	-	-	-	-	-	-	-	-	1	-	-	-	-	-	-	-	-	2	-	-	-	-	-	-	-	-	-	-	-	-	-	-	-	-	-	3
Total	-	-	-	-	-	-	-	-	7	1	-	1	-	1	-	-	-	19	-	-	-	-	-	-	-	-	2	1	-	1	-	1	-	-	-	28
	Ranks and names of the officers killed									Ranks and names of the officers wounded									Ranks and names of the officers missing and prisoners									Observations								
										6th Regiment Colonel Carlos [sic] Ashworth, slightly Major Domingos Antonio Gil, slightly Ensign Joaquim Maria,[793] severely																										

Carlos [sic] Ashworth

Colonel, Commander of the brigade

Chapter 13

The Combats of 31 August 1813

After the battles of the Pyrenees, Soult spent most of August rebuilding and reorganizing his army. By late August he was able to field a force of 45,000 men in nine infantry divisions. On 31 August Soult attacked with his army across the Bidassoa river at several points, including San Marcial, Salain, Vera, Zugarramurdi, and Urdax, to relieve San Sebastian.

The main French assault was on the Heights of San Marcial, which was held by Spanish troops, with support from the 1st Division and Aylmer's Independent Brigade. No Portuguese troops fought at San Marcial, but they did fight in the other four actions. The 9th Brigade fought at Salain, while the 3rd Caçadores of the Light Division fought at Vera.[794] The 3rd Brigade saw action at Zugarramurdi and Ainhoué. The most heavily engaged was the 7th Brigade, which fought at Urdax and Ainhoué. At the same time the French were attacking, British and Portuguese troops were assaulting San Sebastian.

All the French attacks were beaten back, and San Sebastian was captured, except for its citadel.[795] The day was a bloody one for the Portuguese. Those opposing the French attacks lost 462 men killed, wounded, or missing. Those taking part in the assault on San Sebastian lost 670. Unfortunately, not all the casualty reports for the day could be found in the archives. These numbers are taken from the surviving reports plus those listed in Oman's History of the Peninsular War.[796]

Heights above Salain[797]

The 9th Brigade was deployed west of the village of Vera, along the Bidassoa river, when its picquets fired on Taupin's Division around 6 a.m. A heavy mist rising from the river obscured most of the skirmishing, but it lifted in time for Lieutenant Colonel James Miller, the acting commander of the 9th Brigade, to see the French move across the river. The Portuguese defended the slopes for several hours and Inglis's Brigade from the 7th Division was sent to support them. After fighting for four hours the Portuguese were forced to withdraw up the hill. About 10 a.m. the 23rd Infantry moved first and formed to the left of the British brigade. The 11th Infantry held its position until 11 a.m. and retreated to the right of the British brigade. Together the two brigades stopped Taupin's attack but could not hold Darmagnac's Division when it hit them on the flank. The French cautiously pursued them, but eventually withdrew back across the river.

Inglis commanded all the Allied forces there. After the fight he wrote to Dalhousie, the 7th Division commander, on 2 September: 'I find I have neglected requesting your Lordship would be pleased to mention to the Field Marshal that the Portuguese brigade distinguished themselves, and that I am under obligations to Colonel Miller, commanding it; and to Lieutenant-Colonel Anderson, commanding the 11th Portuguese regiment.'[798]

4th Division

9th Brigade (11th and 23rd Infantry, 7th Caçadores)

Report[799] from Lieutenant Colonel Miller to AG Mozinho

Sir,

I have the honour to report to you that yesterday, about six o'clock in the morning, noticing the enemy's movements to attack the position, which the brigade under my command was ordered to defend, I judged it to be my duty to immediately warn the Allied Army's Quartermaster General, Major General Murray.

As I had anticipated, the enemy started, by eight o'clock, to cross the river,[800] which was fordable in every part. By nine o'clock, the enemy columns, in considerable strength, started to attack the centre and flanks of my position, which, extending for one league, demanded all the caution, discipline and steadiness of this brigade, in order to resist the enemy for as long as necessary for the quartermaster general to make the required arrangements.

It is with the greatest satisfaction that I have to tell you that the brigade showed in a high degree all those qualities in the defence of the position until noon, when I thought it to be my duty to withdraw on the brigade of the 7th Division, commanded by Major General Inglis, which was sent to support me. I formed the 11th Regiment, under the command of Lieutenant Colonel Anderson, and the 23rd Regiment, under Major Peacocke, in line on the flanks of that brigade and covered my right flank with the 7th Caçadores Battalion, commanded by Major Lillie.[801]

It is also my duty to state to you, for the information of His Excellency, that the Brigade Major João [sic] Grant King assisted me throughout the action, directing the corps with great intelligence and intrepidity. I must also inform His Excellency the Marshal Marquis de Campo Maior that the corps commanders distinguished themselves performing their duties with activity and zeal and I'm obliged to them for the good outcome of the combat in which the gallantry of the defence matched the good order of the retreat.

I enclose the return[802] of the killed and wounded in the action that I regret to be considerable.

Today we returned to occupy the same position.

God save you, Sir

Camp of Bera 1 September 1813

Manoel de Brito Mozinho

J. Miller

Lieutenant Colonel 23rd Regiment, commanding the 9th Brigade, 4th Division

Vera

The 3rd Caçadores were the only Portuguese troops from the Light Division engaged on 31 August and 1 September. They were part of the force at Vera that attempted to prevent Vandermaesen from crossing the bridge over the Bidassoa river. No casualty returns could be found but Oman's History of the Peninsular War[803] states that the battalion had 8 killed, 12 wounded, and 2 missing.

Light Division

3rd Caçadores

Report[804] from Lieutenant Colonel Silveira to AG Mozinho

I have the honour to send you the return of the dead and wounded on 31 August and 1 September at the bridge of Bera, to lay before His Excellency the Marshal Marquis de Campo Maior. It is my duty to mention to His Excellency that my officers and men distinguished themselves as usual.

I must again recommend to His Excellency the Ensign Jozé Teixeira Pinto, who was wounded, he is the senior and I had already proposed him to lieutenant, as well as the Adjutant Sergeant, who being wounded in the first day refused to go to the rear and remained with the battalion until the end of the action. This distinguished conduct deserves His Excellency's attention.

God save you, Sir
Camp of Bera
2 September 1813
Manoel de Brito Mozinho
Brigadier and Adjutant General

Manuel Pinto da Silveira
Lieutenant Colonel 3rd Caçadores

Zugarramurdi and Urdax

Abbé's Division was on the French left flank and attacked east of the Great Rhune. Rémond's Brigade took Zugarramurdi, while Maucomble's Brigade moved into Urdax. Wellington had left specific instructions for the commanders of the 6th and 7th Divisions about what to do if the French attacked. Wellington was emphatic that the two generals should only make a demonstration against the French and should not commit their forces to an engagement where they might take serious casualties. Upon receiving word that the French were in Zugarramurdi, Lecor was ordered to move against them. Whether Lord Dalhousie chose to ignore Wellington's guidance or Lecor misunderstood his orders is unknown, but the 3rd Brigade attacked at daybreak[805] and 'drove the piquets of the enemy and followed them with great spirit as they drew back towards Ainhoué'.[806]

When word reached General Colville that a French brigade was in Urdax, he ordered Colonel Douglas, the acting commander of the 7th Brigade, to move his brigade to Urdax. Maucomble withdrew to Ainhoué, where he linked up with Rémond's Brigade. Both Lecor and Douglas followed the French to Ainhoué and instead of stopping their pursuit, they attacked the French. They were not able to take the French position and both brigades suffered heavy casualties.

7th Division

3rd Brigade (7th and 19th Infantry, 2nd Caçadores)

Report[807] from General Lecor to AG Mozinho

Sir,
I have the honour to enclose the return of the killed, wounded, and missing from the brigade under my command in the attack on the village of Zugarramurdi, on the 31st instant. In the morning of this day, by order of Lord Dalhousie, I attacked and dislodged the enemy from the village and the heights behind it. The French lost more than us in officers and men.

A company of the 7th Regiment advanced in extended order to flank the enemy position but advancing its right more than it should, a sergeant and eight men were surrounded and captured by a party of French skirmishers.

I cannot mention particularly any individual in the three corps under my command, because all of them did their duty.

Lieutenant Colonel Calheiros,[808] commanding the 7th Regiment, had his horse wounded and conducted himself with great intelligence, the same did Colonel Doyle, 19th Regiment, and Lieutenant Colonel Zulque [sic],[809] 2nd Caçadores Battalion.

After the enemy's retreat to the camp of Ainhoué I was relieved by a brigade from the 3rd Division, and I was ordered to march to Echalar, and today to Lesaca, where I am now with the brigade under my command.

God save you, Sir

Camp of Lesaca, 1 September 1813

Manoel de Brito Mozinho

Carlos Francisco Lecor
Major General

See Table 13.1.

6th Division

7th Brigade (8th and 12th Infantry, 9th Caçadores)

See Table 13.2.

Table 13.1: Return[810] of the Killed, Wounded, and Prisoners in the 3rd Brigade, 7th Division, in the action of 31 August 1813 around the Village of Zagaramurdi [sic]

Camp 1 September 1813	Killed					Wounded			Prisoners		Total
	Captains	Lieutenants	Ensigns	Sergeants	Privates	Ensigns	Sergeants	Privates	Sergeants	Privates	Total
2nd Caçadores Battalion			1		4	1	2	17			25
7th Infantry Regiment					3		2	28	1	8	42
19th Infantry Regiment	1	1			3	2	2	10			19
Total	1	1	1		10	3	6	55	1	8	85

Names of the officers killed:
 Captain João [sic] Ross[811]
 Lieutenant Leslie[812]
 Ensign Francisco Joze Lourenço

Names of the officers wounded:
 Ensign Antonio do Prado,[813] slightly
 Ensign João Vitorino Pereira, slightly
 Ensign Jullio Cézar Augusto, severely[814]

Nicolão [sic] Colthurst
Brigade Major

Table 13.2: 7th Brigade. Return[815] of the Killed, Wounded, Missing and Prisoners in the Infantry Brigade 8th, 12th and 9th Caçadores in the Action of 31 August 1813

	Killed								Wounded								Missing and Prisoners								Total							
	Colonels	Lieutenant Colonels	Majors	Captains	Subalterns	Sergeants	Drummers	Corporals and Privates	Colonels	Lieutenant Colonels	Majors	Captains	Subalterns	Sergeants	Drummers	Corporals and Privates	Colonels	Lieutenant Colonels	Majors	Captains	Subalterns	Sergeants	Drummers	Corporals and Privates	Colonels	Lieutenant Colonels	Majors	Captains	Subalterns	Sergeants	Drummers	Corporals and Privates
9th Caçadores					1		1	6					2	1	1	23								2					2	1	2	31
8th Regiment						2		33	1	1		1	3	6		102								30	1	1		1	4	8		165
12th Regiment								6				1	1			25												1	1			31
Total					1	2	1	45	1	1		2	6	7		150								32	1	1		2	7	9	2	227

Observations

Names and ranks of the officers killed

Lieutenant Manoel Alexandre Santa Clara

Names and ranks of the officers wounded

8th Regiment:
Colonel João [sic] Douglas,[816] severely
Lieutenant Colonel Rafael Ouzoley [sic], severely
Captain Connor, severely[817]
Adjutant João Luis Thomas slightly
Ensign Joaquim Manoel Mascarenhas, severely
Ensign Alexandre Jorge,[818] severely
12th Regiment:
Captain Francisco da Silva Teixeira Pinto, severely
Lieutenant João Maria da Fonseca, severely
9th Caçadores:
Brevet Lieutenant Ignacio Ferreira, severely
Ensign Dom Henrique de Menezes, severely

Names and ranks of the officers missing and prisoners

J Green[819]
Acting Brigade Major

Chapter 14

The October Battles: Banca and the Crossing of the Bidassoa River

The month of September was quiet for Wellington's Army. Wellington was reluctant to push into France for several reasons. The first was that the French still had a sizeable force in Pamplona. Although under a blockade, they could wreak havoc in his rear if he took the bulk of his army over the Pyrenees. The second consideration was political. He was unsure what was happening in Central Europe. If the armistice held, Napoleon might shift troops to reinforce Soult's Army, but if hostilities broke out again, he knew that there was little chance of this happening. So Wellington waited for news. He finally received official word on 15 September that the fighting in Central Europe had started again and he could resume the offensive.

Meanwhile, Soult had been very active and had fortified the likely approaches into France. He occupied a 40km front from the Atlantic Ocean to the upper Nive river. His left flank was high in the mountains, guarding the passes there. His right flank was on the Atlantic Ocean, overlooking the Bidassoa river. Soult thought his positions on the Bidassoa were impregnable and so had most of his army protecting the passes through the Pyrenees. Wellington had the Bidassoa estuary thoroughly scouted and found that it was passable in several places at low tide. Knowing that an assault on the passes would cause heavy casualties, he decided to attack across the Bidassoa instead. On 30 September he ordered a diversionary attack by the Portuguese Division on the French position overlooking Banca. Six days later Wellington attacked across the Bidassoa estuary.

The Attack at Banca, France, 1 October 1813

The Portuguese Division was in the vicinity of Aldudes, France, when it was ordered to attack at Banca, a small village between the Maya and Roncesvalles Passes. The attack had no purpose other than to instil in Soult's mind that Wellington's main attack would be against those passes. The plan was complex, with two flanking columns sent to conduct a night march to get behind the French lines. Lieutenant Colonel John McDonald[820] was to lead a detachment around the eastern flank of the French lines, while Lieutenant Colonel Donald McNeill[821] was to move around the western flank. The objective of both these marches was to be in a position to cut off the retreat of the French garrison when the Portuguese Division attacked. The exact composition of the two detachments is not known, but each likely consisted of their brigades' four grenadier companies. The strength of the two detachments was about 500 men each.

The attack began on the night of 30 September. There was little light because it was a new moon and it had set by 9 p.m.. Not surprisingly, the column under MacDonald got lost but arrived at the Rock of Arrola about 2 a.m. and took the French fortifications there. Lieutenant Colonel McNeill's detachment made it around the French right flank and was in the Baigorrey valley when Buchan's 2nd Brigade launched its assault. The attack was a success, and the French garrison was captured.

Portuguese Division

2nd and 4th Brigades

Letter[822] from General Campbell, Acting Commander of the Portuguese Division, to AG Mozinho

Sir,
I have the honour to enclose, for the information of His Excellency the Marshal Marquis de Campo Maior, a copy of a report that I sent to Lieutenant General Sir Rowland Hill on the attack made yesterday against the enemy posts in Banca Valley by detachments of the Portuguese Division under my command, whose conduct I hope deserves the approbation of His Excellency.
God save you, Sir
Aldudes 2 October 1813
Manoel de Brito Mozinho
Army's Adjutant General

A. Campbell
Brigadier General

Copy[823] in Portuguese of a Report from General Campbell, Acting Commander of the Portuguese Division, to General Hill

Copy
Aldudes 2 October 1813
According to the instructions that yesterday I had the honour to receive from Your Excellency, I arranged the means to surprise the enemy's posts and pickets in the Banca valley.

I ordered Lieutenant Colonel McDonald, 14th Regiment, with a detachment of the 2nd Brigade, to flank the enemy's position on our right, and Lieutenant Colonel McNeill, 10th Regiment, with another detachment from the 4th Brigade, to flank it on the left. The former went by the Arrola Mountain[824] and the latter by the left of the Huessa Mountain.[825]

Lieutenant Colonel McDonald, due to the excessive darkness of the night, lost his way for a short time and was surprised to found himself, at 2 a.m., close to the strong enemy post of the Rock of Arrola; any alarm from this post would have ruined all our projects against the posts in the valley, therefore the lieutenant colonel with his characteristic quickness of decision and intrepid conduct settled to attack and carry the post by assault. In the moment the enemy discovered the party, he rushed forward with two grenadier companies under Captain D. Campbell,[826] 2nd Regiment. They had no ladders, so they climbed on the shoulders of some of their men to penetrate the post, [and] bayoneted almost every enemy without any musket being discharged; the garrison was made of 75 men of the National Guard. Lieutenant Colonel McDonald reported that Captain D. Campbell conducted himself with incredible gallantry. After this enterprise, the detachment moved to the intended point beyond Banca, to which both detachments arrived soon before dawn without being perceived and both commanders took a judicious position to cut off and capture the enemy's picquets.

At dawn Brigadier General Buchan ordered parties from our line to advance and dislodge the enemy, who began to retreat from Banca by the road to Baigorrey[827] where the detachments of Lieutenant Colonels McDonald and McNeill were posted. After some resistance 70 enemy soldiers surrendered and it would have been more if I was acquainted with the hour of the change of the posts, which had taken place a few hours before, and the old picquet had already gone to Baigorrey. The French captain and lieutenant commanding at Banca were killed refusing to surrender even after seeing their men do it.

We did not have anyone killed, but I truly regret to inform Your Excellency that Lieutenant Colonel McDonald was severely wounded; hopefully he is out of danger but I'm afraid we will lose the benefits of his invaluable services, which Your Excellency knows so well that any recommendation is superfluous. I have the honour to be, Sir, your most humble and obedient servant

A. Campbell
Brigadier General

P.S. Lieutenant Colonel McDonald's detachment destroyed an arms depot in the Rock of Arrola. Lieutenant Colonel McNeill's another in Banca.

The Attack across the Bidassoa River, 7 October 1813

On 7 October Wellington attacked across the Bidassoa river. The attack had two prongs. The primary attack was conducted by the 1st and 5th Divisions, and the 1st Brigade across the estuary of the Bidassoa. The second prong was at Vera and consisted of the Light Division and three Spanish divisions.

The 3rd Brigade, commanded by Colonel do Rego Barreto, was part of the main attack. The 5th Division began moving across the estuary at 7:25 a.m., which was low tide. The movement was virtually unopposed, and they took few casualties. They climbed the heights near Hendaye and once there moved south along the crest. This move outflanked the French forces opposing the 1st Division's and the 1st Brigade's attack.

The attack by the Light Division at Vera did not go as well. Its mission was to take the Great Rhune, a heavily fortified height that rises about 800m above the valley below. It was defended by 15,000 French. The Light Division would attack up the western flank, while the Spanish would attack the eastern slopes. Participating in the attack were the 1st and 3rd Caçadores and the 17th Infantry. The fighting was brutal, and the Portuguese took heavy casualties. Among those killed was the commander of the 1st Caçadores, Lieutenant Colonel John Algeo.

To draw attention away from the main effort at the Bidassoa estuary, Wellington ordered Colville's 6th Division, which was in the vicinity of Urdax, to make a demonstration against the French forces just across the border. It was to make a limited attack and avoid taking casualties. Douglas's 7th Brigade was part of the feint. The Portuguese soldiers pressed their attack too enthusiastically and took heavy casualties. Wellington was furious and wrote on 10 October that 'I am sorry to be obliged to express my disapprobation of the conduct of an officer of whom I have always entertained a good opinion; but I must say, that is unworthy of one of his reputation to get his brigade into scrapes, for the sake of the little gloriole of driving in a few piquets, knowing, as he must do, that is not intended he should engage in a serious affair …'[828]

5th Division

3rd Brigade (3rd and 15th Infantry, 8th Caçadores)

Report[829] from Colonel Barreto to AG Mozinho

Sir,
I have the honour to report to you for the information of His Excellency Marshal Beresford Marquis de Campo Maior, on the conduct of the 3rd Brigade under my command on 7 October. The 5th Division was formed in three columns to cross the Bidassoa River by three different fords. The 3rd [Portuguese] Brigade was the centre column and its first objective, once the river was crossed, was the village of Hendaye and after achieving it, to attack from the right an enemy battery posted on a height to the right of that village.

In consequence, the brigade crossed the river in contiguous columns with the Caçadores up front in extended order, all in the best order possible. Immediately after the brigade attacked and took Hendaye and proceeded to evict the enemy from the several heights where he tried to resist. All these movements were executed with great regularity and promptitude, until, achieving our goals we were ordered to halt.

I am completely satisfied witnessing that all individuals did the utmost to carry out their duties, however, despite the good conduct of all, I must beg leave to particularly bring to His Excellency's attention the conduct of Captain Joaquim Antonio Duarte, by the intelligent and conspicuous manner he commanded the 8th Caçadores Battalion[830] during the skirmishes, and that of Major Campbell,[831] who commanded and directed the 15th Infantry Regiment in a most exemplary manner. Also the conspicuous conduct of Lieutenant Colonel Luiz Diogo Pereira Forjaz, commanding a battalion of the 3rd Regiment, deserves His Excellency's approbation; this officer took command of the regiment when Colonel McCreagh was detached with a battalion, by order of the general commanding the division, to protect the artillery; Captain Brackenbury, Aide-de-Camp to General Spry,[832] distinguished himself as he usually does; Brigade Major Carlos [sic] FitzGerald[833] carried out his duties with intelligence and bravery for which he deserves great praise; Captain João Correia Guedes, 15th Regiment, despite not fully recovered from a shell wound suffered when he was a prisoner in San Sebastian, seeing that the regiment was short on officers, volunteered himself and commanded the First Grenadier Company of the 15th Regiment with great bravery.[834] Lieutenant João Antonio Correia Sepulveda, First Grenadier Company of the 15th Regiment, also deserves His Excellency's approbation. Ensign Antonio Peito de Carvalho, 15th Regiment, was very useful to me and he is a meritorious officer; Lieutenant Domingos de Sá Farinha, 8th Caçadores Battalion, distinguished himself in a most conspicuous manner, being lately recommended by his lieutenant colonel[835] for the assault on San Sebastian; Captain Alexandre Marcelino,[836] First Grenadier Company 3rd Regiment, also behaved very well.

God save you, Sir
Camp of Hendaye, 9 October 1813
Manoel de Brito Mozinho

Luiz do Rego Barretto
Colonel[837] commander of the 3rd Brigade

See Table 14.1.

1st Brigade (Independent) (1st and 16th Infantry, 4th Caçadores)

Report[838] from General Wilson to AG Mozinho

Sir,
I have the honour to enclose the return of the casualties in the brigade under my command on the morning of the 7th instant, during the passage of the Bidassoa. Despite the circumstances under which the brigade was employed I am gratified that their number is so small. On this occasion, I have the pleasure to state to you that the general conduct of the corps of this brigade was in accordance with the best I could wish for. I am in debt to the officers in my staff for the assistance they gave me.

The 4th Caçadores Battalion and the 1st Infantry Regiment chanced to be more particularly employed on this occasion and I enclose the reports sent to me by their commanders, all to be laid before His Excellency the Marshal Marquis de Campo Maior.

God save you, Sir
Camp in the Heights of Urogne,[839] 8 October 1813
Manoel de Brito Mozinho

John Wilson
Brigadier General

P.S. I deem it unnecessary to mention the two pieces of artillery in an enemy's redoubt on our left, which the 1st Regiment left behind without reclaiming them in consequence of the rapidity of movements required at the occasion.

1st Infantry

Report[840] from Major O'Hara to General Wilson

Sir,

I have the honour to report to you that every individual in the regiment under my orders carried out gallantly his duty in yesterday's combat. The First Grenadier Company and its commander Captain MacIntosh [sic],[841] deserve a particular mention. I recommend to you that officer.

God save you, Sir

Camp on the right [bank] of the Bidassoa, 8 October 1813

Brigadier Wilson

1st Brigade commander

Walter O'Hara
Major Commander 1st Regiment

4th Caçadores

Report[842] from Lieutenant Colonel Williams to General Wilson

Sir,

A few days ago I had the honour to request that you lay before His Excellency the Marshal the recommendation of Lieutenant Thomás Theotonio[843] to the vacant company in my battalion, now a more strong reason compels me to recommend him by his gallant conduct in the passage of the Bidassoa River in which he was severely wounded.

I beg leave also to recommend Captain Alexandre [sic] McGregor, who took command of his company, despite being very ill due to the wounds suffered at the battles of Salamanca and Vitoria and distinguished himself for the time the action lasted.

The conduct of Captain Caetano Alberto de Souza Canavarro, both in the passage of the river and in the attack, was very conspicuous leading his skirmishers, whence I beg leave to recommend him.

Major Adamson commanding three companies, directed them brilliantly, skirmishing with the enemy.

God save you, Sir

Camp near Urogne, 10 October 1813

Brigadier João [sic] Wilson

E.K. Williams
Lieutenant Colonel 4th Caçadores

Light Division (1st and 3rd Caçadores, 17th Infantry)

Letter[844] from AQMG Harvey, Portuguese Army, to AG Mozinho

Headquarters at Vera 17 October 1813

Sir,

I have the honour to enclose an extract of a letter from Lieutenant Colonel Colborne, commander of the brigade that includes the 1st and 3rd Caçadores Battalions, to be laid before His Excellency the Marshal Marquis de Campo Maior.

I transmit to you for the information of His Excellency, the officers' names that, according to the General Orders of the British Army from the 10th and 15th instant, should enter in the Portuguese service, and also one captain who should leave it to return to the British army.

God save you, Sir

Manoel de Brito Mozinho

Robert John Harvey
Lieutenant Colonel AQMG

Extract[845] of Lieutenant Colonel John Colborne's letter

Translation of an Extract from a letter from Lieutenant Colonel Colborne, Commander of the brigade that includes the 1st and 3rd Caçadores Battalions

Camp 10 October 1813
I beg leave to report on the gallant conduct of some officers of the Caçadores, immediately under my own observation, in the attack on the heights above Vera's church.

The enemy's position could only be approached by a narrow piece of ground which was defended by some redoubts. According to orders, the 1st and 3rd Caçadores Battalions moved up and flanked the enemy's position in an admirable manner. Captains Dobbin[846] and Kirk,[847] 3rd Battalion, who led the first companies, conducted themselves with great gallantry and knowledge of their service. Lieutenant Leitão,[848] from the same battalion, Lieutenant Sobral[849] and Ensign Costa, 1st Battalion, are brave officers who led their men with the greatest resolution against the redoubts.

Adjutants Lisboa,[850] 1st Battalion, and Chrizostomo,[851] 3rd Battalion, and Sergeant Carneiro were very active and their conduct exemplary.

Lieutenant Colonel Algeo[852] died leading his battalion in the attack; this lieutenant colonel's conduct and that of Lieutenant Colonel Silveira[853] was most conspicuous.

1st Caçadores

Report[854] from Major Barros to AG Mozinho

Sir,
I have the honour to transmit to you the enclosed return of the killed and wounded in this battalion in combat on the 7th instant. I must assure you that words cannot describe the conduct of all officers and men in this combat and I am sure they deserved the brigade commander's approbation. Lieutenant Manuel Antonio Sobral commanding a skirmishing party from his company had the opportunity to flank two enemy pieces, which were posted in a high point, and seized them and the enemy party which protected the pieces. Lieutenant Sobral,[855] with his sword, fought and killed two enemy officers. With this party were Adjutant Sergeant João Ramillio and First Sergeant Grigorio Joze dos Santos, who supported the lieutenant in such a praiseworthy manner that I judge all of them worthy of His Excellency the Marshal Marquis of Campo Maior's greatest attention. I also must mention the deepest sorrow felt in this battalion due to the death of Lieutenant Colonel Algeo, who was widely respected for his human qualities and military knowledge. He was killed at the first redoubt seized by the battalion. I beg leave to request that you lay this report before His Excellency the Marshal.
God save you, Sir
Camp at Saint Jean de Luz, 8 October 1813
Manoel de Brito Mozinho

António Lobo Teixeira de Barros[856]
Major

3rd Caçadores

Report[857] from Lieutenant Colonel Silveira to AG Mozinho

I have the honour to enclose the return of the killed and wounded in the battalion under my command in the combat on the Heights of Vera on the 7th instant. It is my duty to report to you, for His Excellency, the Marshal Marquis de Campo Maior's information, that my officers, inferior officers,[858] and men fought with such bravery that induced admiration among all in the brigade, which, I believe, our commander will confirm.

I must praise the conduct of Lieutenant Antonio Correia Leitão, who I have recommended for captain a month ago,[859] and that of Ensign Joaquim Antonio Severo, who volunteered to join the advance party, and was severely wounded, deserves the attention of His Excellency, the Marshal Marquis de Campo Maior. I also must recommend Adjutant Sergeant Thadeo Luiz, who behaved with such gallantry, making himself worthy of His Excellency's consideration.[860] Likewise, soldier Jozé Joaquim Pinto distinguished himself, volunteering to join the advance party. About a month ago, I sent to Lieutenant General Lemos[861] this soldier's justification documents to become cadet. For his distinction and valour, he deserves His Excellency's attention.
God save you, Sir
Camp of Vera, 8 October 1813
Manoel de Brito Mozinho
Brigadier Army's Adjutant General

Manoel Pinto da Silveira
Lieutenant Colonel

17th Infantry

See Table 14.2.

6th Division

7th Brigade[862] (8th and 12th Infantry, 9th Caçadores)

See Table 14.3.

Table 14.1: 3rd Brigade. Return[863] of the Casualties in the Combat with the Enemy on 7 October 1813

Camp in France 7 October 1813	Killed	Wounded					Missing
	Privates	Lieutenant	Ensign	Sergeant	Privates	Privates	Privates
3rd Regiment	1	-	-	1	2		1
15th Regiment	-	-	-	-	2		-
8th Battalion	-	1	1	-	12		5
Total	1	1	1	1	16		6

Officers wounded:
  Lieutenant Joze Vellez Cardozo, severely
  Ensign Placido Joaquim,[864] severely

Luiz do Rego Barretto
Brigade Commander

Table 14.2: 17th Infantry. Return[865] of the Killed, Wounded and Missing in the Action of 7 October 1813

Ranks	Names	Killed	Wounded		Prisoners	Missing
			Severely	Slightly		
Lieutenant	John Augusto [sic] Mathison[866]			1		
Inferior Officers						
Privates		3	3	7		
	Totals	3	3	8		1

Camp of Okalarre, 8 October 1813

John Rolt
Lieutenant Colonel 17th Infantry Regiment Command

Table 14.3: 7th Infantry Brigade Composed of the 8th and 12th Regiments and the 9th Caçadores. Return[867] of the Killed, Wounded, Missing and Prisoners in the Brigade in the Battle at the Heights of Urdax on 7 October 1813

Quarter at Urdax 7 October 1813	Killed									Wounded									Missing and Prisoners									Total								
	Colonels	Lieutenant Colonels	Majors	Captains	Subalterns	Flag Bearers	Sergeants and *Furriés*	Musicians and Drummers	Corporals and Privates	Colonels	Lieutenant Colonels	Majors	Captains	Subalterns	Flag Bearers	Sergeants and *Furriés*	Musicians and Drummers	Corporals and Privates	Colonels	Lieutenant Colonels	Majors	Captains	Subalterns	Flag Bearers	Sergeants and *Furriés*	Musicians and Drummers	Corporals and Privates	Colonels	Lieutenant Colonels	Majors	Captains	Subalterns	Flag Bearers	Sergeants and *Furriés*	Musicians and Drummers	Corporals and Privates
9th Caçadores				2			1		9					3		2		21									3				2	3		3		33
8th Regiment					1		1		10					4		4		65									1					5		5		76
12th Regiment					1				3				1			1		28				1	1				4				2	2		1		35
Total				2	2		2		22				1	7		7		114				1	1				8				4	10		9		144

Ranks and names of the officers killed

Brevet Major Antonio Luiz Sarmento, 9th Caçadores
Captain G.W. Cumming,[868] 9th Caçadores
Lieutenant Murphy,[869] 8th Regiment
Brevet Lieutenant João Joze Baraxo,[870] 12th Regiment

Ranks and names of the officers wounded

Lieutenant Joaquim de Pinho Souza, 4th Company, 9 th Caçadores, slightly
Lieutenant, Antonio Simplício,[871] 1st Company, 9th Caçadores, severely
Brevet Lieutenant Lourenço Joze de Andrade, 1st Company, 9th Caçadores, severely
Lieutenant Manoel Pereira,[872] 8th Regiment, slightly
Ensign Joze Caetano Vivas, 8th Regiment, severely
Ensign Antonio Pita de Castro,[873] 8th Regiment, severely
Ensign Carlos Guedes, 8th Regiment, severely
Captain João Antonio Teixeira de Sampaio, 12th Regiment, severely

Ranks and names of the officers missing and prisoners

Captain Bento Joze da Veiga Cabral, 12th Regiment
Ensign Joze Maria de Souza, 12th Regiment

Observations

Colonel George Brown's[874] horse, 9th Caçadores, was wounded.
Adjutant Luis Ignacio de Goveia's horse, 8th Regiment, was severely wounded

A Simpson[875]
Acting Brigade Major

Chapter 15

The Battle of Nivelle, 10 November 1813

After taking the north bank of the Bidassoa river on 7 October, Wellington made plans for invading France. Soult knew that he did not have the means to conduct offensive operations and had built a line of fortifications based on the Nivelle river from its mouth at Saint-Jean-de-Luz to Espelette 35km to the east. The positions had to cover the passes through the Pyrenees to the mouth of the Nivelle river.

Soult had learned his lesson from the Allies' crossing of the Bidassoa and the western sector of the lines were anchored on Fort Socoa, 2km south of Saint-Jean-de-Luz, and stretched along the south bank of the Nivelle for about 15km as far as Ascain. In the centre of the lines was the Lesser Rhune,[876] a mountain peak 600m high. This is dominated by the Greater Rhune,[877] which lies south of it and towers over it at 900m elevation. Between the two mountains is a steep valley. Any force attacking from the Greater Rhune had to descend 400m into a valley and then climb 200m to reach the Lesser Rhune. The eastern flank of the lines began in the valleys to the east of the Lesser Rhune and continued to Ainhoué[878] and the bridge at Amot.[879] To defend these fortifications, Soult had about 60,000 men. D'Erlon was responsible for the lines to the east with two divisions, Clausel defended the centre with three divisions, while Reille defended from the sea to the positions at Ascain with four divisions.

Wellington had 82,000 men in fifteen divisions: 8 Allied, 1 Portuguese, and 6 Spanish. On paper this gave the Allies 4 to 3 odds, which was not considered sufficient to capture fortified positions. Wellington knew this and chose to mass his forces against the centre of the French line. Feints would be made by smaller forces against the French in the west to pin them in place and prevent them from reinforcing the defenders in the centre. Wellington divided his army into three parts. Hill would be responsible for the attacks in the east. He had the 2nd and 6th Divisions, the Portuguese Division, and two Spanish divisions. In the west was Lieutenant General John Hope, who had replaced Graham.[880] He had the 1st and 5th Divisions, Aylmer's Independent British Brigade, the 1st Brigade, and two Spanish divisions. Beresford was given command of the centre, but since this was the main effort, Wellington was also there. His force included the 3rd, 4th, and 7th Divisions, the Light Division, the 10th Brigade, and two Spanish divisions.

Every Portuguese unit assigned to Wellington's Army would be involved in the battle: almost 25,000 men. Additionally, when the commander of the 7th Division returned to England in late October, as a sign of his confidence in his Portuguese officers Wellington appointed General Lecor its acting commander.[881] This was the first time a Portuguese officer had been given command of a division containing British troops.

Wellington's forces were in place by 9 November and that night there was almost a full moon,[882] which helped the troops move into their starting positions. The attack began at daybreak, about 6 a.m.[883] In the west Hope's force made a demonstration against the right flank of the French lines, but never pressed home the attacks. In the centre the Light Division took the Lesser Rhune, while the 3rd, 4th, and 7th Divisions assaulted the lines to the east of the mountain. On Wellington's right flank Hill's troops were late in starting their attack and did not begin their assault until 9 a.m. They too pushed the French out of their positions. By the end of the day the French had abandoned all their lines along the Nivelle river and moved about 15km to the north side of the Nive river. The Allies were now in France in large numbers.

The Left Wing

Hope's mission was to convince the French commander in the area that there was a threat to his flank and by doing so prevent him from sending help to the centre of the French lines. Hope ordered the 5th Division and 1st Brigade to clear the French advance outposts around Saint Jean de Luz, then bring the French fortifications under fire, but not assault them. The 1st Division and Aylmer's Brigade were to do the same for the fortifications further east. The 3rd Brigade was on the right of the 5th Division's attack and the 1st Brigade was to their right. After clearing the outposts, the 3rd Brigade moved closer to the French lines. The 8th Caçadores took some buildings near the bridge across the Nivelle and were counter-attacked several times by the French. The French abandoned Saint Jean de Luz that night. They spiked their guns and partially destroyed the bridge across the river.

5th Division

3rd Brigade (3rd and 15th Infantry, 8th Caçadores)

Report[884] from Colonel Barreto to AG Mozinho

Sir,
I have the honour to report to you, for the information of His Excellency, the Marshal Commander-in-Chief, Marquis de Campo Maior, that on the 11th I received an order, from the general commanding the Division,[885] to leave behind the 15th Infantry Regiment to cover the artillery and march with the rest of the brigade, by the 2nd Brigade's right, to evict some enemy troops from a very thick wood, which laid in front of the hill where the French camp was, and to flank it by the left to reach a wall, which was in the range of the artillery of the Saint Jean de Luz Fort and of that posted on a fortified hill that protected the fort. All these movements were executed to the approbation of the division commander.

I beg leave to mention particularly the conduct of Lieutenant Domingos de Sá Farinha, 8th Caçadores, who repulsed three French attacks on his post which was established in a house, an important point located between the bridge and the castle. On that night he was the first to discover the enemy's retreat and the first to enter Saint Jean de Luz Fort. This officer deserves His Excellency's consideration. I have the honour to enclose the return of the killed and wounded.
God save you, Sir
Guéthary, 13 November 1813
Manoel de Brito Mozinho

Luiz do Rego Barretto
Colonel, Brigade Commander

See Table 15.1.

1st Brigade (Independent)

See Table 15.2.

The Centre

The Allied Army deployed for its attack on the Lesser Rhune with the Light Division on the left tasked with the mission of taking it. To their right was Giron's Spanish Division, then the 4th, 7th, and 3rd Divisions. The mission of these four divisions was to clear the French fortifications to the right of the Lesser Rhune and seize the bridge at Amotz. Bradford was in reserve. There were more than 10,800 Portuguese troops in this attack. The assaults succeeded in taking the fortifications and by the end of the day the Allied soldiers were over the Nivelle river.

Light Division (1st and 3rd Caçadores, 17th Infantry)

The soldiers were fed at 2 a.m. and moved within 200m of the French picquets. Instead of attacking in two brigade columns, the Light Division would attack up the southeastern side of the Lesser Rhune with the 43rd Foot. The two rifle battalions were to pressure the southern slope of the Lesser Rhune, and the 52nd Foot was to swing around the western edge of the mountain and attack up the western slopes. The 17th Portuguese Infantry was in support of the 43rd Foot, while the 1st and 3rd Caçadores supported the 52nd Foot.

The initial assault by the 43rd Foot went well, and captured the first line of fortifications, but the men bogged down trying to clear the ones behind it. The 17th Infantry moved up in support. Once the 17th Infantry was committed, the 52nd Foot's assault on the western flank of the Lesser Rhune went in, behind the last line of fortifications. The French, being almost surrounded, withdrew. After taking the Lesser Rhune, the 52nd Foot, the Rifles, and the caçadores were sent to assault the next line of fortifications, which they eventually took after suffering heavy casualties.

1st Caçadores

Report[886] from Lieutenant Colonel Snodgrass to AG Mozinho

Sir,
I have the honour to report to you, for the information of His Excellency, Marshal Beresford, Marquis de Campo Maior, that the battalion under my command, on the 10th instant, placed on the Division's left, was particularly engaged in turning the enemy's fortifications. That was the reason for our loss being lower than the other corps which attacked frontally. I must attest to you that I have every reason to be satisfied with the conduct of all officers and men.

I wish to recommend particularly Captain Joze da Roza e Souza, who was severely wounded; Lieutenant Joaquim Achioli da Fonceca,[887] commanding the 5th Company, Lieutenant Manoel Antonio Sobral, commanding the 1st Company on that day, replacing the Captain, who performed the duties of major, and also 1st Sergeant Grigorio Joze dos Santos, 3rd Company. The aforementioned officers are the seniors in their ranks, so if His Excellency the Marshal condescends to promote Captain Manoel Jorge Rodrigues, who also showed zeal and valour, to major, for which he already had been recommended by former commanders, I hope His Excellency will consider the merits of those officers. I enclose the return of the killed and wounded on the 10th.
God save you, Sir
Camp of Arbonne, 12 November 1813
Manoel de Brito Mozinho

K Snodgrass
Lieutenant Colonel, commander 1st Caçadores

3rd Caçadores

Report[888] from Major Pinto to AG Mozinho

Sir
I have the honour to report to you that the battalion temporarily under my command behaved on the 10th instant in a manner that enhanced the glory which the corps had already acquired. The conduct of all the individuals was magnificent but the occasion allowed some of them, particularly those who were with the advanced skirmishing parties, to distinguish themselves. By the zeal and valour showed, I beg leave to particularly mention Captain Guilherme [sic] Dobbin, Lieutenants Affonço Botelho, Joaquim Pedro Sigurado

and Joze Joaquim Teixeira Pinto, the last two being severely wounded;[889] Lieutenant Joze Joaquim Teixeira Pinto with the party under his command captured 60 to 70 enemy soldiers. I also must recommend Sergeants Antonio Alves da Fraga and João Joze Rodrigues; both volunteered for the advanced parties and showed great bravery, the latter was severely wounded. I humbly beg you to lay this report before His Excellency.

God save you, Sir

Quarter in Ahetze, 16 November 1813

Manoel de Brito Mozinho

Brigadier General the Army's Adjutant General

Manuel Caetano Teixeira Pinto
Major, 3rd Caçadores

17th Infantry

See Table 15.3.

4th Division

The 4th Division assaulted in a column of brigades. Anson's Brigade led and took the Ste Barbe Redoubt. After this was taken, the 9th Brigade deployed to the right of it and marched northward. It was not long before they came across two redoubts that protected Sare. The fighting was furious and the 7th Caçadores took heavy casualties before the redoubts fell. After securing the village, the 9th Brigade followed Anson's Brigade as it continued north. They were part of the attack that outflanked the abattis that caused the 6th Division so many problems.

9th Brigade (11th and 23rd Infantry, 7th Caçadores)

Report[890] from Colonel Sá to AG Mozinho

Sir,

The noble conduct of the 9th Brigade, which is temporarily under my command, on the 10th instant, had increased its reputation, acquired in similar occasions, that is already remarkably high. I beg leave to require that you lay before His Excellency the Marshal Marquis de Campo Maior the enclosed reports sent to me by the corps' commanders. I personally witnessed the distinguished conduct of the individuals mentioned in those reports, particularly the gallantry shown by Captain Francisco de Paulla Rozado, 7th Caçadores.[891]

Lieutenant Colonels Miller, commanding the 23rd Regiment, and Anderson, commanding the 11th Regiment, whose zeal and gallantry made them praiseworthy, the latter was bruised. It is my duty to mention particularly the services of Major Lillie, commanding the 7th Caçadores, who directed the battalion in combat in a most intelligent manner and kept it in good order throughout the day.

I must also mention particularly the conduct of Brigade Major King[892] in all the points of the fight; his zeal, activity, and valour make him worthy of the consideration of His Excellency, the Marshal.

Ensign João Antonio Rebocho, 23rd Regiment, acted as my Aide-de-Camp, and I sent him forward with the caçadores to inform me on the enemy's movements and the events at the front. He carried out these duties with great intelligence and activity and deserves the attention of His Excellency, the Marshal.

The Brigade Surgeon, David MacLagan, established the brigade hospital in the village of Sare and with great activity and order, took such effective measures to attend the wounded, that after a quarter of an hour none of them could be found on the field. He continued to follow the brigade and exposed himself to the enemy fire to assist the wounded. His conduct deserves the particular attention of His Excellency.

I enclose the return of the casualties in the brigade on this day.

God save you, Sir

Camp, Bois de S. Pée, 12 November 1813

Manoel de Brito Mozinho

Joze de Vasconcellos
Colonel,[893] 9th Brigade commander

11th Infantry

Report[894] from Lieutenant Colonel Anderson to Colonel Sá

Sir,

I have the honour to report to you for the information of His Excellency, the Marshal Marquis de Campo Maior, the distinguished conduct of the Adjutant, Lieutenant Simão Joze Clemente,[895] and the 1st Sergeant Joze de Mello Cardozo,[896] in the attack of the 10th instant, which was so conspicuous that it is my duty to recommend both to any reward that His Excellency thinks proper.

God save you, Sir

Camp, 12 November 1813

Joze de Vasconcellos

9th Brigade Commander

Alex. Anderson
Lieutenant Colonel, 11th Regiment commander

See Table 15.4.

23rd Infantry

See Table 15.5.

7th Caçadores

Report[897] from Major Lillie to Colonel Sá

Sir,

I have the honour to report to you that in yesterday's action the 7th Caçadores Battalion behaved with its usual gallantry and valour. The conspicuous conduct of Captains Rozado[898] and Derenzy[899] deserves to be mentioned, notwithstanding everyone in the battalion carried out their duties admirably. I will be deprived of the services of Captain Derenzy due to a severe wound which he suffered leading his company in the assault on the village of Sare. I also must mention to you the intelligence and bravery shown by Lieutenants Francisco Xavier,[900] in the assault of the village, and Frederico Cezar,[901] in the assault of the redoubt, both commanding the two vacant companies. I had already recommended those officers to be promoted to these companies; unfortunately, Ensign V. Du Forest[902] and 1st Sergeant Guimaraes, both also recommended for promotion, died on this occasion. I reiterate my recommendation of Adjutant Sergeant Manoel Joachim Alves[903] whose conduct on all occasions was very praiseworthy. I beg leave to request, if the conduct of the battalion met your approbation, that you lay before His Excellency, the Marshal, Marquis de Campo Maior, the names of the individuals who I have the honour to recommend, because I am certain they deserve the praise of His Excellency.

God save you, Sir

11 November 1813

To the 9th Brigade commander

JS Lillie
Major, 7th Caçadores commander

See Table 15.6.

7th Division

The 7th Division advanced in a single brigade column with Inglis's Brigade at its head. The 6th Brigade followed in support. After taking the Grenade Redoubt, the 7th Division was part of the attack that took Sare. The only Portuguese troops that were under fire during the day were the 2nd Caçadores.

6th Brigade (7th and 19th Infantry, 2nd Caçadores)

Report[904] from Colonel Doyle to AG Mozinho

Sir,
I have the honour to report to you that the 6th Brigade, in yesterday's operations, was mainly employed supporting Major General Inglis' Brigade, except for the 2nd Caçadores Battalion, commanded by Lieutenant Colonel Zuhlecke [sic].[905] I'm pleased to inform you that the battalion behaved with its usual gallantry and steadiness.

I beg leave to report with satisfaction that no irregularities were committed by the brigade, and not a single complaint was presented, since we entered in this country.[906] This I attribute to the zeal and desire shown by every officer to carry out His Excellency, the Commander-in-Chief's orders.

I enclose the return of the casualties in the brigade in yesterday's action.
God save you, Sir
Quarters near St Pée, 11 November 1813
Manoel de Brito Mozinho

JM Doyle
Colonel,[907] acting commander

3rd Division

The 3rd Division advanced on a single column front. Keane's Brigade led the assault, preceded by the division's light troops, including the 11th Caçadores. After Sare was taken, the division moved north and came upon a 1.5km-long tangle of abattis in front of the two forts protecting the bridge at Amotz.[908] While Keane tried to advance through the abattis, Power sent the 9th Infantry and the 11th Caçadores to the right to try to get around the end of the abattis and attack the western fort. When the 21st Infantry arrived, he ordered it to make a frontal assault through the abattis in support of the 4th Division. Eventually the redoubts fell, as did the bridge they were protecting. Power and his brigade crossed the bridge and pursued the French for 8km to St Pée.[909]

8th Brigade (9th and 21st Infantry, 11th Caçadores)

Report[910] from General Power to AG Mozinho

Camp, November 12th 1813
Sir,
As His Excellency, Marshal Sir William Beresford Marquis of Campo Mayor witnessed the proceedings of the brigade, under my command, in the attack of the enemy's position, on the 10th instant, it will not be necessary for me, to enter more into the particulars of its operations, than will be requisite, in order to lay before him the merits of some officers, who particularly distinguished themselves.

When I received the order to attack the two redoubts, constructed by the enemy, to defend a road, which led up to their position, and the passage of which was also much obstructed by abbatis in every direction, I ordered Colonel Sutton, as soon as we reached the bottom of the hill, to move his regiment [9th Infantry] in column to the right, covering his left flank with the grenadier companies, until he passed a small wood, and that the ground afforded the facility of employing the regiment collectively in the attack of the left of the redoubts, at the same time, I ordered the 21st regiment to march straight up the road, and having formed then in column in the rear of the first abbatis, I detached the grenadier companies to the left of the hill, whilst the remainder of the regiment pushed through the abbatis, as rapidly as circumstances would admit, to join the assault, with the grenadiers of the 9th Regiment and the 11th Caçadores, who were moving upon our right. The latter battalion, previous to the order for the attack of the redoubts, had been ordered to the ravine, which separated the enemy positions in the rear of Sare and Ainhoe, but observing the movement of the 9th and 21st Regiments, Lieutenant Colonel Durzbach with very great judgement brought up the battalion,[911] to support our right flank, and his gallantry was very conspicuous, as well as that of Major Kilsha, who at the time that the enemy were preparing to advance against them, animated his men by his very gallant exertions, to keep their ground, at the same time, I have equal occasion, to speak most highly of Lieutenant Colonel Paty, who commanded the grenadier companies of the 9th Regiment, and whose exertions were most effectual in the same way, until the 21st Regiment got through the abbatis and joined in the assault, when the result was our driving the enemy from the redoubts, and pursuing them a considerable distance, when it became necessary to reform our column, for farther operations. Lieutenant Colonel Paty and Major Kilsha, being old British captains, I trust their exertions upon this occasion may be thought worthy of their being recommended for the brevet rank of Major in the British service.

In addition to the encomiums, which Lieutenant Colonel Durzbach has bestowed upon Major Kilsha[912] he has particularly mentioned the distinguished gallantry of Captain João Bento de Magalhaes Fontoura, Lieutenant Antonio Pinto de Arauyo and Adjutant Joaquim Teixeira de Mesquita, as well as 1st Sergeant Francisco Duarte de Freitas,[913] 2nd Sergeant Joze de Correia Vianna, who is acting Sergeant Major[914] and 2nd Sergeant João Nunes Cardozo.

Colonel Sutton[915] to whose exertions and gallantry, I am at all times, particularly indebted, but who upon this occasion, in consequence of the unforeseen obstructions he met with, could not bring up the whole of the regiment in time to join in the general assault, has recommended to the favourable consideration of His Excellency, the conspicuous services of Lieutenant Colonel Jacintho do Couto Soares, who was wounded, Lieutenant Colonel Paty, who commanded the grenadier companies, Captains Peacocke[916] and João Barboza,[917] Adjutant Caetano Joze Gomes, Lieutenants Joze Antonio de Aguiar and João Joaquim,[918] Ensigns João Pinto de Villas Boas, João Pita Bezerra and Alexandre Pita Bezerra, the gallantry of the latter two officers who are in the 1st and 2nd Grenadiers [companies] was very distinguished, as well as Captain Peacocke who commanded the 2nd Grenadiers [company] and which justly entitles them to distinct consideration.

Colonel Sutton also speaks very highly of the conduct of the two Sergeant Majors, João Antonio Vianna and Francisco Joze de Val, the latter of whom was recommended also for his activity and gallantry in the battle of Vittoria.[919]

Colonel João Telles,[920] who commanded the 21st Regiment, does not wish to recommend any particular officer, as he says that the whole of them merit equal praise. From my own immediate observation, I can say that nothing could exceed their gallantry, but I must particularize the conduct of Major Telles Jordão[921] who led the grenadiers, as well as Captain Jermyn, who commanded the 1st [Grenadier Company] and Lieutenant Galbraith,[922] the 2nd Grenadier Company.

I cannot close this letter without reporting the gallantry and exertions of my Aide de Camp, Major Johnston, who has upon this, as well as every other occasion, afforded me opportunities of witnessing his very great merit.

I am also indebted to Brigade Major João Leandro de Valladas,[923] for rendering every assistance in his power, in forwarding the execution of my orders.

I have the honour to be, Sir, your most obedient and humble servant

M Power
Major General

To the Adjutant General

21st Infantry

See Table 15.7

The Right Wing

Hill's five divisions were deployed with the 6th Division on the left flank, Giron's Spanish Division in the left centre, the Portuguese Division in the right centre, and the 2nd Division on its right. Further east was Morillo's Spanish Division. The French had two divisions to oppose them. Hill's orders were to evict the French from their positions on the south side of the Nivelle and force them back to the Nive river. The troops began moving forward at 6:30 a.m. but due to the difficult terrain, they did not begin their attacks until 9 a.m., by which time the Lesser Rhune had fallen. This exposed D'Erlon's right flank and he had no choice but to abandon his first line of defences and move his troops into the fortified positions just north of Anhoué on a high ridge overlooking the Nivelle river.

The 6th and Portuguese Divisions crossed the river and deployed in front of the French, while the 2nd Division moved west to attack the redoubts in the vicinity of the Col de Finodetta. The 2nd Division had orders not to assault the position in front of it until the attacks by the other two divisions had reached the crest of the ridge. By this time French morale was beginning to falter and when the assaults went in the French abandoned the ridge after only a token resistance. The French were chased north and crossed the Nive at Ustaritz and Cambo.[924]

6th Division

The division advanced in a column of brigades, with Lambert's Brigade in the lead, followed by the 7th Brigade, and then Pack's Brigade. In front of the division were the 9th Caçadores and four light companies from Lambert's Brigade. Lieutenant Colonel Brown of the 9th Caçadores, commanded the screen. The troops advanced unopposed until they reached the Nivelle river, where they halted. The division commander then ordered the 7th Brigade and Pack's Brigade to move up and form a line. While they were doing this, Lieutenant Colonel Brown found two fords across the river and the division crossed to the north side. There they waited until the Portuguese Division arrived.

As the Portuguese Division was approaching, Lieutenant Colonel Brown and his light troops were sent to the west to clear the area of French skirmishers. After doing so, Brown continued around the flank of the French positions in the hopes of cutting off any French troops trying to escape. Once he was in the rear of the French line, he seized a building near the road to Espelette. Upon the arrival of the Portuguese Division, it deployed to the right of the 6th Division. Both divisions assaulted the ridge and were brought under fire by the defenders. When they reached the redoubts, the French abandoned their positions.

7th Brigade (8th and 12th Infantry, 9th Caçadores)

See Table 15.8.

12th Infantry

Report[925] from Lieutenant Colonel Beatty to Colonel Douglas, 7th Brigade Commander

Ustaritz, 18 November 1813

Sir,

According to your wish I will mention the individuals in the regiment under my command who distinguished themselves in the battle of the 10th instant. So, it is my duty to lay before His Excellency, the Marquis de Campo Maior, the names of Major Madeira,[926] Lieutenant José de Sousa Canavarro, and Adjutant Sergeant Antonio Manuel Varejão.

From the first officer I received every assistance and support in this action as well as in the reconnaissance made by the brigade on 7 October. The second was killed encouraging the men with his example and words in a manner that honours his country and his memory. The Adjutant Sergeant Varejão distinguished himself by his gallantry in both actions.

I do not think it necessary to report more on the conduct of the 12th Regiment, which was such to give me perfect satisfaction. You witnessed it and will be a more impartial judge.

I beg leave to particularly mention the merits of Brigade Major Maher,[927] to whom I am in great debt for the zeal and intrepidity leading the brigade's skirmishers, covering our front.

I have the honour to be, Sir, your most obedient servant

To J. Douglas
7th Brigade Commander

Wm. Beatty
Lieutenant Colonel, 12th Regiment commander

9th Caçadores

Report[928] from Lieutenant Colonel Brown to AG Mozinho

I have the honour to report to you, to be laid before His Excellency, the Marshal Beresford Marquis de Campo Maior, on the conduct of the battalion under my command in the attack made on the 10th instant.

I was the advance guard with the battalion and four light companies from the Division, to cover its march, forcing the enemy to abandon all the advanced posts and retire. Upon arriving before the enemy's main position, I received an order from the division's general[929] to turn by the right of the entrenched heights. We climbed up and despite the enfilading fire from the redoubts behind the heights, arrived on the top with the first troops of the division. Continuing to march, flanking the enemy's right, we crossed the valley behind the heights, and seeing that we were able to cut the enemy's retreat, I tried to seize a post, which the enemy occupied to cover the road to Espoleta.[930] Despite the enemy's strong position and great numbers, double ours, I ordered a bayonet attack and I had the satisfaction of seeing the enemy abandon his position and flee so fast that we could not capture more than an officer, a sergeant, and eighteen men. A similar loss was inflicted on the enemy by our fire and we forced him to abandon two guns, a wagon loaded with gunpowder, and other tools, all of which could be withdrawn by the road.

In this last attack only three companies of the battalion charged with the Division's four light companies. All matched each other in bravery and valour. It's my duty to praise the conduct of the battalion on all occasions, on this day, and mention particularly the officers who led the three companies that charged the enemy, who were Captain Francisco Joaquim Pereira Vallente, Adjutant Andrew Simpson, and Ensign Joaquim Zeferino Serqueira.

God save you, Sir
Quarters at Ustaritz, 18 November 1813
Manoel de Brito Mozinho

G Brown
Lieutenant Colonel, 9th Caçadores commander

Portuguese Division

In addition to its two brigades, the Portuguese Division also had the 3rd and 4th Artillery Brigades.[931] The division advanced in a column of brigades. In front of the column was an advanced guard, led by Lieutenant Colonel Daniel McNeill of the 10th Infantry. When the division reached the river, the artillery deployed and provided covering fire while the division crossed. After reaching the north bank, the division formed into a line to the right of the 6th Division and assaulted the ridge. Once the division was across the river, the Portuguese guns crossed and shelled the French positions as the infantry advanced. Both the infantry and artillery were brought under heavy artillery fire. As the division approached the redoubts, the French pulled out of them and retreated north.

Report[932] from General Hamilton to Beresford

1 mile from Ustaritz
November 13th 1813
Sir
I have the honour to acquaint you that the conduct of the Portuguese Division both Artillery and Infantry in the attack of the enemy's redoubts and entrenchments on the morning of the 10th instant was in every respect such as to merit my entire approbation. I have the honour to transmit the reports of the officers commanding the brigades and their recommendations of those who more particularly distinguished themselves.

To the staff of the Division, Major Pinto[933] Deputy Assistant Adjutant General and Captain Watson of the 1st British Dragoons and Assistant Quartermaster General, and to my Aid [sic] de Camp Lieutenant Dom Gastão da Câmara, I am most indebted for their assistance.

I beg leave most strongly to recommend to your notice Captain Watson. He has been with me nearly four years, and is the only British officer on the staff of the Division and with me, and I feel confident that if you want to give satisfaction to any officer in the Division it is Captain Watson to obtain the brevet of Major, not solely from his conduct on the morning of the tenth, but at the battles of Victoria and Pamplona. I have the honour to be Your Excellency's most obedient and humble servant

John Hamilton
Lieutenant General

His Excellency the Marshal Sir W.C. Beresford
Commander-in-Chief Portuguese Army

4th Brigade (4th and 10th Infantry, 10th Caçadores)

Report[934] from General Campbell to General Hamilton

Sir,
I have the honour to recommend to the particular consideration of His Excellency the conduct of the following officers and inferior officers in yesterday's action: Lieutenant Colonel Daniel [sic] McNeill[935], 10th Regiment, commanding the Division's advance guard, Captain Angus McDonald, 4th Regiment, Captains Armstrong[936] and Anselmo Jozé de Queirós, 10th Caçadores Battalion. The latter, despite having an open wound, received in the battle of Pamplona,[937] carried out his duties with the usual bravery and was again severely wounded (a leg broken by a musket ball), being his third wound.[938] Lieutenant Queirós, 4th Caçadores, already deceased, who Lieutenant General Sir Thomas Graham praised so much, was the brother of this captain.[939]

Adjutant Sergeant Francisco Izidro da Ponte,[940] 10th Caçadores Battalion, and 1st Sergeant Francisco da Silva, 4th Infantry Regiment, both already recommended for their conduct in the battle of Pamplona, were again by their commanders.

Adjutant Sergeant João Francisco do Nascimento Serrão, 4th Regiment, and those of the 10th Regiment, António Alberto[941] and Joaquim da Fonceca, were equally recommended by their respective commanders and by their education, family and conduct are worthy of promotion.
God save you, Sir
Heights of Ainhoué, 11 November 1813
To Lieutenant General John Hamilton

A Campbell
Brigadier General

2nd Brigade (2nd Infantry and 14th Infantry)

Report[942] from General Buchan to General Hamilton

Sir,
I have the greatest satisfaction and pleasure to report to you the good conduct of the brigade under my command in the battle of the 10th instant and particularly its steadiness under a very heavy artillery fire.

I beg leave to mention the names of some officers and inferior officers who distinguished themselves during this day.

2nd Regiment
    Captain Dugald Campbell severely wounded[943]
    2nd Sergeant Manoel Joze Sabino
    Adjutant Sergeant Joze Joaquim Correia

14th Regiment
    Ensign Simão Felis Calça Pina[944]
    Ensign *agregado* Joze Simplicio de Moura
    Sergeant Antonio Joaquim Travassos
God save you, Sir
Quarter in Sarrassin
14 November 1813
To Lieutenant General Hamilton

J Buchan
Brigadier General

See Table 15.9.

2nd Division

The 2nd Division had the mission of taking the redoubt that overlooked the Col de Finodetta,[945] a pass through the mountains that connected Ainhoué with Espelette. The position was 3.5km northeast of Ainhoué and sat on a ridge immediately west of the pass and 50m above it. The redoubt was defended by a brigade of 3,000 men. The division arrived at the foot of the ridge and deployed with the 5th Brigade on the right and Byng's Brigade on the left. The division commander had been ordered to wait until he could see that the Portuguese and 6th Divisions had taken the fortifications to the west before he attacked. When that occurred, he gave the order to assault. The 6th Caçadores provided a screen for its brigade as it attacked up the hill. Unlike the assaults on the positions to the west, here the French did not immediately withdraw. However, when it became apparent that their main redoubt to the west had fallen, the defenders abandoned their position.

5th Brigade (6th and 18th Infantry, 6th Caçadores)

6th Infantry

See Table 15.10.

6th Caçadores

See Table 15.11.

Artillery

List[946] of Officers and Inferior Officers from the 3rd and 4th Artillery Brigades Who Distinguished Themselves particularly in the Attack on the Enemy's Camp and Entrenched Position near Ainhoué on 10 November 1813

1st Lieutenant Joze Joaquim Barreiros, 4th Artillery Regiment
This officer was detached at the beginning of the attack, commanding a half brigade of 9-pounder guns, and owing to the judicious dispositions and well directed fire, he compelled the enemy to retreat while protecting the crossing of the river by the infantry. After this, he moved to the right joining the rest of the brigade by very difficult paths with great energy and celerity. On all occasions he showed zeal, activity, and courage.

2nd Lieutenant Vicente Antonio Buyz, 2nd Artillery Regiment
This officer commanded the 9-pounder brigade, in the absence of the Captain and 1st Lieutenant, on the day of the attack. The energy and activity that he showed, not only when firing, but also in its movements, always a critical circumstance, was essential to posting the guns in the most suitable positions to fire at the enemy with the desired effect.

1st Sergeant Antonio Vicente de Abreu and Corporal Joze Theodoro da Silva, 2nd Artillery Regiment
These inferior officers distinguished themselves by their steady, active, and brave conduct and particularly by the extreme accuracy of the fire of the pieces they managed. The corporal, being detached with the howitzer, directed the fire so well that the enemy was forced to abandon a redoubt at the time when our infantry was ready to storm it; on another occasion, when moving the artillery by a path which the enemy blocked with an abattis, he took an axe and alone open the way.
Espelette 18 November 1813

Alex. Tulloh
Lieutenant Colonel
Artillery commander

Return[947] **of the Casualties and Spent ammunition, in the Attack near Ainhoué, by the 3rd and 4th Artillery Brigades, on 10 November 1813**

Round shot 6 pounder: 16
Round shot 9 pounder: 162
Shells 5 and ½ inches: 22
3 Drivers wounded
3 Beasts killed
1 Carriage 6-pounder broken

Ainhoué, 11 November 1813

Alex. Tulloh
Lieutenant Colonel, Commander

See Table 15.12.

Table 15.1: 3rd Brigade. Return[948] of the Casualties in the Combat with the Enemy on 10 November 1813

		Officers									
		Colonels	Lieutenant Colonels	Majors	Captains	Lieutenants	Ensigns	Sergeants	Drummers	Corporals and Privates	Total
3rd Regiment	Killed	-	-	-	-	-	-	-	-	-	-
	Wounded	-	-	-	-	-	1	-	-	-	1
	Missing	-	-	-	-	-	-	-	-	-	-
15th Regiment	Killed	-	-	-	-	-	-	-	-	-	-
	Wounded	-	-	-	-	-	-	-	-	-	-
	Missing	-	-	-	-	-	-	-	-	-	-
8th Battalion [Caçadores]	Killed	-	-	-	-	-	-	-	-	3	3
	Wounded	-	-	-	-	-	-	3	-	10	13
	Missing	-	-	-	-	-	-	-	-	5	5
Totals		-	-	-	-	-	1	3	-	18	22

3rd Regiment: Ensign Francisco Antonio de Almeida severely wounded, lost a leg.

Luiz do Rego Barretto
Colonel Brigade Commander

Table 15.2: Return[949] of the Killed, Wounded and Prisoners in the 1st Infantry Brigade in the Action before St Jean de Luz on 10 November 1813

Corps	Killed									Wounded									Prisoners and Missing									Total								
	Colonels	Lieutenant Colonels	Majors	Captains	Subalterns	Flag Bearers	Sergeants and *Furriés*	Musicians and Drummers	Corporals and Privates	Colonels	Lieutenant Colonels	Majors	Captains	Subalterns	Flag Bearers	Sergeants and *Furriés*	Musicians and Drummers	Corporals and Privates	Colonels	Lieutenant Colonels	Majors	Captains	Subalterns	Flag Bearers	Sergeants and *Furriés*	Musicians and Drummers	Corporals and Privates	Colonels	Lieutenant Colonels	Majors	Captains	Subalterns	Flag Bearers	Sergeants and *Furriés*	Musicians and Drummers	Corporals and Privates
1st Infantry	-	-	-	-	-	-	1	-	-	-	-	-	-	-	-	1	-	4	-	-	-	-	-	-	-	-	-	-	-	-	-	-	-	2	-	4
16th Infantry	-	-	-	-	-	-	-	-	-	-	-	-	1	-	-	-	-	-	-	-	-	-	-	-	-	-	-	-	-	-	1	-	-	-	-	-
4th Cacadores	-	-	-	-	-	-	-	-	3	-	-	-	-	-	-	1	-	13	-	-	-	-	-	-	-	-	-	-	-	-	-	-	-	1	-	16
Total	-	-	-	-	-	-	1	-	3	-	-	-	1	-	-	2	-	17	-	-	-	-	-	-	-	-	-	-	-	-	1	-	-	3	-	20
	Ranks and names of the officers killed									Ranks and names of the officers wounded									Ranks and names of the officers missing and prisoners									Observations								
16th Regiment										Captain Manuel Joze Xavier																		slightly								

John Wilson
Brigadier General

Table 15.3: 17th Infantry. Return[950] of the Killed, Wounded, and Missing in the action of 10 November 1813

Ranks	Killed	Wounded		Prisoners	Missing
		Severely	Slightly		
Adjutant Antonio Sardinha de Andrade	-	1	-	-	-
Lieutenant Joze da Costa	-	1	-	-	-
Brevet Lieutenant Joaquim Joze de Santana	-	-	1	-	-
Inferior Officers	-	-	-	-	-
Drummers	-	-	-	-	-
Corporals and Privates	1	13	1	-	-
Totals	1	15	2	-	-

Camp beyond Mont la Rhune 11 November 1813

John Rolt
Lieutenant Colonel 17th Infantry Regiment commander

Table 15.4: 11th Infantry. Return[951] of the Casualties against the Enemy on 10 November 1813

Camp 10 November 1813	Officers						Sergeants	Drummers	Corporals and Privates	Horses	Observations
	Lieutenant Colonel	Majors	Captains	Lieutenants	Ensigns	Staff					
Killed	-	-	-	-	-	-	-	-	1	-	
Wounded	1	-	1	1	-	-	2	-	23	-	
Missing	-	-	-	-	-	-	-	-	-	-	
Total	1	-	1	1	-	-	2	-	24	-	

Officers' Names:

Killed	Wounded	Meritorious Action	Missing
Rank and Name	Rank and Name	Rank and Name	Rank and Name
	Lieutenant Colonel Alexander Anderson, slightly		
	Brevet Captain Ignacio Pereira de Lacerda, slightly		
	Adjutant Lieutenant Simão Joze Clemente, slightly		

Alex. Anderson
Lieutenant Colonel

Table 15.5: 23rd Infantry. Return[952] of the Casualties in the Action against the Enemy on 10 November 1813

Camp St Jean de Luz 10 November 1813	Officers							Sergeants	Drummers	Corporals and Privates	Total	Horses	Observations
	Colonel	Lieutenant Colonel	Majors	Captains	Lieutenants	Ensigns	Staff						
Killed	-	-	-	-	-	-	-	-	-	2	2	-	
Wounded	-	-	-	-	-	-	-	1	-	11	12	-	
Missing	-	-	-	-	-	-	-	-	-	-	-	-	
Total	-	-	-	-	-	-	-	1	-	13	14	-	

J. Miller
Lieutenant Colonel, commander

Table 15.6: 7th Caçadores. Return[953] of the Casualties in the Action against the Enemy on 10 November 1813

Camp Bois 10 November 1813	Officers						Sergeants	Buglers	Corporals and Privates	Total	Observations
	Lieutenant Colonel	Majors	Captains	Lieutenants	Ensigns	Staff					
Killed	-	-	-	-	2	-	1	-	6	9	
Wounded	-	-	1	-	-	-	4	-	63	68	
Missing	-	-	-	-	-	-	-	-	-	-	
Total	-	-	1	-	2	-	5	-	69	77	

Officers killed: Ensign, 2nd Company, Valentin Duforest; Ensign, 3rd Company, Joze Joaquim da Costa Pereira
Officers wounded: Captain, 2nd Company, B.V. Derenzy, dangerously[954]

João [sic] Scott Lillie
Major, commander

Table 15.7: 21st Infantry. Return[955] of Killed, Wounded, and Missing

Camp 11 November 1813	Killed									Wounded									Missing and Prisoners									Total								
	Colonel	Lieutenant Colonels	Majors	Captains	Subalterns	Flag Bearers	Sergeants	Musicians and Drummers	Corporals and Privates	Colonel	Lieutenant Colonels	Majors	Captains	Subalterns	Flag Bearers	Sergeants	Musicians and Drummers	Corporals and Privates	Colonel	Lieutenant Colonels	Majors	Captains	Subalterns	Flag Bearers	Sergeants	Musicians and Drummers	Corporals and Privates	Colonel	Lieutenant Colonels	Majors	Captains	Subalterns	Flag Bearers	Sergeants	Musicians and Drummers	Corporals and Privates
Total																1		13																1		13
Observations	Name and rank of the officers killed									Nome and rank of the officers wounded									Name and rank of the officers missing or prisoners									Observations								
3 privates severely wounded																																				

João Telles
Colonel, 21st Regiment

Table 15.8: 7th Brigade. Return[956] of the Killed, Wounded, and Prisoners in the Action on 10 November 1813

Camp 11 November 1813	Killed								Wounded								Prisoners and Missing								Total								Observations
	Colonel	Lieutenant Colonels	Majors	Captains	Subalterns	Sergeants	Drummers	Corporals and Privates	Colonel	Lieutenant Colonels	Majors	Captains	Subalterns	Sergeants	Drummers	Corporals and Privates	Colonel	Lieutenant Colonels	Majors	Captains	Subalterns	Sergeants	Drummers	Corporals and Privates	Colonel	Lieutenant Colonels	Majors	Captains	Subalterns	Sergeants	Drummers	Corporals and Privates	
9th Caçadores								2					1	2		6													1	2		8	
8th Infantry								5					1			6													1			11	
12th Infantry					1			7						1		37													1	1		44	
Total					1			14					2	3		49													3	3		63	
	Name and rank of the officer killed								Name and rank of the officer wounded								Name and rank of the officer prisoner or missing																
	Adjutant, 12th Regiment, Joze de Souza Pereira Canavarro								Ensign, 9th Caçadores, Estevão Joze Neiva, severely[957] Ensign, 8th Infantry, Cazimiro Candido de Lacerda, slightly																								

J Maher
Brigade Major

Table 15.9: Return[958] of the Killed, Wounded, Prisoners and Missing in the Portuguese Division under the command of Lieutenant General Hamilton in the Action of 10 November 1813

		Killed									Wounded									Prisoners and Missing									Total										
		Colonels	Lieutenant Colonels	Majors	Captains	Subalterns	Flag Bearers	Sergeants and Furriers	Musicians and Drummers	Corporals and Privates	Colonels	Lieutenant Colonels	Majors	Captains	Subalterns	Flag Bearers	Sergeants and Furriers	Musicians and Drummers	Corporals and Privates	Colonels	Lieutenant Colonels	Majors	Captains	Subalterns	Flag Bearers	Sergeants and Furriers	Musicians and Drummers	Corporals and Privates	Colonels	Lieutenant Colonels	Majors	Captains	Subalterns	Flag Bearers	Sergeants and Furriers	Musicians and Drummers	Corporals and Privates	Killed Mules
Artillery	3rd Brigade																		2																		2	2
Artillery	4th Brigade																		1																		1	1
Infantry — 2nd Brigade	2nd Regiment									4				2	2		1		16													2	2		1		20	
Infantry — 2nd Brigade	14th Regiment									5									6									4									15	
Infantry — 2nd Brigade	4th Regiment									4		1					1		12											1					1		16	
Infantry — 4th Brigade	10th Regiment									6				1	4				17													1	4				23	
Infantry — 4th Brigade	10th Caçadores							1		1				1	6		1	1	20													1	6		2	1	21	
Total								1		20		1		4	12		3	1	74									4		1		4	12		4	1	98	3

Names and ranks of the officers wounded

2nd Regiment
1st Grenadier Company Captain Dugald Campbell, severely; 2nd Grenadier Company Captain João Rozendo,[959] slightly; Lieutenant Dom José Maria Carlos de Noronha, severely; Ensign José Pedro Tavares, slightly[960]

10th Regiment
Lieutenant Colonel Donald MacNeill, slightly; Captain Guilherme [sic] Gordon, severely; Lieutenant Pedro Pinto,[961] slightly; Lieutenant Manoel Martiniano Girão, slightly; Brevet Lieutenant João Rodarte,[962] slightly; Ensign Fortunato José Barreto, severely;

10th Caçadores
Captain Ancelmo José de Queiros, severely; Lieutenant João Honorato Rolim, slightly; Lieutenant João Allão Correia, slightly; Ensign Francisco de Paula Bastos, severely; Ensign José Pinto Montenegro, severely; Ensign Ignacio Antonio de Paiva, slightly; Ensign Filipe Diogo da Costa, slightly

J Hamilton
Lieutenant General

Table 15.10: 6th Infantry. Return[963] of the Casualties in the Action of 10 November 1813

Casualties	Officers						Sergeants	Drummers	Corporals and Privates	Total	Horses
	Lieutenant Colonel	Majors	Captains	Lieutenants	Ensigns	Staff					
Killed	-	-	-	-	-	-	-	-	-	-	-
Wounded	-	-	-	-	-	-	-	-	7	7	-
Missing	-	-	-	-	-	-	-	-	-	-	-
Total	-	-	-	-	-	-	-	-	7	7	-

Maxwell Grant
Lieutenant Colonel

Table 15.11: Return[964] of the Killed, Wounded, and Missing in the 6th Caçadores Battalion in the Combat of 10 November 1813

	Killed									Wounded									Prisoners and Missing									Total								
	Lieutenant Colonel	Major	Captains	Lieutenants	Ensigns	Sergeants and Furriés	Buglers	Corporals and Privates	Total	Lieutenant Colonel	Major	Captains	Lieutenants	Ensigns	Sergeants and Furriés	Buglers	Corporals and Privates	Total	Lieutenant Colonel	Major	Captains	Lieutenants	Ensigns	Sergeants and Furriés	Buglers	Corporals and Privates	Total	Lieutenant Colonel	Major	Captains	Lieutenants	Ensigns	Sergeants and Furriés	Buglers	Corporals and Privates	Total
Bivouac 10 November 1813	-	-	-	-	-	-	-	-	-	-	-	-	-	-	1	-	9	10	-	-	-	-	-	-	-	8	8	-	-	-	-	-	1	-	17	18
Total	-	-	-	-	-	-	-	-	-	-	-	-	-	-	1	-	9	10	-	-	-	-	-	-	-	8	8	-	-	-	-	-	1	-	17	18

P Fearon
Lieutenant Colonel, Commander

Table 15.12: Return[965] of the Killed and Wounded in the Portuguese Artillery Brigades

Quarter at Ibarren 15 November 1813	Artillerymen — Killed								Artillerymen — Wounded								Men employed in the park — Killed								Men employed in the park — Wounded								Beasts — Killed			Beasts — Wounded		
	Majors	Captains	1st Lieutenants	2nd Lieutenants	Sergeants and *Furriés*	Drummers	Corporals and Privates	Total	Majors	Captains	1st Lieutenants	2nd Lieutenants	Sergeants and *Furriés*	Drummers	Corporals and Privates	Total	1st Lieutenants	2nd Lieutenants	Sergeants	*Alvaita res*[966] and Farriers	Buglers	Corporals and Privates	Artificers	Total	1st Lieutenants	2nd Lieutenants	Sergeants	*Alvaita res* and Farriers	Buglers	Corporals and Privates	Artificers	Total	Horses	Mules	Total	Horses	Mules	Total
Mountain Brigade on the 10th[967]													1			1																						
1st Brigade Reserve on the 10th[968]															1	1																						
Brigades under the command of Lieut. Col. Tulloh on the 10th and 12th[969]															1	1														4		4		5	5			
Totals													1		2	3														4		4		5	5			

A Dickson
Lieutenant Colonel, Commander

Chapter 16

The Battle of the Nive, 9–13 December 1813

After his defeat on 10 November, Soult had to choose between defending the Nive river or falling back 25km to Bayonne. The Nive river was 35km long and 20m in width, but it was fordable in many places. The heavy rains of November had given it a fast-moving current that could make crossing difficult, but not impossible. Its northern bank was dominated by the hills along the southern bank, which would expose any defensive positions to Allied artillery. Soult knew that he could not fortify the whole river and thus decided to move his army 25km north and conduct a mobile defence based on the fortress at Bayonne.

The French Army had 65,000 men in eight infantry divisions.[970] Soult's plan placed his army in such a position that should Wellington make a move on Bayonne, he would expose his flank and the marshal would attack. If Wellington chose to ignore the fortress and cross the Nive upstream, the marshal would use the smallest force possible to hold back the main Allied attack, while he would take most of his army and attack the Allied force in the west.

Wellington wanted to cease operations and move his army into winter quarters. To do this, he needed to consolidate his position and make it difficult for Soult. His plan was to force the French back across the Adour river, which was the next major river after the Nive. To achieve this, Hill, with the 2nd and Portuguese Divisions, plus Morillo's Spanish Division, would attack near Cambo and turn the French left flank. Beresford would attack at Ustaritz with the 3rd and 6th Divisions. General Hope was to make a demonstration along the coast with the 1st and 5th Divisions, Aylmer's Brigade, and the 1st and 10th Brigades. The Light Division, which was in a position on Hope's right, was also to take part in the demonstration. The 4th and 7th Divisions were in reserve behind Beresford's troops.

On the right flank, the assault began at daybreak.[971] Hill's force crossed the river but became bogged down in the muddy countryside. By late afternoon they had linked up with the 6th Division and reached the outskirts of Villefranque, having taken almost 8 hours to cross the river and march less than 15km. There they found D'Erlon and four divisions waiting for them on a ridge behind the village. The 7th Brigade took the village but could not hold it when the French counter-attacked. Hill ordered them to attack again, this time with support from Pringle's Brigade, but this second attack also failed. By this time it had become too dark[972] to continue and the fighting stopped. During the night D'Erlon slipped away and in the morning Hill marched the 10km to the outskirts of Bayonne unopposed.

On the left flank, Hope's troops marched at daybreak. He advanced with the 1st Brigade on the left, the 5th Division in the centre and the 1st Division on the right. The 10th Brigade followed the 1st Division. The Light Division marched about the same time and was about 5km to the right of the 1st Division. The force met the French line of outposts at Anglet. After driving in their picquets, they came up to two French brigades holding the village. A heavy firefight ensued until the French left flank was in danger of being turned. The French retreated about a kilometre to their fortifications at Beyris. The 1st and 3rd Brigades, and the 1st and 3rd Caçadores of the Light Division, were part of the attack. Hope, having obeyed his orders to only make a demonstration against Bayonne, withdrew most of his troops towards St Jean-de-Luz, leaving the 1st, 3rd, and 10th Brigades in an exposed position on the Barrouillet Heights, about 500m northeast of Bidart along the road to Bayonne. The nearest unit to them was the 5th Division about 5km to the south. The Light Division had a picquet line on the Bassussarry Heights about 2km to the east.

During the night Soult shifted the four divisions that were in front of Hill to his right flank. This gave him eight divisions to attack Hope. In the west was Reille with two divisions, who was ordered to attack down the coastal road. In the centre the attack would be made by Clausel with two divisions. Behind him were D'Erlon's four divisions.

The troops began moving up at daybreak on 10 December and the assault began about 9 a.m. The ground was soaked from the rain and the terrain was broken by hedges, walls, and woods, which slowed the advance. Clausel's two divisions surprised the Light Division's outposts and pushed them back 2km to Arcangues. After the repulse of the initial attack, Clausel chose to engage in an artillery duel rather than continue the attack.

In the west, Reille's attack began about 9:30 and caught the picquet lines by surprise, pushing them back to the Barrouillet Heights. There were heavy casualties on both sides, but especially among the Portuguese. The Allied line was about to be outflanked in the east when reinforcements arrived in mid-afternoon. Reille called off his attacks and retreated north about a kilometre.

The next day, 11 December, the positions around the Barrouillet Heights were quiet until about 10 a.m. when Wellington ordered Greville's Brigade of the 5th Division to drive the French outposts back. It was very costly for the British. The move broke an unspoken ceasefire and Soult sent in two divisions in retaliation. The French attacked the Allied outposts and quickly overthrew them. Instead of stopping, they continued to the Barrouillet Heights, where they came close to breaking the 5th Division's lines. The Allies rallied, rushed in reinforcements, and the French withdrew.

On 12 December there was fighting between the outposts throughout the lines. Eventually the 5th Division and the 1st and 10th Brigades were withdrawn from the front lines. Soult saw that Wellington had moved the 7th Division closer to the west and decided the time had come to attack in the east. He ordered Clausel and D'Erlon to move their six divisions back to Bayonne. From there they crossed the Nive river to attack Hill's force. Late in the afternoon the Allied pontoon bridge was swept away by the fast current. Any reinforcements would have to march 10km south to the bridge at Ustaritz, and then 10km north to reach General Hill's troops on the outskirts of Bayonne.

Hill's position was on heights overlooking the Adour river and was 5km long. The centre of the position was 500m south of St Pierre d'Irube. The 2nd Division was on the left and centre, with its 5th Brigade in the centre of the heights. On the right flank was Byng's Brigade. Supporting the brigades on the heights were the 3rd and 4th Artillery Brigades. The Portuguese Division was in reserve.

Soult's plan called for a three-division-wide attack with Abbé's Division attacking up the road from Bayonne, which the 5th Brigade sat astride. The French began manoeuvring about 7 a.m. and by 8 a.m. the assault had begun. The French pushed the skirmishers back and a firefight began with the 5th Brigade. General Stewart, the commander of the 2nd Division, sent in his reserves. By 11:30 the 2nd Division was beginning to be pushed off the ridge when the last reserve of seven companies was committed. This caused the French to halt their advance. The French effort on the left of the line was not pressed, while that on the right of the line had been stopped by Byng's Brigade. Hill ordered the Portuguese Division to move up and counter-attack the French. Across the front the Allies moved forward, and it was enough to convince the French to retreat. Within a few days all fighting had stopped and both armies went into winter quarters.

The Right Wing: Combats of 9 and 13 December 1813

6th Division

The 6th Division crossed the Nive river in the vicinity of Ustaritz on 9 December and marched 6km to Villefranque, where they ran into the first serious French resistance. The 7th Brigade troops were ordered to clear the village. They took it after some heavy fighting and then were forced from it by a French counter-attack. To retake the village, Hill committed the whole of the 6th Division, with support from the 6th Caçadores of the 5th Brigade and Pringle's Brigade, both of the 2nd Division. Although having three times more troops, the Allies could not take the village before nightfall, when Hill called off the attack.

On 12 December the division was sent across the Nive to support the left wing but saw no action. The next day, when Soult attacked Hill at St Pierre d'Irube, the division crossed the Nive for the third time in four days and marched 17km north to the Allied positions. There the division was kept in reserve except for the 9th Caçadores, which was attached to Byng's Brigade on the right of the Allied lines. The 9th Caçadores was the only unit of the 6th Division to see action on 13 December.

7th Brigade (8th and 12th Infantry, 9th Caçadores)

Report[973] from Colonel Douglas to AG Mozinho

Ville Franche December 18th 1813
Sir,
I had the honour of forwarding to you a return of the officers who had distinguished themselves under my command in the late movements of the army, together with the return of casualties. I herewith mention them again and I am obliged to make this communication in English as your messenger says he was directed to bring back an answer with him.

It costs me considerable time to make a report in Portuguese myself and particularizing the conduct of officers is too delicate a subject to put in the hands of others.
I have the honour to be Sir your most obedient and humble servant

J Douglas
Colonel[974] commandant of the Brigade

To Brigade General Mozinho

Return[975] of the officers who had distinguished themselves in the operations connected with the passage of the Nive:

Lieutenant Colonel George [sic] Brown[976]
Capitão Valente[977]
Lieutenant Adjutant Andrew Simpson

All from the 9th Caçadores Battalion

J Douglas
Colonel 7th Brigade commander

See Tables 16.1 and 16.2.

Report[978] from Colonel Douglas to the AG Mozinho

Sir,
The 9th Caçadores Battalion was detached from the brigade under my command by an order from General Clinton, on the action of the 13th instant. The report from Major Cerqueira[979] about the operations on that day was sent to the headquarters before General Byng acquainted me with the gallant conduct of Major Cerqueira, commanding the battalion following Lieutenant Colonel Browne's wound.[980] The battalion attacked with General Byng's brigade and his conduct was praised by the general.
God save you, Sir
Quarters in Ville Franche, 28 December 1813
Adjutant General of the Army

J Douglas
Colonel 7th Brigade commander

9th Caçadores

Report[981] from Major Cerqueira to Colonel Douglas

Camp near Bayonne, 13 December 1813

Sir,

I have the honour to enclose the return of the killed and wounded of the Caçadores Battalion that is under my command due to the lieutenant colonel's wound. I must report to you, for the information of His Excellency the Marshal, that the conduct of the officers, inferior officers, and men of the battalion was, on this day, particularly good. In this my part was small, all owed to the brave lieutenant colonel, who remained in the field during the time the battalion was engaged, despite his wound.

It is my duty to recommend to the Marshal the constant good conduct of Captain Francisco Joaquim Pereira Valente,[982] who was wounded; the activity, valour and zeal with which Adjutant Andrew Simpson[983] conveyed my orders; and the courage with which Ensign Joaquim Manoel da Silva Rocha[984] and Adjutant Sergeant Joze Marques Salgueiral charged the enemy with the bayonet.

God save you, Sir

Colonel Douglas, Brigade commander

Luiz Maria Cerqueira
Major, 9th Caçadores

2nd Division

The 5th Brigade crossed the Nive river by a ford at daybreak on 9 December. The 6th Caçadores led the way and were surprised to find the river deeper than expected. The first two or three sections of the caçadores were washed away by the current. The rest made it across by linking arms to keep from falling, while their ammunition pouches were placed on their heads to keep their cartridges dry. The 6th Caçadores were part of the force that cleared Villefranque and their casualties were heavy. One officer described it as 'the sharpest work for a few minutes that I ever was engaged in, the 2 Companies had 12 men Killed and 26 Wounded, an unusually large proportion of the former but it is accounted for by the fact, that our men and the French at one time, were actually firing at each other through the same hedge'.[985]

By 11 December the 5th Brigade was located on a height 500m south of St Pierre d'Irube and deployed on both sides of the road to Saint-Jean-Pied-de-Port. In front of their position was the Hiriberry Farm. The 6th Infantry was deployed to the right of the road, while the 18th Infantry Regiment was to the left, just above the farm. The 6th Caçadores deployed picquets across the brigade's front. Throughout the night the picquets reported large numbers of French troops to their front, so when the French assault began about 8 a.m. the next morning they were not caught by surprise. The attack was preceded by a large screen of light infantry which outnumbered the caçadores. The fighting was intense and the caçadores were pushed back up the hill, although some pockets of them held their ground. A counter-attack stopped the first assault, but the French came on again. By 11:30 a.m. the French had almost reached the top of the ridge when a second counter-attack forced them back down the hill. By noon the Portuguese Division had come up to support the 5th Brigade and Hill ordered it and the 2nd Division to counter-attack the French. The Portuguese fixed bayonets and charged down the hill, driving the French before them. The 5th Brigade took about 20 per cent casualties and the toll was especially heavy among the brigade's senior leaders. Major Matias José de Sousa, the commander of the 18th Infantry, was killed, Ashworth[986] and Colonel Grant, the commander of the 6th Infantry, were seriously wounded, and Lieutenant Colonel Fearon, the commander of the 6th Caçadores, was slightly wounded.

5th Brigade (6th and 18th Infantry, 6th Caçadores)

Report[987] from General Ashworth to AG Mozinho

Sir,

I have the honour and pleasure to report to you, for His Excellency the Marshal, Commander-in-Chief, Marquis de Campo Maior's information, on the conduct of the three corps, which composed the 5th Infantry Brigade, on the 13th instant, in the action against the enemy. Their conduct was most brilliant and emulated the best troops.

As I am told that Lieutenant Colonel Maxwell Grant, the 6th Regiment's Commander, had already informed His Excellency on the behaviour of that regiment, mentioning the officers who distinguished themselves more conspicuously, I do not have anything more to add than confirm the information given by that brave officer, who, in spite of being already severely wounded, seeing that I was also wounded and that the command of the brigade devolved to him, refused to abandon the field until the end of the action.

The conduct of the 6th Caçadores Battalion was the best possible and I beg leave to recommend Lieutenant Colonel Peter Fearon,[988] the battalion commander, to His Excellency's attention. Since he commanded the battalion, he has always shown to be a brave and intelligent officer. He strongly praises Captains Henrique [sic] Temple[989] (severely wounded on the 9th instant) and Ricardo [sic] Brunton (likewise wounded in the 13th); the latter already recommended several times, for his bravery, to His Excellency the Marshal. Lieutenant Colonel Fearon also mentions particularly Ensigns Brackhausen[990] [sic] and Pedro Pinto de Araujo,[991] and adds that Ensign Melchior Vilhena behaved in such a praiseworthy manner as to clean any previous stain on his character. I am again informed of the good conduct of Private Joze Manoel Henriques de Carvalho, from the same caçadores battalion. His Excellency the Marshal had already allowed this private to be proposed to be an ensign.

About the 18th Regiment, with which I had to be most of the day, I have nothing to say but to praise its brilliant conduct, particularly the two courageous bayonet charges with which the regiment repelled the enemy completely. I deeply regret the death of its commander, Major Mathias Joze de Souza, who had carried out his duties very well throughout the day but was unfortunately killed near the end of the action. Captain Hugh Lumley,[992] of the same regiment, on the 11th instant, when the enemy made a reconnaissance in force, was with his company in a picquet and his conduct earned the thanks of Lieutenant General Stewart, 2nd Division Commander; on the 13th he equally showed himself to be a most brave and intelligent officer. Captain Manoel Pereira Borges,[993] Lieutenants Fernando de Magalhaes and Luiz [sic] Apellius,[994] as well as Ensign Bernardino Coelho Soares,[995] all from the 18th Regiment, distinguished themselves and deserve to be particularly mentioned.

I must not omit to mention 1st Sergeant João Manoel Bento, 3rd Company 6th Caçadores Battalion, who, in all occasions offered, behaved with great dignity.[996] I beg leave also to recommend to His Excellency, 2nd Sergeant Vitorino Vieira Borges, 18th Regiment, serving for some time as Adjutant Sergeant,[997] and 2nd Sergeant Antonio Ozorio, 2nd Grenadier Company, from the same regiment, for their valour and activity. Both gave every indication that they could be able officers.

Brigade Major Antonio Pereira Quinland and my Aide-de-Camp, Captain Filippe Rickets [sic],[998] carried out their duties in a very satisfactory manner. Both officers deserve His Excellency's attention.

I also must mention particularly the zeal and tireless activity with which the surgeons from the brigade's three corps took care of the wounded, especially Surgeon Bernardo Maria de Moraes, from the 18th Regiment, acting as Staff Surgeon, who repeatedly showed his intelligence and worth. The surgeons informed me that they received every help they needed from their assistants.

God save you, Sir

Cambo, 17 December 1813

Manoel de Brito Mozinho

Carlos [sic] Ashworth
Brigadier General

P.S. Just now Lieutenant Colonel Maxwell Grant, 6th Regiment, informs me that he forgot to mention the officers from the regiment who were wounded and that he wishes that His Excellency the Marshal, Marquis de Campo Maior, knows that these officers conducted themselves with great gallantry and their absence will be considerably felt in the service. The same I must tell about the officers wounded in the 18th Regiment, particularly Ensign Joaquim Jeronimo da Cunha Reys,[999] a promising young officer, who had repeatedly conducted himself very well.

Report[1000] from Lieutenant Colonel Grant, 5th Brigade Acting Commander, to AG Mozinho

Sir,

As a result of Brigadier Ashworth's wound, the 5th Brigade's command devolved to me before I also had to leave it because of a wound I received,[1001] but I feel it is my duty to report to you, for the information of His Excellency the Marshal, Commander-in-Chief, on his brilliant conduct against the enemy on this day.

The 6th Infantry Regiment was under my orders for most of the day and behaved in such a manner that I believe no other troops could exceed.

The nature of the place and of the operations did not allow me to witness the conduct of every individual but I must mention the behaviour and activity of my Major, Manoel Luis Correia,[1002] as of Captains Francisco Pinto Henriques and Joze Cardozo de Carvalho,[1003] Ensigns Antonio Ferreira Borges[1004] and Manuel Joze Pimentel,[1005] 1st Sergeant João Luis,[1006] and 2nd Sergeant Francisco de Paula Melo. Notwithstanding the general good behaviour of the regiment, I mention particularly these because they led the columns which charged with the bayonet two times and completely repelled the enemy.

For the conduct of the 6th Caçadores Battalion and of the 18th Regiment, in the short time they were under my command, I can report it was the best possible.

God save you, Sir

Camp at Saint Pierre D' Uribe, 13 December 1813, 5 o'clock in the afternoon

Manoel de Brito Mozinho

Maxwell Grant
Lieutenant Colonel
5th Brigade, Acting Commander

Portuguese Division

The division was in reserve for most of the battle. On the morning of 13 December it was in the vicinity of Horlopo, about a kilometre south of the heights defended by the 2nd Division. About 11:30 a.m. Hill ordered it to move up to the heights and push the French back. The road to Bayonne was the axis of advance. The 2nd Brigade would attack to the left of the road, while the 4th Brigade was to attack to the right. Hill led the 2nd Brigade as it marched to the heights. The arrival of the two brigades was enough to stop the French assault. The 14th Infantry pursued the French down the hill. Its 1st Battalion soon found itself far in advance of the rest of the 2nd Brigade and in danger of being captured. Lecor noticed their predicament and led the regiment's 2nd Battalion in a bayonet charge to rescue them.

After the heights had been cleared of the French, Hill noticed that a strong French force still occupied the Croix de Mouguerre Heights about 300m to the northeast. Byng was ordered to take the hill and the 4th Brigade was sent to help. After some bitter fighting, the French evacuated the hill.

Report[1007] from General Lecor to AG Mozinho

Sir,

I have the honour to transmit to you, for the information of His Excellency, the Marshal Marquis de Campo Maior, the return of the killed and wounded of the Division under my command in the action of the 13rd instant in front of Bayonne. I have the satisfaction to ensure His Excellency that the conduct of the corps was very gallant, particularly the 2nd Battalion of the 14th Infantry Regiment, which, under my immediate command, charged the enemy brilliantly. The bayonet charge was made to support and relieve the 1st Battalion of the 14th, which was forced to give some ground to avoid being surrounded when attacked by a superior force of *voltigeurs*.[1008] The enemy turned and fled, abandoning the position and leaving behind some prisoners.

It is my duty to acquaint His Excellency with the distinguished manner with which the two brigade commanders, Brigadiers Antonio Hipolito da Costa and J. Buchan, carry out their duties. I must also mention the gallant conduct of the corps commanders, Colonel Jorge de Avilez, 2nd Regiment, Colonel Luis Maria,[1009] 10th Regiment, Major Rodrigo Vito Pereira, the 14th Regiment's acting commander, Lieutenant Colonel Hill,[1010] 4th Regiment, Brevet Major Pamplona,[1011] 10th Caçadores, and Lieutenant Colonel Tulloh, the artillery commander, who behaved with his usual intelligence until he was severely wounded.

I beg leave to strongly request His Excellency's protection for the hapless widow of one of the brave officers fallen in the field of honour, Captain Urbano Xavier Henriques, 14th Regiment, who died leading his company.

Brigadier Generals Costa and Buchan submitted to me the names of the officers who had the fortune to distinguish themselves on this occasion. I forward this list to be laid before His Excellency.[1012]

I would be failing my duties if I forgot to mention the staff officers who assisted me in the necessary arrangements before and during the action, showing their zeal, intelligence, and activity. I have the honour to recommend them to His Excellency. They were:

Cavalry Lieutenant Dom Gastão da Câmara, Aide-de-Camp to General Hamilton[1013]
Lieutenant Joze Ferreira da Cunha, my Aide-de-Camp
Lieutenant Grifits[1014] [sic] from His British Majesty's Army

Beside the officers mentioned by the brigade commanders, I must mention Ensign Antonio Lobo da Silva,[1015] 14th Regiment, who was recommended to me in the course of the action, for his gallant conduct commanding a party from the regiment which joined the Caçadores in the front.
God save you, Sir
Quarters in Moguerre, 16 December 1813
Manoel de Brito Mozinho

Carlos Frederico Lecor
Major General

P.S. Major Pereira commanded the 2nd Battalion of the 14th Regiment when I ordered the charge with the bayonet and only after the brave Major Travassos[1016] fell wounded did the command of the regiment devolve to Major Pereira.

See Table 16.3.

Return[1017] **of the Officers Killed and Wounded in the Portuguese Division from the Action on 13 December 1813**

Officers killed:

    Captain Luis Manoel de Carvalho, 10th Regiment

    Lieutenant Antonio de Abreu, 10th Regiment

    Captain Urbano Xavier Henriques, 14th Regiment

Officers wounded:

2nd Regiment

    Lieutenant Colonel John Gomersall, slightly

    Captain Manoel Alexandrino Pereira, slightly

14th Regiment

    Major Jacintho Alexandre Travassos, severely, died later of his wounds

    Lieutenant Daniel Donovan, severely

    Ensign João Lampreia de Sarre, severely

    Ensign Jose Cezario Peniz Pereira, severely

    Adjutant Thomas Antonio Cabreira, severely

4th Regiment

    Captain Angus McDonald, slightly

    Captain Domingos Correa de Mesquita, slightly

    Ensign Bernardino de Sena, severely

10th Regiment

    Captain Manoel Martiniano Girão, severely

    Captain Pedro Pinto de Moraes Sarmento, slightly

    Ensign Antonio de Padua Ferreira Passos, severely

    Ensign Antão de Sá Valente, slightly

    Ensign Pedro Paulo Ferreira Passos, slightly

10th Caçadores Battalion

    Captain Frederick Armstrong, slightly

    Lieutenant Miguel Correa de Mesquita, severely

    Lieutenant Jose Alão Correa, slightly

    Lieutenant Jose de Souza Cirne, slightly

    Ensign José Maria de Souza, slightly

    Ensign António de Souza Cirne, slightly

Artillery

Return[1018] **of the Casualties in the 3rd and 4th Artillery Brigades in the Passage of the Nive in Cambo on 9 December 1813**

    1 soldier killed

    1 soldier wounded

    1 beast killed

Camp before Bayonne 10 December 1813

Alex. Tulloh

Lieutenant Colonel commander

List[1019] of the Artillery Officers Who Distinguished Themselves in the Battle of 13 December 1813

João da Cunha Preto, Brevet Major, 1st Artillery Regiment
This officer commanded the brigades after the wounding of the lieutenant colonel[1020] and showed his military talents and was praised by the generals on the field.

Joze Joaquim Barreiros, 1st Lieutenant, 4th Artillery Regiment, Adjutant of the Brigades[1021]
This officer, who had distinguished himself in the Ainhoué attack[1022] and his name being laid before His Excellency, the Marshal Marquis de Campo Maior, showed again his bravery and intelligence. He commanded a division of the 9-pounder brigade in the advanced posts and for his services there he received public thanks from General Rowland Hill.

João Joze Lodovice, 1st Lieutenant, 1st Artillery Regiment[1023]
This officer has shown his knowledge and bravery and for that deserves His Excellency the Marshal's approbation.

Vicente Antonio Buyz, 2nd Lieutenant, 2nd Artillery Regiment[1024]
This officer, whose services in the Ainhoué attack were laid before His Excellency the Marshal, again showed his intelligence and bravery in the battle of the 13th.

Cambo, 14 December 1813

Alex. Tulloh
Lieutenant Colonel commander

The Left Wing: Combats of 9, 10, and 11 December 1813

Light Division (1st and 3rd Caçadores, 17th Infantry)

The Portuguese units of the Light Division were involved in the fighting on 9, 10, and 11 December. The 1st and 3rd Caçadores fought in the combat that forced back the French outposts at Anglet on 9 December. That evening the division moved to the Bassussarry Heights about 2km east of the Barrouillet Heights. The next day the 1st Caçadores were responsible for the outlying picquets and were not surprised[1025] by the swarm of French skirmishers who attacked their outposts. They were able to give enough warning for the battalion to assemble to meet the threat and to send their baggage to the rear. The 1st Caçadores also skirmished on 11 December. The 3rd Caçadores and the 17th Infantry were in the fighting on 10 and 11 December but, like the 1st Caçadores, their casualties were also light.

1st Caçadores

Report[1026] from Lieutenant Colonel Snodgrass to AG Mozinho

I have the honour to enclose the returns of the killed and wounded in the actions of the 9th, 10th, and 11th instant. I inform you that on the 9th the battalion under my command, at the head of the 2nd Brigade of the Light Division, attacked the enemy's advanced posts and after some resistance they fell into our hands. The conduct of the officers and men in this attack was very creditable and gallant, but I must particularly mention Captains W.O.B. McMahon[1027] and Martinho de Magalhaes Peixoto,[1028] who led their companies in the skirmish line, showing great activity and valour. I also have every reason to recommend again Lieutenants Joaquim Achioli da Fonseca and Manoel Antonio Sobral.[1029]

On the 10th our advanced posts were attacked and the battalion being forward quickly formed and sustained the enemy while the brigade assembled and the baggage was removed, until receiving the order to retreat, which the battalion did in good order.

On the 11th there was some exchange of fire with the enemy, the battalion kept the posts assigned to it and behaved with the same steadiness as in the previous days.

I beg you to lay this report before His Excellency the Marshal Marquis de Campo Maior.

God save you, Sir

Camp in the neighbourhood of Arcangues, 12 December 1813

Manoel de Brito Mozinho

K. Snodgrass

Lieutenant Colonel

1st Caçadores commander

See Table 16.4.

3rd Caçadores

Report[1030] from Lieutenant Colonel Silveira to AG Mozinho

Sir,

I have the honour to enclose the return of the killed and wounded in the battalion under my command in the combats of the 9th, 10th and 11th, to be laid before His Excellency the Marshal, Marquis de Campo Maior.

It is my duty to acquaint you, for the information of His Excellency, of the good conduct of the officers, inferior officers, and men, which is already customary.

God save you, Sir

Camp near Arbonne, 12 December 1813

Manoel de Brito Mozinho

Manoel Pinto da Silveira

Lieutenant Colonel, commander

See Tables 16.5, 16.6, and 16.7.

17th Infantry

See Table 16.8.

4th Division

The 4th Division was in reserve for most of the operations of 9–13 December. During the battle on 10 December it was at Arbonne, about 4km from where the 5th Division and two Portuguese brigades were, and 5km from Arcangues, where the Light Division was. The 7th Caçadores and one company of the 11th Infantry saw action that day. Where they were committed to the fight is not known. However, they probably had outposts in the gap between the Barrouillet Heights and Arcangues.

9th Brigade (11th and 23rd Infantry, 7th Caçadores)

7th Caçadores

See Table 16.9.

1st Brigade (Independent) (1st and 16th Infantry, 4th Caçadores)

The 1st Brigade was on the left of the advance of Hope's forces as they moved forward on 9 December and reached the banks of the Adour River before being recalled. The 1st Infantry and the 4th Caçadores were part of the attack at Anglet, while the 16th Infantry was in reserve. After the combat the 1st, 3rd, and 10th Brigades were placed in a position on the Barrouillet Heights, about 500m northeast of Bidart along the road to Bayonne. The 3rd Brigade was on the left of the line, the 10th Brigade in the centre, and the 1st Brigade to the right.

On the morning of 10 December Soult attacked the Allies' left flank. The 1st Brigade was initially assaulted by Level's Division and was able to prevent the French from breaking through their lines. However, they were then assaulted by Boyer's Division, which was supported by French cavalry. The 16th Infantry was caught by the cavalry in the open and badly cut up. They held on until reinforcements arrived, but the 1st Brigade paid a heavy price. It started the battle with about 2,100 men and by the end of the day only 1,800 were still with the colours. Among the casualties were the 16th Infantry's commander, Colonel Pizarro, and Major O'Hara, a battalion commander in the 1st Infantry, both of whom were captured.

Report[1031] from General Campbell to AG Mozinho

I have the honour to report to you, for the information of His Excellency, the Marshal, Marquis de Campo Maior, that on the reconnaissance made over Bayonne on the 9th, and on the attack made by the enemy yesterday's morning [the 10th] against this part of our position, the 1st Portuguese Infantry Brigade under my command was heavily engaged and I regret to say that we sustained a severe loss, as His Excellency can see in the enclosed returns.

On the first occasion mentioned we were on the extreme left of the army and we reconnoitred to the banks of the Adour, a little further from Bayonne.

Yesterday we held our position for a considerable amount of time against a strong enemy attack, until the arrival of other troops. On this occasion the conduct of the 4th Caçadores was very gallant. The enemy, stopping his attack on the Light Division, brought a formidable force against my brigade, which was, for a moment, due to the intricacy of the field, almost surrounded. We escaped this critical situation under a spirited charge made by the enemy's cavalry supported by his infantry. I have the pleasure to inform you of the good conduct of all the officers in general, but I am much obliged for the able and judicious cooperation that I received from Lieutenant Colonel E.K. Williams, and Major Pedro [sic] Adamson, both from the 4th Caçadores Battalion, Lieutenant Colonel Jozé Antonio Vidigal and Major Antonio Pedro de Brito, 16th Regiment, and Captain Guilherme [sic] Queade, 1st Regiment. I beg leave to recommend the latter officer to His Excellency's favourable consideration, as also Captain Murphy,[1032] Brigadier General Wilson's Aide-de-Camp, who voluntarily joined the 4th Caçadores Battalion, for this battalion was very short on officers, and I witnessed his gallant conduct.[1033] I must also particularly recommend the Brigade Major, Lieutenant Rodrigo Luciano de Abreu and Lieutenant Jozé Jorge Loureiro, my Aide-de-Camp, both rendered me great services and are very worthy officers. I never saw anyone exceed his duties as Adjutant Sergeant Henrique, 16th Regiment.[1034]

I sincerely regret the loss of Colonel Francisco Homem de Magalhães Pizarro, 16th Regiment, and Major Walter O'Hara, 1st Regiment, both prisoners, and I believe, wounded.[1035] They gallantly fell into the enemy's hands carrying out their duties.

I must add that the conduct of the 16th Regiment was not what it should have been; on this subject I will very soon inform His Excellency.

God save you, Sir

Camp near Bidart, 11 December 1813

Manoel de Brito Mozinho

Arch. Campbell

Brigadier General

See Tables 16.10 and 16.11.

4th Caçadores

Report[1036] from Lieutenant Colonel Williams to General Campbell.

Camp 11 December 1813

Sir,

I beg leave to mention some individuals of the 4th Caçadores Battalion for their gallant conduct on the 9th and 10th instant and request that their names be laid before His Excellency the Marshal Marquis of Campo Maior. They are: Captain Caetano Alberto Canavaro, Ensigns Antonio de Gouvea Cabral[1037] and João Oliva, Adjutant Sergeant Antono Pinto da Matta,[1038] and Sergeants Luiz Maximo do Sobral, Manoel Monteiro Pereira e Joze Rodrigues Valente, the former lately commanding a company.

I am much obliged to Captain Murphy, Brigadier Wilson's Aide-de-Camp, who voluntarily joined my battalion. Major Adamson with his usual bravery and intelligence helped me in every possible manner.

I have the honour to be, Sir, your most obedient and faithful servant

A. Campbell

E.K. Williams
Lieutenant Colonel
4th Caçadores

10th Brigade (Independent) (13th and 24th Infantry, 5th Caçadores)

During the initial advance to Bayonne, the 10th Brigade was in reserve. The only units to see any combat on 9 December were two companies of the 5th Caçadores who were involved in the fighting near Anglet. After the French had been pushed back towards Bayonne, the 10th Brigade occupied the Barrouillet Heights, just to the east of the main road to Saint-Jean-de-Luz, close to Lake Mouriscot. The 5th Caçadores were in a line of outposts in the front and the 13th and 24th Infantry were on the crest of the heights. The brigade defended the heights from the French attack on 10 December and took part in the heavy skirmishing on 11 December, when the Allies attacked the French about 10 a.m. A few hours after the fighting had ceased, the French attacked the Allied outposts. The skirmishing continued the next day with all the units in the brigade taking casualties. Although the fighting was at its heaviest on 10 December, the constant skirmishing between the outposts eroded the strength of the brigade. By the end of the campaign the 10th Brigade had lost 17 per cent of its men, mostly through the fighting at the outposts.

Report[1039] from General Bradford to AG Mozinho

Cantonment in front of Bidart

15th December 1813

Sir,

I have the honour to report for the information of His Excellency the Marquis of Campo Mayor, that the 5th Caçadores and part of the 24th Regiment, that were most engaged in the late affairs which the left column has had with the enemy, have performed their duty to my satisfaction.

On the 9th when a reconnaissance was made beyond Anglet, the brigade being in reserve to the 5th Division, only two companies of the 5th Caçadores were engaged, and they conducted themselves well.

On the 10th the 5th Caçadores supported by some companies of the 24th Regiment were in advance when the enemy made an attack, which was very creditably sustained.

On the 11th the Caçadores drove in handsomely the enemy's picquets, supported by the 13th Regiment.

I beg leave to recommend to His Excellency's notice Captain Bunbury[1040] of the 5th Caçadores who in charge of two companies of that battalion sustained the advance on the 10th in a very gallant manner, until a severe wound obliged him to quit the field, also Lieutenant Jose Antonio de Sá[1041] and Ensign Joaquim Jose Antonio Nogueira,[1042] whose conduct on the 9th, 10th, and 11th most particularly merit His Excellency's favour.

Of the 13th Regiment, I beg leave to mention in terms of praise, Lieutenant Colonel João Carlos de Saldanha, Captain Antonio de Mendonça,[1043] Lieutenant Lourenço Justiniano Lima[1044] and Sergeants Antonio Jose Vannes, Joaquim Ervilhero and Antonio Teixeira who set the most gallant example to their corps.

Of the 24th Regiment I beg leave again to recommend Captain Romão Soares, whose gallant conduct I have twice before had occasion to notice to His Excellency, who has already been pleased to give him the brevet rank of Captain. This officer with 4 companies of the 24th Regiment had charge of a post on the right of the position which the enemy attempted with very superior numbers to carry, but were driven back with considerable loss, and Captain Romão took the colonel, 3 other officers and 60 men prisoners. The 2 grenadier companies of the 24th Regiment were employed upon this occasion, they have always distinguished themselves. I beg also to mention particularly the conduct of Captain Lemos[1045] of the 24th Regiment who with his company drove the enemy down the main road on the 10th and on the 11th I regret to say he was severely wounded. Sergeant Padua with a few men made an officer and 8 prisoners.

I cannot conclude my report without mentioning the gallant conduct shown upon every occasion by my Aid de Camp [sic] Major Rainey[1046] who I am concerned to say received a severe wound on the 10th instant. I have the honour to be, Sir, your most obedient and humble servant

Thomas Bradford
Major General
To the Adjutant General

P.S. I have the honour to transmit herewith returns of the killed and wounded on the 9th, 10th, 11th, 12th instant of the brigade under my command.

See Tables 16.12, 16.13, 16.14, and 16.15.

5th Division

On 9 December the 5th Division was in the left centre of the advance towards Bayonne. It marched in three brigade columns with the 3rd Brigade in the centre. The division had orders to push the French back to Bayonne. The only serious opposition they ran into was at Anglet and the 3rd Brigade was part of the attack that cleared the village. That evening the 3rd Brigade was ordered to take up a position on the Barrouillet Heights while the division withdrew and bivouacked 5km to the south. The 3rd Brigade was on the far left, with the 10th and 1st Brigades to its right. The 8th Caçadores provided the outposts.

On 10 December the brigade was attacked by Leval's Division, but was able to hold its position. The 3rd Infantry took part in the counter-attack that drove the French back, while the 15th Infantry stayed in reserve. The next morning the 15th Infantry was sent with Greville's Brigade to force the French picquets back to their own lines. The 15th Infantry was on the left of the 9th Foot and remained there with them in a forward position after the French picquets had retreated. They were still there when the French attacked in the afternoon. They and the 9th Foot were ordered to hold their position until the rest of the Allies had pulled back to the heights. The fighting was heavy, and the 15th Infantry lost 20 per cent of its men, most of whom were captured. The brigade was not involved in the fighting on 12 December.

3rd Brigade (3rd and 15th Infantry, 8th Caçadores)

Report[1047] from Colonel Barreto to AG Mozinho

Sir,

I have the honour to enclose the returns of the killed, wounded and missing in the brigade under my command on the 9th, 10th and 11th instant, for the information of His Excellency, the Marshal Marquis de Campo Maior. It is with great satisfaction that I inform you of the gallant conduct of the brigade's three corps in the several actions with the enemy and I beg leave to request that you lay this report before His Excellency, so that the officers who had distinguished themselves could be rewarded by His Excellency, as he usually does for their meritorious services to His Royal Highness.

On the 9th, the brigade, being the 5th Division's centre column, marched in good and regular order, to the advanced fortifications of Bayonne; four companies from the 15th Regiment, under my direct command, attacked an enemy advanced post forcing the enemy to abandon it; the brigade kept its order and steadiness until ordered to return to the cantonments.

On the 10th, the brigade was under arms in our advanced posts, and when the enemy tried to break them, the 3rd Regiment was ordered to charge the enemy by the right of the main road, which was done by the whole regiment with great gallantry driving the enemy before them. The conduct of this regiment, of its commander and officers, was very brave and conspicuous. The 15th Regiment protected the artillery[1048] with great steadiness and I felt in it every disposition to be engaged.

On the 11th, the 3rd Regiment was detached to the right, the 15th Regiment on the left of the 9th British, in an advanced position close to the enemy; in the afternoon an order arrived to all the corps to fall back; the 15th and the 9th British should cover this movement. Under heavy artillery and musketry fire, the 15th Regiment held the enemy and kept his position, covering the retreat of the 9th British. Finally, the regiment fell back with great steadiness, despite its right flank being threatened, thanks to the effective measures taken by its commander, Major Archibald Campbell.

In all these occasions all the officers carried out their duties perfectly, but I must mention particularly those who distinguished themselves. Some I witnessed myself, others were recommended by their respective commanding officers. The whole I recommend in view of any reward that His Excellency wishes to give.

Captain Brackenbury, General Spry's Aide-de-Camp, an officer of great valour, was slightly wounded on the 9th and on the 11th, never quitting the battlefield, distinguished himself particularly on the 10th in the attack of the 3rd Regiment, observed by me and General Hope, who positively requested me to recommend that officer to His Excellency the Marshal's attention.

I received the greatest assistance from the Brigade Major, Captain Fitzgerald,[1049] who on all occasions exerted himself with great courage.

Ensign Antonio Peito de Carvalho, 15th Infantry Regiment, who I used to help deliver my orders to the corps on all these occasions, and despite being wounded on the 11th kept carrying on his duties regardless of the danger, deserves that I recommend him to be promoted.[1050]

Colonel Miguel [sic] McCreagh[1051] behaved with his characteristic bravery and merit.

Major Archibald Campbell, the 15th Regiment commander, who Major General Hay saw conducting himself with great gallantry on the 11th and his dispositions were so well made, leaving no doubt of his merits.[1052]

I transmit and personally confirm the names of the officers who distinguished themselves and are recommended by the corps commanding officers:

3rd Regiment:

    Major Joaquim Rebello da Fonceca Rozado[1053]
    Captain, 5th Company, Thome de Avellar[1054]
    Lieutenant, 1st Grenadier Company, Mariano Joze Barrozo[1055]
    Ensign Caetano Joze da Fonceca[1056]
    Adjutant Sergeant Antonio de Almeida Rozado[1057]

15th Regiment:
    Major Antonio Joze Soares Vasconcellos
    Captain, 4th Company, Antonio Ignacio Cayola
    Lieutenant Joze Gomes Menacho[1058]
    Ensign Sebastião Severino dos Reis
    Adjutant Sergeant Antonio Mendes Bello

8th Caçadores Battalion:
    Lieutenant Domingo de Sá Farinha[1059]

This battalion, owing to its shortage of officers, was only partially engaged, but in one of the parties this officer distinguished himself most conspicuously.

Surgeon Joze Machado de Assunção, 15th Regiment, doing the duties of Brigade Surgeon, deserves to be mentioned for his zeal and activity taking care of the wounded.

Lieutenant Colonel Diogo Pereira Forjaz, 3rd Regiment, died gloriously and I deeply regret the loss of such a brave officer.

I enclose the report from Colonel McCreagh on Major Rozado, 3rd Regiment.

I cannot conclude without again requesting that you call the attention of His Excellency the Marshal to those brave officers, both from the staff and from the regiments, and also the sergeants. They deserve to be promoted for their brilliant conduct on the battlefield.

God save you, Sir
Guitariz, 13 December 1813
Manoel de Brito Mozinho

Luiz do Rego Barretto
Colonel, 3rd Brigade Commander

See Tables 16.16, 16.17, and 16.18.

Table 16.1: Return[1060] of the Killed, Wounded and Prisoners in the 7th Brigade in the Action on 9 December 1813[1061]

Quarter at Ville Franque 10 December 1813		Killed								Wounded								Prisoners and Missing								Total								Names and ranks of the officers killed	Names and ranks of the officers wounded	Names and ranks of the officers prisoners and missing	Observations
		Lt Cols	Majors	Captains	Lieutenants	Ensigns	Sergeants and *Furriers*	Drummers	Corporals and Privates	Lt Cols	Majors	Captains	Lieutenants	Ensigns	Sergeants and *Furriers*	Drummers	Corporals and Privates	Lt Cols	Majors	Captains	Lieutenants	Ensigns	Sergeants and *Furriers*	Drummers	Corporals and Privates	Lt Cols	Majors	Captains	Lieutenants	Ensigns	Sergeants and *Furriers*	Drummers	Corporals and Privates				
9th Caçadores Battalion				1					1			1	1		1		29											2	1		1		30	Brevet Major João [sic] Mellik Arrison[1062]	9th Caçadores: Captain Joaquim de Pinho e Souza, severely; Lieutenant Joaquim Izequiel da Cunha, severely 8th Infantry: Adjutant Luis Ignacio de Gouvea, severely; Lieutenant Matheos Joze Roxo, severely; Ensign João Antonio do Carmo, severely 12th Infantry: Captain Antonio Joze Carneiro, severely		
Infantry	8th								5				1	2	1		18												1	2	1		23				
	12th											1			1		19								2			1			1		21				
Total				1					6			2	2	2	3		66								2			3	2	2	3		74				

J Maher
Brigade Major

Table 16.2: Return[1063] of the Killed, Wounded, and Prisoners in the 7th Brigade in the action on 13 December 1813

Quarters at Saint Pierre 14th December 1813		Killed								Wounded								Prisoners and Missing								Total								Observations
		Lt Cols	Majors	Captains	Lieutenants	Ensigns	Sergeants and Furriers	Drummers	Corporals and Privates	Lt Cols	Majors	Captains	Lieutenants	Ensigns	Sergeants and Furriers	Drummers	Corporals and Privates	Lt Cols	Majors	Captains	Lieutenants	Ensigns	Sergeants and Furriers	Drummers	Corporals and Privates	Lt Cols	Majors	Captains	Lieutenants	Ensigns	Sergeants and Furriers	Drummers	Corporals and Privates	
9th Caçadores Battalion									10	1		1		2	6	1	32								2	1		1		2	6	1	44	
Infantry	8th								1																								1	
	12th																																	
Total									11	1		1		2	6	1	32								2	1		1		2	6	1	45	

Names and ranks of the officers killed

Names and ranks of the officers wounded: Lieutenant Colonel George [sic] Brown,[1064] severely; Captain Francisco Joaquim Pereira Valente, slightly; Ensign Pedro Paulo da Silveira severely; Ensign Manoel Bernardino Freire, severely

Names and ranks of the officers prisoners and missing

J Maher
Brigade Major

Table 16.3: Return[1065] of the Killed, Wounded, Prisoners, and Missing in the Portuguese Division under the Command of Major General Lecor in the Action on 13 December 1813

Corps		Killed: Colonels	Lieutenant Colonels	Majors	Captains	Subalterns	Flag Bearers	Sergeants and *Furriéis*	Musicians and Drummers	Corporals and Privates	Wounded: Colonels	Lieutenant Colonels	Majors	Captains	Subalterns	Flag Bearers	Sergeants and *Furriéis*	Musicians and Drummers	Corporals and Privates	Prisoners and Missing: Colonels	Lieutenant Colonels	Majors	Captains	Subalterns	Flag Bearers	Sergeants and *Furriéis*	Musicians and Drummers	Corporals and Privates	Total: Colonels	Lieutenant Colonels	Majors	Captains	Subalterns	Flag Bearers	Sergeants and *Furriéis*	Musicians and Drummers	Corporals and Privates	Mules: Killed	Wounded	Missing
Art.	3rd Brigade											1							5											1								5		5	
Art.	4th Brigade								1										1																			2	1		
Infantry 2nd Brigade	2nd Regiment				1			1		12		1		1			8		105											1		2			9		117			
Infantry 2nd Brigade	14th Regiment							1		19			1		4		2	1	116							1		8			1		4		4	1	143			
Infantry 4th Brigade	4th Regiment									7				2	1		2		70													2	1		2		77			
Infantry 4th Brigade	10th Regiment				1	1				15				2	3		3	1	83													3	4		3	1	98			
Infantry 4th Brigade	10th Caçadores									3				1	5		4	1	33													1	5		4	1	36			
Total					2	1		2		57		2	1	6	13		19	3	413							1		8		2	1	8	14		22	3	478			

Names and ranks of the officers wounded[1066]

Major General Carlos Frederico Lecor, slightly
Lieutenant Colonel Alexander Tulloh, severely

N.B. 4th Artillery Brigade: the soldiers were killed and wounded on 9 December. 10th Regiment: two of the soldiers died in that day

Carlos Frederico Lecor
Major General

Table 16.4: 1st Caçadores. Return[1067] of the Killed, Wounded, Missing and Prisoners on 10 December 1813

Killed							Wounded							Missing and Prisoners							Total							
Lieutenant Colonel	Major	Captains	Subalterns	Sergeants	Buglers	Corporals and Privates	Lieutenant Colonel	Major	Captains	Subalterns	Sergeants	Buglers	Corporals and Privates	Lieutenant Colonel	Major	Captains	Subalterns	Sergeants	Buglers	Corporals and Privates	Lieutenant Colonel	Major	Captains	Subalterns	Sergeants	Buglers	Corporals and Privates	Observations
-	-	-	-	-	-	3	-	-	-	-	-	-	11	-	-	-	-	-	-	-	-	-	-	-	-	-	14	Name and rank of officers killed / Name and rank of officers wounded / Name and rank of officers prisoners or missing

Camp of Arangues, 10 December 1813

K Snodgrass
Lieutenant Colonel
1st Caçadores commander

Table 16.5: 3rd Caçadores. Return[1068] of the Killed, Wounded, Missing and Prisoners in the Action on 9 December 1813

	Killed							Wounded							Missing							Prisoners							Total						
	Superior Officers	Captains	Subalterns	Staff	Sergeants and *Furriés*	Buglers and Musicians	Corporals and Privates	Superior Officers	Captains	Subalterns	Staff	Sergeants and *Furriés*	Buglers and Musicians	Corporals and Privates	Superior Officers	Captains	Subalterns	Staff	Sergeants and *Furriés*	Buglers and Musicians	Corporals and Privates	Superior Officers	Captains	Subalterns	Staff	Sergeants and *Furriés*	Buglers and Musicians	Corporals and Privates	Superior Officers	Captains	Subalterns	Staff	Sergeants and *Furriés*	Buglers and Musicians	Corporals and Privates
Total														1																					1
	Names of the officers killed							Names of the officers wounded							Names of the officers missing							Names of the officers prisoners							Observations						

Cantonment of Arbonne, December 10th 1813

Manoel Pinto da Silveira
Lieutenant Colonel, commander

Table 16.6: 3rd Caçadores. Return[1069] of the Killed, Wounded, Missing and Prisoners in the Action on 10 December 1813

	Killed							Wounded							Missing							Prisoners							Total						
	Superior Officers	Captains	Subalterns	Staff	Sergeants and *Furriés*	Buglers and Musicians	Corporals and Privates	Superior Officers	Captains	Subalterns	Staff	Sergeants and *Furriés*	Buglers and Musicians	Corporals and Privates	Superior Officers	Captains	Subalterns	Staff	Sergeants and *Furriés*	Buglers and Musicians	Corporals and Privates	Superior Officers	Captains	Subalterns	Staff	Sergeants and *Furriés*	Buglers and Musicians	Corporals and Privates	Superior Officers	Captains	Subalterns	Staff	Sergeants and *Furriés*	Buglers and Musicians	Corporals and Privates
Total							1	1	1	1				12															1	1	1				13
	Names of the officers killed							Names of the officers wounded Major Manoel Caetano Teixeira Pinto severely Captain Daniel Kirk severely[1070] Ensign Manoel Martins Taveira severely							Names of the officers missing							Names of the officers prisoners							Observations						

Cantonment of Arbonne, 12 December 1813

Manoel Pinto da Silveira
Lieutenant Colonel, commander

Table 16.7: 3rd Caçadores. Return[1071] of the Killed, Wounded, Missing and Prisoners in the Battle on 11 December 1813

	Killed							Wounded							Missing							Prisoners							Total						
	Superior Officers	Captains	Subalterns	Staff	Sergeants and *Furriés*	Buglers and Musicians	Corporals and Privates	Superior Officers	Captains	Subalterns	Staff	Sergeants and *Furriés*	Buglers and Musicians	Corporals and Privates	Superior Officers	Captains	Subalterns	Staff	Sergeants and *Furriés*	Buglers and Musicians	Corporals and Privates	Superior Officers	Captains	Subalterns	Staff	Sergeants and *Furriés*	Buglers and Musicians	Corporals and Privates	Superior Officers	Captains	Subalterns	Staff	Sergeants and *Furriés*	Buglers and Musicians	Corporals and Privates
Total							1					1		6																			1		7
	Names of the officers killed							Names of the officers wounded							Names of the officers missing							Names of the officers prisoners							Observations						

Cantonment of Arbonne, 12 December 1813

Manoel Pinto da Silveira
Lieutenant Colonel, commander

Table 16.8: 17th Infantry. Return[1072] of the Killed, Wounded, Missing and Prisoners on 10 December 1813

Ranks	Killed	Wounded		Prisoners	Missing
		Severely	Slightly		
Corporals and Privates			1	9	
Total			1	9	

Observation: on the 9th, 11th, 12th, and 13th the regiment did not have any casualties.
Camp of Arbonne, 16 December 1813

John Rolt
Lieutenant Colonel, 17th Regiment commander

Table 16.9: 7th Caçadores. Return[1073] of the Casualties in the Action against the Enemy on 10 December 1813

Camp Arbonne 11 December 1813	Officers						Sergeants	Buglers	Corporals and Privates	Total
	Lieutenant Colonel	Major	Captains	Lieutenants	Ensigns	Staff				
Killed										
Wounded		1			1				3	5
Missing										
Total		1			1				3	5

Names of the officers wounded:
Major João [sic] Scott Lillie, slightly;
Ensign Vicente Joze de Almeida, severely

JS Lillie
Major, commander

Table 16.10: Return[1074] of the Killed, Wounded, Prisoners, and Missing in the 1st Infantry Brigade on 9th December 1813

Corps	Killed									Wounded									Prisoners and Missing									Total									Observations
	Colonels	Lieutenant Colonels	Majors	Captains	Subalterns	Flag Bearers	Sergeants and Furriers	Musicians and Drummers	Corporals and Privates	Colonels	Lieutenant Colonels	Majors	Captains	Subalterns	Flag Bearers	Sergeants and Furriers	Musicians and Drummers	Corporals and Privates	Colonels	Lieutenant Colonels	Majors	Captains	Subalterns	Flag Bearers	Sergeants and Furriers	Musicians and Drummers	Corporals and Privates	Colonels	Lieutenant Colonels	Majors	Captains	Subalterns	Flag Bearers	Sergeants and Furriers	Musicians and Drummers	Corporals and Privates	
1st Infantry	-	-	-	-	-	-	-	-	2	-	-	-	-	1	-	3	-	40	-	-	-	-	-	-	-	-	-	-	-	-	-	1	-	3	-	42	
16th Infantry	-	-	-	-	-	-	-	-	-	-	-	-	-	-	-	-	-	-	-	-	-	-	-	-	-	-	-	-	-	-	-	-	-	-	-	-	
4th Caçadores	-	-	-	-	-	-	-	-	3	-	-	-	1	2	-	4	1	29	-	-	-	-	-	-	-	-	-	-	-	-	1	2	-	4	1	32	
Total	-	-	-	-	-	-	-	-	5	-	-	-	1	3	-	7	1	69	-	-	-	-	-	-	-	-	-	-	-	-	1	3	-	7	1	74	
	Ranks and names of the officers killed									Ranks and names of the officers wounded									Ranks and names of the officers missing and prisoners																		
	Ensign Caetano Gomes da Silva, 1st Regiment, slightly; Captain Caetano Alberto Canavarro, 4th Caçadores, slightly; Brevet Captain Antonio Vicente Queiros, ditto, severely; Ensign Luiz de Vasconcellos[1075], ditto, slightly;																																				

A Campbell
Brigadier General

Table 16.11: Return[1076] of the Killed, Wounded, Prisoners, and Missing in the 1st Infantry Brigade on 10 December 1813

Corps	Killed									Wounded									Prisoners and Missing									Total								
	Colonels	Lieutenant Colonels	Majors	Captains	Subalterns	Flag Bearers	Sergeants and Furriés	Musicians and Drummers	Corporals and Privates	Colonels	Lieutenant Colonels	Majors	Captains	Subalterns	Flag Bearers	Sergeants and Furriés	Musicians and Drummers	Corporals and Privates	Colonels	Lieutenant Colonels	Majors	Captains	Subalterns	Flag Bearers	Sergeants and Furriés	Musicians and Drummers	Corporals and Privates	Colonels	Lieutenant Colonels	Majors	Captains	Subalterns	Flag Bearers	Sergeants and Furriés	Musicians and Drummers	Corporals and Privates
1st Infantry	-	-	-	1	1	-	-	-	29	-	-	-	3	5	-	4	-	44	1	-	1	-	-	-	-	-	-	1	-	1	4	6	-	4	-	73
16th Infantry	-	-	-	-	-	-	-	-	104	-	-	-	1	1	-	2	-	33	-	-	-	2	1	-	1	1	67	-	-	-	3	2	-	3	1	204
4th Caçadores	-	-	-	-	1	-	-	-	8	-	-	-	1	1	-	-	-	19	-	-	-	1	-	-	-	-	-	-	-	-	2	2	-	-	-	27
Total	-	-	-	1	2	-	-	-	141	-	-	-	5	7	-	6	-	96	1	-	1	3	1	-	1	1	67	1	-	1	9	10	-	7	1	304

Ranks and names of the officers killed

1st Regiment
Captain Joze Colaço da Silva
16th Regiment
Lieutenant Domingos Vicente de Freitas
4th Caçadores
Ensign Joze Maria[1077]

Ranks and names of the officers wounded

1st Regiment
Captain Joaquim Ferreira dos Santos, slightly; Captain Joze Soares Barrão, ditto; Captain Vitorino Joze de Almeida, ditto; Lieutenant Sebastião Gustavo,[1078] severely, amputated; Ensign Adjutant Joze Fernandes da Silva, severely; Ensign Antonio Felles de Matos, ditto; Ensign Anselmo Joze Mendes, ditto; Ensign Francisco Maria Jordão, ditto[1079]

16th Regiment
Captain Carlos [sic] Lempriere, severely[1080]; Lieutenant Aurelio Joze de Moraes, ditto
4th Caçadores; Captain Joze Maria da Cunha, severely; Ensign Joze Cardozo[1081]

Ranks and names of the officers missing and prisoners

Major O'Hara,[1082] 1st Regiment, severely wounded

16th Regiment:
Colonel Francisco Homem de Magalhaes Pizarro; Captain Joze Bruno[1083]; Captain Joaquim Joze Xavier; Ensign Fernando Teles da Silva Penalva; Captain Joze Bernardino de Faria, 4th Caçadores

Observations

N.B. Nine of the Caçadores wounded were made prisoners.

A Campbell
Brigadier General

Table 16.12: 10th Brigade. Return[1084] of the Killed, Wounded, and Prisoners in the Brigade on 9 December 1813

Regiments	Killed										Wounded										Prisoners and Missing									
	Colonels	Lieutenant Colonels	Majors	Captains	Lieutenants	Ensigns	Sergeants	Drummers	Corporals and Privates	Total	Colonels	Lieutenant Colonels	Majors	Captains	Lieutenants	Ensigns	Sergeants	Drummers	Corporals and Privates	Total	Colonels	Lieutenant Colonels	Majors	Captains	Lieutenants	Ensigns	Sergeants	Drummers	Corporals and Privates	Total
5th Caçadores Battalion	-	-	-	-	-	-	-	-	1	1	-	-	-	-	-	-	-	1	5	6	-	-	-	-	-	-	-	1	-	1
13th Regiment	-	-	-	-	-	-	-	-	-	-	-	-	-	-	-	-	-	-	-	-	-	-	-	-	-	-	-	-	-	-
24th Regiment	-	-	-	-	-	-	-	-	-	-	-	-	-	-	-	1	-	-	-	1	-	-	-	-	-	-	-	-	-	-
Total	-	-	-	-	-	-	-	-	1	1	-	-	-	-	-	1	-	1	5	7	-	-	-	-	-	-	-	1	-	1

Names and ranks of the officers killed

Names and ranks of the officers wounded

Ensign Nicolao Lopes, slightly wounded

Names and ranks of the officers prisoners and missing

G Lenon [sic]
Brigade Major

Table 16.13: 10th Brigade. Return[1085] of the Killed, Wounded, and Prisoners in the Brigade on 10 December 1813

Regiments	Killed										Wounded										Prisoners									
	Colonels	Lieutenant Colonels	Majors	Captains	Lieutenants	Ensigns	Sergeants	Drummers	Corporals and Privates	Total	Colonels	Lieutenant Colonels	Majors	Captains	Lieutenants	Ensigns	Sergeants	Drummers	Corporals and Privates	Total	Colonels	Lieutenant Colonels	Majors	Captains	Lieutenants	Ensigns	Sergeants	Drummers	Corporals and Privates	Total
5th Caçadores Battalion	-	-	-	1	-	-	-	-	8	9	-	-	-	2	1	2	8	-	43	56	-	-	-	-	-	1	1	-	4	6
13th Regiment	-	-	-	-	-	-	-	-	3	3	-	-	-	1	-	2	-	-	22	25	-	-	-	-	-	-	-	-	-	-
24th Regiment	-	-	1	1	-	-	1	-	6	9	-	-	-	-	-	1	4	-	56	61	-	-	-	-	-	-	-	-	6	6
Total	-	-	1	2	-	-	1	-	17	21	-	-	-	3	1	5	12	-	121	142	-	-	-	-	-	1	1	-	10	12

Names and ranks of the officers killed

Major Joaquim Anacleto Ferreira da Costa, 24th Regiment; Captain Joaquim Antonio Callado, 24th Regiment; Captain Francisco de Paula Arraes, 5th Caçadores Battalion

Names and ranks of the officers wounded[1086]

Captain 2nd Company Antonio Carlos de Mendonça,[1087] 13th Regiment, slightly wounded Adjutant Jozé Climaco Brancamp and Ensign Francisco de Paula Salema, both from the 13th Regiment, slightly wounded; Ensign Nicolao Lopes, 24th Regiment, severely wounded[1088]

5th Caçadores:
Captain Thomas Bunbury, severely; Captain Manoel Joaquim de Menezes, slightly; Lieutenant Jozé Carrasco,[1089] slightly; Ensign Antonio Augusto, severely

Names and ranks of the officers prisoners

Ensign Francisco Neri;[1090] 5th Caçadores

G Lenon [sic]
Brigade Major

Table 16.14: 10th Brigade. Return[1091] of the Killed, Wounded, and Prisoners in the Brigade on 11 December 1813

Regiments	Killed										Wounded										Prisoners									
	Colonels	Lieutenant Colonels	Majors	Captains	Lieutenants	Ensigns	Sergeants	Drummers	Corporals and Privates	Total	Colonels	Lieutenant Colonels	Majors	Captains	Lieutenants	Ensigns	Sergeants	Drummers	Corporals and Privates	Total	Colonels	Lieutenant Colonels	Majors	Captains	Lieutenants	Ensigns	Sergeants	Drummers	Corporals and Privates	Total
5th Caçadores Battalion	-	-	-	-	1	-	-	-	-	1	-	-	-	-	-	-	-	-	9	9	-	-	-	-	-	-	-	-	12	12
13th Regiment	-	-	-	-	-	-	1	-	8	9	-	-	-	2	-	2	4	-	45	53	-	-	-	-	-	-	-	-	30	30
24th Regiment	-	-	-	-	-	-	1	-	1	2	-	-	-	1	-	2	1	-	19	23	-	-	-	-	-	-	-	-	8	8
Total	-	-	-	-	1	-	2	-	9	12	-	-	-	3	-	4	5	-	73	85	-	-	-	-	-	-	-	-	50	50
	Names and ranks of the officers killed										Names and ranks of the officers wounded										Names and ranks of the officers prisoners									
	Lieutenant Luiz Pedro[1092], 5th Caçadores										Captain Joaquim Antonio de Almeida, 13th Regiment, and Captain Antonio Francisco de Paula Pontes, from the same regiment, both slightly wounded; Adjutant Diogo Ignacio de Souza, 13th Regiment, slightly wounded; Ensign Francisco de Paula Salema, severely wounded; Captain Luis Manoel Lemos, 24th Regiment, severely; Ensigns Francisco Pinto[1093] and Antonio Caetano,[1094] both from the 24th Regiment, both severely wounded																			

G Lenon [sic]
Brigade Major

Table 16.15: 10th Brigade. Return[1095] of the Killed, Wounded, and Prisoners in the Brigade on 12 December 1813

Regiments	Killed										Wounded										Prisoners									
	Colonels	Lieutenant Colonels	Majors	Captains	Lieutenants	Ensigns	Sergeants	Drummers	Corporals and Privates	Total	Colonels	Lieutenant Colonels	Majors	Captains	Lieutenants	Ensigns	Sergeants	Drummers	Corporals and Privates	Total	Colonels	Lieutenant Colonels	Majors	Captains	Lieutenants	Ensigns	Sergeants	Drummers	Corporals and Privates	Total
5th Caçadores Battalion	-	-	-	-	-	-	-	-	-	-	-	-	-	-	-	-	-	-	2	2	-	-	-	-	-	-	-	-	-	-
13th Regiment	-	-	-	-	-	-	-	-	-	-	-	-	-	-	-	-	-	-	4	4	-	-	-	-	-	-	-	-	-	-
24th Regiment	-	-	-	-	-	-	-	-	1	1	-	-	-	-	-	-	-	-	4	4	-	-	-	-	-	-	-	-	-	-
Total	-	-	-	-	-	-	-	-	1	1	-	-	-	-	-	-	-	-	10	10	-	-	-	-	-	-	-	-	-	-
	Names and ranks of the officers killed										Names and ranks of the officers wounded										Names and ranks of the officers prisoners									

G Lenon [sic]
Brigade Major

Table 16.16: Return[1096] of the Casualties in Combat of the 3rd Brigade on 9 December 1813

Camp 9 December 1813	Killed										Wounded										Prisoners and Missing									
	Colonels	Lieutenant Colonels	Majors	Captains	Lieutenants	Ensigns	Staff	Sergeants	Drummers	Corporals and Privates	Colonels	Lieutenant Colonels	Majors	Captains	Lieutenants	Ensigns	Staff	Sergeants	Drummers	Corporals and Privates	Colonels	Lieutenant Colonels	Majors	Captains	Lieutenants	Ensigns	Staff	Sergeants	Drummers	Corporals and Privates
3rd Regiment	-	-	-	-	-	-	-	-	-	-	-	-	-	-	-	-	-	3	-	8	-	-	-	-	-	-	-	-	-	-
15th Regiment	-	-	-	-	-	-	-	-	-	2	-	-	-	-	-	-	-	-	-	20	-	-	-	-	-	-	-	-	-	1
8th Battalion	-	-	-	-	-	-	-	1	-	-	-	-	-	-	1	1	-	1	-	11	-	-	-	1	-	-	-	1	1	10
Total	-	-	-	-	-	-	-	1	-	2	-	-	-	-	1	1	-	4	-	39	-	-	-	1	-	-	-	1	1	11

Luiz do Rego Barretto
Colonel, brigade commander

Names of the officers

Wounded:
Lieutenant Domingos de Sá Pereira Farinha, slightly;
Ensign Rodrigo Navarro, severely;
Aide-de-Camp to Major General Spry, Captain Eduardo [sic] Brackenbury, slightly.

Prisoner:
Captain Antonio Carllos[1097]

Table 16.17: Return[1098] of the Casualties in Combat on 10 December 1813 in the 3rd Infantry Brigade

Camp 10th December 1813	Killed										Wounded										Prisoners and Missing									
	Colonels	Lieutenant Colonels	Majors	Captains	Lieutenants	Ensigns	Staff	Sergeants	Drummers	Corporals and Privates	Colonels	Lieutenant Colonels	Majors	Captains	Lieutenants	Ensigns	Staff	Sergeants	Drummers	Corporals and Privates	Colonels	Lieutenant Colonels	Majors	Captains	Lieutenants	Ensigns	Staff	Sergeants	Drummers	Corporals and Privates
3rd Regiment	-	1	-	-	-	-	-	-	-	6	-	-	1	-	4	2	-	4	-	69	-	-	-	-	-	-	-	-	-	2
15th Regiment	-	-	-	-	-	-	-	-	-	-	-	-	-	-	-	-	-	-	-	3	-	-	-	-	-	-	-	-	-	1
8th Battalion	-	-	-	-	-	-	-	-	-	1	-	-	-	-	-	-	-	-	-	4	-	-	-	-	-	-	-	-	-	-
Total	-	1	-	-	-	-	-	-	-	7	-	-	1	-	4	2	-	4	-	76	-	-	-	-	-	-	-	-	-	3

Names of the officers

Killed:
Lieutenant Colonel Luis Diogo Forjaz

Wounded:
Major Joaquim Rebelo da Fonceca Rozado, slightly;
Lieutenant Amaro dos Santos Barrozo, severely;
Lieutenant Ignacio da Cunha Gasparinho, severely;
Lieutenant Antonio Bernardo,[1099] severely;
Lieutenant Joze Maria Crivas, slightly;
Ensign Joaquim de Souza,[1100] severely;
Ensign Antonio Coelho Seabra, severely[1101]

Luiz do Rego Barretto
Colonel, brigade commander

Table 16.18: Return[102] of the Casualties in Combat of the 3rd Infantry Brigade on 11 December 1813

Camp 11th December 1813	Killed										Wounded										Prisoners and Missing									
	Colonels	Lieutenant Colonels	Majors	Captains	Lieutenants	Ensigns	Staff	Sergeants	Drummers	Corporals and Privates	Colonels	Lieutenant Colonels	Majors	Captains	Lieutenants	Ensigns	Staff	Sergeants	Drummers	Corporals and Privates	Colonels	Lieutenant Colonels	Majors	Captains	Lieutenants	Ensigns	Staff	Sergeants	Drummers	Corporals and Privates
3rd Regiment	-	-	-	-	-	-	-	-	-	-	-	-	-	-	1	-	1	2	-	17	-	-	-	-	-	-	-	-	-	4
15th Regiment	-	-	-	-	-	-	-	-	-	18	-	-	-	1	2	3	-	3	-	32	-	-	-	-	-	-	-	-	-	82
8th Battalion	-	-	-	-	-	-	-	-	-	1	-	-	-	-	-	-	-	1	1	14	-	-	-	-	-	-	-	-	-	3
Total	-	-	-	-	-	-	-	-	-	19	-	-	-	1	3	3	1	6	1	63	-	-	-	-	-	-	-	-	-	89

Names of the officers

Wounded:

3rd Regiment:
Lieutenant Adjutant Antonio Franco da Roza, slightly;
Lieutenant Alexandre [sic] Campbell,[1103] severely;

15th Regiment:
Captain João Correa Guedes, slightly;
Lieutenant Joze Antonio Franco, severely;
Lieutenant João de Sepulveda[1104], slightly;
Ensign Joze Maria Callado de Oliveira, slightly;
Ensign Antonio Peito[105], slightly;
Ensign Jeronimo Caetano de Almeida, severely

Luiz do Rego Barretto
Colonel, brigade commander

Chapter 17

An Overview of the Campaign of 1814

After the battle of Nive Wellington's Army went into winter quarters. There were both political and military reasons for doing so. Wellington was still unsure whether the Coalition in Central Europe would continue operations and invade France, or would stop at the French border. Militarily he ceased operations because

> In military operations there are some things which can not be done; one of them is to move troops in this country during or immediately after a violent rain fall. I believe I shall lose many more men than I shall ever replace, by putting any troops in camp in this bad weather; but I should be guilty of an useless waste of men, if I were to attempt an operation during the violent falls of rain which we have here.[1106]

At the beginning of January 1814 Soult was able to muster about 80,000 men, many of whom were national guards. In mid-January he was ordered to send two infantry divisions, his dragoon division, and a light cavalry brigade north to reinforce Napoleon. For Soult, these were drastic cuts in the numbers of his troops, for it amounted to 45 per cent of his infantry and 55 per cent of his cavalry. Just as importantly, these were some of his best troops. He was left with about 40,000 men to defend the 40km-long Adour river. Of those men, 8,000 were part of the garrison of Bayonne.

Since both armies were in winter quarters, fighting was limited in January. However, the Portuguese Division and the 8th Brigade saw action in the early days of January, when the French attacked on 3 January near La Bastide de Clarence and reached Bon Loc[1107] before they were stopped. Heavy rains prevented the Allies from forcing them back until 6 January.

The situation remained quiet until mid-February when the Allies began their offensive. Wellington planned to split his army in two. One part, commanded by Hope, would be responsible for besieging Bayonne. It consisted of the 1st and 5th Divisions, plus the 1st and 10th Brigades, Aylmer's British Brigade, General Vandeleur's Light Cavalry Brigade, and 16,000 Spanish troops. In addition to besieging Bayonne, they were to protect the Allies' supply lines from Saint Jean de Luz which was only 25km south of the fortress.

The rest of Wellington's Army would be a mobile force that would cross the Adour river upstream of Bayonne and drive Soult's Army further away from the fortress. It comprised six Allied divisions, the Portuguese Division, and a Spanish division. Its total strength was 52,000 men. Wellington further divided this force into three parts. On the right was Hill, with the 2nd and Portuguese Divisions, and Morillo's Spanish Division. In the centre was the 3rd Division, and on the left was Beresford with the 4th and 7th Divisions. In reserve, following Beresford, were the 6th and Light Divisions.

Operations began on 15 February, when Hill attacked Harispe's Division near Garris. The 5th Brigade and the Portuguese Division were both involved in the fighting. At the same time the 3rd Division threatened Leval's Division at Bon Loc. Harispe could not hold his position and his troops fell back in disorder across the Bidouze river at St Palais. They were unable to hold the bridge and had to retreat further east to Arriverayte,[1108] to defend the Saison river. Because Harispe had retreated further than expected, the French forces that were holding the Bidouze river had to retreat. Beresford's forces advanced on 15 February and faced little opposition. Soult, seeing the danger to his eastern flank, ordered all troops in the vicinity of Bayonne, except for its garrison, to march east.

Heavy rains caused the numerous rivers in the area to flood and made it exceedingly difficult to march over the muddy roads. By 18 February operations had ceased and did not begin again until 22 February, when the 6th and Light Divisions were sent to reinforce Hill. The next day the 7th Division attacked Foy's Division in the vicinity of Hastingues and drove them back across the Gave Réunis river.[1109] Manoeuvring by the Allies forced Soult to give up his position on the Saison and the Gave d'Oloron rivers and to fall back towards Orthez, where he defended along the Gave de Pau river.

During the hiatus in operations from 18 to 22 February, Hope's forces made final preparations for investing Bayonne. On 24 February a bridge was thrown across the Adour river, downstream of the city. Allied forces crossed and invested the city from the north. Once the north bank of the Adour had been secured, Hope decided it was time to clear the various enemy outposts on the northern bank of the river. On 27 February he ordered the 1st Division to take the Heights of St Etienne, about 750m north of the river. The 10th Brigade supported the attack. Hope opted to blockade the city and starve it into surrendering.

Soult turned to face his pursuers at Orthez and on 27 February Wellington caught up with him. All seven of the Portuguese infantry brigades that were part of the mobile force took part in the battle. The French were not able to stop the Allies and by the end of the day had to retreat east. Wellington lost contact with the French and, not knowing which direction they had taken, he sent Beresford north towards Bordeaux and Hill eastward. Hill found the French rearguard at Aire[1110] on 2 March. The Portuguese Division as well as the 5th and 7th Brigades were involved in the fighting. Initially Costa's 2nd Brigade attacked up the ridge that the French occupied and took it. They had not been there long when they were counter-attacked by a smaller number of French soldiers and thrown back in great disorder. Hill was incensed by the 2nd Brigade's performance and blamed its commander, who was relieved of his command a few days later.

After the combat at Aire, Soult continued to withdraw his army eastward and eventually stopped at Vic Bigorre,[1111] 50km to the southeast. Wellington chose not to pursue him and turned his attention to Bordeaux. After resting his troops, Soult went on the offensive and attacked Hill. There was a cavalry skirmish at Viella on 13 March between the 4th Cavalry and the French 10th Chasseurs and on 15 March Soult reached Aire. Wellington decided to go on the offensive again and the Allies caught the French at Vic Bigorre on 19 March. The French were in danger of being surrounded. Soult decided not to risk his army and broke off the fighting. The 8th Brigade lost more than 100 men in the combat. The French withdrew to Tarbes and Wellington followed closely. On 20 March the French rearguard – three divisions commanded by Clausel – was positioned on a ridge to the east of Tarbes. There was some heavy fighting on their right, and when their flank was about to be turned, the French withdrew. Some Portuguese troops were involved in the combat but did not play a major role.

The French retreated from Tarbes and Soult marched his army 150km east to Toulouse, where he planned to make a stand. He succeeded in evading the Allies' pursuit and had several days to prepare the defences of the city. Wellington arrived there on 27 March. Rather than trying a river assault to take the city, he sent Hill about 15km upstream to cross the river there. Once again Wellington was foiled by heavy rains. The river was too wide for the pontoon bridge and Hill was recalled. Wellington then tried to bridge the river about 20km downstream of the city. This was accomplished on 4 April and Beresford, with the 3rd, 4th, and Light Divisions, crossed. Heavy rains broke the bridge that evening and the Allies on the north bank were cut off for three days.

The rain let up on 7 April and communications were established between the two wings of Wellington's Army. The 6th Division crossed the river and reinforced Beresford. The Portuguese on the north bank of the river were the 7th, 8th, and 9th Brigades, plus the troops of the Light Division. Deployed on the south side of the river, in front of the Toulouse suburbs, were the 5th Brigade on the left, and the 2nd Division and the Portuguese Division on the right. The attack began early on the morning of 10 April when Hill ordered that the first defensive line south of the city be cleared. After doing so, he stopped the attack.

Across the river the terrain was dominated by a high ridge called Mont Rave. Beresford sent the 4th and 6th Divisions on a long flanking march to attack it from the east, while Freire's Spanish Division attacked its western flank. The 3rd and Light Divisions attacked the western suburbs and walls of the city. The assaults on Mont Rave were successful but at a heavy cost to the 7th Brigade, which took over 17 per cent casualties. Among them were its brigade commander, as well as both regimental commanders.

After losing his position on Mont Rave, Soult withdrew his army to the suburbs east of Toulouse. There he stayed for about 24 hours and that night, 11 April, marched his army east. The next day Wellington received word that Napoleon had abdicated on 6 April. On 13 April Soult heard the news. An armistice was reached between the armies on 17 April. The military governor of Bayonne had also received news of Napoleon's abdication but refused to surrender. Instead, on 14 April he sallied forth and attacked Hope's troops on the north bank of the Adour. The attack caught the Allies by surprise and their casualties were heavy. The French then withdrew back into the city, and it did not capitulate until 26 April. The long war was finally over. In June Wellington's Army began to disband. The Portuguese, who had been fighting for six years, soon began the long march back to their homeland.

The Portuguese Army

The Allied Army, after six months of campaigning and several major engagements, began the year of 1814 in winter quarters in southwest France, south of the river Adour. The arduous fights in the Pyrenees and southern France had taken a heavy toll on the Portuguese Army, both in the number of men and officers but also on its brigades and regimental commanders.

The field army had difficulty in getting replacements for the losses in its regiments and battalions, and some of them were very understrength. Beresford tried to persuade the Portuguese government in Lisbon to bolster recruitment, but the government insisted it could not completely strip the country of the manpower needed to rebuild agriculture and industry after years of economic destruction. The efforts of the authorities to obtain more men were frustrated by new recruits refusing to show up for duty when ordered to do so and desertion by those who initially obeyed the call.

Another problem was the lack of general officers to command the brigades since there were not many Portuguese general officers capable of field command and many of the most experienced were incapacitated. At the beginning of March Brigadier Generals João Lobo Brandão de Almeida and Luís Inácio Xavier Palmeirim left Portugal to take command of vacant brigades but they arrived in France only after the Battle of Toulouse. A critical shortage of officers in the regiments and battalions became so extreme that by the end of the war several battalions were commanded by captains. Compounding the problem was the fact that by this point of the war very few British officers were entering Portuguese service, and those who did usually came in as subalterns.

The financial situation was untenable. The immense debt of the Portuguese commissariat in Spain led to the fall of its credit and consequent difficulties in supplying the army, both with food and with the animals needed for transport and the artillery. Furthermore, the payment of the troops was in arrears by several months. These problems were somewhat mitigated by the arrival of 200,000 dollars from the government in early January 1814.[1112]

From November 1813 Beresford was employed by Lord Wellington as a de facto corps commander, although this formation was never formally called a corps. Beresford recalled General D'Urban from his cavalry brigade to return to his role as quartermaster general. The other departments of the Portuguese Headquarters had been led by the same officers since 1812.

The Infantry

On 1 January 1814 the infantry brigades were composed and commanded as follows:

Portuguese Division, commanded by Major General Carlos Frederico Lecor, consisting of:
  2nd Brigade commanded by Brigadier General António Hipólito da Costa, about 2,100 men:
    2nd Infantry commanded by Colonel Jorge de Avilez[1113]
    14th Infantry commanded by Major Rodrigo Vito Pereira da Silva
  4th Brigade commanded by Brigadier General John Buchan, about 2,350 men:
    4th Infantry commanded by Lieutenant Colonel *agregado* John Hill[1114]
    10th Infantry commanded by Colonel Luís Maria de Sousa Vahia
    10th Caçadores commanded by Captain José Rodrigues Lima

  5th Brigade commanded by Colonel Henry Hardinge,[1115] 2nd Division, about 2,300 men:
    6th Infantry commanded by Brevet Lieutenant Colonel Manuel Luís Correia[1116]
    18th Infantry commanded by Brevet Major Manuel Pereira Borges[1117]
    6th Caçadores commanded by Lieutenant Colonel Peter Fearon[1118]
  8th Brigade commanded by Major General Manley Power, 3rd Division, about 2,100 men:
    9th Infantry commanded by Lieutenant Colonel Charles Sutton[1119]
    21st Infantry commanded by Colonel João Teles de Meneses
    11th Caçadores commanded by Lieutenant Colonel Charles Kilsha[1120]
  9th Brigade commanded by Colonel José de Vasconcelos e Sá,[1121] 4th Division, about 2,400 men:
    11th Infantry commanded by Lieutenant Colonel Alexander Anderson
    23rd Infantry commanded by Lieutenant Colonel James Miller[1122]
    7th Caçadores commanded by Major John Lillie
  3rd Brigade commanded by Colonel Luís do Rego Barreto,[1123] 5th Division, about 1,550 men:
    3rd Infantry commanded by Major Joaquim Rebelo Fonseca Rosado[1124]
    15th Infantry commanded by Brevet Lieutenant Colonel Archibald Campbell[1125]
    8th Caçadores commanded by Captain Joaquim António Duarte[1126]
  7th Brigade commanded by Colonel James Douglas,[1127] 6th Division, about 2,150 men:
    8th Infantry commanded by Lieutenant Colonel Walter Birmingham[1128]
    12th Infantry commanded by Lieutenant Colonel William Beatty
    9th Caçadores commanded by Major Luís Maria Cerqueira[1129]
  6th Brigade commanded by Colonel John Doyle,[1130] 7th Division, about 2,350 men:
    7th Infantry commanded by Lieutenant Colonel Francisco Xavier Calheiros[1131]
    19th Infantry commanded by Lieutenant Colonel Francisco José da Costa Amaral
    2nd Caçadores commanded by Lieutenant Colonel George Zulke
  Portuguese units in the Light Division, around 1,750 men:
    1st Caçadores commanded by Lieutenant Colonel Kenneth Snodgrass[1132]
    3rd Caçadores commanded by Captain Luís Evaristo de Figueiredo[1133]
    17th Infantry commanded by Lieutenant Colonel John Rolt

1st Brigade (Independent) commanded by Brigadier General Archibald Campbell, about 1,900 men:
   1st Infantry commanded by Colonel Thomas Hill[1134]
   16th Infantry commanded by Lieutenant Colonel José António Vidigal[1135]
   4th Caçadores commanded by Lieutenant Colonel Edmund Williams[1136]
10th Brigade (Independent) commanded by Major General Thomas Bradford, about 1,700 men:
   13th Infantry commanded by Lieutenant Colonel João Carlos de Saldanha
   24th Infantry commanded by Colonel William McBean [sic][1137]
   5th Caçadores commanded by Lieutenant Colonel Thomas Saint Clair

During the campaign of 1814 there were few changes in the command of the brigades. In March 1814, after the combat at Aire, Costa was relieved from the command of the 2nd Brigade and recalled to Portugal. He was replaced first by Colonel Avilez, 2nd Infantry, and then by Lieutenant Colonel John MacDonald, 14th Infantry. General Almeida arrived in the army after the battle of Toulouse and was appointed to command the brigade on 21 April 1814.

General Campbell left for Britain on sick leave on 15 January 1814, being replaced in command of the 1st Brigade by Colonel Hill, 1st Infantry. He returned to France and took command of the brigade after the end of the war.

Colonel Hardinge replaced General Ashworth in command of the 5th Brigade on 16 January 1814.[1138]

The Cavalry
The cavalry consisted of the following units:

Colonel Viscount de Barbacena's Brigade, about 1,000 men:
   1st Cavalry commanded by Lieutenant Colonel Henry Watson
   6th Cavalry commanded by Lieutenant Colonel Richard Diggens
   11th Cavalry commanded by Lieutenant Colonel Martinho Correia Morais e Castro
   12th Cavalry commanded by Lieutenant Colonel António Carlos Cary
4th Cavalry commanded by Colonel John Campbell, about 250 men, attached to Major General Henry Fane's cavalry brigade.

The Artillery
The 1st Artillery had four brigades with the field army:

Brevet Lieutenant Colonel Sebastião José de Arriaga's Brigade of 9-pounder guns
Brevet Major João da Cunha Preto's Brigade of 6-pounder guns
Brevet Captain António da Costa e Silva's Mountain Brigade of 3-pounder guns
Captain Pedro de Roziers Brigade, which was without guns

The 2nd Artillery had one brigade:

Captain João Eduardo Pereira Amado's[1139] Brigade of 9-pounder guns.

Major Preto's and Captain Amado's brigades were attached to the Portuguese Division.
   Lieutenant Colonel Alexander Tulloh commanded these brigades until he was wounded at the Nive and was replaced by Lieutenant Colonel Victor Arentschild, 1st Artillery, in March 1814.

The Engineers
Two companies of the Artificers Battalion were under the command of Major José Jerónimo Granate, Royal Corps of Engineers. They took part in the blockade of Fort Blaye near Bordeaux in the first days of April 1814.

Chapter 18

The Actions of 3–6 January 1814

Although both the French and the Allies went into winter quarters after the battles of Nive, both maintained a line of picquets in front of their cantonments. In early January Soult took action to secure his lines of communication between Saint-Jean-Pied-de-Port and Bayonne and attacked the Allied outposts along the La Joyeuse river in the vicinity of La Bastide de Clarence and Bon Loc, which were manned by the 4th Infantry of the 4th Brigade and the 11th Caçadores of the 8th Brigade.

The French attacked with two brigades and the Portuguese retreated 12km northwest to Briscous. In the south the French sent infantry and cavalry 12km to the southwest. There they forced the British cavalry back across the Joyeuse river and liberated Bon Loc, which was picqueted by the 11th Caçadores. The commander of the caçadores counter-attacked and at the end of the day the village was back in Allied hands. However, because the outposts in the north had retreated, the 11th Caçadores abandoned the village and the French retook it.

Wellington ordered the men of the Portuguese Division, as well as the 3rd and 7th Divisions, out of their cantonments to counter the French. Heavy rains prevented them from moving into position until 6 January. The 10th Infantry and the 10th Caçadores of the 4th Brigade led the attack in the north. The French chose not to stand and pulled back across the Joyeuse river but did not leave La Bastide-Clarence. In the south the Allies skirmished with the French, who quickly withdrew.

Bon Loc, 3 January 1814

3rd Division

8th Brigade (9th and 21st Infantry, 11th Caçadores)

Report[1140] from General Power to AG Mozinho

Hasparren, January 6th 1814

Sir,

I have the honour to enclose to you, to be laid before Marshal Sir William Beresford, a report which I have received from Lieutenant Colonel Kilsha, commanding the 11th Caçadores, of the conduct of that Battalion, on the 3rd instant, when the enemy made a movement in the whole of our front and advanced upon the village of Bunlock.[1141] At the same time that they attacked the whole line of our picquets, I understand from other reports, nothing could exceed the gallantry of the above battalion upon the above occasion, as well as the able disposition made by Lieutenant Colonel Kilsha.

I beg leave also at the same time, to report for His Excellency's information, the good conduct of the 9th Regiment commanded by Colonel Sutton, which regiment was on the left of the 3rd Division, on the road to La Bastide and covered the town of Hasparren.

I have the honour to be Sir, your most obedient and humble servant

M. Power
Major General

To the Adjutant General

P.S. Lieutenant Colonel Kilsha is very lavish in the praise of 1st Sergeant Joze Antonio da Fonseca, whose individual courage and exertions, was beyond description. He commanded the advanced picquets until the battalion came to his support.

11th Caçadores

Report[1142] from Lieutenant Colonel Kilsha to General Power

Sir,

I have the honour to inform His Excellency that on the 3rd of this month a party of enemy cavalry forced the retreat of the picquet of British cavalry posted in the village of Bonloc and the enemy's party, passing the village, discovered the advanced picquet of the 11th Caçadores Battalion posted just outside the village. The picquet immediately started to fire and forced their retreat.

I promptly marched with the battalion to support the picquet, according to your orders. When I arrived, I found the French occupying a position in the church and in the part of the village at the right of the bridge with a cavalry squadron and two hundred *chasseurs*. I ordered two companies to occupy the best positions to defend the passage of the bridge and posted another two companies in a wood, on the left of the bridge, from which they could cross fire; the other two companies remained as a reserve to act according to the circumstances.

The French tried to cross the bridge two times, attacking with cavalry and infantry, but were repelled and on the latter the two companies near the bridge advanced and seized the church's position. The enemy retired to the heights, firing until the night. The battalion under my command behaved with great gallantry and steadiness, and all the officers deserve my complete approbation.

It is my duty to mention particularly the excellent conduct of 1st Sergeant Joze Antonio da Fonceca, who was posted at twenty paces from the bridge with a small party with orders to defend it until the last, which he did with great bravery and the fire of his party stopped the enemy at the centre of the bridge forcing them to retreat. I enclose the return of the killed and wounded.

God save you, Sir
Hasparren 6 January 1814
Major General Power

Charles Kilsha
Lieutenant Colonel 11th Caçadores

See Table 18.1.

La Bastide de Clarence, 3-6 January 1814

Portuguese Division

Report[1143] from General Lecor to AG Mozinho

Sir,

I have the honour to enclose the returns of the killed, wounded, and missing in the 4th Infantry Brigade on the 3rd to 6th instant. I have the satisfaction to inform you that from the men missing on the 3rd 8 have re-joined.

Brigadier Buchan, on the 6th, strongly recommended Ensign José da Cunha Mello and Adjutant Sergeant Antonio José dos Santos,[1144] whose conduct deserved the approbation of General Fane. He requests that you lay their names before His Excellency the Marshal Marquis de Campo Maior.

God save you, Sir
Maison du Malde, 8 January 1814

Carlos Frederico Lecor
Major General

Brigadier General Mozinho

See Tables 18.2 and 18.3.

Table 18.1: 8th Brigade. Return[1145] of the Killed, Wounded, Prisoners, and Missing on 3 January 1814

	Killed									Wounded									Prisoners and Missing									Total									
	Colonels	Lieutenant Colonels	Majors	Captains	Subalterns	Flag Bearers	Sergeants and *Furriéis*	Musicians and Drummers	Corporals and Privates	Colonels	Lieutenant Colonels	Majors	Captains	Subalterns	Flag Bearers	Sergeants and *Furriéis*	Musicians and Drummers	Corporals and Privates	Colonels	Lieutenant Colonels	Majors	Captains	Subalterns	Flag Bearers	Sergeants and *Furriéis*	Musicians and Drummers	Corporals and Privates	Colonels	Lieutenant Colonels	Majors	Captains	Subalterns	Flag Bearers	Sergeants and *Furriéis*	Musicians and Drummers	Corporals and Privates
9th Regiment																		2																			2
21st Regiment																																				
11th Caçadores													1	1		1		7																		10
Total													1	1		1		9																		12
	Names and ranks of the officers killed									Names and ranks of the officers wounded									Names and ranks of the officers missing and prisoners									Observations									
										Captain A. de Borgh,[1146] slightly / Ensign Joze Maria da Maré, slightly																		Charl. Sutton / Colonel 9th Regiment commander									

N.B. Major General Power commanded the division on this day.

Table 18.2: Return[147] of the Killed, Wounded, and Missing in the 4th Infantry Brigade on 3 January 1814

		Killed									Wounded									Prisoners; Missing									Total									Mules		
		Colonel	Lieutenant Colonels	Majors	Captains	Subalterns	Flag Bearers	Sergeants and *Furriéis*	Musicians and Drummers	Corporals and Privates	Colonel	Lieutenant Colonels	Majors	Captains	Subalterns	Flag Bearers	Sergeants and *Furriéis*	Musicians and Drummers	Corporals and Privates	Colonel	Lieutenant Colonels	Majors	Captains	Subalterns	Flag Bearers	Sergeants and *Furriéis*	Musicians and Drummers	Corporals and Privates	Colonel	Lieutenant Colonels	Majors	Captains	Subalterns	Flag Bearers	Sergeants and *Furriéis*	Musicians and Drummers	Corporals and Privates	Killed	Wounded	Missing
Artillery / 2nd Brigade	3rd Brigade																																							
Artillery / 2nd Brigade	4th Brigade																																							
Infantry / 2nd Brigade	2nd Regiment																																							
Infantry / 2nd Brigade	14th Regiment																																							
Infantry / 4th Brigade	4th Regiment									1							1		8									12							1		21			
Infantry / 4th Brigade	10th Regiment																																							
Infantry / 4th Brigade	10th Caçadores Battalion																																							
Total										1							1		8									12							1		21			
		Names and ranks of officers killed									Names and ranks of officers wounded									Names and ranks of officers prisoners and missing									Names and ranks of officers prisoners and missing											

Observation: Eight prisoners and missing men have already returned.

Carlos Frederico Lecor
Major General
Headquarters Maison du Malde, 6 January 1814

Table 18.3: Return[1148] of the Killed, Wounded, and Missing in the 4th Infantry Brigade on 6 January 1814

			Killed									Wounded									Prisoners; Missing									Total									Mules		
			Colonel	Lieutenant Colonels	Majors	Captains	Subalterns	Flag Bearers	Sergeants and *Furriéis*	Musicians and Drummers	Corporals and Privates	Colonel	Lieutenant Colonels	Majors	Captains	Subalterns	Flag Bearers	Sergeants and *Furriéis*	Musicians and Drummers	Corporals and Privates	Colonel	Lieutenant Colonels	Majors	Captains	Subalterns	Flag Bearers	Sergeants and *Furriéis*	Musicians and Drummers	Corporals and Privates	Colonel	Lieutenant Colonels	Majors	Captains	Subalterns	Flag Bearers	Sergeants and *Furriéis*	Musicians and Drummers	Corporals and Privates	Killed	Wounded	Missing
Artillery																																									
Infantry	2nd Brigade	3rd Brigade																																							
		4th Brigade																																							
	4th Brigade	2nd Regiment																																							
		14th Regiment																																							
		4th Regiment																																							
		10th Regiment																		2																		2			
		10th Caçadores Battalion																		7																		7			
Total																				9																		9			

Names and ranks of officers killed Names and ranks of officers wounded Names and ranks of officers prisoners and missing

Carlos Frederico Lecor
Major General
Headquarters Maison du Malde, 7 January 1814

Chapter 19

The Battles of February 1814

Both armies stayed in winter quarters through the rest of January. In mid-February Wellington ordered his army onto the offensive. On 14 February Hill began manoeuvring against Harispe's Division in the vicinity of Hellette,[1149] while Picton moved against Villatte's Division at Bon Loc, 9km to the north. The following day the French withdrew from the La Joyeuse river line 20km to the east to the Bidouze river. Instead of crossing the Bidouze at Saint Palais, Harispe halted 3km west of the river at Garris. The 2nd Division attacked while the Portuguese and Spanish divisions attempted to cut off the French line of retreat by outflanking them. The French withdrew across the La Joyeuse river at Saint Palais but did not destroy the bridge there. They continued north to the Saison river at Arriverayte.

Heavy rain brought operations to a halt until 23 February, when Beresford attacked Foy's outposts at Hastingues, 30km northwest of Garris. The next day the Allied forces began preparations to cross the Saison and the Gave d'Oloron rivers. Soult retreated to the east and stopped at Orthez along the Gave de Pau river. Wellington arrived there on 26 March and attacked the next day. The French were in defensive positions on a ridge to the northwest of the city and repulsed the first attacks but by 2:30 p.m. the Allies had broken through the French lines and Soult ordered a retreat.

Garris and Saint Palais, 15 and 16 February 1814

The French turned to fight the advancing Allied 2nd Division on the Motte de Garris, a high ridge with a deep ravine in front of it, located just to the north of Garris. Stewart was reluctant to assault the hill, but Wellington ordered him to attack, while Morillo's Spanish Division would manoeuvre to cut the French route of retreat to Saint Palais.

The 2nd Division attacked with Pringle's Brigade on the left, the 5th Brigade in the centre, and Byng's Brigade on the right. The 6th Caçadores provided a screen for the 18th Infantry as it attacked the ridge, while the 6th Infantry was in reserve. The heaviest fighting was on the Allies' left flank, where the French counter-attacked after being pushed off the hill. While the fighting was going on, Morillo moved on the French left to cut the road to Saint Palais. Harispe ordered his troops to break off the attacks and withdraw. In the confusion of the retreat, the French raced for the bridge at Saint Palais and Harispe lost control of his men. Rather than trying to defend the bridge, he sent them on towards Arriverayte.[1150] He was able to damage the bridge at Saint Palais, which slowed the Allied pursuit. The 5th Brigade took part in the pursuit the next day and lost some men in skirmishing. Most sources erroneously state that only the Portuguese Division was involved in the fight and fail to mention the 5th Brigade of the 2nd Division.

2nd Division

5th Brigade (6th and 18th Infantry, 6th Caçadores)

Report[1151] from Colonel Hardinge to AG Mozinho

Sir,
I have the honour to enclose, for the information of His Excellency the Marshal Marquis de Campo Maior, the returns of the killed, wounded and missing in the brigade under my command in the action of the 15th instant and in the skirmish of the 16th.

I have the satisfaction to notice that the returns showed such a small loss given the strong position seized and the enemy numbers. But it is with great regret that I had to include among the killed Lieutenant Colonel Peter Fearon, a most excellent officer. In him the 6th Caçadores Battalion has lost a commander that will be forever deeply missed.

The 18th Regiment, under the command of Lieutenant Colonel Pynn, covered by the 6th Caçadores Battalion, led off the attack, the 6th Regiment, under Lieutenant Colonel Grant,[1152] was the reserve. The brigade gained the heights at the same time as the British brigades, which attacked the flanks. The attack being made through an intricate terrain and at an hour approaching the night, prevented me from making a fair judgement of the conduct of the officers and men, to inform His Excellency the Marshal.

I deem unnecessary to praise Lieutenant Colonels Pynn and Grant, whose bravery and zeal His Excellency had witnessed in other more important occasions.
God save you, Sir
Burgaine on Sauveterre, 18 February 1814
Manoel de Brito Mozinho

H. Hardinge
Colonel

6th Infantry
See Table 19.1.

18th Infantry
See Table 19.2.

Combat of Hastingues, 23 February 1814

On 23 February the 2nd Caçadores of the 6th Brigade was ordered to drive the French outposts from Hastingues, which is on the south bank of the Gave de Pau. The fighting was sharp between the light troops and the French withdrew across the river in boats. The caçadores lost no men killed, but five officers were wounded, four of them junior officers. This was a critical loss, since prior to the skirmish the battalion had only had ten captains and subalterns.

7th Division

6th Brigade (7th and 19th Infantry, 2nd Caçadores)
See Table 19.3.

2nd Caçadores

Report[1153] from Lieutenant Colonel Zuhlcke, 2nd Caçadores, to Colonel Doyle

Sir,

I beg you to recommend to the particular attention of His Excellency the Marshal Marquis de Campo Maior Lieutenant Adjutant Joze Manoel Vannez, Lieutenants Ricardo Antonio Paulo Soares and Joze Antonio Gabriel do Carmo e Lima, Ensigns Antonio do Prado,[1154] Luis Figueira, and Felix do Prado,[1155] the last four wounded. They all distinguished themselves in the combat of the 23rd of this month by the zeal and activity carrying out their duties. The ensigns are not only the seniors in the battalion, but I think the seniors in all the caçadores battalions.

I have the honour to inform you that when the enemy was expelled from the village, I decided to collect the battalion over the road by which the enemy retired. Our left was overextended and the right not coming out of the village I sent Major Pamplona[1156] and the adjutant to move the left promptly and I went to the village to collect and lead the right to the post I determined. At that point, the adjutant arrived with the news that the major was severely wounded. The absence of such an active officer as Major Pamplona is a great loss to the service, particularly because the battalion has only an officer per company, which is very insufficient, and the battalion recruiting in the Beira Baixa province has the disadvantage that almost no sergeant is qualified to aspire to be an officer. I beg you to lay this report before His Excellency.

God save you, Sir

Quarters in Hastingues 25 February 1814

John Doyle

6th Brigade Commander

Jorge [sic] H. Zuhlcke
Lieutenant Colonel 2nd Caçadores

The Battle of Orthez, 27 February 1814

Soult deployed his eight divisions, totalling about 30,000 men, on the high ground northwest of Orthez. His lines stretched 7km from the city to Baights.[1157] The heights were a kilometre from the river and rose 100m in height. Wellington deployed Beresford's three divisions on the left with the 4th Division on the far left and the Light Division to their right, with the 7th Division behind the 4th Division. In the centre was the 3rd Division with the 6th Division to its right. Hill, with the 2nd and Portuguese Divisions, was sent on a march to cross the Ousse river upstream of Orthez to outflank the French on the right. Beresford was supposed to attack first and once he was committed, the 3rd and 6th Divisions were to attack the centre. Hill's mission was to hit the French left flank as quickly as possible. Things initially went according to the plan and Beresford's attack with the 4th Division captured the town of Saint-Boès, but he was unable to gain a foothold on the heights. By 11 a.m. Beresford's attack had stalled, and Wellington ordered the 3rd, 6th, and Light Divisions to assault the ridge. The 3rd Division deployed with Brisbane's Brigade in the lead and the 8th Brigade in support. The division made it to the crest of the ridge before its attack also stalled. It was reinforced by the 6th Division, and helped by the attack of Colborne's Brigade of the Light Division and the 7th Division to their left. Before long, the French line began to collapse from the pressure.

On the Allies' right, Hill had the 2nd Brigade make a demonstration against the Orthez bridge, while he moved the rest of his troops upstream to the ford at Souars. He crossed the river and soon encountered Harispe's Division, on the French left flank. During the advance the 5th Brigade was in reserve and was not engaged. Hill's troops greatly outnumbered the French and Harispe ordered his division to withdraw. He turned and fought several times when he reached suitable terrain, but he could not hold off the advancing Allies. Soult saw that his route of retreat was about to be cut off and ordered a general withdrawal to the east. By 4 p.m. most of the fighting was over.

The Left Wing

4th Division

The 9th Brigade was in reserve until Saint-Boès was captured. It was on the right of Ross's Brigade during the assault on the ridge. The attacks were screened by the 10th Caçadores. The brigade attacked twice,[1158] but both times failed to reach the top. Casualties were heavy, especially among the senior leaders, with two battalion commanders wounded.

9th Brigade (11th and 23rd Infantry, 7th Caçadores)

11th Infantry

Report[1159] from Lieutenant Colonel Anderson to Colonel Sá

Sir,

I have the honour to lay before you, for the information of His Excellency the Marshal, a list of the individuals, from the regiment under my command, who particularly distinguished themselves in the action of the 27th February, notwithstanding the general good behaviour of everyone, which deserves His Excellency the Marshal Marquis de Campo Maior's approbation.

During the action, I received every assistance from Lieutenant Colonel Donahoe, who was severely wounded,[1160] as well as from Captains Joze Maria Softer[1161] and João de Govea Ozorio, Lieutenant Manoel do Nascimento,[1162] Ensign Dom Gil Eanes da Costa,[1163] and Adjutant Sergeant Joze Jacinto Godinho.[1164] These officers behaved with the greatest gallantry.

God save you, Sir
Camp, 2 March 1814
Joze de Vasconcellos e Sá
9th Brigade Commander

Alex. Anderson
Lieutenant Colonel 11th Regiment

See Table 19.4.

23rd Infantry

Report[1165] from Captain Pereira to Colonel Sá

Sir,

In consequence of the wounds of Lieutenant Colonel Melo[1166] and Captain King[1167] in yesterday's battle, the command of the regiment devolved to me. It's my duty to report to you that on the two brilliant charges, made against the enemy, and in the time they manoeuvred as skirmishers, the officers, inferior officers and men behaved in a most gallant manner, which you personally witnessed. But some of them particularly distinguished themselves and deserve every attention. They are Lieutenant Antonio Rodrigues Medeiros,[1168] the Adjutants, Ensigns Joao Gomes de Almeida and Antonio Roque de Andrade, Ensign Joao Antonio Rebocho,[1169] Adjutant Sergeant Manuel Antonio da Fonceca[1170] and 1st Sergeants Joze Tavares and Joze Maria Ilharco. These three sergeants, besides their good conduct in the battle, come from good families, have sufficient knowledge and their age and physical constitution allows them to become very good officers.

I beg leave to require that you lay this report before His Excellency the Marshal Marquis de Campo Maior in order to secure his approbation.

God save you, Sir
Camp, 28 February 1814
Colonel Joze de Vasconcellos e Sa

Francisco Joze Pereira[1171]
Captain commanding the 23rd Regiment

7th Caçadores

Report[1172] from Lieutenant Colonel Lillie to Colonel Sá

Sir,

The 7th Caçadores Battalion behaved with its usual gallantry and valour in the action of the 27th of last month. It is my duty to mention particularly the captain from the 6th Company B.V. Derenzy, whose conduct in previous actions has been mentioned frequently; the same in the case of Adjutant Sergeant Joze de Moreira. I hope, if you think them worthy of some praise, that their names will be laid before His Excellency the Marshal Marquis of Campo Maior, Commander in Chief of the Army.

I enclose the return of the killed and wounded on that occasion.

God save you, Sir

1 March 1814

Joze de Vasconcellos

J S Lillie
Major 7th Caçadores Battalion Commander

7th Division

The division was in reserve on the left flank for much of the morning. When it was committed to the assault on the ridge in support of the 4th Division, the 6th Brigade moved to Saint-Boès as the reserve for the attack. Only the 2nd Caçadores fought in the attack and its casualties were light.

6th Brigade (7th and 19th Infantry, 2nd Caçadores)

See Table 19.5.

Light Division (1st and 3rd Caçadores, 17th Infantry)

After the attacks on the heights by the 4th Division stalled, the 1st Caçadores was sent to protect the right flank of the 9th Brigade of the 4th Division as it attacked the heights again. When the 4th Division fell back to Saint-Boès, the 1st Caçadores stayed with it during the next assault and captured two guns. After the battle was over, the caçadores did not receive orders to rejoin their division, so they stayed with the 9th Brigade until 1 March, when Captain Harry Smith, the brigade major of Colborne's Brigade, tracked them down.[1173]

The 3rd Caçadores deployed as skirmishers to the front of the Light Division and covered the gap between the 4th and Light Divisions, when the 52nd Foot assaulted the ridge at the end of the battle. The 17th Infantry was not engaged.

1st Caçadores

Report[1174] from Major Rodrigues to AG Mozinho

Sir,

I have the honour to enclose the returns of the killed, wounded and missing in this battalion on the 25th 26th and 27th of February and I beg leave to report that the battalion behaved with its usual gallantry and met the approbation of the Brigade Commander, Colonel Barnard.[1175] I strongly recommend Manoel Joaquim de Mello, 2nd Sergeant of the 6th Company, who distinguished himself taking a howitzer and a gun, the first the enemy lost on the 27th, advancing against the artillery position with five or six men with great intrepidity. This action was witnessed by Lieutenant Colonel Snodgrass[1176] before being wounded and he instructed me to do justice to the sergeant. This sergeant cannot read and was appointed 2nd Sergeant by Colonel Avillez[1177] for his bravery on all occasions and for saving the battalion's records under a heavy fire in Alenquer. All this for the information of His Excellency Marshal Beresford Marquis de Campo Maior.

God save you, Sir

Mont de Marsan, 2 March 1814

Manoel de Brito Mozinho

Manoel Jorge Rodrigues

Major 1st Caçadores Battalion commander

3rd Caçadores

Report[1178] from Major Pinto to AG Mozinho

Sir,

I have the honour to enclose the return of the killed and wounded in this battalion, which was temporarily under my command, in the action of the 27 February. In this combat every officer and soldier behaved extremely well but it is my duty to mention Captain Joaquim Joze Pimentel Jorge for his conduct leading the two companies detached, covering our left flank. He kept his men in front of the enemy in such an order and steadiness as on a parade.

God save you, Sir

Quarter in Mont de Marsan, 2 March 1814

Brigadier General Manoel de Brito Mozinho

Manoel Caetano Teixeira Pinto

Major 3rd Caçadores commander

See Table 19.6.

17th Infantry

Report[1179] from Lieutenant Colonel Rolt to AG Mozinho

Sir,

I have the honour to report that in the action of the 27th instant the 17th Regiment under my command did not have any individuals killed, wounded, or missing.

God save you, Sir

Camp, 28 February 1814

Manoel de Brito Mozinho

John Rolt

Lieutenant Colonel 17th Regiment commander

The Centre

3rd Division

When the 3rd Division assaulted the heights, Brisbane's Brigade was on the right and Keane's Brigade was on the left. The 8th Brigade followed Keane's Brigade. The 11th Caçadores had been detached that morning to cover the left flank of the division as it advanced. On reaching the top of the ridge the 8th Brigade was sent to the right flank to expand the division's front. Eight companies from the 88th Foot were attached to the brigade. Its formation was the 21st Infantry on the left, the 9th Infantry in the centre, and the 88th Foot on the right. To the immediate right of the 88th Foot was Captain Turner's artillery brigade of 9-pounder guns. The brigade did not have its caçadores battalion with it, so its four grenadier companies and the grenadier company of the 88th Foot acted as a screen. A charge by the French 21st Chasseurs down the road caught the grenadier companies in the open and the carnage was deadly. The French cavalry continued to the guns on the brigade's right and began to cut down the gunners until reinforcements arrived and fired on them. After stopping this attack, the brigade was ordered to advance, but did not see any further combat that day. The brigade's casualties were not high. However, losses were heavy among the leadership of the grenadiers serving as light troops. Of the four grenadier company commanders, one was killed and another severely wounded. Losses were similar in the 11th Caçadores. Its battalion commander and one company commander were killed, while another company commander died of his wounds.

8th Brigade (9th and 21st Infantry, 11th Caçadores)

Report[1180] from General Power to AG Mozinho

Grenade, March 1st 1814
Sir,
I have the honour to make a report to you, for the information of His Excellency Marshal Sir William Beresford, respecting the conduct of the Brigade, under my command, on the 27th ultimo.

The 11th Caçadores were detached on a separate service, by order of Lieutenant General Sir Thomas Picton, so that I had no opportunity of observing them, but I understand that the conduct of the officers and men was very exemplary and I have very sincerely to lament the loss of Lieutenant Colonel Kilsha, who was killed, whilst leading on the battalion in a most gallant manner. In him the service has lost a most valuable and zealous officer. Major Francisco de Paula Rozado, who commanded the battalion, after his death, particularly recommended Lieutenant Antonio Pinto de Araujo[1181] and 1st Sergeant João Nunes Cardozo,[1182] for their very distinguished gallantry. This battalion had also two captains killed, de Silva[1183] and Joze Bento.[1184]

The service on which the 9th and 21st Regiments were employed was executed with that promptness and bravery, which has been their characteristic, ever since I have had the honour of commanding the brigade. Lieutenant General Sir Thomas Picton desired me to gain a position, which the enemy occupied on their left, not far from the high road to Orthez, on which they had a considerable column formed, with some pieces of artillery, under a heavy fire from which, these two battalions[1185] marched with great firmness, supported by eight companies of the 88th British Regiment, and covered by their own grenadier companies, until we arrived at such a distance, as to be able to charge the enemy's column, which gave way and we remained masters of the position, where I was ordered to halt. However from another position, across a small ravine, they kept up a very heavy fire, for a considerable time, which was opposed by the right battalion of the 9th Regiment with the grenadier companies of the brigade as well as the 88th Regiment which lined the front of our position *en tirailleurs* whilst the remainder were held in reserve. The enemy's cavalry in some force during this period charged along a road which led to our position to drive us from it, but they were so well received, by the advance above mentioned, that they were immediately repulsed, with some loss of men and horses, and the enemy's *tirailleurs* were also driven back and retreated with the column opposed to us, to which they belonged, soon after which, I was ordered to advance, to join the other brigades of the 3rd Division, but we were not afterwards engaged.

During the advance of my brigade to the enemy's position, I am sorry to observe, that Captain Jermyn of the 2nd Grenadiers [Company], of the 21st Regiment was killed and Lieutenant Galbraith[1186] who commanded the 1st Grenadiers [Company], very severely wounded. The grenadier companies of the 9th Regiment were commanded by Captain Peacocke[1187] who has been acting as my Aide de Camp, during the absence of Major Johnstone, but as he belongs to the 2nd Grenadiers of that regiment and as there was no other captain, and more particularly, as he volunteered his services, upon this occasion, I accepted them. I beg leave to recommend him to His Excellency's consideration as a very gallant, and zealous officer in the field, and I also have very particular reason to be satisfied with Adjutant Caetano Joze Gomes,[1188] of the 9th and Adjutant Joze Antonio Pereira de Eça, of the 21st Regiment, whose coolness, gallantry and exertions, merit from me, the highest eulogium, I can bestow on them.
I have the honour to be Sir your most obedient humble servant

M. Power
Major General

To the Adjutant General

P.S. Brigade Major Valladas[1189] gave me every assistance in forwarding the execution of my orders and the brigade is much indebted to Staff Surgeon Lesassier[1190] for his exertions as well as for his arrangements, respecting the care of the wounded.

See Table 19.7.

6th Division

The 7th Brigade was on the left as they assaulted the ridge. The brigade was screened by its caçadores, and the 8th Infantry was on the left and the 12th Infantry on the right. Upon reaching the top of the ridge the Allied troops were engaged in a prolonged firefight. Hoping to bring more firepower against the French troops, Picton ordered Turner's Artillery Brigade to the top of the ridge. The guns had just begun firing when the 21st Chasseurs charged them and some disordered infantry companies of the 88th Foot and Portuguese grenadiers. The chasseurs sabred their way through the infantry and were cutting down the gunners when the 8th Infantry intervened, killing many of the cavalrymen and taking their squadron commander prisoner.

7th Brigade (8th and 12th Infantry, 9th Caçadores)

Report[1191] from Colonel Douglas to AG Mozinho

Sir,

I have the great satisfaction to report, for the information of His Excellency Marshal Beresford Marquis de Campo Maior, that the 7th Infantry Brigade, in the action of the 27th instant, had again the opportunity to show its steadiness under fire, which had met with His Excellency's approbation so many times and testify to the merits of the commanders of its three corps.

Two enemy cavalry squadrons[1192] made a desperate charge to capture the 3rd Division's artillery, but they met the 8th Regiment and were received with great steadiness, a proof of Lieutenant Colonel Birmingham's merits.[1193] I can assure His Excellency that of the part of the cavalry squadron who faced us only less than a quarter escaped and the commanding officer was made prisoner.

I recommend to His Excellency for promotion, Brigade Major João [sic] Maher[1194] and Ensign Holman,[1195] Lieutenant of the 52nd Regiment of His Britannic Majesty's Army; this is the third time I recommend both officers. I beg leave to request to His Excellency the promotion of the Adjutant Sergeants Marques[1196] from the 9th Caçadores, and João de Mattos Cotrim, 8th Regiment, both for gallant conduct against the enemy.

I enclose the return of the killed and wounded from the brigade in the last actions.

I have the honour to be, Sir, your most obedient servant

3 March 1814
Manoel de Brito Mozinho

J Douglas
Colonel Brigade Commander

See Table 19.8.

The Right Wing

Portuguese Division

The division was part of General Hill's flanking movement to the right but neither brigade was heavily engaged.

See Table 19.9.

Table 19.1: 6th Infantry. Return[1197] of the Killed, Wounded, Missing, and Prisoners on 15 and 16 February 1814

Killed									Wounded									Missing and Prisoners									Total									
Colonel	Lieutenant Colonels	Majors	Captains	Subalterns	Flag Bearers	Sergeants and *Furriés*	Musicians and Drummers	Corporals and Privates	Colonel	Lieutenant Colonels	Majors	Captains	Subalterns	Flag Bearers	Sergeants and *Furriés*	Musicians and Drummers	Corporals and Privates	Colonel	Lieutenant Colonels	Majors	Captains	Subalterns	Flag Bearers	Sergeants and *Furriés*	Musicians and Drummers	Corporals and Privates	Colonel	Lieutenant Colonels	Majors	Captains	Subalterns	Flag Bearers	Sergeants and *Furriés*	Musicians and Drummers	Corporals and Privates	Observations
-	-	-	-	-	-	-	-	-	-	-	-	-	-	-	1	-	5	-	-	-	-	-	-	-	-	-	-	-	-	-	-	-	1	-	5	
Name and rank of the officers killed									Nome and rank of the officers wounded									Name and rank of the officers missing or prisoners																		

Observation: On the 15 four privates were wounded; on the 16 one sergeant and one private.

Maxwell Grant
Lieutenant Colonel

Table 19.2: 18th Infantry. Return[1198] of the Casualties in the Action of 15 February 1814

Killed									Wounded									Missing and Prisoners									Total									
Colonel	Lieutenant Colonels	Majors	Captains	Subalterns	Flag Bearers	Sergeants and *Furriés*	Musicians and Drummers	Corporals and Privates	Colonel	Lieutenant Colonels	Majors	Captains	Subalterns	Flag Bearers	Sergeants and *Furriés*	Musicians and Drummers	Corporals and Privates	Colonel	Lieutenant Colonels	Majors	Captains	Subalterns	Flag Bearers	Sergeants and *Furriés*	Musicians and Drummers	Corporals and Privates	Colonel	Lieutenant Colonels	Majors	Captains	Subalterns	Flag Bearers	Sergeants and *Furriés*	Musicians and Drummers	Corporals and Privates	Observations
								2							2	1	12									6							2	1	20	
Name and rank of the officers killed									Name and rank of the officers wounded									Name and rank of the officers missing or prisoners																		

Henry Pynn
Lieutenant Colonel 18th Regiment

Table 19.3: Return[1199] of the Killed, Wounded, and Missing in the 6th Brigade in the combat of 23 February 1814

Hastingues 24 February 1814	Officers Wounded			Sergeants	Privates			
	Majors	Lieutenants	Ensigns	Wounded	Killed	Wounded	Prisoners and Missing	Total
2nd Caçadores Battalion	1	1	3	1	-	27	-	33
7th Infantry Regiment	-	-	-	1	-	4	-	5
19th Infantry Regiment	-	-	-	-	-	2	-	2
Total	1	1	3	2	-	33	-	40

Names of the officers [wounded]
Major Francisco Antonio Pamplona, severely;
Lieutenant Joze do Carmo Lima, severely;
Ensign Luis Antonio Figueira, severely;
Ensign Francisco Feliz do Prado, severely;
Ensign Antonio do Prado Fragozo, slightly

JM Doyle
Colonel Acting Commander

Table 19.4: 11th Infantry. Return[1200] of the casualties suffered against the enemy on 27 February 1814

	Officers						Sergeants	Drummers	Corporals and Soldiers	Total	Horses	Observations
	Lieutenant Colonel	Majors	Captains	Lieutenant	Ensign	Staff						
Killed	-	-	-	-	-	-	-	-	17	17	1	
Wounded	-	2	2	1	4	-	10	2	109	130	1	One of the drummers wounded is a Drummer Major
Missing	-	-	-	-	-	-	2	-	18	20	-	
Total	-	2	2	1	4	-	12	2	144	167	2	

Ranks and Names of the officers wounded	Observations
Brevet Lieutenant Colonel Daniel Donahoe	Severely
Major João Correia Guedes	Severely
Captain Joze Maria da Costa	Severely
Lieutenant Ignacio Pereira de Lacerda	Slightly
Lieutenant Antonio de Gouvea[1201]	Slightly
Ensign Thomas de Magalhaens	Severely
Ensign Joaquim Maria[1202]	Slightly
Ensign António de Carvalho Savedra	Severely
Ensign Valentim de Almeida	Slightly
From the missing some were made prisoners	Alex. Anderson Lieutenant Colonel 11th Regiment

Table 19.5: Return[1203] of the Casualties in the 6th Brigade in the Combat of 27 February 1814

Mont de Marsan 4 March 1814	Privates Wounded	Total
2nd Caçadores Battalion	3	3
7th Infantry Regiment	-	-
19th Infantry Regiment	-	-
Total	3	3

JM Doyle
Colonel 6th Brigade commander

Table 19.6: 3rd Caçadores. Return[1204] of the Killed, Wounded, Missing, and Prisoner in the Battalion on 27 February 1813

	Killed							Wounded							Missing							Prisoners							Total						
	Lieutenant Colonel	Major	Captains	Subalterns	Sergeants	Buglers	Corporals and Privates	Lieutenant Colonel	Major	Captains	Subalterns	Sergeants	Buglers	Corporals and Privates	Lieutenant Colonel	Major	Captains	Subalterns	Sergeants	Buglers	Corporals and Privates	Lieutenant Colonel	Major	Captains	Subalterns	Sergeants	Buglers	Corporals and Privates	Lieutenant Colonel	Major	Captains	Subalterns	Sergeants	Buglers	Corporals and Privates
Total							2						1	13							1													1	16

Manoel Caetano Teixeira Pinto
Major 3rd Caçadores commander

Table 19.7: 8th Infantry Brigade. Return[1205] of the Killed, Wounded, Prisoners, and Missing in Yesterday's Action 27 February 1814

28 February 1814	Killed									Wounded									Prisoners and Missing									Total										
	Colonels	Lieutenant Colonels	Majors	Captains	Subalterns	Flag Bearers	Sergeants and *Furriers*	Musicians and Drummers	Corporals and Privates	Colonels	Lieutenant Colonels	Majors	Captains	Subalterns	Flag Bearers	Sergeants and *Furriers*	Musicians and Drummers	Corporals and Privates	Colonels	Lieutenant Colonels	Majors	Captains	Subalterns	Flag Bearers	Sergeants and *Furriers*	Musicians and Drummers	Corporals and Privates	Colonels	Lieutenant Colonels	Majors	Captains	Subalterns	Flag Bearers	Sergeants and *Furriers*	Musicians and Drummers	Corporals and Privates	Total
9th Regiment									8					2		4		54														2		4		62	68
21st Regiment		1		1										1				45											1		1	1				45	47
11th Caçadores				1					2				1	1		2		23													2	1		2		25	31
Total		1		2					10				1	4		6		122											1		3	4		6		132	146

	Killed	Wounded	Prisoners and Missing	Total
	Names and ranks of the officers killed	Names and ranks of the officers wounded	Names and ranks of the officers missing and prisoners	Observations
	Lieutenant Colonel Carlos [sic] Kilsha, 11th Caçadores; Captain Samuel Jermyn, 21st Regiment; Captain Antonio Rodrigues da Silva, 11th Caçadores	Lieutenant Paulo Joze Ferreira, 9th Regiment; Ensign Bento Pereira de Araujo, 9th Regiment; Lieutenant Guilherme [sic] Galbraith, 21st Regiment; Captain Joze Bento de Magalhães (died later), 11th Caçadores; Ensign Francisco Duarte de Freitas, severely, 11th Caçadores		M Power Major General

Table 19.8: Return[1206] of the Killed, Wounded and Missing in the 7th Infantry Brigade in the Battle of 27 February 1814

Camp 28 February 1814	Killed									Wounded									Prisoners and Missing									Total								
	Colonels	Lieutenant Colonels	Majors	Captains	Lieutenants	Ensigns	Sergeants and *Furriés*	Drummers	Corporals and Privates	Colonels	Lieutenant Colonels	Majors	Captains	Lieutenants	Ensigns	Sergeants and *Furriés*	Drummers	Corporals and Privates	Colonels	Lieutenant Colonels	Majors	Captains	Lieutenants	Ensigns	Sergeants and *Furriés*	Drummers	Corporals and Privates	Colonels	Lieutenant Colonels	Majors	Captains	Lieutenants	Ensigns	Sergeants and *Furriés*	Drummers	Corporals and Privates
9th Caçadores Battalion									1							1	1	17																1	1	18
8th Regiment									1							1		18																1		19
12th Regiment															1			11															1			11
Total									2						1	2	1	46															1	2	1	48
Observations	Names and ranks of the officers killed									Names and ranks of the officers wounded									Names and ranks of the officers missing and prisoners									Observations								
										Ensign Evaristo Joze Ferreira, slightly																										

J Maher
Brigade Major

Table 19.9: Return[1207] of the Killed, Wounded, and Missing in the Portuguese Division under the Command of Major General Lecor on 27 February 1814

			Killed										Wounded										Prisoners and Missing										Total										Mules		
			Colonels	Lieutenant Colonels	Majors	Captains	Subalterns	Flag Bearers	Sergeants and *Furriéis*	Musicians and Drummers	Corporals and Privates	Colonels	Lieutenant Colonels	Majors	Captains	Subalterns	Flag Bearers	Sergeants and *Furriéis*	Musicians and Drummers	Corporals and Privates	Colonels	Lieutenant Colonels	Majors	Captains	Subalterns	Flag Bearers	Sergeants and *Furriéis*	Musicians and Drummers	Corporals and Privates	Colonels	Lieutenant Colonels	Majors	Captains	Subalterns	Flag Bearers	Sergeants and *Furriéis*	Musicians and Drummers	Corporals and Privates	Killed	Wounded	Missing
Artillery		3rd Brigade																																								
		4th Brigade																																								
Infantry	2nd Brigade	2nd Regiment									1									8																		9			
		14th Regiment																																							
	4th Brigade	4th Regiment																																							
		10th Regiment													1	1		1	1	2													1	1		1	1	2			
		10th Caçadores Battalion									1							1	1	7																1	1	8			
Total											2				1	1		1	1	17													1	1		1	1	19			

Names and ranks of the officers killed

Names and ranks of the officers wounded
10th Regiment, Captain Manuel Martiniano de Sousa Girão, severely
10th Caçadores, Ensign Francisco Izidro da Ponte, slightly

Names and ranks of the officers prisoners and missing

Camp before Orthez, 27 February 1814

Carlos Frederico Lecor
Major General

Chapter 20

The Combats of March 1814

Wellington's cavalry lost contact with the French after Orthez. He knew that they were moving either north towards Bordeaux or eastward. Since both were realistic possibilities, Wellington split his army and sent Beresford towards Bordeaux and Hill to the east. The 3rd and 6th Divisions found two French divisions at Cazères-sur-l'Adour on 1 March, but the French continued to retreat to Aire.[1208] Hill, with the 2nd and Portuguese Divisions, arrived there the next day. Soult continue to withdraw but left a rearguard to cover his retreat. The 2nd Brigade was involved in heavy fighting, but the French withdrew when their right flank collapsed. The French continued eastward and stopped at Vic Bigorre.[1209]

Wellington chose not to pursue Soult. Instead, he moved on Bordeaux, the third largest city in France. Operations resumed on 13 March when Soult took advantage of Wellington's absence and marched west. There was a cavalry skirmish with the 4th Cavalry Regiment on 13 March at Viella and Soult reached Aire on 15 March. On learning of the French advance, Wellington ordered Hill back on the offensive. Soult decided to retreat rather than fight and returned to Vic Bigorre. On 19 March Wellington closed in on the French, who had the Adour river to their rear and were in danger of being trapped before they could withdraw. Soult realized the threat and ordered his army to retreat. Wellington sent the 3rd Division to clear the French out of the village. The 8th Brigade was the only Portuguese troops involved in the fight.

The French continued their retreat and headed south. On 20 March their rearguard stopped at Tarbes, 20km away. There was a fight between the rearguard and the 95th Rifles, but no Portuguese troops were significantly engaged. The French were able to break contact and marched east to Toulouse, where Soult decided to make another stand and prepared the city's defences.

The Fighting at Aire and Barcelonne, 2 March 1814

On 2 March Clausel commanded the rearguard as Soult and the rest of the French Army retreated towards Tarbes. He deployed his two divisions south of the town on a ridge about a kilometre to the west of the Grave river[1210] which flowed into the Adour river. The ridge was about 50m higher than the river valley below. Hill arrived near the town and saw that the French were retreating. He expected Clausel's force to abandon the ridge as soon as he advanced, so he quickly deployed his troops on a five-brigade front. The 2nd Division would attack the northern section of the ridge, while the Portuguese Division attacked the centre. The 2nd Division quickly pushed the French in their sector off the ridge and into Aire and came close to capturing the bridge across the Adour. But in the event the enemy troops were able to escape across the river and destroy the bridge.

In the centre, Costa was ordered to take the hill, with Buchan in support. Costa made it to the top of the ridge but was counter-attacked and his brigade fled down the hill, taking numerous casualties. The commander of the 2nd Division saw the collapse of the attack and sent a brigade along the top of the ridge to hit the French in the flank. While this was happening, the 4th Brigade was ordered to send its 10th Caçadores plus the brigade's four grenadier companies to take the ridge in the centre. The combination of these attacks was successful and the remaining French retreated to the south.

The French troops on the right bank of the Adour river thought they were safe, not knowing the Allied 6th Division was on the same side of the river and only a few kilometres away. The 7th Brigade was ordered to pursue the retreating French and the 9th Caçadores encountered them at Barcelonne[1211] and engaged their rearguard.

Portuguese Division

Letter[1212] from General Rowland Hill to Beresford

Aire 6 March 1814

My dear Beresford

I received your letter respecting the Algarve's Brigade[1213] and allow me to certify you that it was with great sadness that I was compelled to inform Lord Wellington of my disapprobation of the conduct of the brigade on the 2nd instant.

On that day the enemy was posted in a height to cover the road to this town. I gave orders that the height should be attacked by the 2nd Division and by General Lecor's Division. This last had in the front Brigadier Costa's brigade supported by Brigadier Buchan's.

The head of the 2nd Division and Costa's brigade reached the top of the height and at that point the last was thrown into confusion by the opposition of an inferior number of the enemy. Some companies of the brigade rallied after, but their conduct was bad for the rest of the day. In my opinion the cause of this bad behavior [sic] was the poor dispositions and the lack of talent of his commander,[1214] who is a capable man and had the best intentions, but is unfit to command a brigade in combat.

At the same time I must advert you that, according to all reports and my personal observation, the staff of this Division[1215] and Brigadier Costa's brigade officers did not show the necessary activity excepted Colonel Avillez,[1216] Captain Hamilton[1217] and a few others.

The conduct of the Portuguese troops since I had the honor [sic] to command some of them, had been so admirably good in all occasions, that you may easily imagine my surprise and distress with what happened on the 2, which I expect will not happen again.

Faithfully yours

R. Hill

P.S. I thought that your Adjutant General[1218] would come here yesterday after seeing Lecor. I would have a longer conversation with him than when he was here to hand me your letter. I hope that he was able to obtain the information that you want.

See Table 20.1.

6th Division

7th Brigade

See Table 20.2.

The Cavalry Skirmish at Viella, 13 March 1814

In mid-March Fane's Light Cavalry Brigade manned outposts with its left flank along the Leéz river,[1219] a tributary of the Adour. The 4th Cavalry was part of the brigade and had the responsibility for the outposts in the vicinity of Viella, a village about 3km west of the Larcis river[1220] and 4km south of the Adour river. On 13 March the regiment had 250 men in two squadrons. One squadron was at the Larcis river, where the road to Viella goes south to Lembeye and then on to Vic Bigorre. The other squadron was on the heights about 2km to the east of Viella. From these heights the road from Vic Bigorre could be watched. This position was about a kilometre from the Le Saget river. Soult sent out a strong cavalry screen as he advanced from Vic Bigorre. His left flank was screened by two cavalry regiments. One regiment advanced up the Lembeye road from Conchez-de-Béarn, which ran parallel to the Larcis river. The French 10th Chasseurs[1221] moved up the road from Maridan. The cavalry regiment coming from Conchez-de-Béarn approached the ford over the Larcis river and saw that it was heavily guarded by a Portuguese squadron of cavalry and twenty infantrymen. The 10th Chasseurs crossed the La Saget river at a ford near the broken bridge. When they were about 100m away, Campbell charged and broke the French, pursuing them for a short distance. Realizing he might be cut off by the cavalry regiment across the river, he ordered his regiment to withdraw to Jellemalle,[1222] 10km to the north. The French chased the Portuguese cavalry most of the way until they reached the safety of the Allied lines. Among the casualties was 18-year-old Lieutenant Bernardo de Sá Nogueira, the future 1st Marquess de Sá da Bandeira and five times prime minister of Portugal, who was severely wounded and captured.

4th Cavalry

Letter[1223] from General Fane, Commanding the Cavalry attached to General Hill's Corps to Lieutenant Colonel Arbuthnot, Beresford's British Military Secretary

Near Garlin 16th March 1814
Sir,
I inclose, to be laid before His Excellency Marshal Sir W.C. Beresford, a report I have received from Colonel Campbell,[1224] commanding the 4th Portuguese dragoons, at present under my orders, of an affair he had with the enemy's cavalry on the 13th March instant.

The line of the enemy's advance, and the nature of the country, prevents my being an eyewitness of the business he details. But Lieutenant General Sir W. Stewart, who chanced to be present, bears ample testimony to the bravery and good conduct of all concerned.
I have the honour to be, Sir, your most obedient servant

H. Fane
Major General

Lieutenant Colonel Arbuthnot

Report[1225] from Colonel Campbell to General Fane

Jellemalle
13 March 1814
Sir,
I have the honour to inform you that shortly after I received your last communication letting me know of the retreat of the post, on the Lembeye road, I occupied the ford of the Leéz river at the junction of this road with that of Vic Bigorre by one of my squadrons and a subaltern and twenty men of the 14 Portuguese Infantry.

With the other squadron I occupied the heights of Viella.

The two squadrons of the enemy had advanced on the Lembeye road with about 200 infantry within 2,000 yards of the ford.

Three squadrons of the 10th (Chasseurs a Cheval) crossed the river in front of Viella, and presuming on their strength drove in my advanced guard and arrived to within 100 paces of my squadron.

I charged them, put them into confusion and pursued them for a while.

I have the great satisfaction to tell you that the conduct of my Regiment exceeds all encomiums that I can give it.

We left about thirty of the enemy on the ground either dead or most severely wounded. We took several prisoners but as my duty obliged me to retire with all expedition to prevent the force on the Conchez[1226] road from cutting off my retreat, I lost again all but one.

One of my brave Lieutenants, Lieutenant Bernardo de Sa Nogueira, was wounded severely in the charge and as he fell senseless all our attempts to carry him off were fruitless and he remained a prisoner. I understand however that he is doing very well.

The rest of my loss took place during the retreat, which the nature of the ground made so difficult, giving the enemy such advantage as chasseurs; on descending the declivity some of the horses fell by which I lost several men.

I beg your permission to mention my Adjutant, Luis Nogueira Velho,[1227] the eldest Lieutenant as the bravest dragoon officer I have yet seen, he was first in the charge. I am most particularly indebted to Captain Pedro Raimundo,[1228] to Lieutenants Bernardo de Sa Nogueira and Fellipe Neri de Oliveira and Ensign Jose Teixeira Homem de Brederode. These officers were most active in the charge and covering my retreat.

I am also particularly indebted to Ensign the Viscount de Asseca, who acting as my orderly officer was of the foremost in the charge and most useful in the retreat.

I beg you to do me the favour of forwarding to His Excellency Sir William Carr Beresford Commander in Chief of the Portuguese Army my recommendation of these gallant officers who merit his approbation in the highest degree; and I am very desirous also that the list of standard bearers, non commissioned officers and privates which I send may be also laid before His Excellency as I consider it my duty to mention them.

My Lieutenant Colonel, the Count de Penafiel, was at my side and to him and all the rest of the officers of this squadron I am indebted for their steady and cool conduct in their respective places.

By the dispositions which Captain Dom Thomas de Mascarenhas made at the bridge I was enabled to make good my junction with his squadron and I afterwards effected my retreat on the infantry in the rear. I have the honour to be, Sir, your most obedient and humble servant
To Major General Fane

John Campbell
Colonel 4 Portuguese Cavalry

List[1229] of the Individuals Who had Distinguished Themselves in the Action, of 13th instant, against the Enemy, being this the 10th French Chasseurs, near Viella

Standard Bearers: Christovão da Costa and João Lopes
Adjutant Sergeant: Joze Antonio Moreira
Sergeants: João Tavares de Almeida and Joaquim Amancio de Aguiar
Privates:
   1st Company: 12- Angelo Pereira and 14- Francisco Antonio, wounded
   4th Company: 20- João de Mendonça and 11- Jacinto Rodrigues
   5th Company: 14- Joze Antonio
   6th Company: 10- Feles Joaquim and 19- Manoel Simoens Penedo
   7th Company: 21- João Caetano and 15- Joze de Almeida
   8th Company: 33- Manoel Cordeiro, 53- Gonsalo Alves and 48- Joaquim Simoens

Jellemale 13 March 1814

John Campbell
Colonel 4 Portuguese Cavalry

See Table 20.3

The Combat at Vic Bigorre, 19 March 1814

On 19 March the French rearguard deployed 3km north of Vic Bigorre to give the rest of the army time to retreat. Its left flank was on the l'Échez river and its right was unsupported. Much of the terrain was vineyards. About 2 p.m. the 3rd Division attacked the French left and centre. The 8th Brigade was part of the attack. The 11th Caçadores screened the 21st Infantry as it advanced, while the 9th Infantry was in reserve. As the fighting intensified, Power ordered two companies from the 9th Infantry to support the 21st Infantry. The 3rd Division was about to break the French line when French reserves arrived. The fighting continued until the Light Division and the KGL Heavy Cavalry Brigade threatened the French right. The French withdrew a few kilometres south of the town, where they bivouacked for the night.

3rd Division

8th Brigade (9th and 21st Infantry, 11th Caçadores)

Report[1230] from General Power to AG Mozinho

La Granje, March 21st 1814
Sir,
I have the honor [sic] to report for the information of His Excellency, Marshal Sir William Beresford, that I had great reason to be satisfied with the conduct of the brigade under my command, but particularly the 21st Regiment which was most engaged, in the advance made upon Vic Bigorre, by the 3rd Division, on the 19th instant.

The 9th Regiment commanded by Colonel Sutton was the greater part of the time in reserve, but he speaks in very favorable [sic] terms of the companies which were engaged and of their Captains Barbosa[1231] and Leopoldo.[1232] He also mentions the conduct of Adjutant Caetano Joze Gomes, who I particularly recommended to His Excellency's consideration, for his gallantry at the battle of Orthez on the 27th ultimo.

Colonel João Telles de Menezes, of the 21st Regiment, does not wish to particularize any officers of that corps alledging [sic] that they all acquitted themselves bravely, but I beg leave, as the conduct of the following officers fell more especially under my own observation, to recommend Major Telles Jordão,[1233] who had a horse killed under him, and was afterwards himself severely wounded in the arm having the bone broke, Captain Azevedo,[1234] Lieutenant Joze Manuel Saccoto and Adjutant Antonio Pereira d'Eça, whose conduct was very exemplary.

I must also take this opportunity of noticing my acting Aide de Camp Captain Peacocke,[1235] whose exertions and gallantry were very conspicuous, and who received a severe contusion in the leg, and had a horse wounded. In justice to Brigade Major João Leandro de Valladas, I cannot omit at the same time mentioning his exertions.

I have the honor [sic] to enclose herewith an amended return of killed and wounded, as that which was given in to the Adjutant General of the 3rd Division on the next day was not quite correct.
I have the honor [sic] to be Sir, your very obedient humble servant

M. Power
Major General

To the Adjutant General

See Table 20.4.

Table 20.1: Return[1236] of the Killed, Wounded, Prisoners, and Missing in the Portuguese Division under the Command of Major General Carlos Frederico Lecor in the Action of Aire on 2 March 1814

	Killed									Wounded									Prisoners and Missing									Total								
	Colonels	Lieutenant Colonels	Majors	Captains	Subalterns	Flag Bearers	Sergeants and *Furriéis*	Musicians and Drummers	Corporals and Privates	Colonels	Lieutenant Colonels	Majors	Captains	Subalterns	Flag Bearers	Sergeants and *Furriéis*	Musicians and Drummers	Corporals and Privates	Colonels	Lieutenant Colonels	Majors	Captains	Subalterns	Flag Bearers	Sergeants and *Furriéis*	Musicians and Drummers	Corporals and Privates	Colonels	Lieutenant Colonels	Majors	Captains	Subalterns	Flag Bearers	Sergeants and *Furriéis*	Musicians and Drummers	Corporals and Privates
Headquarter in the camp before Aire 3rd March 1814																																				
Artillery — 2nd Brigade — 3rd Brigade																																				
Artillery — 2nd Brigade — 4th Brigade																																				
Infantry — 2nd Brigade — 2nd Regiment							1		5				1	1		2		52									3				1	1		3		60
Infantry — 2nd Brigade — 14th Regiment									1				2			3		32									1				2			3		34
Infantry — 4th Brigade — 4th Regiment																																				
Infantry — 4th Brigade — 10th Regiment																																				
Infantry — 4th Brigade — 10th Caçadores Battalion									2				1			1		8									2				1	1		1		12
Total							1		8				4	1		6		92									6				4	1		7		106

Names and ranks of the officers killed

Names and ranks of the officers wounded

2nd Regiment:
Captain Manoel de Azevedo, severely; Ensign José Correia de Freitas, slightly

14th Regiment:
Captain Potter,[1238] severely; Captain Pedro Alexandrino[1239], severely

Caçadores:
Captain Augusto Hardecastle [sic],[1240] severely

Carlos Frederico Lecor
Major General
The horse of Major Vitto,[1237] 14th Regiment Commander was killed

Table 20.2: Return[124] of the Killed, Wounded, and Prisoners in the 7th Infantry Brigade in the Battle of 2 March 1814

	Killed									Wounded									Prisoners and Missing									Total									Observations
	Colonels	Lieutenant Colonels	Majors	Captains	Lieutenants	Ensigns	Sergeants and Furriers	Drummers	Corporals and Privates	Colonels	Lieutenant Colonels	Majors	Captains	Lieutenants	Ensigns	Sergeants and Furriers	Drummers	Corporals and Privates	Colonels	Lieutenant Colonels	Majors	Captains	Lieutenants	Ensigns	Sergeants and Furriers	Drummers	Corporals and Privates	Colonels	Lieutenant Colonels	Majors	Captains	Lieutenants	Ensigns	Sergeants and Furriers	Drummers	Corporals and Privates	
9th Caçadores Battalion													1			2		6													1			2		6	
8th Regiment																																					
12th Regiment																																					
Total													1			2		6													1			2		6	
	Names and ranks of the officers killed									Names and ranks of the officers wounded 9th Caçadores, 1st Company Captain Ignacio Ferreira da Rocha, slightly									Names and ranks of the officers missing and prisoners																		

Camp 3 March 1814

J Maher
Brigade Major

Table 20.3: 4th Cavalry. Return[1242] of the Killed, Wounded, Prisoners and Missing in the Action on 13 March 1814 against the Enemy Cavalry near Viella

Jellemale 13 March 1814	Senior Staff		Minor Staff									Officers									
	Colonel	Lieutenant Colonels	Adjutant	Paymaster	Quarter Master	Adjutant Sergeant	Quarter Master Sergeant	Standard Bearers	Assistant Surgeon	Chaplain	Artificers	Captains	Lieutenants	Ensigns	Sergeants	Furriéis	Trumpeters	Farriers	Corporals and Privates	Totals	Horses
Killed	-	-	-	-	-	-	-	-	-	-	-	-	-	-	-	-	-	-	2	2	2
Wounded	-	-	-	-	-	-	-	-	-	-	-	-	-	-	-	-	-	-	4	4	2
Prisoners	-	-	-	-	-	-	-	-	-	-	-	-	1	-	-	-	-	1	6	8	6
Missing	-	-	-	-	-	-	-	-	-	-	-	-	-	-	-	-	-	-	6	6	6
Total	-	-	-	-	-	-	-	-	-	-	-	-	1	-	-	-	-	1	18	20	16

Name and rank of the officers: Lieutenant, 4th Company, Bernardo de Sá Nogueira
N.B. The missing men were detached to several posts and have not joined yet.

John Campbell
Colonel 4 Portuguese Cavalry

Table 20.4: Return[1243] of the Killed, Wounded, Missing and Prisoners in the 8th Infantry Brigade on 19 March 1814 at *Vic Bigorre*

Corps	Killed													Wounded													Missing and Prisoners													Total												
	Colonels	Lieutenant Colonels	Majors	Captains	Lieutenants	Ensigns	Staff	Flag Bearers	Sergeants	Furriéis	Musicians and Drummers	Corporals and Soldiers	Total	Colonels	Lieutenant Colonels	Majors	Captains	Lieutenants	Ensigns	Staff	Flag Bearers	Sergeants	Furriéis	Musicians and Drummers	Corporals and Soldiers	Total	Colonels	Lieutenant Colonels	Majors	Captains	Lieutenants	Ensigns	Staff	Flag Bearers	Sergeants	Furriéis	Musicians and Drummers	Corporals and Soldiers	Total	Colonels	Lieutenant Colonels	Majors	Captains	Lieutenants	Ensigns	Staff	Flag Bearers	Sergeants	Furriéis	Musicians and Drummers	Corporals and Soldiers	Total
9th												1	1									1			6	7																						1			7	8
21st						1						10	11			1		2	2			2			77	84																1		2	3			2			87	95
11th Caç.												2	2						1						6	7																			1						8	9
Total						1						13	14			1		2	3			3			89	98																1		2	4			3			102	112

Names and Ranks of the Officers Killed:

Ensign Vitorino Joaquim Avondanho, 21st Regiment

Names and Ranks of the Officers Wounded:

Major Joaquim Telles Jordão, severly
Lieutenant Manuel Antonio Pereira, slightly
Lieutenant João Manuel Cerqueira, slightly
Ensign Luis Pereira de Eça, severely
Ensign Joze Maria Ignocencio, slightly
Captain Thomas Peacocke, 9th Regiment, slightly

Names and Ranks of the Officers Missing and Prisoners:

Observations:

Captain Peacocke was wounded carrying out the duties of aide de camp of the brigade commander

M. Power
Major General

Chapter 21

The Battle of Toulouse, 10 April 1814

Soult halted at Toulouse, a walled city located along the east bank of the Garonne river, with its suburbs of Saint Cyprien on the west bank. Although Wellington was near Toulouse by 27 March, heavy rains caused the rivers to rise and made crossing them difficult, while at the same time turning the roads into quagmires. Wellington delayed attacking, which gave the French time to improve the defences of the city. These improvements included constructing field fortifications on a ridge to the east of the city, known as Mont Rave. This ridge was about 4km long and 80m high. Between the city and Mont Rave was the Royal Canal,[1244] which had only two bridges spanning its 6m width, although it was possible to use the lock gates to cross over.

If Wellington wanted to take the city, he would have to attack it from the east, which meant moving his army across the Garonne river and then the Ers river.[1245] He spent the first eight days of April trying to cross the flooded Garonne and it was not until late on 9 April that he was in position to move on the city. He left Hill with the 2nd and Portuguese Divisions on the left bank with orders to make a demonstration against the Saint Cyprien suburbs. Hill did this with the 2nd Division and kept the 5th Brigade and the Portuguese Division in reserve.[1246]

For the main attack, Wellington deployed his forces in a semi-circle. In the north was the 3rd Division and to its right was the Light Division. They were to make demonstrations against the fortifications but not to become seriously engaged. To the left of the two divisions was the Spanish Corps that was to attack the northern end of Mont Rave. After crossing the Garonne Beresford was to march past the front of the ridge and attack its southern slope with the 4th and 6th Divisions. To defend the ridge, Soult had three divisions in entrenchments on its top.

The attacks were supposed to be simultaneous; however, Beresford's march was slowed by the soggy ground and the Spanish began their assault long before he was in position. Their initial assault went well but was repulsed with heavy losses. Soult, seeing the opportunity to catch Beresford in the flank, ordered Taupin's Division to move along the ridge and attack. Taupin hit the Allies as they were climbing the ridge, but the British had time to deploy into line and fire several volleys into the French columns. The situation was chaotic. Rather than stand and face the deadly fire, Taupin's troops fell back in great disorder, down to the other side of the Royal Canal. The 4th Division captured the redoubts on the southern end of the ridge, while the 6th Division took the entrenchments to its north.

Picton could hear the fight on the ridge and saw the Spanish assault fail. He assumed that Beresford's attack had also failed. Contrary to his orders to only make a demonstration, he decided to attack the French positions to his front. To get to them, he had to attack across the Royal Canal. Brisbane's Brigade assaulted the lines unsuccessfully three times, while the 8th Brigade and the other British brigade made demonstrations against the fortifications to the left.

A coordinated Allied attack began about 3 p.m. from both ends of the ridge. The Spanish attacked the northern redoubts, while the 6th Division advanced along the ridge to clear it from the south. The 6th Division attacked with Pack's Brigade on the right and the 7th Brigade on its left. It was successful in taking the redoubts in the centre of the ridge and forced the French to retreat. Both the Portuguese and British brigades took heavy casualties. While the 6th Division was reorganizing itself, a French counter-attack retook the two redoubts. The 6th Division's commander responded by sending his reserve to force the French out of the redoubts once again.

This achieved,, he sent his light troops to harass the rear of the Great Redoubt that the Spanish were attacking. Soult, fearing that his men would be trapped between the Spanish in the north and the 6th Division in the south, ordered them to abandon the Great Redoubt and retreat to Toulouse.

Once the French had pulled off the ridge, Wellington ordered no further attacks. The French retreated into Toulouse and it was quiet the next day. On the night of 11 April Soult withdrew from the city and Wellington entered it on 12 April.

4th Division

9th Brigade (11th and 23rd Infantry, 7th Caçadores)
Prior to the battle of Toulouse, the commander of the 7th Caçadores, Major John Lillie, had incurred the wrath of Wellington and was placed under arrest on 30 March. Wellington was incensed that a caçadores took a wagon from St Lys to transport ammunition and never returned it, which was a violation of the general orders. Lillie marched with his battalion as a prisoner and was not reinstated to the command of his battalion until 8 April.[1247] The 9th Brigade attacked up the ridge with both of its regiments, preceded by a screen of the 7th Caçadores. The brigade lost 38 dead and 64 wounded. About half the casualties were in the 23rd Infantry.[1248] Among the wounded was the commander of the 7th Caçadores, Major John Lillie, who suffered da fractured knee.[1249]

> Report[1250] from Colonel Sá to AG Mozinho
>
> Sir,
> I notify you, for the information of His Excellency the Marshal Marquis de Campo Maior, that in the battle of the 10th instant, the 9th Brigade, under my command, had the loss reported by the corps commanders on the returns enclosed. I must also report that all the officers and men carried out their duties with great gallantry, but some particularly distinguished themselves: Captain Derenzy,[1251] 7th Caçadores Battalion, who commanded the battalion since the wounding of Major Lillie in the beginning of the action, Lieutenant Joaquim Joze de Almeida,[1252] wounded three times, and Adjutant Sergeant Antonio Joze Moreira, both from the 7th Caçadores. I recommend the Adjutant of the 23rd Regiment, Ensign Antonio Roque de Andrade,[1253] who, on several occasions, I sent with my orders to direct the skirmishers and behaved with great intelligence and valour. It is my duty to request the favour of His Excellency to those mentioned.
> God save you, Sir
> Camp before Toulouse, 12 April 1814
> Manoel de Brito Mozinho
>
>   Joze de Vasconcellos
>   Colonel 9th Brigade Commander

7th Caçadores

> Report[1254] from Captain Derenzy to Colonel Sá
>
> In the absence of the Major,[1255] who was severely wounded, it is my duty, since the battalion command devolved to me, to enclose the return of the killed and wounded in yesterday's battle.
> I have the pleasure to inform you that the conduct of all individuals was most conspicuous, showing gallantry, steadiness and valour, not only in the attack on the enemy posts until the seizing of the height but also during all day, under a heavy artillery fire, repelling all the enemy's efforts to dislodge the battalion. All the officers behaved with their usual valour but as it is not possible to reward all of them, I beg leave to particularly recommend to His Excellency the Marshal, Captain Francisco Xavier,[1256] Lieutenant Joaquim Joze de Almeida, both severely wounded, and Ensign Firmino Joze Pereira Rangel.[1257] The three are the

senior in their ranks. Also worthy of His Excellency's attention is Adjutant Sergeant António José Moreira for his distinguished conduct even after he was severely wounded.

God save you, Sir

Heights above Toulouse, 11 April 1814

Joze de Vasconcellos

Brigade commander

B.V. Derenzy

Captain Commanding the 7th Caçadores

6th Division

7th Brigade (8th and 12th Infantry, 9th Caçadores)

The 6th Division started its assault on Mont Rave with three brigades abreast. Lambert's Brigade was on the left, the 7th Brigade in the centre, and Pack's Brigade on the right. As they were moving up the ridge, General Taupin's Division assaulted down it and hit the junction between Lambert's Brigade and Anson's Brigade of the 4th Division to his left. Once the French counter-attack was beaten back, both divisions continued their assault and took the redoubts and trenches on the southern half of the ridge. Beresford was reluctant to continue to move along the ridge to take more of the entrenchments until he could get artillery support and coordinate with the Spanish so that their attacks would happen simultaneously.

About 3 p.m. Beresford ordered the 7th Brigade to attack along the western slope of the ridge, while Pack's Brigade attacked along the crest. The 12th Infantry was in reserve. The attack succeeded, but at a heavy cost. Colonel Douglas was severely wounded and lost his leg, while Lieutenant Colonel Birmingham, 8th Infantry, was killed. Both brigades were disorganized by the fight and a French counter-attack retook the redoubts. General Clinton ordered the 12th Infantry and 91st Foot, the two brigades' reserves, to retake the redoubts. This they did, but could not hold it when the French counter-attacked a second time. By this point the two brigades were spent and Clinton sent Lambert's Brigade to take the redoubts for a third time. This achieved, they held them for the rest of the battle. Clinton had achieved his objective, but rather than stopping he sent his light troops, including the 9th Caçadores, to harass the French forces holding the Great Redoubt at the northern end of the ridge.

The 7th Brigade lost 17 per cent of its total strength in the battle and only two other brigades in Wellington's Army suffered more.[1258] Casualties among its senior leaders were particularly heavy, with the loss of brigade, regimental, and battalion commanders.

Report[1259] from Lieutenant Colonel Beatty,[1260] to AG Mozinho

Sir,

The command of the brigade having devolved upon me in consequence of the severe wound of Colonel Douglas,[1261] and the death of Lieutenant Colonel Birmingham, it becomes my duty to lay before His Excellency Marshal Beresford, Commander-in-Chief of the Army, the names of those officers whose intrepid and zealous conduct attracted my particular observation. I have the honour to strongly recommend Major Ignacio Luis Madeira de Mello,[1262] who so effectually assisted me in the first part of the action and was severely wounded leading the regiment[1263] after I succeeded in the command of the brigade; Brigade Major Maher,[1264] who in this, as in other occasions, showed the most meritorious zeal, intelligence and activity, and despite the pain from a severe contusion did not leave the field; Captain Green, 12th Regiment, whose gallant and lively conduct, commanding the regiment after Major Madeira was wounded, deserves notice; Ensign Guedes[1265] and Adjutant Sergeant Antonio Manoel Varejão.[1266] The latter I had recommended many times to His Excellency and again yesterday he distinguished himself and was dangerously wounded.

The conduct of every corps in the brigade was most soldierly and creditable.

God save you, Sir

Camp before Toulouse, 11 April 1814

Manoel de Brito Mozinho

Wm Beatty
Lieutenant Colonel Commander of the 7th Brigade

Report[1267] from Lieutenant Colonel Beatty to General Clinton, 6th Division Commander[1268]

Camp before Toulouse

April 11th 1814

Sir,

The command of the brigade having devolved upon me in the action of yesterday, in consequence of the severe wound which deprived us of Colonel Douglas, and the death of Lieutenant Colonel Birmingham, it becomes my duty to offer to your notice the names of those officers whose conduct attracted my particular observation and I hope you will consider them deserving your recommendation to Marshal Beresford.

Major Madeira, Captain Green, Ensign Guedes and Sergeant Major[1269] Varejão of the 12th Regiment and Captain Maher of the 8th (Brigade Major) were those who had opportunities of manifesting their zeal, activity and intrepidity under my own eye.

Major Madeira had on a very recent occasion distinguished himself, as you Sir, will no doubt recollect. He has given repeated proofs of his military merit, and it is but justice to entreat your interposition in his favour.

Major Sullivan[1270] succeed to the command of the 8th Regiment after the fall of Lieutenant Colonel Birmingham, and as he is only a British Captain and of many years standing, I trust he may through your patronage reap the same benefit, that has generally accrued to officers under similar circumstances.

Both Major Sullivan and the commanding officer of the 9th Caçadores, sent me in the names of individuals in their respective corps who had distinguished themselves by their good conduct, and those I have forwarded to the Adjutant General of the Portuguese Army. But tho' I have not the smallest doubt of their merits, it was not in my power to enforce them by my own testimony, the duties of my [illegible word] having occupied [me] during almost the whole of the battle with the 12th Regiment and in another part of the field.

I have the honour to be, Sir, your most obedient servant

Wm Beatty
Lieutenant Colonel commander of the Portuguese Brigade

Lieutenant General Sir Henry Clinton K.B.

Report[1271] from Lieutenant Colonel Beatty to AG Mozinho

Sir,

I have the honour to forward the enclosed reports which arrived after I sent my own this morning. I hope they arrive in time to deserve the consideration of His Excellency the Marshal Commander-in- Chief of the Army.

God save you, Sir

Camp, 11 April 1814

Manoel de Brito Mozinho

Wm Beatty
Lieutenant Colonel Commander of the 7th Brigade

8th Infantry

Report[1272] from Major Sullivan to the 7th Brigade Commander

Camp, Toulouse
11 April 1814
Sir,
After His Royal Highness, the Prince Regent lost the services of the late Lieutenant Colonel Birmingham, the command of the 8th Regiment devolved upon me. I have the satisfaction to report to you, for the information of His Excellency Marshal Beresford Marquis de Campo Maior, the brave conduct of the officers and men of the regiment under my command during yesterday's action; I beg leave to recommend particularly Captains Vicente Mateus Aires, 2nd Company, Simão J. Clemente, 5th Company, and Luis Appellius, 8th Company, for their good example and Ensign Joze Alves, who commanded the skirmishers, and also Adjutant João Luis Thomas for his activity in the duties assigned to him.

I also recommend Surgeon Joaquim Vieira de Souza and Assistant Surgeon Antonio Xavier Climaco for their zeal and attention to caring and dressing the wounded.
God save you, Sir
7th Brigade Commander

Benj. Sullivan
Major Commander of the 8th Infantry Regiment

9th Caçadores

Report[1273] from Major Figueiredo to AG Mozinho

Sir,
I have the honour and the satisfaction to report to you, for the information of His Excellency Marshal Beresford Marquis de Campo Maior, the brave conduct of the officers of the 9th Caçadores Battalion. Among them I must recommend Captain Antonio Simplicio de Moraes Fontoura, 6th Company, Captain Ignacio Ferreira da Rocha, 1st Company; Lieutenants Miguel da Cunha and Joaquim Manuel da Silva Rocha, not only for their bravery but also for their zeal in making up the battalion's shortage in officers. I must not omit the conduct of Surgeon João Pedro Baptista, who not only took good care of the wounded of the battalion but also of the brigade, as he had done before on all occasions offered to him. In the same way the Chaplain Joze da Costa, who heard, on the battlefield, the confession of the wounded in need.
God save you, Sir
Camp before Toulouse, 11 April 1814
Brigadier Adjutant General
Manoel de Brito Mozinho

Luis Evaristo de Figueiredo
Major Commander

See Table 21.2.

Light Division (1st and 3rd Caçadores, 17th Infantry)
The Light Division was deployed against the northern defences of Toulouse, just to the right of the Spanish. Kempt's Brigade was on the right and Colborne's Brigade was on the left. The 17th Infantry was in reserve. In a line of skirmishers to the front were the two caçadores battalions, with the 3rd Caçadores on the right and the 1st Caçadores on the left. The division was only supposed to make a demonstration and not become heavily involved. The 1st Caçadores were the only troops seriously engaged. After the initial Spanish attack on the north of the ridge was beaten back with

great loss, the French chased the Spanish down the ridge. Many of the fleeing troops ran through the 1st Caçadores' skirmish line and suddenly the Portuguese light troops had French to their front. The 1st Caçadores' commander ordered his reserve companies to move forward in line to protect his skirmishers and a deadly firefight followed.[1274] The French broke off their pursuit and returned to their entrenchments. By the end of the day the 1st Caçadores' casualties were more than those of all the other Portuguese units in the division, and 36 per cent of the division's total.

1st Caçadores

Report[1275] from Major Rodrigues to AG Mozinho

Sir,

I have the honour to enclose the return of the killed and wounded in this battalion on the battle of the 10th instant. It is my duty to assure you that all the officers and men carried out their duties. They particularly showed their steadiness and courage in the charge made by the reserve companies, forcing the enemy, who was pursuing the Spanish from the Bellevue Redoubts,[1276] to retire. The skirmishers, who received the fleeing Spanish, retired in the best order, compelling many Spanish to turn around and fire against the enemy and cover the retreat.

God save you, Sir

Camp of Toulouse, 12 April 1814

Manoel de Brito Mozinho

Manoel Jorge Rodrigues
Major 1st Caçadores Acting Commander

3rd Caçadores

Report[1277] from Lieutenant Colonel Cerqueira to AG Mozinho

Sir,

I have the honour to enclose, for His Excellency Marshal Beresford Marquis de Campo Maior's information, the return of the killed and wounded of the battalion under my command, in the battle of the 10 instant, before Toulouse. It's also my duty to report that the battalion attacked the two first redoubts and remained defending them, with its characteristic gallantry.[1278] The general conduct of the officers was excellent, so I recommend to His Excellency the seniors in the battalion: Major Manoel Caetano Teixeira, Captains Joaquim Jozé Pimentel Jorge, and Guilherme [sic] Dobbin.

God save you Sir

Quarter before Toulouse, 11 April 1814

Manoel de Brito Mozinho

Brigadier, Army's Adjutant General

Luis Maria Cerqueira
Lieutenant Colonel 3rd Caçadores Commander

See Table 21.2.

Letter[1279] from Colonel Barnard, Commander of the 2nd Brigade of the Light Division, to Lieutenant Colonel Cerqueira, 3rd Caçadores

Toulouse, 11 April 1814
I beg you to express to the officers and men of the battalion under your command my approbation of their gallant conduct in the action of the 10th instant, of which I will make a favourable representation to Marshal Beresford.
I have the honour to be your most obedient servant

AF Barnard
Colonel Commander of the 2nd Brigade of the Light Division

Lieutenant Colonel Cerqueira
3rd Caçadores commander

17th Infantry

Report[1280] from Lieutenant Colonel Rolt, 17th Infantry, to AG Mozinho

Sir,
I enclose the return of the killed and wounded in the 17th Infantry Regiment under my command and I have the honour to recommend to His Excellency the Marshal Marquis de Campo Maior the Captain of the 1st Grenadier Company Manoel Bernardo da Silva Reboxo. This officer has been with the regiment in all the actions, always carrying out his duties in the best way, leading his company, or acting as the major, when the post was vacant. I have already proposed this officer to be promoted to major and again I recommend him to His Excellency for his good conduct and being for twelve years captain.
God save you, Sir
Camp before Toulouse
11 April 1814
Manoel de Brito Mozinho

John Rolt
Lieutenant Colonel 17th Regiment Commander

See Table 21.3.

Artillery
Arriaga's 1st Artillery Brigade of 9-pounders and Preto's 3rd Artillery Brigade of 6-pounders were under the command of Lieutenant Colonel Victor von Arentschild[1281] during the battle and were in direct support of the Spanish Corps. They were on Pujade Hill and fired on the redoubts on the north end of the ridge, while being under fire from the French heavy guns on the ridge throughout the day. By the end of the battle the guns had little ammunition left.

Report[1282] from Brevet Colonel Dickson, Commander of the Artillery, to AG Mozinho

Sir,
It is with the greatest pleasure that I forward to you the enclosed report from Lieutenant Colonel Victor von Arentschild, the commander of the brigades from the Portuguese Artillery. He mentions the military conduct of the officers and men who distinguished themselves on the 10th of this month; to this I have only to add that I noticed with satisfaction the steadiness and valour of the Portuguese artillery during the battle under a heavy enemy fire from its fortified position. This conduct was witnessed with great pleasure and admiration by the officers of the Allied Army. For this reason, I beg you to particularly recommend the

officers mentioned in Lieutenant Colonel Arentschild's report to His Excellency Marshal Beresford Marquis de Campo Maior's favourable attention.

God save you, Sir

Headquarters Toulouse, 13 April 1814

Brigadier Manoel de Brito Mozinho

A Dickson
Colonel Artillery Commander

Report[1283] from Lieutenant Colonel Victor von Arentschild, Commander of the Artillery Brigades, to Brevet Colonel Dickson

Sir,

It is my duty to inform you of the military conduct of some officers of the brigades under my command in the battle of the 10th instant. The conduct of Captain Michell, who was attached to the 4th Spanish Division, commanded by the Count de Espoletta,[1284] was so brave and precise, equal to his character and honour, but also a great advantage to the service of that division. A little time after, this officer joined the other brigades on the position in front of the enemy's redoubts. From it all the brigades fired and during the action, Lieutenant Colonel Arriaga, Major Cunha, and Captain Charles Mitchell [sic], behaved with their usual bravery and sustained the fire from the enemy's redoubts with great steadiness deserving my complete approbation.

I must not omit the cooperation of 1st Lieutenant João Xavier da Costa Vellozo;[1285] of the two 2nd Lieutenants, Joze Maria da Costa Ribeiro[1286] and Pedro Xavier Fragozo and particularly of Captain Teodoro Joze Duarte, the Army Artillery Commander Colonel Dickson's Aide-de-Camp, who joined the service voluntarily and whose services I praise very much. I beg leave to request that you lay this report before His Excellency Marshal Beresford Marquis de Campo Maior and Commander-in-Chief of the Army.

I have the honour to enclose, to your information, the return of killed and wounded on the brigades.

God save you, Sir

Quarters before Toulouse, 11 April 1814

Colonel Alexander Dickson

Army's Artillery commander

Victor von Arentschild
Lieutenant Colonel Commander of the Artillery Brigades

See Table 21.4.

Table 21.1: 7th Brigade. Return[1287] of the Killed and Wounded in the Brigade Composed by the 8th, 12th Regiments and 9th Caçadores Battalion

Camp 10 April 1814		Killed									Wounded									Total								
		Colonel	Lieutenant Colonel	Majors	Captains	Lieutenants	Ensigns	Sergeants	Drummers	Corporals and Privates	Colonel	Lieutenant Colonel	Majors	Captains	Lieutenants	Ensigns	Sergeants	Drummers	Corporals and Privates	Colonel	Lieutenant Colonel	Majors	Captains	Lieutenants	Ensigns	Sergeants	Drummers	Corporals and Privates
Regiments	9th Caçadores									3				1	1		7		29				1	1		7		32
	8th Regiment		1			1	1			10	1					3	9		114	1	1			1	4	9		124
	12th Regiment									16			1	2	2	2	11		140			1	2	2	2	11		156
	Total																			1	1	1	3	4	6	27		312

Observations

Colonel Douglas's horse was killed
Captain Maher's horse was severely wounded
Major Madeira's horse was severely wounded

J Maher
Brigade Major

Names and ranks of the officers killed

8th Regiment:
Lieutenant Colonel Birmingham
Lieutenant Joaquim Manoel Mascarenhas
Ensign João Benedito

Names and ranks of the officers wounded

9th Caçadores:
Captain Ignacio Ferreira da Rocha, severely; Lieutenant Joaquim Manoel da Silva Rocha, severely

8th Regiment:
Colonel João [sic] Douglas,[1288] severely; Ensign Cazemiro Candido de Lacerda, slightly; Ensign Luis Pinto,[1289] slightly; Ensign Joze Maximo, slightly

12th Infantry:
Major Ignacio Luis Madeira, severely; Captain Joze Antonio da Costa, severely; Captain Antonio Joze Carneiro[1290], severely; Lieutenant Antonio Alvares da Silva, slightly; Lieutenant Joze de Mesquita e Souza, slightly; Ensign Manoel Antonio Teixeira, severely; Ensign Joze Manoel Carneiro, slightly

Table 21.2: 3rd Caçadores. Return[1291] of the Killed, Wounded, and Missing on 10 April 1814

	Killed							Wounded							Missing							Prisoners							Total						
	Superior Officers	Captains	Subalterns	Staff	Sergeants and *Furriéis*	Buglers and Musicians	Corporals and Privates	Superior Officers	Captains	Subalterns	Staff	Sergeants and *Furriéis*	Buglers and Musicians	Corporals and Privates	Superior Officers	Captains	Subalterns	Staff	Sergeants and *Furriéis*	Buglers and Musicians	Corporals and Privates	Superior Officers	Captains	Subalterns	Staff	Sergeants and *Furriéis*	Buglers and Musicians	Corporals and Privates	Superior Officers	Captains	Subalterns	Staff	Sergeants and *Furriéis*	Buglers and Musicians	Corporals and Privates
Camp before Toulouse April 10th 1814	-	-	-	-	-	-	2	-	-	-	-	-	-	20	-	-	-	-	-	-	-	-	-	-	-	-	-	-	-	-	-	-	-	-	22
	Names of the officers killed							Names of the officers wounded							Names of the officers missing							Names of the officers prisoners							Observations						

Luis Maria Cerqueira
Lieutenant Colonel 3rd Caçadores Commander

Table 21.3: 17th Infantry. Return[1292] of the Killed, Wounded, and Missing in the action of 10 April 1814

Ranks	Killed	Wounded		Prisoners	Missing	Total
		Severely	Slightly			
Corporals and Privates	-	3	1	-	-	4

John Rolt
Lieutenant Colonel 17th Regiment Commander

Table 21.4: Return[1293] of the Killed and Wounded in the Artillery Brigades at the battle of 10 April in the Vicinity of the City of Toulouse

Headquarters Toulouse 19 April 1814	Killed														Wounded													
	Artillerymen					Drivers					Beasts			Artillerymen					Drivers					Beasts		
	Officers	Sergeants and *Furriés*	Drummers	Corporals and Privates	Total	Officers	Sergeants and *Furriés*	Buglers	Corporals and Privates	Total	Horses	Mules	Total	Officers	Sergeants and *Furriés*	Drummers	Corporals and Privates	Total	Officers	Sergeants and *Furriés*	Buglers	Corporals and Privates	Total	Horses	Mules	Total
1st Brigade Lieutenant Colonel Arriaga	-	-	-	-	-	-	-	-	-	-	1	2	3	-	1	-	1	2	-	-	-	-	-	-	-	-
3rd Brigade Major João da Cunha	-	-	-	-	-	-	-	-	-	-	-	-	-	-	-	-	4	4	-	-	-	-	-	-	1	1
4th Brigade Captain Michell	-	-	-	1	1	-	-	-	1	1	-	2	2	-	-	-	3	3	-	-	-	3	3	-	-	-
Total	-	-	-	1	1	-	-	-	1	1	1	4	5	-	1	-	8	9	-	-	-	3	3	-	1	1

The killed horse belonged to Lieutenant Colonel von Arentschild [sic]. It was his personal horse.

A Dickson
Colonel Artillery Commander

Chapter 22

The Siege of Bayonne, February–April 1814

While Wellington manoeuvred against Soult's mobile force, Hope had the mission of besieging the fortress of Bayonne and protecting the Allied supply lines from Saint Jean de Luz and other ports along the Bay of Biscay. To do this, he had the 1st and 5th Divisions, Aylmer's Brigade, Vandeleur's Light Cavalry Brigade, the 1st and 10th Independent Brigades, and 16,000 Spanish. The Portuguese troops numbered about 5,100 officers and men.

Hope planned to invest the city from all sides, but to do this he had to get forces across the Adour river. He crossed 4km downstream of Bayonne on 26 February and the next day ordered the 1st Division and the 10th Brigade to clear the fortified suburb of St Etienne. The roads and parks of this suburb had many entrenchments, while the houses and shops were loop-holed. The defence was stubborn, but after inflicting many casualties the defenders withdrew to the citadel.

Rather than try to batter the walls down and then make a costly assault, Hope decided to starve them out. It was quiet for the next two months until on 13 April both sides received word that Napoleon had abdicated. The French made a final sortie with 6,000 men at 3 a.m. on the morning of 14 April. Heavy casualties were inflicted on both sides before the French retreated into the city. The fortress capitulated on 26 April.

Clearing the Suburbs, 27 February 1814

Once his troops had safely crossed the river, Hope's next goal was to evict the French from the suburbs. His first target was to take St Etienne, about 750m from the walls of the citadel. The suburbs were on heights that would give him a good position to emplace siege guns. The 10th Brigade and the 1st Division were ordered to take St Etienne. The 5th Caçadores and the 24th Infantry led the 10th Brigade's attack, with the 13th Infantry in reserve. According to Captain John Dobbs, a company commander in the 5th Caçadores, they cleared them to within a half-pistol shot of the walls of the citadel.[1294]

10th Brigade (Independent) (13th and 24th Infantry, 5th Caçadores)

Report[1295] from General Bradford to AG Mozinho

St Etienne February 28th 1814

Sir,

I have the honour to report for the information of Marshal Sir William Carr Beresford, Marquis of Campo Mayor, that I had every reason to be satisfied with the good conduct of the brigade under my command yesterday in the attack made upon the heights of St Etienne. The regiments most engaged were the 5th Caçadores commanded by Lieutenant Colonel St Clair,[1296] and the 24th Regiment by Colonel MacBean, who I regret to say was severely wounded. After gaining the points which completed the investment, several attempts were made by the enemy to retake the post on which our left rested, aided by a very heavy fire of grape and round shot from the Fort and gun boats, this point as essential to preserve, was however maintained with the utmost gallantry by Lieutenant Colonel Emidio Ayres da Costa,[1297] a very brave officer, commanding some companies of the 24th Regiment and Lieutenant Colonel St Clair of the Caçadores battalion. The good conduct of these troops was very conspicuous and I beg leave to recommend to His Excellency's notice the following officers who distinguished themselves.

5th Caçadores:
  Lieutenant Almada[1298]
  Sergeant Antonio Bello de Vales

24th Regiment:
  Captain Francisco Joaquim de Souza Alcanforado[1299]
  Ensign Bernardo de Azeredo Pinto[1300]
  Lieutenant Antonio Lobo da Silva
  Sergeant of the 4th Company Joaquim Maria de Carvalho,[1301] this sergeant also highly distinguished
    himself at the assault of St Sebastian.

I take this opportunity of again requesting that His Excellency will have the goodness faborable [sic] to consider the memorial I transmitted on the part of the Brigade Major Lennon for promotion, as this officer has been very active in the performance of his duties on the late occasion.
    I have the honour to be Sir your most obedient and humble servant

T. Bradford
Major General

P.S. I beg leave to transmit the enclosed letter from Lieutenant Colonel João Carlos de Saldanha relative to a most excellent officer of his corps, who I am sorry to say was severely wounded on picket this day.

To the Adjutant General

13th Infantry

Report[1302] from Lieutenant Colonel João Carlos de Saldanha to General Bradford

Sir,
I have the honour to report for the information of His Excellency the Marshal Marquis de Campo Maior that the conduct of Lieutenant Francisco Candido da Silveira[1303] from the 13th Regiment, under my command, was excellent during the time he was employed defending the post which I ordered him. I think that his conduct made him worthy of His Excellency's consideration.
I have the honour to be Sir your most obedient servant

João Carlos de Saldanha
Lieutenant Colonel 13th Regiment Commander
St Etienne 28 February 1814

See Table 22.1.

The French Sortie, 14 April 1814

By mid-April 1814 the 1st Brigade was responsible for manning the siege lines closest to the river on the west side of the fortress. The 10th Brigade was to its left, with its headquarters at Lostau.[1304] Although news reached the army on 13 April that Napoleon had abdicated, Hope had also received intelligence that the French garrison might make one last sortie. Word had filtered down to the troops that the war was over, but apparently not the suggestion that the French might still attack.

The sortie was primarily against the suburb of St Etienne, which was held by the 1st Division. The fighting in the 1st Division sector was very heavy, while that against the Portuguese quickly petered out. Captain Dobbs of the 5th Caçadores wrote about this last sortie:

We occupied a gentleman's country house in rear of the outposts, and having heard the night before of the Peace having been concluded at Paris, the Governor of Bayonne having likewise been informed of it, we retired to rest under the impression that the last shot had been fired – what was our astonishment to be awakened a little before daylight by the enemy's balls flying through our windows. A few minutes found us under arms, and on the left of the Germans, with whom we advanced to the relief of the troops engaged, driving the French into their fortress. Being in command of a wing of the Caçadores, I had them in column in front of the citadel, waiting to see if any further attack would take place, when a ball from the walls wounded one of my men, on which I moved the column behind a house on my left, remaining myself on the look out. Suddenly I felt a blow on the shin, and on looking down found that a ball had entered between the two bones, carrying in a piece of the trowsers, which I believe was the last shot fired.[1305]

10th Brigade (Independent) (13th and 24th Infantry, 5th Caçadores)

Report[1306] from General Bradford to AG Mozinho

Petit Basque
near S. Etienne
April 14th 1814
Sir
I have the honour to transmit to you a return of the killed and wounded of the brigade under my command in the sortie made by the enemy this morning.

    As the attack of the enemy was not made upon that part of the line occupied by my brigade, we had not the good fortune to be in the way of rendering any further assistance in repelling the sortie than in supporting with part of the reserve of the picket the attack made by the Germans to recapture the village of St. Etienne.
I have the honour to be, Sir, your most obedient servant

T Bradford
Major General

See Table 22.2.

1st Brigade (Independent) (1st and 16th Infantry, 4th Caçadores)

Report[1307] from Colonel Hill to AG Mozinho

Sir,
I have the honour to transmit enclosed, for the information of His Excellency the Marshal Marquis de Campo Maior, the return of the casualties in a sortie made by Bayonne's garrison this morning.
God save you, Sir
Lostau, Siege of Bayonne
14 April 1814
Manoel de Brito Mozinho

T.N. Hill
Colonel[1308] Commander

See Table 22.3.

Table 22.1: 10th Brigade. Return[1309] of the Killed, Wounded, and Prisoners in the Brigade on 27 February 1814

Regiments	Killed										Wounded										Prisoners and Missing									
	Colonels	Lieutenant Colonels	Majors	Captains	Lieutenants	Ensigns	Sergeants	Drummers	Corporals and Privates	Total	Colonels	Lieutenant Colonels	Majors	Captains	Lieutenants	Ensigns	Sergeants	Drummers	Corporals and Privates	Total	Colonels	Lieutenant Colonels	Majors	Captains	Lieutenants	Ensigns	Sergeants	Drummers	Corporals and Privates	Total
5th Caçadores Battalion	-	-	-	-	-	-	-	-	3	3	-	-	-	-	-	1	3	-	18	22	-	-	-	-	-	-	-	-	5	5
13th Regiment	-	-	-	-	-	-	-	-	1	1	-	-	-	-	1	-	-	-	5	6	-	-	-	-	-	-	-	-	-	-
24th Regiment	-	-	-	-	-	-	1	-	5	6	-	-	-	1	-	1	1	-	33	37	-	-	-	-	-	-	-	-	3	3
Total	-	-	-	-	-	-	1	-	9	10	1	-	-	1	1	2	4	-	56	65	-	-	-	-	-	-	-	-	8	8
	Names and ranks of the officers killed										Names and ranks of the officers wounded										Names and ranks of the officers prisoners and missing									

Colonel MacBean, 24th Regiment, severely wounded; Captain Antonio Xavier da Rocha, 24th Regiment, severely wounded; Ensign Francisco Magalhães, 24th Regiment, slightly wounded; Lieutenant Francisco Candido, 13th Regiment, severely wounded; Adjutant Sebastião Luiz Soares, 5th Caçadores Battalion, severely wounded[1310]

T Bradford
Major General

Table 22.2: 10th Brigade. Return[1311] of the Killed, Wounded, and Prisoners in the 10th Brigade on 14 April 1814

Regiments	Killed										Wounded										Prisoners and Missing									
	Colonels	Lieutenant Colonels	Majors	Captains	Lieutenants	Ensigns	Sergeants	Drummers	Corporals and Privates	Total	Colonels	Lieutenant Colonels	Majors	Captains	Lieutenants	Ensigns	Sergeants	Drummers	Corporals and Privates	Total	Colonels	Lieutenant Colonels	Majors	Captains	Lieutenants	Ensigns	Sergeants	Drummers	Corporals and Privates	Total
5th Caçadores Battalion	-	-	-	-	-	-	-	-	-	-	-	-	-	1	-	-	1	-	1	3	-	-	-	-	-	-	-	-	-	-
13th Regiment	-	-	-	-	-	-	-	-	2	2	-	-	-	1	-	-	-	-	5	6	-	-	-	-	-	-	-	-	-	-
24th Regiment	-	-	-	-	-	-	-	-	3	3	-	-	-	-	-	-	-	-	4	4	-	-	-	-	-	-	-	-	3	3
Total	-	-	-	-	-	-	-	-	5	5	-	-	-	2	-	-	1	-	10	13	-	-	-	-	-	-	-	-	-	-

Names and ranks of the officers killed

Names and ranks of the officers wounded: Major General Bradford, severely wounded but not in danger; Captain Dobbs,[1312] 5th Caçadores Battalion, severely wounded but not in danger; Captain Clearey,[1313] 13th Regiment, severely wounded but not in danger

Names and ranks of the officers prisoners and missing

Table 22.3: Return[134] of the Killed, Wounded, Prisoners, and Missing in the 1st Infantry Brigade on 14 April 1814 at Lostau, siege of Bayonne

	Killed									Wounded									Prisoners and Missing									Total								
	Colonels	Lieutenant Colonels	Majors	Captains	Subalterns	Flag Bearers	Sergeants and *Furriéis*	Musicians and Drummers	Corporals and Privates	Colonels	Lieutenant Colonels	Majors	Captains	Subalterns	Flag Bearers	Sergeants and *Furriéis*	Musicians and Drummers	Corporals and Privates	Colonels	Lieutenant Colonels	Majors	Captains	Subalterns	Flag Bearers	Sergeants and *Furriéis*	Musicians and Drummers	Corporals and Privates	Colonels	Lieutenant Colonels	Majors	Captains	Subalterns	Flag Bearers	Sergeants and *Furriéis*	Musicians and Drummers	Corporals and Privates
1st Infantry	-	-	-	-	-	-	-	-	1	-	-	-	-	-	-	-	-	1	-	-	-	-	-	-	-	-	-	-	-	-	-	-	-	-	-	2
16th Infantry	-	-	-	-	-	-	-	-	-	-	-	-	-	-	-	-	-	2	-	-	-	-	-	-	-	-	-	-	-	-	-	-	-	-	-	2
4th Caçadores	-	-	-	-	-	-	-	-	2	-	-	-	-	-	-	-	-	5	-	-	-	-	-	-	-	-	-	-	-	-	-	-	-	-	-	7
Total	-	-	-	-	-	-	-	-	3	-	-	-	-	-	-	-	-	8	-	-	-	-	-	-	-	-	-	-	-	-	-	-	-	-	-	11
	Rank and name of the officers killed									Rank and name of the officers wounded									Rank and name of the officers missing or prisoners									Observations								

T. N. Hill
Colonel Commander

Appendix A

Portuguese Officers' Biographies

Amarante, Count de. Francisco da Silveira Pinto da Fonseca Teixeira[1315]
Born on 1 September 1763, he entered the army as a cadet in the Almeida Cavalry Regiment on 25 April 1780. He was promoted to ensign in the Bragança Cavalry Regiment on 22 April 1790 and to lieutenant on 17 December 1792. On 17 December 1799 he was promoted to captain and appointed ADC to the military government of Beira province on 15 February 1800. In 1801, during the War of the Oranges against Spain, he distinguished himself in the defence of Trás-os-Montes province and was promoted on 14 March 1801 to major on the staff and commander of the *Companhias Francas*[1316] raised in the northern provinces. He was appointed major *agregado* in the Bragança Cavalry Regiment on 28 June 1802 and lieutenant colonel *agregado* on 14 March 1803. He became one of the leading officers in the Portuguese uprising against French rule in 1808 in northern Portugal. On 21 July 1808 he was promoted to colonel of the 6th Cavalry, to brigadier general on 4 January 1809, and on 15 February 1809 was appointed Military Governor of Trás-os-Montes. In March 1809 General Silveira faced Soult's invasion, the French corps entering Portugal through Trás-os-Montes. Realizing that his force was no match for the French, he retired, harassing the enemy with his irregulars. After Soult moved from Chaves to Oporto, Silveira returned and retook Chaves, capturing the French hospital and garrison, and then followed Soult closely. With Soult established in Oporto and extending his control over northern Portugal, Silveira brought his force to Amarante, on the Tâmega river, blockading French access to Trás-os-Montes. From 18 April to 2 May 1809 he defended the bridge at Amarante and the Tâmega line, with only 2,000 men, against the French. Finally a French division under General Loison took the bridge, opened the passage to Trás-os-Montes and advanced to the Douro valley. Silveira retreated to the Douro and joined Beresford, who was already on the Upper Douro, advancing in conjunction with Wellington, who was moving against Soult in Oporto. He was promoted to major general on 21 May 1809. From June 1809 to 1812 he commanded in Trás-os-Montes a division composed mainly of provincial militia regiments and some regular cavalry and artillery. His mission was to defend the province and observe and report on French movements in northern Spain. During Massena's invasion of Portugal, General Silveira took every opportunity to harass the French lines of communication and small isolated corps, according to the strategy adopted by Wellington. In the first days of August 1810 he successfully attacked Puebla de Sanabria in Spain, near the Trás-os-Montes border, which had been garrisoned by the French with a Swiss battalion, forcing their surrender. For his outstanding services he was created Count de Amarante on 13 May 1811 and was promoted to lieutenant general on 1 January 1812. In July 1812 his small division advanced to Zamora, where he blockaded the French garrison until the end of August, when he was forced to retreat by a French raid intended to rescue the garrisons of Toro, Astorga, and Zamora. On 26 February 1813 he was appointed commander of the Portuguese Division, and led it at Vitoria and in the pursuit of the French to the Pyrenees. The division distinguished itself in the Pyrenees, but the Count resigned his command on 3 September 1813, frustrated with the manner in which his division, and the Portuguese Army in general, was employed. He returned to his post of Military Governor of Trás-os-Montes until 1820, when he tried to resist the Liberal Revolution. Abandoned by some of his closest family members, all high-ranking officers, and deserted by most of his regiments, he escaped to Spain. He returned to Portugal to die on 29 May 1821 at the age of 58.

Barbosa, Jerónimo Soares
Born in 1788, he entered the army on 15 October 1811 as a cadet in the 13th Infantry, being appointed cadet flag bearer. He was promoted to ensign on 5 May 1812. He was with his regiment throughout the war, fighting in all major engagements. On 7 October 1812, during the siege of Burgos, the besieged French made a sortie and in the ensuing fight Ensign Barbosa distinguished himself. For his gallant conduct he was promoted to lieutenant on 14 November 1812. In 1815 he became seriously ill and died on 26 April 1816.

Barreto, Luís do Rego[1317]
He was born on 28 October 1777 and entered the army on 1 March 1790 in the Viana Infantry Regiment. He was appointed cadet in the regiment on 31 October 1792 and cadet flag bearer on 26 July 1798. He was promoted to ensign on 24 June 1802 and to lieutenant on 24 July 1807. He was promoted to major on 24 July 1808 and was sent to Beira province, to raise the Beira Caçadores Battalion. This was renamed the 4th Caçadores Battalion and he was promoted to lieutenant colonel and its commander on 21 January 1809. He distinguished himself commanding the battalion throughout the first three years of the war, being mentioned by Wellington in his dispatches several times. He was promoted to colonel of the 15th Infantry on 5 February 1812 and led the regiment with distinction at Badajoz, Salamanca, Vitoria, and San Sebastian. From October 1813 to the end of the war he commanded the 3rd Brigade, 5th Division and led it at the Bidassoa, Nivelle and Nive. He was promoted to brigadier general on 12 October 1815. In 1816 he joined the royal court in Rio de Janeiro. In 1817 he was appointed to command a force assembled to suppress a republican uprising in the province of Pernambuco. For his success he was promoted to major general on 25 April 1817 and appointed governor of that province, in which he remained until 1821. He returned to Portugal and was appointed Military Governor of Minho province in September 1822. He was promoted to lieutenant general on 28 July 1827 and made Viscount de Geraz do Lima in April 1835. He died on 7 September 1840.

Barros, António Lobo Teixeira de
He was born on 22 December 1777 and entered the army as a cadet in the Miranda Cavalry Regiment on 1 May 1790. He was promoted to ensign on 30 September 1796. On 31 August 1808 he was promoted to brevet captain and adjutant in the Beira Caçadores Battalion, renamed the 4th Caçadores Battalion in November 1808. On 6 December 1809 he was promoted to captain in the 4th Caçadores. On 2 June 1812 he was promoted to major in the 1st Caçadores. He was severely wounded on 22 November 1810 and slightly at Vera and Nive. On 9 November 1813 he was promoted to lieutenant colonel in the 12th Caçadores, to colonel of the 9th Infantry on 22 January 1820 and to brigadier general on 18 December 1820. He died on 25 August 1829.

Câmara, Joaquim da[1318]
He was born in 1783 and entered the army as a cadet in the Cais Cavalry Regiment on 2 April 1791. He was promoted to ensign[1319] on 8 April 1797 and on 31 July 1797 was promoted to captain and ADC. On 24 June 1802 he was appointed captain *agregado* in the 2nd Olivença Infantry Regiment, on 14 November 1802 captain *agregado* in the Lisbon Infantry Regiment, and captain *efetivo* on 20 January 1806. He was promoted major in the 10th Infantry on 11 January 1809 and lieutenant colonel in the 13th Infantry on 6 June 1810. In May 1811 he took command of the regiment and led it at Badajoz, Salamanca, Burgos, and Vitoria. At the combat of Tolosa he was seriously wounded, preventing him from returning to the army. On 10 September 1813 he was promoted to colonel and appointed the commander of the *Guarda Real de Polícia*.[1320] On 12 October 1815 he was promoted to brigadier general. He died in 1817.

Canavarro, Caetano Alberto de Sousa
He was born in 1785 and entered the army as a cadet in the Chaves Infantry Regiment on 10 September 1801. He was promoted to ensign in the 12th Infantry on 4 August 1808 and to lieutenant in the 4th Caçadores on 21 January 1809. He was promoted to captain in the 4th Caçadores on 5 October 1811. He was severely wounded at Nive. On 22 June 1815 he was promoted to major in the 1st Caçadores Battalion of the *Divisão dos Voluntários Reais do Príncipe*.[1321] He was promoted to lieutenant colonel in the division on 22 January 1818. On 12 January 1824 he was promoted to colonel of the 13th Infantry, on 14 February 1831 to brevet brigadier general, and on 6 November 1833 to major general. He died on 12 November 1843.

Cerqueira, Luís Maria
Born *c.* 1775, he entered the army on 2 August 1792. He was appointed cadet a month later in the Chaves Infantry Regiment. On 13 September 1794 he was promoted to ensign in the Bragança Cavalry Regiment. He was promoted to captain on 31 August 1808 and appointed ADC to Major General Manuel Pinto Bacelar. On 20 August 1809 he was appointed captain in the 4th Caçadores and was present in all the battalion's actions until 22 June 1811, when he was promoted to major in the 9th Caçadores. He was present in most of the engagements of the battalion, commanding it at Orthez, and was severely wounded at Burgos and Sorauren. On 29 January 1814 he was promoted to lieutenant colonel *agregado* and on 15 March to lieutenant colonel *efetivo* in the 3rd Caçadores, which he commanded at Toulouse. He was promoted to colonel and DAG on 6 February 1818. On 15 October 1818 he was promoted to brevet brigadier general. He died in January 1819.

Correia, Sebastião Pinto de Araújo
He was born on 21 March 1780 and entered the army on 16 August 1799 in the Viana Infantry Regiment, where he was appointed cadet on 1 July 1804. On 1 April 1805 he was appointed major *agregado* in the Braga Militia Regiment. During the Portuguese uprising in 1808 he was appointed a staff officer in the Portuguese force raised in the northern provinces under General Bernardim Freire de Andrade. This force marched from Oporto to Coimbra and joined Wellington. He was promoted to major in the 6th Caçadores on 21 January 1809 and to lieutenant colonel and commander of the battalion on 13 May 1809. He commanded it at Bussaco, Fuentes D'Oñoro, where he was severely wounded, and in the Pyrenees. He was promoted to colonel in the 18th Infantry on 10 July 1813, to brigadier general on 12 October 1814, and to major general and appointed AG and Military Secretary of the *Divisão dos Voluntários Reais do Príncipe* on 24 June 1815. He was promoted to lieutenant general on 24 June 1817. In November 1818 he was shipwrecked when making the passage from Montevideo to Rio de Janeiro.

Figueiredo, Luís Evaristo Guedes de
He was born *c.* 1779 and entered the army as a private in the Chaves Infantry Regiment on 2 June 1796. There he was promoted to sergeant on 16 August 1799. He was promoted to ensign in the Trás-os-Montes Caçadores Battalion on 21 July 1808. This battalion was later renamed the 3rd Caçadores Battalion and he was promoted to lieutenant on 21 March 1809 and to captain on 10 January 1810. He was promoted to major in the 9th Caçadores on 8 February 1814. He commanded the battalion at Tarbes and Toulouse. He transferred to the 9th Infantry on 17 February 1820 and on 18 December 1820 was promoted to lieutenant colonel in the 13th Infantry. On 5 April 1821 he took command of the 21st Infantry. On 16 June 1823 he was dismissed from his regiment, probably due to political reasons, but on 19 December 1823 he returned to the army as a lieutenant colonel on the staff. He was appointed governor of the small coastal fort of Esposende, in Minho province, on 16 September 1824. No information was found about him after 1824.

Lecor, Carlos Frederico

He was born on 6 October 1764 and entered the army as an artillery soldier in Tavira Fortress on 13 October 1793. On 17 March 1794, already a sergeant, he was promoted to adjutant in Portimão Fortress. On 2 December 1794 he was promoted to 1st lieutenant in the Algarve Artillery Regiment. On 1 March 1797 he was promoted to captain in the *Legião de Tropas Ligeiras*,[1322] to major on 13 May 1802, and to lieutenant colonel *agregado* on 1 August 1805, and was appointed ADC to General Marquis de Alorna. He was promoted to colonel of the 23rd Infantry on 23 November 1808. From January 1809 he commanded several provisional brigades and detached corps on the Portuguese border. On 8 May 1811 he was promoted to brigadier general and on 9 March 1813 he was appointed to command the Portuguese brigade in the 7th Division, which he led at Vitoria and the Pyrenees. On 10 July 1813 he was promoted to major general and commanded the 7th Division at Nivelle. He remained the acting commander until he was appointed commander of the Portuguese Division on 3 December 1813. He was wounded at Nive, where the division distinguished itself. On 22 June 1815 he was promoted to lieutenant general and commander of the *Divisão dos Voluntários Reais do Príncipe*, which was shipped to southern Brazil to invade the *Banda Oriental*, which would become modern Uruguay. In February 1818 he was made Baron da Laguna. Hostilities ended in 1820 with General Lecor obtaining the full integration of the region in the United Kingdom of Portugal and Brazil, with the name of *Cisplatina* province. When Brazil declared its independence in 1822, General Lecor declared his allegiance to the new country and assumed command of the Brazilian troops in the *Cisplatina*. He retired in 1832 with the rank of Marshal of the Brazilian Army. He died on 2 August 1836.

Meneses, João Teles de[1323]

He was born in 1763 and entered the army on 13 August 1782. He was appointed a cadet on 30 April 1785. He fought in the campaigns of Roussillon and Catalonia. He was promoted to ensign on 21 February 1794, to lieutenant on 14 February 1798, and to captain on 15 August 1805. When the French disbanded the Portuguese Army in 1808, he sailed to Brazil to join the royal court and was promoted to major *agregado* in the Maranhão Infantry Regiment on 4 August 1808. Returning to Portugal, he was appointed major in the 2nd Infantry on 3 September 1809 and promoted to lieutenant colonel on 10 January 1810. He campaigned and fought in many engagements with his regiment until he was promoted to colonel of the 21st Infantry on 10 July 1813. He commanded it at Nivelle, Nive, Orthez, and Toulouse. On 12 October 1815 he was promoted to brigadier general, and on 17 December 1815 he was appointed second-in-command of the Elvas Fortress; on 21 April 1817 he became the Governor of Almeida Fortress. No information could be found on him after 1817.

Mozinho, Manuel de Brito

He was born in 1763. He was commissioned as an ensign on 13 March 1787, probably in the Estremoz Artillery Regiment, and was promoted to 1st lieutenant on 24 October 1789. In 1800 he was an infantry major and an ADC in the military government of Alentejo province. In 1807 he was already a lieutenant colonel but still an ADC in the same government. In 1808 he took part in the disbandment of the Portuguese Army under the orders of his father, General João de Brito Mozinho, who had been appointed to that task in Alentejo. He, his father and his brother were appointed to several posts in the Portuguese force sent to France under the command of General Marquis de Alorna. At the end of July 1808 he and his relatives were allowed to return to Portugal and on 10 December 1808 he was appointed adjutant general of the Portuguese division assembled at Tomar under the command of General António José de Miranda Henriques, the *Exército de entre Tejo e Mondego*.[1324] Meanwhile he was promoted to colonel of the 22nd Infantry on 5 January 1809, but never joined the regiment[1325] because on 14 March 1809[1326] Beresford appointed him Adjutant General of the Portuguese Army. Throughout the Peninsular War he was one of Beresford's most trusted officers. In his position as AG, he was vital in the effort to raise the Portuguese Army and to turn it into an effective fighting force. He accompanied Beresford on every campaign and was often praised for his zeal and assistance. He remained AG of the Portuguese Army until September 1820. On 8 May 1811 he was promoted to brigadier general, on 12 October 1815 to major general, and on 13 May 1820 to lieutenant general. He died in 1824.

Pereira, Francisco José

He was born on 12 October 1783 and entered the army as a volunteer on 1 January 1798 in the Almeida Infantry Regiment. He was made a sergeant on 1 April 1807. He was promoted to ensign in the 23rd Infantry on 14 January 1809 and appointed quartermaster on 14 August 1809. On 16 March 1810 he was promoted to lieutenant and to captain on 30 June 1810. He was present with his regiment in most of the major engagements of the war, where he was wounded several times. For his conduct at Orthez he was promoted to brevet major, and then to major in the 12th Infantry on 15 December 1814. In 1818 the 12th Infantry was dispatched to Bahia in Brazil and fought the Brazilian forces, in consequence of the declaration of independence, until 1823. Meanwhile he was promoted to brevet lieutenant colonel on 6 February 1818 and to lieutenant colonel on 14 December 1818. He was promoted to colonel of the 6th Infantry Regiment on 5 June 1824, to brigadier general on 4 April 1833 and to major general on 2 July of the same year, and was appointed Military Governor of Oporto. In May 1837 he was made Baron de Vilar Torpim. He died on 28 September 1846.

Pinto, Manuel Caetano Teixeira

He was born *c.* 1776 and entered the army in the Chaves Infantry Regiment on 1 January 1788. He was appointed cadet and flag bearer on 30 March 1790 and promoted to ensign on 24 June 1802. He was promoted to lieutenant in the Trás-os-Montes Caçadores Battalion on 21 July 1808. The battalion was renamed the 3rd Caçadores and he was promoted to captain on 21 January 1809. For his conduct at Badajoz he was promoted to brevet major on 5 May 1812 and given temporary command of the battalion until August 1812. He commanded it at Salamanca. On 27 August 1813 he was promoted to major and was the acting commander of the battalion at Nivelle, Nive, where he was severely wounded, and Orthez. He was promoted to lieutenant colonel in the 10th Caçadores on 5 May 1814, to brevet colonel on 22 January 1819, to brevet brigadier general on 20 August 1823 and to brigadier general on 14 February 1831. He retired from the army with the rank of major general on 2 January 1832. No more information was found on him after 1832.

Pizarro, Francisco Homem de Magalhães Quevedo

He was born on 27 September 1776 and entered the army as a cadet in the Chaves Cavalry Regiment on 28 February 1791. He joined the navy and was admitted as an *aspirante*[1327] on 2 August 1793. On 5 November 1796 he was promoted to 2nd lieutenant. He served on the 70-gun warship *Afonso de Albuquerque*, which was part of a Portuguese squadron that operated in the Mediterranean with the British Fleet under Admiral Nelson, from 1798 to 1800. The squadron distinguished itself in the blockade of Malta, in an attack on Tripoli, and in the retaking of Naples in 1799. He was promoted to 1st lieutenant on 27 July 1799. After resigning his commission in the navy, he was appointed lieutenant colonel *agregado* in the Chaves Militia Regiment. He distinguished himself in the uprising against the French in 1808 and on 10 February 1809 was appointed in the regular army as a lieutenant colonel *agregado* in the 12th Infantry and on 5 February 1812 became lieutenant colonel *efetivo*. He took command of the regiment at Salamanca when its commander was wounded. On 11 August 1812 he was promoted to brevet colonel and continued to command the regiment at Burgos and during the retreat to Portugal in the autumn of 1812. On 6 October 1812 he was promoted to colonel of the 16th Infantry. He commanded the regiment at Vitoria, San Sebastian, Bidassoa, and Nivelle. At Nive he was taken prisoner by the French and remained in captivity until the end of the war. On 24 June 1815 he was promoted to brigadier general in the *Divisão dos Voluntários Reais do Príncipe* and was appointed commander of the 2nd Brigade. He was promoted to major general on 24 June 1817 and was appointed Governor of the Brazilian province of Maranhão in 1818. Falling ill, he returned to Portugal, where he died on 6 January 1819, probably of tuberculosis.

Resende, Count de, Luís Inocêncio Benedito de Castro

He was born on 5 December 1777. He was appointed major on 6 September 1796, major *agregado* in the 1st Regiment of Rio de Janeiro in Brazil on 23 April 1797 and ADC to his father, the Viceroy and Captain General of Brazil between 1790 and 1801. He was appointed major *agregado* in the Lisbon Infantry Regiment on 27 September 1802 and major *efetivo* on 19 January 1807. He was promoted to lieutenant colonel in the 10th Infantry on 9 December 1808 and to colonel on 3 November 1809. He led the regiment in all its engagements until he was promoted to brigadier general on 5 February 1812 and appointed commander of the 6th Division's Portuguese brigade. At Salamanca he was wounded so severely that he was forced to leave the army at the end of August 1812 and was invalided home for the rest of the war. He was promoted to major general on 12 October 1815 and appointed Governor of Abrantes on 17 December 1815. He died on 7 January 1824.

Rodrigues, Manuel Jorge

Born on 23 April 1777, he entered the army as a volunteer on 18 September 1794 and on 24 June 1807 was promoted to ensign in the 8th Infantry. On 21 January 1809 he was promoted to captain in the 1st Caçadores. Promoted to major on 9 November 1813, he temporarily commanded the battalion several times, including at Tarbes and Toulouse. He was promoted to lieutenant colonel on 22 June 1815 in the *Divisão dos Voluntários Reais do Príncipe*, commanding the 1st Caçadores Battalion of the division. After the Brazilian declaration of independence in September 1822 he chose to join the new Brazilian Army. In Brazil he rose to the rank of general and was made Baron de Taquary. He died on 14 May 1845.

Sá, José de Vasconcelos e

He was born on 19 March 1775 and entered the army as a cadet in the Freire Infantry Regiment on 25 October 1785. He fought in the campaigns of Roussillon and Catalonia. He was promoted to ensign in the Cascais Infantry Regiment on 19 September 1794 and appointed adjutant. He was promoted to captain on the staff on 21 November 1795 and ADC to the Military Governor of Algarve, General Francisco da Cunha e Meneses, better known as Monteiro Mór. On 7 February 1797 he was promoted to major on the staff of Castro Marim Fortress, and to lieutenant colonel on the staff on 17 December 1799, keeping his post of ADC. He was appointed lieutenant colonel in the Lagos Infantry Regiment on 16 July 1800 and on 2 June 1804 became its colonel. In 1808 he chose to go to France with the Portuguese corps taken from the disbanded army, under the command of General Marquis de Alorna. In 1810 he was one of the Portuguese officers ordered to join Massena's staff to assist him in the invasion of Portugal. In 1811 he deserted the French Army and presented himself to Wellington. He was brought before a court to justify his conduct and was acquitted on 30 December 1811 and returned to the army, being appointed colonel *agregado*[1328] in the 8th Infantry on 21 February 1812. He commanded the regiment at Burgos and in the retreat to Portugal in the autumn of 1812. On 10 July 1813 he was appointed colonel of the 23rd Infantry but, being the senior colonel, took command of the 9th Brigade, part of the 4th Division, on 7 October 1813. He commanded the brigade at the Bidassoa, Nivelle, Nive, Orthez, and Toulouse. He was promoted to brigadier general on 17 June 1815, major general on 25 April 1817, and lieutenant general on 28 December 1826. He was created Baron de Albufeira in October 1823. He died on 4 September 1842.

Saldanha, João Carlos[1329]

He was born on 17 November 1790 and entered the army as a cadet on 28 September 1805 in the Lippe Infantry Regiment. As a member of the higher nobility, he was appointed captain *agregado* on 24 June 1806 and captain *efetivo* a year later. On 28 February 1809 he was appointed ADC to Lieutenant General António de Miranda Henriques, commander of the Portuguese Corps concentrated between the Tagus and Mondego rivers. He was promoted to major in the 1st Infantry on 9 December 1809 and to lieutenant colonel on 5 February 1812. He campaigned throughout the war with his regiment until 20 September 1813, when he was appointed lieutenant colonel in the 13th Infantry. He commanded the regiment at the Bidassoa, Nivelle, and Nive. On 22 June 1815 he was promoted to colonel in the *Divisão dos Voluntários Reais do Príncipe*. In Brazil he was the commander of the 1st Infantry Regiment of the division. On 2 January 1818 he was promoted to brevet brigadier general and to brigadier general on 13 May 1820. On 9 December 1821 he was appointed the Military Governor of the province of Rio Grande do Sul in southern Brazil, from which he resigned in the following year, after Brazil's declaration of independence, returning to Portugal. He was promoted to major general on 6 February 1825, to lieutenant general on 5 July 1833, and to marshal of the army on 23 September 1833. He was made successively Count, Marquis, and finally Duke de Saldanha in 1846. He would become one of the most influential military and political figures in Portugal during the nineteenth century. He rose to the rank of marshal general and commander in chief in the Portuguese Army, was ambassador to different countries, and was several times appointed a minister and prime minister of the Portuguese Liberal Monarchy. He died on 21 November 1876.

Savedra, José Pinto da Cunha

He was born in 1789 and joined the LLL in Oporto in June 1808. Despite having no previous military experience, he was appointed a captain in the Legion, though his commission was only officially recognized on 3 January 1809. An English speaker, he was appointed ADC to Major General John Hamilton on 24 January 1810. He accompanied General Hamilton in his duties of inspecting and reporting on the progress of the army's discipline and organization. On 12 July 1810 he was appointed an AAG and later assigned to the Portuguese Division. On 24 July 1813 he was promoted to major on the staff, remaining as the division's AAG. He was with the Portuguese Division in all its campaigns and actions, working for several divisional commanders, who praised his assistance on numerous occasions. On 15 October 1818 he was promoted to lieutenant colonel in the 20th Infantry and on 9 April 1821 to lieutenant colonel in the 13th Infantry. On 22 June 1821 he retired from the army as a colonel. He died on 19 September 1855.

Silveira, António de Lacerda Pinto da[1330]

He was born *c.* 1774 and entered the army as a cadet on 18 May 1797. He was appointed lieutenant colonel in the Moncorvo Militia Regiment on 17 December 1798. In 1808, during the Portuguese uprising, he served on the staff of Colonel Francisco da Silveira's force. On 21 January 1809 he was appointed lieutenant colonel in the regular army and commander of the 6th Caçadores. On 26 August 1809 he took command of the 12th Infantry. He was promoted to colonel on 5 February

1812. He commanded the regiment at Fuentes D'Oñoro and Salamanca, where he was wounded. He returned to Portugal to recover and on 10 July 1813 he was appointed colonel of the 22nd Infantry. He was promoted to brigadier general on 12 October 1815 and to major general on 13 May 1820. He died on 24 January 1839.

Silveira, Manuel Pinto da

A half-brother of Count de Amarante, he was born *c.* 1778 and entered the army on 30 August 1794. He was appointed cadet on 1 January 1795 in the Miranda Cavalry Regiment, where he was promoted to ensign on 20 January 1797. He was promoted to lieutenant in the 2nd Oporto Infantry Regiment on 18 March 1800. He was promoted captain in the Trás-os-Montes Caçadores Battalion on 21 July 1808. On 10 March 1810 he was promoted to major in the 4th Caçadores but on 22 July 1810 he returned to the 3rd Caçadores. He was severely wounded at Badajoz and for his conduct was promoted to brevet lieutenant colonel on 14 April 1812. He returned in August 1812 to command the battalion at Vitoria, Bidassoa, and Nive. On 15 March 1814 he was appointed lieutenant colonel of the 22nd Infantry and its colonel on 12 October 1815. He was promoted to brigadier general on 18 December 1820 and was appointed Governor of Almeida on 4 June 1823, remaining in this post until February 1832. He was promoted to brevet major general on 2 January 1832. He died in 1836.

Appendix B

British and Foreign Officers' Biographies

Peter Adamson was born on 23 September 1779. Commissioned as an ensign in the 71st Foot on 12 July 1800, he was promoted to lieutenant on 26 September, and to captain on 21 April 1808. He was appointed a major in the 4th Caçadores on 10 December 1811 and served with them at Ciudad Rodrigo, Badajoz, Salamanca, Burgos, Vitoria, San Sebastian, Nivelle, and Nive. On 4 May 1814 he was promoted to lieutenant colonel and given command of the 6th Caçadores. He was released from the Portuguese Army on 24 August 1820 and went on half-pay in the British Army. He died in 1865.

John Henry Algeo was commissioned in the 4th Foot on 18 August 1799 and by 1805 he was a captain in the 34th Foot. On 11 April 1810 he joined the Portuguese Army as a major in the 1st Caçadores. On 14 April 1812 he was promoted to lieutenant colonel and given command of the 1st Caçadores. He led them at Ciudad Rodrigo, Badajoz, Salamanca, and Vitoria, and was killed at the crossing of the Bidassoa river on 7 October 1813.

Victor Von Arentschild was born on 5 May 1778 in Göttingen. He was commissioned in the Hanoverian Artillery in 1794 and as a captain in the KGA on 22 March 1805. He was commissioned as a major in the Portuguese 4th Artillery Regiment on 2 April 1809 and commanded an artillery brigade at Bussaco, Pombal, Redinha, Sabugal, and Fuentes D'Oñoro. He was promoted to lieutenant colonel on 24 March 1812 in the 1st Artillery Regiment. He commanded two Portuguese artillery brigades at Toulouse. He was promoted to colonel in the 1st Artillery Regiment on 12 October 1815 but was released from the Portuguese Army on 26 August 1820. Upon returning to Hanover, he was promoted to major general and died on 20 January 1841.

Lawrence Arnot was born *c.* 1780. He was commissioned in 1796 in Myers' Regiment and in 1803 exchanged into the 53rd Foot. On 25 September 1808 he was promoted to captain in the 56th Foot. He was commissioned as a major in the Portuguese 10th Infantry on 2 January 1812 but transferred to the 12th Infantry on 5 May 1812. He led its 2nd Battalion in the 1812 and 1813 campaigns and died on 27 August 1813 of wounds he received at Sorauren on 28 July.

Charles Ashworth was born *c.* 1784 and was commissioned as an ensign in the 68th Foot on 13 October 1798. He was promoted to captain in the 55th Foot on 12 March 1801 and went to the West Indies with them in June 1802. While there he was promoted to major in the 8th West India Regiment on 8 August 1804. He exchanged into the 62nd Foot on 2 January 1808. Major Ashworth was commissioned as a lieutenant colonel in the Portuguese 6th Infantry on 14 August 1809. On 28 February 1810 he was promoted to colonel and led the regiment at Bussaco. On 14 March 1811 he was given command of the Portuguese brigade that his regiment was in and led it at Fuentes D'Oñoro, Arroyo Molinos, Almaraz, Vitoria, the Pyrenees, Nivelle, and Nive, where he was seriously wounded. He was promoted to brigadier general on 10 July 1813. He did not recover from his wounds in time to participate in the 1814 campaign. He was promoted to major general on 12 October 1815 and was released from the Portuguese Army on 26 August 1820. He died on 13 August 1832.

William Beatty was commissioned on 28 October 1795 as an ensign in the 27th Foot. On 16 January 1804 he was promoted to captain in the 64th Foot and was a major in the regiment when he was appointed a lieutenant colonel in the Portuguese 12th Infantry on 6 October 1812. He led the regiment at Nivelle, Nive, Orthez, and Toulouse, where he assumed command of the 7th Brigade. He left the Portuguese Army on 1 October 1814 and died in 1815.

Thomas Bradford was born on 1 December 1777 and was commissioned as an ensign on 30 October 1792, promoted to major on 9 September 1795, and to brevet lieutenant colonel on 1 January 1801. On 18 May 1809 he was appointed a lieutenant colonel in the 34th Foot but exchanged into the 82nd Foot on 21 December 1809. He was promoted to brevet colonel on 30 July 1810 and joined the Portuguese Army as a brigadier general on 19 December 1811. He was given command of a brigade and led it at Salamanca, Burgos, Vitoria, San Sebastian, Nive, and Bayonne. He was promoted to major general in the British Army on 4 June 1813 and in the Portuguese Army on 10 July 1813. General Bradford stayed in the Portuguese Army until 1 October 1814. He continued to serve in the British Army in Britain, France, and India. He was promoted to general in 1841 and died on 28 November 1843.

Gustavus Brown was born on 25 December 1775 in Arneburg, Saxony-Anhalt. He was commissioned as an ensign in the Lowenstein Chasseurs on 1 November 1794 and appointed a captain in the 60th Foot on 30 December 1797. He was commissioned as a major on 21 April 1810 in the 2nd Caçadores and fought with them at Bussaco. On 3 November 1810 he was promoted to lieutenant colonel in the 7th Infantry and given command of the 9th Caçadores on 6 June 1811. He led them at Salamanca, Burgos, the Pyrenees, the Bidassoa, Nivelle, and Nive. He remained in the Portuguese Army after the war and was promoted to brevet colonel on 22 October 1815 and to colonel on 26 September 1818. In April 1820 he went to Rio de Janeiro and was promoted to brigadier general. He retired from the Portuguese Army on 10 April 1821 and from the British Army on 7 July 1825. In 1826 he joined the newly formed Army of Brazil and was appointed a major general. He campaigned with that army against the Argentinians for the control of what is now Uruguay. In 1831 he was discharged from the Brazilian Army and died in Dresden on 8 May 1865.

John Buchan was born *c.* 1782 and was commissioned in the Scotch Brigade in 1795. He served with the regiment in India until he became a captain in the 2nd Ceylon Regiment in 1802. He was promoted to major in 1804 and on 30 March 1809 to lieutenant colonel in the 4th West India Regiment. He was commissioned as a colonel on 22 June 1811 in the Portuguese 22nd Infantry. He fought at Vitoria and commanded the 7th Infantry during the Pyrenees. He was promoted to brigadier general on 10 July 1813 and took command of Costa's Brigade in the 2nd Division. He commanded the brigade at Nivelle and on 20 November 1813 he was given command of the 4th Brigade, which he led at Nive. He was promoted to major general on 12 October 1815 but was released from the Portuguese Army on 26 August 1820. He was promoted to major general in the British Army in 1830 and to lieutenant general in 1841. He died on 2 June 1850.

Archibald Campbell was born on 12 March 1769 and was commissioned as an ensign in the 77th Foot on 18 December 1787. He went with the regiment to India in 1788 and spent thirteen years there. While in India he was promoted to lieutenant on 26 April 1791 and to captain in the 67th Foot on 17 May 1799, and exchanged into the 88th Foot. He returned to Britain in 1801 and was promoted to major and was in the 71st Foot on 18 April 1805. He fought at Roliça, Vimeiro, and at Corunna. He was the senior EOPS officer and was commissioned as a colonel in the Portuguese

4th Infantry on 24 March 1809 and given command of a brigade on 29 September 1809. He led it at Bussaco, Albuera, Arroyo Molinos, the 1st and 2nd Sieges of Badajoz, Alba de Tormes, Vitoria, the Pyrenees and Nivelle. He was promoted to brigadier general on 8 May 1811. On 23 November 1813 he took command of the 1st Brigade and led it at Nive. He was promoted to major general on 12 October 1815 and given command of the Lisbon Division. He was promoted to lieutenant general on 13 May 1820 but was released from Portuguese service on 26 August 1820. He led the British forces in the 1st Burmese War from 1824 to 1826. He was promoted to major general on 27 May 1825 and returned to Britain in 1829. He was promoted to lieutenant general on 28 June 1838 and died on 6 October 1843.

John Campbell was born in 1780 and was commissioned as a cornet in the 7th Light Dragoons on 30 October 1800. He was promoted to lieutenant on 23 July 1803 and to captain on 23 January 1806, and exchanged into the 10th Foot on 26 February 1807. He was one of the original twenty-four EOPS officers and was commissioned as a lieutenant colonel in the Portuguese 15th Infantry on 14 April 1809, but was transferred to the 4th Cavalry on 24 September 1809. He led them at Fuentes del Maestro in January 1812 and was promoted to colonel on 5 February 1812. He was given command of his brigade until it was disbanded on 12 July 1813 and the 4th Cavalry was assigned to General Fane's Brigade. He saw action at Viella and at Tarbes. He chose to stay in the Portuguese Army after the war ended and was promoted to brigadier general on 12 October 1815 and to major general on 13 May 1820. He left the Portuguese Army in 1820 and the British Army on 23 September 1824. He was involved in Portuguese politics in the early 1820s and joined the forces that opposed the Liberals. He was readmitted into the Portuguese Army on 24 July 1830 and retired on 26 October 1832. He died on 19 December 1863.

Richard Collins was born *c*. 1774 and was commissioned as an ensign in the 82nd Foot in January 1794. He was promoted to lieutenant in September of the same year, to captain in the 2nd West India Regiment in 1799, and to major in the 12th West India Regiment in February 1802, and exchanged into the 83rd Foot on 9 May 1805. He was promoted to lieutenant colonel on 17 August 1809. He was commissioned as a colonel in the Portuguese 11th Infantry on 22 October 1810, and then assumed the command of the brigade it was assigned to. He was appointed commander of a provisional brigade on 22 March 1811 and led it at Albuera, where he was shot in the left leg, which was amputated on 16 May 1811. He went back to Britain in July 1811 to recover but returned to Portugal in October 1811. He was given command of the 7th Division's Portuguese Brigade on 27 February 1812 and led it at Salamanca. His brigade was part of the rearguard during the retreat to Portugal in the autumn of 1812. He died of exhaustion at Gouveia, Portugal, on 18 February 1813.

Bartholomew Derenzy was born in December 1791. He was commissioned as an ensign in the 81st Foot on 26 May 1806 and promoted to lieutenant on 16 March 1808. On 11 February 1811 he was commissioned as a captain in the 1st Battalion LLL, which became the 7th Caçadores. He fought at Pombal, Redinha, Campo Maior, Olivença, the 1st Siege of Badajoz, Albuera, Ciudad Rodrigo, 3rd Badajoz, Salamanca, Vitoria, the Pyrenees, San Sebastian, Bidassoa, Nivelle, Nive, Orthez, and Toulouse. He was promoted to brevet major in the Portuguese Army on 10 April 1814 and remained in the Portuguese Army after the war. He was promoted to major on 12 October 1815 in the 12th Caçadores, but he remained in command of the 7th Caçadores until 20 June 1816. He was released from Portuguese service on 26 August 1820. He was on half-pay in the British Army until he exchanged into the 11th Foot in 1821. He was promoted to major on 4 January 1833, to lieutenant colonel on 26 February 1841, to colonel on 11 November 1851, and to major general on 31 August 1855. He died on 22 November 1861.

Alexander Dickson was born on 3 June 1777. He entered the Royal Military Academy at Woolwich on 5 April 1793, was commissioned as a 2nd lieutenant in the Royal Artillery on 6 November 1794, then promoted to 1st lieutenant on 7 October 1795, to captain-lieutenant on 14 October 1801, to 2nd captain on 19 July 1804, and to captain on 10 April 1805. He was commissioned as a major in the Portuguese artillery on 14 August 1809 and given command of three Portuguese artillery brigades. He led them at Bussaco, the siege of Olivença, Albuera, and the 2nd Siege of Badajoz. He commanded the artillery at Ciudad Rodrigo and Badajoz. He was promoted to brevet major in the British Army on 6 February 1812 and to brevet lieutenant colonel on 27 April 1812. He was promoted to lieutenant colonel in the Portuguese 4th Artillery on 24 March 1812. He led the Portuguese artillery at Almaraz, the Salamanca Forts, at Salamanca, and Burgos. He was Wellington's chief of artillery during the campaigns of 1813 and 1814 and led it at Vitoria, San Sebastian, the Bidassoa, Nivelle, Nive, and Toulouse. He was promoted to brevet colonel in the 4th Artillery on 9 November 1813. He resigned his Portuguese commission on 1 October 1814. Upon returning to England, he reverted to his Royal Artillery rank of captain. He served in a variety of staff jobs and was promoted to major on 26 June 1823, to lieutenant colonel on 2 April 1825, to brevet colonel on 27 May 1825, to colonel on 1 July 1836 and to major general on 10 January 1837. He died on 22 April 1840.

James Douglas was born on 14 January 1785. He was commissioned as an ensign in the 45th Foot on 2 May 1800, purchased his lieutenancy on 19 June 1800, and attended the Royal Military College at Great Harlow. He purchased his captaincy on 16 September 1802. He was one of the original twenty-four EOPS officers. He was commissioned as a lieutenant colonel in the Portuguese 16th Infantry on 31 March 1809, but from 16 October 1809 he served as an ADC to Beresford. He was transferred to the 8th Infantry on 18 February 1810 and led it at Bussaco. Promoted to colonel on 5 February 1812, he led the regiment at Salamanca and commanded his brigade until 4 October 1812. He led his regiment until August 1813, when he was given command of the 7th Brigade, which he led at Nivelle, Nive, Orthez, and Toulouse, where he lost his left leg. He left the Portuguese Army on 12 October 1815. He was promoted to colonel in 1819, to major general in 1830, to lieutenant general in 1838, and to general in 1854. He died on 6 March 1862.

John Doyle was born in 1781. He was commissioned as an ensign in the 107th Foot on 31 May 1794, promoted to lieutenant in the 108th Foot on 21 June 1794, exchanged into the 92nd Foot, promoted to captain in the 81st Foot on 9 July 1803, exchanged into the 5th Foot on 3 September 1803, and on 7 December 1804 he exchanged back into the 81st Foot. He was one of the original twenty-four EOPS officers and was commissioned as a lieutenant colonel in the Portuguese 16th Infantry on 31 March 1809. He transferred to the 19th Infantry on 5 April 1811. He led the regiment at Fuentes D'Oñoro, the 1st Siege of Badajoz, Ciudad Rodrigo, Vitoria, the Pyrenees, Nivelle, and Nive. He was promoted to colonel on 5 February 1812, took command of the 6th Brigade in early November 1813 and led it in the campaign of 1814. He retired from the Portuguese Army on 1 October 1814. In 1823 he was asked to return to Portugal by the Portuguese royal family, and he became involved in the 1824 April Liberal Revolt. He was arrested by Dom Miguel in 1828 and imprisoned for several months. He returned to Ireland and was promoted to brevet colonel on 27 May 1825 but left the British Army on 29 October 1825. In 1831 he went to Portugal again and fought in the civil wars, as a major general supporting Dom Pedro. He died on 9 August 1856.

Benjamin D'Urban was born on 16 February 1777. He was commissioned as a cornet in the 2nd Dragoon Guards on 22 April 1794, promoted to lieutenant on 1 July 1794, to captain the next day, to captain en second in the 29th Light Dragoons on 23 April 1796, to captain on 5 July 1796, and to major on 21 November 1799. In late 1800 he was a student at the Royal Military College at High Wycombe. He exchanged into the 25th Light Dragoons on 22 January 1801 and then into the 89th Foot on 21 December 1802. By 7 January 1808 he was a lieutenant colonel in the 2nd West India Regiment. In the autumn of 1808 he was appointed the AQMG of General David Baird's Division that went to Spain. In late 1808 he joined the LLL in Castille. He was commissioned as a colonel in the Portuguese Army on 22 April 1809 and appointed the Portuguese Quartermaster General. He was promoted to brigadier general on 8 May 1811 and given command of a Portuguese cavalry brigade in June 1812. He led it at Salamanca, Majalahonda, Vitoria, and the Pyrenees. In mid-October 1813 he resumed his duties as the QMG, but in February 1814 he returned to the command of his cavalry brigade. He was promoted to major general on 12 October 1815. He resigned his commission in the Portuguese Army on 18 January 1820. He was promoted to colonel in the British Royal Staff Corps in April 1816, was promoted to major general in the British Army on 12 August 1819, and to lieutenant general on 10 January 1837. In January 1847 he was appointed the commander-in-chief of the British forces in Canada. He died on 25 May 1849 in Montreal.

Thomas Dursbach was either German or Austrian but little is known of his background. He was born *c*. 1776. He joined the LLL in 1808 and was commissioned a major in the 1st Infantry on 30 March 1809. On 6 June 1811 he was promoted to lieutenant colonel and given command of the 11th Caçadores. He led the battalion at Badajoz, Vitoria, the Pyrenees, and Nivelle. He died from sickness on 12 December 1813.

Peter Fearon was commissioned as an ensign in the 69th Foot on 16 March 1804, exchanged into the 31st Foot on 14 April 1804, was promoted to lieutenant on 21 December 1804, and to captain on 17 August 1809. He was appointed a major in the 1st Battalion of the LLL on 22 July 1810, which became the 7th Caçadores. He fought with them at Albuera. He was promoted to major in the 1st Infantry on 8 February 1812 and was with it at Ciudad Rodrigo, Salamanca, Burgos, Vitoria, and the Pyrenees. On 27 August 1813 he was promoted to lieutenant colonel and given command of the 6th Caçadores. He led them at Nivelle, Nive, and Garris, where he was killed on 15 February 1814.

Maxwell Grant was born in 1780 and was commissioned as an ensign in the 42nd Foot in June 1795. He served with the regiment for the next twenty-two years. On 4 September 1795 he was promoted to lieutenant, and to captain on 9 July 1803. He was commissioned as a major in the Portuguese 6th Infantry on 26 August 1809 and promoted to lieutenant colonel on 30 June 1810. He was appointed its commander on 14 March 1811 and led it at Fuentes D'Oñoro, Arroyo Molinos, Almaraz, Vitoria, the Pyrenees, Nivelle, Nive, Garris, Orthez, and Aire. He was promoted to colonel on 12 October 1815 and to brigadier general on 13 May 1820 but was released from the Portuguese Army on 26 August 1820. He died on 22 October 1823.

John Hamilton was born on 4 August 1755. He joined the Army of the East India Company as a cadet in the Bengal Native Infantry in 1771 and spent the next twenty-four years in India. He advanced through the ranks and was promoted to lieutenant colonel in the 81st Foot on 23 December 1795. He was promoted to brevet colonel in 1802 and to brigadier general in 1804. Hamilton was related by marriage to Beresford and it was likely through him that he was accepted into the Portuguese Army as a major general on 13 September 1809 and appointed the Inspector General of the Infantry on 6 December 1809. On 15 March 1810 he was given command of the

Portuguese Division and led it at Albuera, the 2nd Siege of Badajoz, and Alba de Tormes. He was promoted to lieutenant general on 5 February 1812. In early 1813 he went to Britain but returned to Spain in mid-autumn and commanded the Portuguese Division at Nivelle. He gave up his command on 3 December 1813 and retired from the Portuguese Army on 1 October 1814. He died on 24 December 1835.

Henry Hardinge was born on 30 March 1785. He was commissioned as an ensign in the Queen's Rangers on 8 October 1798, purchased a lieutenancy in the 4th Foot on 25 March 1802 and his captaincy in the 54th Foot on 7 April 1804. He attended the Royal Military College at High Wycombe from 7 February 1806 to 30 November 1807. He fought at Roliça, Vimeiro, and in the Corunna campaign. He was one of the original twenty-four EOPS officers and was commissioned as a lieutenant colonel in the Portuguese Army on 10 June 1809 and became a DQMG. He was promoted to colonel on 10 July 1813 and took command of the 5th Brigade on 22 December 1813. He led the brigade through the rest of the war. Colonel Hardinge returned to England after the war was over but did not resign his Portuguese commission until 15 October 1818. He fought at Waterloo and served on the Army Staff. He was promoted to colonel on 19 July 1821. He served as the Secretary of War from July 1828 to July 1830 and from 1841 to 1844. Colonel Hardinge was promoted to major general on 22 July 1830 and to lieutenant general on 22 November 1841. He was appointed Governor-General of India in May 1844, Master General of the Ordnance on 5 March 1852, and commander-in-chief of the British Army on 28 September 1852. He was promoted to general on 20 June 1854 and to field marshal on 2 October 1855. He died on 24 September 1856.

Robert John Harvey was born on 21 February 1785. He was commissioned as an ensign in the 53rd Foot on 8 October 1803, purchased a lieutenancy in the 60th Foot on 24 March 1804, exchanged into the 4th Dragoons on 14 September 1804, and purchased his captaincy in the 53rd Foot on 2 January 1806. He was commissioned as a major and assigned to the Portuguese QMG Department on 25 July 1811 and promoted to lieutenant colonel on 14 April 1812. At the end of the Peninsular War he was one of Wellington's ADCs in Paris. He returned to England in 1815, went on half-pay on 14 October 1815, and resigned his Portuguese commission on 12 December 1815. He was promoted to colonel on 22 July 1830, to major general on 23 November 1841, and to lieutenant general on 11 November 1851. He died on 18 June 1860.

Dudley St Leger Hill was born in 1787. He was commissioned as a second lieutenant in the 95th Rifles on 27 August 1804 and was promoted to first lieutenant on 10 October 1805. He fought at Roliça, Vimeiro, the Corunna campaign, Talavera, the river Coa, and Bussaco. On 26 September 1810 he was commissioned as a major in the 2nd LLL Battalion, which became the 8th Caçadores. He commanded them at Badajoz, Salamanca, Burgos, Villa Muriel, Vitoria, San Sebastian, and Bayonne. He was promoted to major in the British Army on 27 April 1812, to lieutenant colonel in the Portuguese Army on 28 January 1813, and to brevet lieutenant colonel in the British Army on 21 June 1813. On 12 October 1815 was promoted to brevet colonel in the Portuguese Army and to colonel of the 2nd Infantry on 15 October 1818. He was released from the Portuguese Army on 26 August 1820. He died on 21 February 1851 in Ambala, India.

Thomas Noel Hill was born on 24 February 1784. He was commissioned as a cornet in the 10th Light Dragoons on 25 September 1801, purchased his lieutenancy on 2 February 1803 and his captaincy on 28 February 1805, and exchanged into the 53rd Foot on 25 April 1806. He was one of the original twenty-four EOPS officers and was commissioned as a lieutenant colonel in the

Portuguese 13th Infantry on 31 March 1809. He transferred to the 1st Infantry on 3 July 1809 and was promoted to colonel on 5 February 1812. He led them at Bussaco, Ciudad Rodrigo, Salamanca, Burgos, Vitoria, San Sebastian, and Bayonne. He resigned from the Portuguese Army on 1 October 1814. He was an AAG on the Army Staff during the Waterloo campaign and was with the Army of Occupation in France until 1818. He was promoted to colonel on 27 May 1825 and died on 8 January 1832.

Charles Kilsha was born in 1782 and was commissioned as an ensign on 22 November 1798 in the 77th Foot, then stationed in India. He was promoted to lieutenant in October 1801 and to captain on 30 November 1809. He was commissioned as a major in the Portuguese Army on 16 November 1810 and worked at the Infantry Recruit Depot at Peniche. He was assigned to the 11th Caçadores on 1 July 1811. He was with them at Badajoz, Vitoria, Pyrenees, and Nivelle. He was promoted to brevet lieutenant colonel on 7 December 1813 and given command of the battalion on 12 December. He was killed at Orthez on 27 February 1814.

John Lillie was born in 1790. He was commissioned as an ensign in the 6th Foot on 3 March 1807. He was commissioned as a captain in the 1st LLL Battalion on 17 December 1808 and fought with it along the border with Spain, at Bussaco, Redinha, Pombal, Olivença, and the 1st Siege of Badajoz. On 4 May 1811 the 1st Battalion was renamed the 7th Caçadores and he fought with it at Albuera, El Bodon, Alfaiates, Ciudad Rodrigo, and Badajoz. He was promoted to major on 11 December 1812. He stayed with the 7th Caçadores, fighting with them at Salamanca, Burgos, the retreat to Portugal, Vitoria, and the Pyrenees. Major Lillie was given command of the 7th Caçadores on 28 July 1813 and led them at Bidassoa, Nivelle, Nive, Orthez, and Toulouse. He was promoted to lieutenant colonel in the 7th Infantry on 4 May 1814. He was released from the Portuguese Army on 1 October 1814. He died as a lieutenant colonel unattached on half-pay on 29 June 1868.

William MacBean was born in 1782 and went on his first campaign as a cadet in the services of the Seven United Provinces in 1794. In February 1796 he was commissioned as an ensign in the 6th Foot, and was promoted to lieutenant in October 1796, and to captain on 24 October 1804. He was one of the original twenty-four EOPS officers and was commissioned as a lieutenant colonel in the Portuguese 19th Infantry on 24 March 1809. He served with the regiment at Bussaco but was transferred to the 24th Infantry on 14 November 1810. He was promoted to colonel on 5 February 1812, and led the regiment at Ciudad Rodrigo, Salamanca, San Sebastian, Bidassoa, Nivelle, Nive, Adour, and Bayonne. He resigned his Portuguese commission on 31 October 1814. He went to India in 1820 and commanded a brigade in the 1st Anglo-Burmese War. He was promoted to brevet colonel on 19 July 1821, to major general on 22 July 1830, to lieutenant general on 23 November 1841, and to general on 20 June 1854. He died on 25 May 1855.

Michael McCreagh was born in 1785 and was commissioned as an ensign in the 39th Foot on 1 February 1802. He purchased his lieutenancy in the regiment on 25 June 1802 and exchanged into the 37th Foot. On 14 September 1804 he purchased his captaincy in the 7th West India Regiment and exchanged into the 1st Foot on 14 October 1807. He was one of the original twenty-four EOPS officers and was commissioned as a major in the Portuguese 7th Infantry on 3 July 1809 and promoted to lieutenant colonel on 14 August 1809. He was given command of the 5th Caçadores on 3 November 1810 and led them at Albuera, Salamanca, Burgos, and Vitoria. He was promoted to lieutenant colonel in the British Army on 3 October 1811. He was promoted to colonel in the 3rd Infantry on 10 July 1813 and led it at San Sebastian, Bidassoa, Nivelle, and Nive. He elected to stay in the Portuguese Army and was promoted to brigadier general on 12 October 1815. He was given command of the 12th Brigade on 28 November 1816 and released from the Portuguese Army on 26 August 1820. He died on 31 August 1834.

John McDonald was born on 10 September 1788. He was commissioned as an ensign in the 88th Foot on 17 December 1803 and was promoted to lieutenant on 21 March 1805. He was commissioned a captain in the Portuguese 2nd Infantry on 31 March 1809, promoted to major on 15 November 1809 and given command of its 2nd Battalion. He led it at Bussaco, Redinha, Campo Mayor, the 1st Siege of Badajoz, and Albuera. He was transferred to the 14th Infantry in late March 1812 and led it at Badajoz. He was promoted to lieutenant colonel on 14 April 1812 and given command of the regiment. He led it in the 1812 campaign, at Vitoria, the Pyrenees, and at Banca, where he was severely wounded. He spent six months recuperating but was back with the regiment by April 1814 and temporarily commanded the 2nd Brigade at Toulouse. On 11 April 1814 he was arrested and charged with homicide. On 17 April 1814 he was found guilty by a court martial and sentenced to death by strangulation. On 13 September 1815 the sentence was reduced to dismissal from the Portuguese Army. After returning to Britain, he was placed on half-pay on 24 October 1815. His dismissal from the Portuguese Army did not affect his career in the British Army. He died on 24 June 1866 as a full general.

George Madden was born on 3 January 1777. He was commissioned as a cornet in the 14th Light Dragoons on 14 March 1789, purchased his lieutenancy in the 12th Light Dragoons on 12 July 1791, was promoted to captain on 29 June 1793 and to major on 13 March 1800. He was court-martialled on 31 August 1800, found guilty of conduct unbecoming of an officer, and was sentenced to dismissal from the army. Upon returning to England, he was allowed to sell his commission. Subsequently he was commissioned as a brigadier general in the Portuguese Army and given command of a cavalry brigade on 10 September 1809. He led it at Fuente de Cantos and Gebora. He was reinstated in the British Army as a lieutenant colonel on 3 March 1812, with a date of rank of 4 July 1805. In early 1812 his brigade was disbanded and on 4 October he was appointed the commander of the 6th Division's Portuguese Brigade, which he led in the Pyrenees. On 4 June 1813 he was promoted to brevet colonel in the British Army and on 10 July to major general in the Portuguese Army. In August 1813 he objected to an officer who was junior to him being placed in temporary command of the 6th Division. Wellington resolved the issue by relieving Madden of his command on 19 August. He retired from the Portuguese Army on 1 October 1814. He was promoted to major general on 12 August 1819 and died on 28 November 1828 in Portsmouth.

James Miller was commissioned in the 74th Foot on 21 September 1800, and was promoted to lieutenant on 4 June 1803 and to captain on 26 September 1806. He was commissioned as a major in the Portuguese 23rd Infantry on 7 May 1810. He fought with it at Bussaco, the 1st Siege of Badajoz, Albuera, Ciudad Rodrigo, and Badajoz. He was promoted to lieutenant colonel and given command of the regiment on 14 April 1812. He led it at Vitoria, the Pyrenees, the Bidassoa, Nivelle, and Nive. On 12 February 1814 he resigned his commission in the Portuguese Army and returned to the 74th Foot. He was severely wounded at Toulouse. He returned to Scotland to recuperate but died on 4 June 1814.

Walter O'Hara was born *c.* 1789. He was commissioned as an ensign in the 91st Foot on 9 March 1809 and purchased his lieutenancy on 9 November 1810. He was commissioned as a captain in the 7th Cacadores on 6 June 1811. He fought at Ciudad Rodrigo, Badajoz, Salamanca,

Vitoria, and the Pyrenees. He was promoted to major in the 1st Infantry on 27 August 1813. He commanded the regiment's grenadier companies at Nivelle. He was wounded and captured at Nive on 10 December. He temporarily commanded the 1st Infantry in January 1814 and led it at Bayonne from February to April 1814. He chose to stay with the Portuguese Army and was transferred to the 9th Infantry on 12 October 1815 and was promoted to lieutenant colonel in the 2nd Infantry on 22 January 1820. He was released from the Portuguese Army on 26 August 1820. He retired from the British Army on 3 April 1826 and moved to Canada. He died on 13 January 1874 in Toronto.

Bryan O'Toole was an Irish Catholic officer who was probably born in France in 1773. After serving in the Royal French Army, he joined Hompesch's Hussars as a cornet in 1792. On 1 October 1794 he joined the Irish Brigade and was appointed a lieutenant and adjutant in Conway's Regiment. He was promoted to captain lieutenant on 31 December 1795, and to captain on 30 December 1797 in the Hompesch Mounted Rifles, but exchanged into the 39th Foot on 9 July 1803. He was commissioned as a lieutenant colonel in the 2nd Caçadores on 9 November 1811. He led them at Ciudad Rodrigo, Salamanca, Burgos, and Valladolid. He was given command of the 7th Caçadores on 3 October 1812 and led them at Vitoria and the Pyrenees. He was severely wounded at Sorauren on 28 July 1813 and went to Britain to recover from his wounds. He was promoted to colonel on 12 October 1815 and given command of the 8th Infantry. He was released from the Portuguese Army on 26 August 1820 and returned to Ireland. He died on 27 February 1825.

Denis Pack was born on 7 October 1775 and was commissioned in the 14th Light Dragoons on 30 November 1791. He purchased his lieutenancy on 12 March 1795, his captaincy in the 5th Dragoon Guards on 27 February 1796, his majority in the 4th Dragoon Guards on 25 August 1798, and his lieutenant colonelcy in the 71st Foot on 6 December. He was appointed a brigadier general in the Portuguese Army on 7 July 1810 and given command of an infantry brigade. He was promoted to colonel in the British Army on 25 July 1810. He led his brigade at Bussaco, Ciudad Rodrigo, Salamanca, Burgos, Vitoria, Villafranca, and Tolosa. On 4 June 1813 he was promoted to major general in the British Army, resigned his Portuguese commission, and took command of a British brigade in the 6th Division. He fought in the Pyrenees, Nivelle, Nive, Orthez, and Toulouse. He commanded the British 9th Brigade at Waterloo. He died in London on 24 July 1823.

Thomas Peacocke was born *c.* 1775. He was commissioned as an ensign in the 20th Foot on 9 December 1806, promoted to lieutenant on 27 February 1808, and exchanged into the 44th Foot on 14 April 1808. He was commissioned as a captain in the Portuguese 23rd Infantry on 11 April 1810. He fought with it at Bussaco, Pombal, Redinha, Campo Mayor, and Albuera. He was promoted to major on 5 May 1812 and given command of its 1st Battalion, which he led in the final days of the 1812 campaign, at Vitoria, the Pyrenees, Salain, Bidassoa, and Nivelle. He was given command of the Convalescent Depot in Lisbon on 26 February 1814 and commanded it until 12 October 1815, when he was promoted to lieutenant colonel and made an AQMG. He was appointed DQMG on 4 January 1817. He was released from the Portuguese Army on 26 August 1820. He continued to be promoted in the British Army and died as a major general on 21 June 1856.

Manley Power was born in 1773 and commissioned in the 20th Foot in 1785. He moved through the ranks, usually without purchase, until on 20 June 1801 he purchased his lieutenant colonelcy.

In June 1805 he exchanged into the 32nd Foot and was promoted to brevet colonel on 25 July 1810. On 5 August 1811 he was appointed a brigadier general in the Portuguese Army and given command of the brigade that garrisoned Elvas. In July 1812 he was transferred to the 3rd Division's Portuguese Brigade and led it at Salamanca, Vitoria, the Pyrenees, Nivelle, Orthez, and Toulouse. He was promoted to major general in both the Portuguese and British Armies on 4 June 1813. After the war ended, he was sent to Canada to fight against the Americans. He returned to England in May 1815 and was a brigade commander in the Army of Occupation in France from July 1815 to November 1818. Although General Power no longer served in the Portuguese Army, his name remained in the Portuguese officers' lists until 1818. He was a lieutenant general when he died on 7 July 1826.

Henry Pynn was born on 27 August 1770 in Harbour Grace, Newfoundland. He was commissioned as a lieutenant in the South Devon Militia on 28 June 1798 and appointed an ensign in the 82nd Foot on 7 August 1799. He was promoted to lieutenant on 28 November 1799 and to captain on 30 May 1805. He was commissioned as a major in the Portuguese 3rd Infantry on 17 April 1809, promoted to lieutenant colonel on the staff on 21 April 1810, and transferred to the 18th Infantry on 16 May 1810. He fought with it at Bussaco, Fuentes D'Oñoro, Vitoria and the Pyrenees and led it at Garris, Orthez, Aire, and Toulouse. He was promoted to colonel on 12 October 1815 and appointed lieutenant governor of Valença on 17 December 1815. He was promoted to brigadier general on 13 May 1820 but was released from the Portuguese Army on 26 August 1820. He died a lieutenant colonel on 25 April 1855.

John Rolt was born in 1784. He purchased his ensigncy in the 58th Foot in March 1810, was promoted to lieutenant in September 1801, and to captain on 5 September 1805. He was commissioned as a major in the Portuguese 13th Infantry on 18 February 1810 and fought with them at Bussaco and Badajoz. On 14 April 1812 he was promoted to lieutenant colonel in the 17th Infantry, which he led at Vitoria, Nivelle, Nive, Orthez, and Toulouse. He was promoted to colonel of the 17th Infantry on 12 October 1815 but was released from the Portuguese Army on 26 August 1820. He died a major general on 8 November 1856.

Kenneth Snodgrass was born in 1784. He was commissioned as an ensign in the 90th Foot on 22 October 1802, was promoted to lieutenant on 14 August 1804, exchanged into the 52nd Foot on 4 September 1804, and was promoted to captain on 10 October 1808. He was commissioned as a major on 24 November 1812 in the Portuguese 13th Infantry. He fought with it at Vitoria, Tolosa, San Sebastian, and Bidassoa. He was promoted to lieutenant colonel on 9 November 1813 and given command of the 1st Caçadores. He led them at Nivelle, Nive, and Orthez. He was promoted to brevet colonel on 6 October 1818 and was appointed commander of the 16th Infantry on 11 May 1819. He was released from Portuguese service on 26 August 1820. He went on half-pay and in 1828 emigrated to Australia. He died on 14 October 1853.

William Frederick Spry was born in 1770. He was commissioned as an ensign in the 70th Foot in 1782 and went to India as a captain in the 77th Foot in August 1788. He served in India for the next nine years. While there, he was promoted to major on 12 November 1795 and to brevet lieutenant colonel on 1 January 1800. He was promoted to colonel on 25 July 1810. He was commissioned as a brigadier general in the Portuguese Army on 16 August 1810 and given command of the 5th Division's Portuguese Brigade, which he led at Bussaco, Fuentes D'Oñoro, Badajoz, Salamanca, and Villa Muriel. He was promoted to major general in the British Army on 4 June 1813 and to major general in the Portuguese Army on 10 July 1813. He led his brigade at Vitoria and San Sebastian, but his health was poor, and he returned to Britain. He died on 16 January 1814.

Thomas William Stubbs was born on 7 June 1776. He was commissioned as an ensign in the 50th Foot on 27 July 1793 and was promoted to lieutenant on 16 May 1795. In 1797 he converted to Catholicism to marry a Portuguese lady and resigned his commission in the British Army in early 1800. He was commissioned as a captain in the Setúbal Infantry Regiment on 30 December 1800. On 4 November 1806 he was promoted to major in the same regiment, which was renamed the 7th Infantry. After the French invasion of Portugal in 1807, he resigned his commission on 11 January 1808 and went to Britain. He returned to Portugal after the French were expelled and on 19 October 1808 rejoined the 7th Infantry. He was promoted to lieutenant colonel on 23 November 1808 in the 23rd Infantry, which he led at Bussaco. On 20 February 1811 he was promoted to colonel and led the regiment at the Siege of Olivença, the 1st Siege of Badajoz and Albuera. In May 1812 he was given command of the 4th Division's Portuguese Brigade and led it at Castrillo, Salamanca, Vitoria, and the Pyrenees. On 31 July 1813 he was promoted to brigadier general and was appointed Governor of Almeida on 14 August 1813. He was promoted to major general on 12 October 1815 and to lieutenant general on 28 December 1826. He was created Viscount of Vila Nova de Gaia in 1835. He died on 27 April 1844.

Benjamin Sullivan was born in India *c.* 1786 and was commissioned as an ensign in the 10th Foot on 20 September 1800. He was promoted to lieutenant in the 84th Foot on 23 November 1803 and to captain in the 3rd Ceylon Regiment on 9 April 1804, and exchanged into the 33rd Foot on 6 May 1813. He was commissioned as a major in the Portuguese 8th Infantry on 9 November 1813 and fought at Orthez and Toulouse. He was released from Portuguese service on 26 August 1820. He emigrated to Australia in 1828 and died on 26 April 1860.

Alexander Tulloh was born *c.* 1777. He was commissioned as a lieutenant in the Royal Artillery on 14 August 1794 and promoted to 2nd captain on 19 July 1804. He was in France in 1803 when war broke out and was a prisoner of war until 1811. He was promoted to captain on 8 May 1811. He joined the Portuguese Army on 18 September 1811 as a major in the 3rd Artillery and commanded all the Portuguese artillery at Badajoz. He was promoted to lieutenant colonel on 17 July 1812. During the campaigns of 1812 and 1813 he served as the chief of artillery for the Portuguese artillery under Hill and at Vitoria for all artillery under Hill's command. He fought at Nivelle and Nive, where he was severely wounded. He returned to England to recover from his wounds but never returned to Portugal. He was dismissed from the Portuguese Army on 26 September 1818. He was placed on half-pay as a captain in the British Army on 1 August 1820 and died on 28 May 1826.

Edmund Keynton Williams was born in 1778. He was commissioned as a lieutenant in the Provisional Cavalry of Monmouth on 12 May 1798 but joined the 4th Foot as an ensign on 30 August. He purchased his lieutenancy in the 4th Foot on 18 April 1800, exchanged into the 81st Foot on 9 July 1803, and was promoted to captain on 25 September 1807. He was commissioned as a major in the 4th Caçadores on 7 May 1810. He fought with them at Bussaco, Redinha, Almeida, and Ciudad Rodrigo. In February 1812 he took command of the battalion and led it at Badajoz, Salamanca, Burgos, Vitoria, Tolosa, San Sebastian, Bidassoa, Nivelle, and Nive. He was promoted to lieutenant colonel of the 4th Caçadores on 14 April 1812, to brevet major in the British Army on 8 October 1812 and to brevet lieutenant colonel in the British Army on 21 June 1813. He was promoted to colonel in the 14th Infantry on 12 October 1815 and was released from Portuguese service on 26 August 1820. He was a major general when he died on 7 December 1849.

John Wilson was born in 1780. He was commissioned as an ensign in the 28th Foot on 26 March 1794, was promoted to lieutenant on 12 August 1795, to captain in the 97th Foot on 18 January 1799, and to major on 27 May 1802. He was commissioned as a colonel in the Portuguese Army on 16 September 1809, appointed the chief of staff to General Silveira in March 1810, and promoted to brigadier general on 8 May 1811. He became the commander of the 1st Brigade on 19 July 1813 and led it at San Sebastian and Nivelle. He was appointed governor of Minho province in early 1814 and was promoted to major general on 12 October 1815. He was released from Portuguese service on 26 August 1820. While he was in Portuguese service he continued to be promoted in the British Army. He was a full general when he died on 22 June 1856.

George Henry Zulke was commissioned as a *fahnenjunker* in the Hesse-Cassel Grenadier Guards on 1 February 1794. He quit the Hesse-Cassel Regiment and was commissioned as an ensign in the British 60th Foot on 25 December 1797 and was promoted to lieutenant on 2 August 1800. He was commissioned as a major in the 2nd Caçadores on 22 October 1810 and fought with the battalion at Fuentes D'Oñoro, the 1st Siege of Badajoz, Ciudad Rodrigo, Salamanca, Burgos, and Valladolid. In November 1812 he was given command of the battalion and led it at San Munoz, Vitoria, the Pyrenees, Zugarramurdi, Nivelle, Nive, Orthez, and Blaye. While in command he was promoted to lieutenant colonel on 30 July 1813 and to colonel of the 21st Infantry on 15 October 1818. He resigned his Portuguese commission on 26 June 1820. After he returned to England, he was a half-pay major, but was promoted to colonel on 10 January 1837. He died on 14 June 1846.

Notes

1. Picton to Flanagan, 24 June 1813, 'Some Unpublished Letters of Sir Thomas Picton', pt 2, pp. 17–18; Larpent, *Private Journal*, 23 August 1813, vol. 2, p. 70; Wellington to Liverpool, 25 July 1813, Wellington, *Despatches*, vol. 6, pp. 627–8.
2. Oman, Charles *History of the Peninsular War*, 7 vols. Oxford: AMS, 1980, vol. 2, p. vi.
3. Ibid, vol. 5, pp. viii–ix.
4. Military Historical Archives.
5. Salamanca, Vitoria, Sorauren, Nivelle, Nive, Orthez, and Toulouse.
6. Burgos, San Sebastian, and Bayonne.
7. Such as Villa Muriel during the retreat to Portugal in the autumn of 1812, three actions in the Pyrenees, and the crossing of the Bidassoa river.
8. The reports and returns in the archives were not organized by brigade or division and were scattered among several files.
9. One of the reports in French was by Colonel Richard Collins and the other by General Benjamin D'Urban.
10. Some of the reports in English still had the Portuguese translations attached to them in the archives.
11. For example, Wellington's 1st Division had no Portuguese units assigned to it and is only mentioned twenty-one times. The 2nd Division, which had a Portuguese Brigade assigned to it and also worked closely with the Portuguese Division, is mentioned sixty times.
12. Muir, R., *Salamanca 1812*. New Haven: Yale, 2001.
13. The Prince's Royal Volunteers Division.
14. The Treasury.
15. The Marshal of the Forces was usually referred to as the Marshal.
16. During the War of the Oranges the marshal general was the Duke de Lafões, who decided to command the field army in person instead of the Count of Goltz, who was the marshal of the forces.
17. Beresford ordered the sword to be replaced by a cane.
18. Borrego, p. 61.
19. Silva, A.D., *Collecção da Legislação Portugueza (...) 1763 a 1774*. Lisbon, 1826, pp. 84–106.
20. Silva, A.D., *Collecção da Legislação Portugueza (...) 1802 a 1810*. Lisbon, 1826, pp. 788–92.
21. Caçadores battalions and the Loyal Lusitanian Legion.
22. *Depósitos Provinciais de Recrutas e Remonta*.
23. AHM 1-14-218-2 ms 39.
24. Silva, *1811–1820*, pp. 162–73.
25. Ibid; pp. 271–7.
26. Silva, *1802–1810*, pp. 666–705.
27. This rank did not exist in the British Army. It was the most junior sergeant's rank.
28. This rank did not exist in the British Army. It was the first promotion for a private, like the modern rank of lance corporal.
29. National Caçadores of Oriental Lisbon and Occidental Lisbon.
30. National Artillerymen of Oriental Lisbon and Occidental Lisbon.
31. Silva, *1802–1810*, pp. 892–4.
32. Commerce Royal Volunteers.
33. Oporto's Royal Volunteers Corps.
34. The literal translation is 'hunters'.
35. Silva, *1763–1774*, pp. 84–106; Silva, *1791–1801*, pp. 673–4.
36. Centeno, João Torres, *O Exército Português na Guerra Peninsular. Do Rossilhão ao fim da Segunda Invasão Francesa*. Lisbon: Prefácio, 2008, p. 82. Silva, *1763–1774*, pp. 84–106; Silva, *1802–1810*, pp. 788–92.
37. Silva, *1802–1810*, pp. 559–63.
38. Ibid.; pp. 624–5.
39. Chosen from the subaltern officers.
40. Chosen from the regiment's cadets.
41. Guns' Wooden Parts Artificer.
42. Guns' Metal Parts Artificer. British regiments had an armourer, who had similar duties to the Portuguese artificers.

43. Silva, *1802–1810*, pp. 772–3.
44. Ibid.; pp. 781–3.
44. Orders of the Day, 23 November 1809 and 27 November 1809.
45. Decree of 29 October 1807, in Amaral, vol. 3, pp. 122, 194.
46. Warre, p. 97.
47. It should be noted that, on paper, some of the British commanders were second-in-command of the regiment. However, despite not being the senior officer in the regiment, they led the regiment on campaign.
48. 'To the Valour of the Regiment …'
49. Roughly translated: 'You can judge what is more excellent/ To be King of the world or King of this People.'
50. Quinta Nova, Jorge, *Os Voluntários Reaes*. Online, 2020.
51. Martelo, David, *Os Caçadores. Os galos de combate do exército de Wellington*. Lisbon: Tribuna da História, 2007, p. 29.
52. Silva, *1791–1801*, pp. 289–90.
53. *Collecção de Papeis Oficiaes da Junta Provisional do Governo Supremo (...)*. Porto, 1808, pp. 42–5.
54. Ibid.; p. 44.
55. Gil, Coronel Ferreira, *A Infantaria Portuguêsa na Guerra da Peninsula*, 2 vols. Lisbon, Tipografia da Cooperativa Militar, 1912, vol. 1, p. 275.
56. Ibid., p. 285.
57. Silva, *1802–1810*, p. 623.
58. The *Atiradores* Company was an elite company. It was redesignated as a caçadores company in February 1810.
59. Silva, *1802–1810*, pp. 646–7.
60. AHM 1-14-70-7 ms 11–13. Letter from General Bernardim Freire de Andrade to Dom Miguel Forjaz, dated Coimbra, 28 October 1808.
61. AHM 1-14-70-7 ms 15–18. Letter from General Bernardim Freire de Andrade to Dom Miguel Forjaz, dated Oporto, 4 November 1808.
62. Silva, *1802–1810*, pp. 758–60.
63. Ibid.; p. 772; Order of the Day dated 23 November 1809.
64. Order of the Day dated 20 February 1810.
65. Silva, *1811–1820*, p. 44.
66. Ibid.; Order of the Day dated 4 May 1811.
67. Ibid.
68. Roughly translated: 'Distinguished you shall be in our history/By the laurels collected in victory.'
69. Silva, *1811–1820*, pp. 287–8.
70. Centeno, vol. 1, p. 82; Silva, *1763–1774*, pp. 84–106; Silva, *1802–1810*, pp. 788–92.
71. Silva, *1802–1810*, pp. 625–6.
72. In the Portuguese cavalry this rank is called *Alféres* or Ensign, as in the Infantry. It is equivalent to a British cornet.
73. Riding master.
74. Saddlery Artificer. In the British cavalry there was the rank of Saddle Sergeant. Probably the duties of both were similar.
75. Order of the Day dated 23 November 1810. The regiment had four squadrons of two companies each.
76. There were four, one for each squadron.
77. *The Royal Military Calendar*, 5 vols. London: 1820, vol. 4, p. 54.
78. Warre, p. 114.
79. Silva, *1802–1810*, pp. 622–3.
80. The Bombardier Company specialized in firing howitzers and mortars.
81. These artificers were responsible for the gunpowder. They were considered 2nd sergeants.
82. Silva, *1802–1810*, pp. 777–9.
83. Silva, *1811–1820*, p. 188.
84. The Artificers Battalion.
85. A field brigade, like the British Royal Artillery's brigades, was the equivalent of a battery or company in other armies.
86. Silva, *1811–1820*, pp. 188–90.
87. Riding master.
88. A man who treated the animals' diseases and wounds. He was not a veterinarian but someone with practical knowledge. In the British Corps of Artillery Drivers there was a veterinary surgeon; probably his duties were similar.
89. *Regulamento Provisional do Real Corpo de Engenheiros*. Lisbon, 1812.
90. Composed of artificers (carpenters, smiths, masons, sawyers, coopers, etc.), miners and sappers.
91. Composed of pontoniers but also of carpenters, smiths, and caulkers.

92. Silva, *1811–1820*, pp. 281–3.
93. Some sources state it was 16 December 1809, but we found no documentation supporting this. It probably came into existence on 15 March 1810 when General Hamilton was appointed to command two brigades in eastern Portugal.
94. Two weeks later, on 6 October, the 8th Cavalry replaced the 2nd Cavalry.
95. He was not alone, for Wellington had the same problem finding officers who were competent to command British brigades and even divisions in the years 1809–1811.
96. General Beresford claimed in a letter to his sister that he was not given a choice.
97. Beresford, Marcus de la Poer, *Marshal William Carr Beresford: The Ablest Man I Have Yet Seen With the Army*. Newbridge: Irish Academic Press, 2017, pp. 55–61.
98. Ibid., p. 66.
99. Ibid., p. 76.
100. Much of the information on the EOPS officers is taken from the research of Ron McGuigan and is used here with his permission.
101. Major John Fane, Lord Burghersh, 2nd West India Regiment, was replaced on the list by Major Charles Ashworth, 62nd Foot. Ashworth was commissioned a lieutenant colonel *agregado* in the Portuguese Army on 14 August 1809, but not promoted to lieutenant colonel in the British Army until 18 January 1810. He retired from the Portuguese Army as a major general in 1825. Ashworth's biography is in Appendix B.
102. *General Regulations and Orders for the Army*. London: Adjutant General's Office, 1811, p. 29.
103. Griffith, Robert, *Riflemen: The History of the 5th Battalion 60th (Royal American) Regiment 1797–1818*. Warwick: Helion, 2019, p. 209.
104. Lieutenant General William Beresford.
105. Includes brevet rank.
106. Wellington had the same problem finding competent officers to command British brigades and even divisions in the years 1809–1811. Many were sent out who were not suitable but who could not be fired without cause. However, by 1812 Wellington's reputation was such that he could reject candidates nominated by his superiors in London.
107. The brigade was formed on 4 October 1810.
108. The brigade was formed in the summer of 1811.
109. For more information see Nunes, J. Lucio, 'As Brigadas da Cavalaria Portuguesa na Guerra Peninsular'. *Revista Ocidente*, 1954.
110. It should be noted that on paper some of the British commanders were second-in-command of the regiment. However, despite not being the senior officer in the regiment, they led the regiment on campaign.
111. Majors, lieutenant colonels, and colonels.
112. Brito, Pedro de, 'British Officers in the Portuguese Service 1809–1820'. Academia.edu. 2020, pp. 5, 9–10.
113. John Hamilton, George Elder, John Wilson, John Browne, Benjamin D'Urban, Archibald Campbell, Charles Sutton, Thomas Hill, John Doyle, Henry Pynn, John Campbell, and Victor von Arentschild.
114. Denis Pack, Thomas Bradford, Manley Power, Archibald Campbell, Charles Sutton, James Dawes Douglas, Henry Hardinge, John Doyle, Thomas Hill, Alexander Dickson, Edmund Williams, and Maxwell Grant.
115. George Madden, John Buchan, Charles Ashworth, Robert Nixon, John Waters, William McBean, George Elder, Michael McCreagh, Alexander Tulloh, Gustavus Browne, Bryan O'Toole, Dudley Hill, Richard Armstrong, John Hill, Henry Pynn, Alexander Anderson, Kenneth Snodgrass, Victor von Arentschild, John Rolt, and George Zulke.
116. Nicholas Trant, Robert Wilson, John Hamilton, Denis Pack, Archibald Campbell, Benjamin D'Urban, John Wilson, William Harvey, William Cox, William Spry, Richard Blunt, Manley Power, Thomas Bradford, Charles Ashworth, William Stubbs, Henry Watson, John Buchan, George Madden, and Robert Arbuthnot.
117. Richard Collins, Thomas Stubbs, Robert Arbuthnot, William McBean, John Brown, John Doyle, Thomas Noel Hill, John Dawes Douglas, George Elder, Henry Hardinge, Havilland Le Mesurier, Charles Sutton, Alexander Dickson, John Campbell, William Warre, Michael McCreagh, Henry Watson, Victor von Arentschild, Allan William Campbell, Henry Pynn, Richard Armstrong, Maxwell Grant, Bryan O'Toole, Donald McNeill, Alexander Anderson, Edmund William, John Rolt, John Prior, Dudley Hill, Robert Harvey, Charles Turner, Edward Hawkshaw, and Archibald Ross.
118. Burnham, Robert and Ron McGuigan, *The British Army against Napoleon: Facts, Lists, and Trivia, 1805–1815*. Barnsley: Frontline, 2010, pp. 212–13.
119. The 15 January 1812 Return for the forces in Spain showed a strength of 324,993 in 366 battalions and 195 squadrons. However, only 258,156 officers and men were listed as effectives/available for duty. Another 42,056 were hospitalized and 22,805 were on detached duty.
120. On 1 December 1811 the Army of the South had 81,703 officers and men, of whom 65,715 were available to march. Another 5,376 were detached and 10,612 were in hospital. The army had 86 battalions and 63 squadrons.

121. On 1 December 1811 the Army of Portugal had 74,928 officers and men, of whom 59,183 were with the colours. Another 5,837 were detached and 9,898 were in hospital. The army had 98 battalions and 37 squadrons.
122. AHM 1-14-57-4 ms 3. Note: the dead include those who died from their wounds later.
123. AHM 1-14-57-5 ms 4. Ditto.
124. Campbell was transferred to the 7th Infantry in mid-October and was replaced by Lieutenant Colonel José António Vidigal, who commanded until Colonel Francisco Homem de Magalhães Pizarro was assigned to the regiment in mid-November.
125. McBean went on sick leave on 2 September and was replaced by Lieutenant Colonel Inácio Emídio Aires da Costa.
126. From April 1812 the senior officer in the regiment was Lieutenant Colonel Walter Birmingham but for an unclear reason Gomersall, 16th Infantry, was appointed to command the 21st Infantry on 18 June, on the eve of Salamanca. He kept the command until the end of the campaign.
127. Miller fell ill on 7 July and Major Francisco de Paula Azeredo took command until Miller returned at the end of October.
128. Ward commanded the battalion until he was superseded by Lieutenant Colonel Bryan O'Toole at the end of October.
129. Resende was severely wounded at Salamanca and was replaced by Colonel James Douglas, 8th Infantry. On 4 October Brigadier General George Madden took command of the brigade.
130. During the time he was in command of the brigade, Douglas was replaced by Colonel José de Vasconcelos e Sá.
131. Silveira was incapacitated after Salamanca and was replaced by Lieutenant Colonel Francisco Homem de Magalhães Pizarro until mid-November.
132. The regiment's commander Colonel John Doyle was absent on a six-month leave, since May 1812, and did not return until the end of the campaign.
133. O'Toole was transferred to the 7th Caçadores at the end of October and was replaced by Major George Zulke.
134. Brevet Lieutenant Colonel Manuel Pinto da Silveira returned in September after recovering from his wound and took command.
135. D'Urban, Benjamin, *The Peninsular War Journal: 1808–1817*. London: Greenhill Napoleonic Library, 1988, p. 267.
136. Ibid., p. 257.
137. Watson was severely wounded at Salamanca and was replaced by Lieutenant Colonel João Luis da Silva Souto e Freitas.
138. Sousa was wounded at Majadahonda and was replaced by Major Edward Knight.
139. Barbacena was severely wounded and captured at Majadahonda. He was exchanged later in 1812 and returned to the Allied Army.
140. Possibly a battalion from the French 101st Infantry Regiment.
141. AHM 1-14-243-1 ms 28.
142. These reports could not be found.
143. Beresford.
144. Arthur Crookshank, 38th Foot.
145. For two hundred years there has been a question about whether the eagle was captured by the 12th Caçadores or was it found by them on the battlefield after the battle. Power's report clearly states that they captured it.
146. AHM 1-14-243-1 ms 22–4. The original is in English.
147. The Right Brigade was commanded by Lieutenant Colonel John Wallace, 88th Foot.
148. The Left Brigade was commanded by Lieutenant Colonel James Campbell, 94th Foot.
149. The 3rd Division.
150. Charles Sutton, 23rd Foot.
151. John Gomersall, 58th Foot, commanded the 21st Infantry but at the time he was a brevet lieutenant colonel in the 16th Infantry.
152. James Johnston, 40th Foot.
153. Marshal Beresford.
154. Brackenbury, Henry, 'A Letter from Salamanca'. *Blackwood Magazine*, February 1899, p. 382.
155. The author was probably Luís do Rego Barreto, the commander of the 15th Infantry.
156. Henriques, Mendo Castro, *Salamanca – 1812. Companheiros de Honra*. Lisbon: Prefácio, 2002, p. 76.
157. AHM 1-14-219-46 ms 2–3.
158. Marshal Beresford.
159. Luís do Rego Barreto.
160. The 1st and 2nd Battalions of the 27th Line Infantry Regiment, in General Pierre Berlier's Brigade, Clausel's 2nd Division.

161. Edward Brackenbury, 61st Foot.
162. Dudley Hill, 2nd West Indies Regiment.
163. AHM 3-12-9-36.
164. Spry means the Portuguese Brigade.
165. Died of his wounds.
166. Dudley Hill.
167. Edward Beyrimhof, Baron de Daubraya, 3rd Dragoon Guards.
168. José Joaquim da Silva Pereira.
169. Correia de Melo, José, 'Journal' in Chaby, Cláudio de, *Excerptos Historicos e Collecção de Documentos relativos à Guerra denominada da Peninsula e às anteriores de 1801, e do Rossillon e Cataluña*, 6 vols. Lisbon. Imprensa Nacional, 1863–1882, vol. 4, pp. 555–6.
170. Barrallier, Joseph, 'Adventure at the Battle of Salamanca'. *United Services Magazine*, October 1851, p. 274.
171. AHM 1-14-243-1 ms 31–4.
172. He was the colonel of the 23rd Infantry.
173. Stubbs is referring to the French counter-attack on the 4th Division. Clausel's 2nd Division in front and Bonnet's 8th Division from the flank.
174. This was the attack by the 4th Division on the French centre.
175. Stubbs leaves out that his brigade, as well as the rest of the Division broke from this attack and ran to the rear. He is also referring to the situation when the regrouped troops at the base of the hill resisted the French onslaught.
176. Stubbs means the moment when the French attack faltered due to the 6th Division intervention and the reformed 4th Division started again a forward movement.
177. Alexander Anderson, 42nd Foot.
178. John King, 48th Foot.
179. Despite the glowing recommendation of Stubbs, King was not appointed a major in the Portuguese Army.
180. Oman, vol. 5, p. 465.
181. AHM 1-14-243-1 ms 3–4.
182. Luís de Castro.
183. Francisco de Melo.
184. Lawrence Arnot, 56th Foot.
185. Edward Marlay, 82nd Foot, was a captain in the 8th Infantry.
186. Jorge de Lemos, 12th Infantry.
187. AHM 1-14-243-1 ms 51–2.
188. Francisco Homem de Magalhães Quevedo Pizarro.
189. Jorge de Lemos.
190. Count de Resende.
191. António de Lacerda Pinto da Silveira.
192. AHM 1-14-243-1 ms 15–17.
193. William White, 38th Foot.
194. He died of his wounds. He was the son of Colonel Silveira, the regiment's commander.
195. AHM 1-14-243-1 ms 18.
196. John Green, 83rd Foot.
197. Daniel Donovan, 27th Foot.
198. AHM 1-143-243-1 ms 11–14.
199. Henry Clinton, commander of the 6th Division.
200. This was a ridge known as the El Sierro, which was about 50m higher than the plain the Allies were advancing over. Standing at its bottom and having to climb it in the face of enemy fire may have made it appear higher than it was.
201. Lieutenant Colonel Brown's 9th Caçadores were on the far right of the 6th Division's line.
202. The French were most likely the 31st Light Infantry Regiment of Ferey's 3rd Division.
203. Adjutant Sergeant Manuel da Silva Rocha.
204. Captain Synge, Pack's ADC, probably meant that the 4th Division was the left-most division of all the divisions in the centre of the Allied line.
205. Tottenham, F.St.L, 'Captain Synge's Experiences at Salamanca'. *The Nineteenth Century and After*, vol. LXXII, July–December 1912, p. 58.
206. AHM 1-143-243-1 ms 58–60.
207. Bernardo António Zagalo.
208. General Cole commanded the 4th Division.
209. Edmund Williams, 81st Foot.
210. Peter Adamson, 71st Foot.
211. The Greater Arapile.

212. Promoted to lieutenant in the 8th Caçadores for his conduct.
213. Promoted to lieutenant in the 12th Caçadores for his conduct.
214. Peter Fearon, 31st Foot.
215. Thomas Hill, 55th Foot.
216. José António Vidigal.
217. The reserve consisted of the four grenadier companies, two from each regiment.
218. Neil Campbell, 54th Foot.
219. Charles Synge, 10th Light Dragoons.
220. Pack mistakenly wrote that the 4th Division was to his left. It was to the right of his brigade.
221. The French 120th Line Regiment.
222. AHM 1-143-243-1 ms 1–2.
223. From the letter of the 4th: 'The Caçadores Battalion had one man killed and another wounded in a skirmish on the morning of that day [the 22nd July]. On this occasion Captain Jorge Firmino Pereira Amado's Company's conduct was most gallant under the orders of his Captain who distinguished himself.'
224. Jorge Firmino Pereira Amado.
225. Francisco Xavier Calheiros, 7th Infantry commander.
226. Bryan O'Toole, 39th Foot, 2nd Caçadores commander.
227. Francisco da Costa Amaral, 19th Infantry commander.
228. Nicholas Colthurst, 83rd Foot, captain in the 7th Infantry.
229. Charles Turner, 11th Foot.
230. AHM 1-14-243-1 ms 41.
231. AHM 1-14-256-4 ms 42.
232. AHM 1-14-243-1 ms 47–8.
233. AHM 1-14-256-4 ms 48.
234. Henry Watson, 48th Foot.
235. 1st Cavalry.
236. 1st Cavalry.
237. AHM 3-12-9-43.
238. Died of his wound.
239. Edward Marlay.
240. Died of his wound.
241. Died of his wound.
242. Ralph Wylde, 89th Foot.
243. Died of his wound.
244. AHM 1-14-256-4 ms 44.
245. AHM 3-12-9-37.
246. John Wardlaw, 52nd Foot.
247. Edmund Williams.
248. John Webb, 79th Foot.
249. Alexander McGregor, 95th Foot.
250. Died of his wounds.
251. Died of his wounds.
252. AHM 1-14-256-4 ms 41.
253. AHM 1-14-243-1 ms 45.
254. George Lennon, 27th Foot, captain in the 24th Infantry.
255. AHM 1-14-256-4 ms 46.
256. AHM 1-14-256-4 ms 47.
257. Jones, John, *Journal of the Sieges Carried on by the Army under the Duke of Wellington in Spain, between the Years 1811 & 1814*. 3rd edn, 3 vols. Cambridge: Ken Trotman, 1998, vol. 1, pp. 274–5.
258. AHM 1-14-174-17 ms 3–4.
259. The report from Ensign Lobo is in the archive but the document had a page missing so we chose not to present it here.
260. Michael McCreagh, 1st Foot.
261. Promoted to lieutenant in the regiment for his conduct.
262. Promoted to lieutenant in the 2nd Caçadores for his conduct.
263. AHM 1-14-174-17 ms 8–9. The original is in English.
264. Sergeant Gaspar José de Brito was promoted to ensign in the 5th Caçadores for his conduct.
265. Henry Perry, 28th Foot, was killed.
266. A town in Alentejo Province.
267. AHM 1-14-174-17 ms 11.
268. AHM 1-14-174-17 ms 12–13.

269. He probably meant the breach made to enter the first enceinte.
270. Edward Cocks, 79th Foot, was killed.
271. Barbosa was mistaken. The 12th Foot did not serve in the Peninsula.
272. AHM 1-14-145-35 ms 3–5.
273. Arriaga's brigade was composed of six howitzers.
274. Brevet Major Sebastião José de Arriaga, 1st Artillery.
275. Pedro L'Huylier de Roziers, 1st Artillery.
276. He was court-martialled for insubordination, sentenced to a month in prison, and placed in the position of *agregado*.
277. This is confirmed by Oman, vol vi, p. 40. He was detached to get the guns from the Royal Navy collected at Reinosa.
278. Dickson's recommendation was approved and Júdice's penalty was lifted on 9 December 1812.
279. AHM 1-14-256-4 ms 77.
280. He was killed on 9 October 1812; see Jones, p. 314.
281. Alexander Dickson, Royal Artillery, was a lieutenant colonel in the 4th Artillery.
282. AHM 1-14-256-4 ms 80.
283. AHM 1-14-256-4 ms 84.
284. AHM 1-14-256-4 ms 83.
285. AHM 1-14-256-4 ms 79.
286. José de Vasconcelos e Sá.
287. Villamuriel de Cerrato.
288. AHM 1-14-174-16 ms 3.
289. George Ramsay, 9th Earl of Dalhousie, was the commander of the 7th Division.
290. The 2nd Battalion.
291. Promoted to ensign in the regiment for his conduct.
292. John Ross, 92nd Foot, was in the 19th Infantry.
293. AHM 1-14-174-16 ms 5. The original is in English.
294. 2nd Battalion.
295. George Zulke, 60th Foot, was a major in the 2nd Caçadores.
296. Francis D'Oyley, 1st Foot Guards.
297. Long's Brigade consisted of the 9th and 13th British Light Dragoons and the 2nd King's German Legion Hussars.
298. Wellington, Duke of, *The Dispatches of Field Marshal the Duke of Wellington, During his Various Campaigns in India, Denmark, Portugal, Spain, the Low Countries, and France, from 1799 to 1818.* Edited by Lt-Col. John Gurwood. London: John Murray; 1834–9, vol. 9, pp. 550–3. The report was in English.
299. Henry Goldfinch, Royal Engineers.
300. According to Thomas Bunbury, when the order came to retreat, Goldfinch blew up two arches in the bridge. Bunbury, Thomas, *Reminiscences of a Veteran*, 3 vols. Uckfield: Naval & Military Press, 2009, vol. 1, p. 166.
301. António Hipólito da Costa.
302. Archibald Campbell, 71st Foot.
303. Alexander Tulloh, Royal Artillery, was lieutenant colonel in the 3rd Artillery.
304. Hamilton was writing about the French making a reconnaissance.
305. William Stewart.
306. Henry Cadogan.
307. John Cameron.
308. Frederick Watson, 1st Royal Dragoons, AQMG in the Portuguese army.
309. Thomas Bunbury, 91st Foot, a captain in the 20th Infantry.
310. AHM 1-14-256-4 ms 73.
311. João Teles de Meneses e Melo.
312. AHM 1-14-256-4 ms 75–6.
313. Aldealengua.
314. AHM 1-14-256-4 ms 65. The original is in French.
315. 'Unpublished letter from Major General William Pringle to Major General John Oswald dated 27 October 1812.' *The Waterloo Association Online*, 26 July 2020.
316. AHM 1-14-256-4 ms 61.
317. At Villa Muriel on 25 October 1812.
318. AHM 1-14-256-4 ms 69.
319. AHM 1-14-256-4 ms 74.
320. Costa's Brigade.
321. Morata de Tajuna.

322. José Pinto Saavedra, AAG attached to the Portuguese Division.
323. AHM 1-14-256-4 ms 78.
324. João Rosendo de Mendonça.
325. António Maria Pinto died the next day.
326. AHM 1-14-256-4 ms 82.
327. AHM 1-14-256-4 ms 66.
328. AHM 1-14-256-4 ms 69.
329. AHM 3-12-9-42.
330. The officers of the 8th Caçadores were wounded at Villa Muriel on 25 October 1812.
331. At the siege of Burgos.
332. Charles Western, 29th Foot.
333. Died of his wounds.
334. James Leech, 86th Foot.
335. Edward Owens, 38th Foot, was killed at Villa Muriel on 25 October 1812.
336. Oman, vol. 6, p. 757.
337. Avilez broke a leg at Buenza and was replaced by Lieutenant Colonel John Gomersall until his return in the first days of December.
338. MacDonald was severely wounded at Banca on 1 October and was replaced by Major Jacinto Alexandre Travassos, who kept the command until he was mortally wounded at Nive. He was replaced by Major Rodrigo Vito Pereira da Silva.
339. Campbell was severely wounded at Sorauren and was replaced by Major António Eliseu de Almeida until Major John Hill took command in the last days of October. His promotion to the regiment as lieutenant colonel *agregado* was from 15 November but was published only in mid-December.
340. During the time that Vahia commanded the brigade, the regiment was commanded by Lieutenant Colonel Donald McNeill.
341. Armstrong was severely wounded at Sorauren and was replaced by Brevet Major Francisco António Pamplona until 24 December, when Pamplona was appointed to the 2nd Caçadores.
342. Rangel was promoted to brigadier general at the end of July, leaving the command to Colonel Sebastião Pinto de Araújo Correia, who was promoted to the regiment on the same day. Correia's ill-health forced him to return to Portugal on sick leave in October. The command devolved to Major Matias José de Sousa, who was killed at Nive.
343. Mitchell was temporarily in command because Lieutenant Colonel Sebastião Pinto de Araújo Correia had been on leave since December 1812 and only returned after Vitoria. Correia was in command for only a few weeks because he suffered an incapacitating injury on 7 July. Mitchell commanded until September, when Lieutenant Colonel Peter Fearon was transferred to the battalion and took command.
344. Birmingham was the senior officer, but he went on leave in May 1813 and did not return to the regiment. He later surfaced as the commander of the 8th Infantry at Nivelle. In the first days of August Colonel João Teles de Meneses was promoted to the regiment and took command.
345. Brevet Lieutenant Colonel Charles Kilsha succeeded in command after Dursbach died on 12 December from illness. The exact date he took command is unknown, but he commanded the 11th Caçadores at Nive in mid-December.
346. On the last day of July Colonel José de Vasconcelos e Sá was promoted to the regiment and took command. He soon went on sick leave, so Miller commanded the regiment through the rest of the year, and for some time the 9th Brigade. When Sá returned at the beginning of October he immediately took command of the brigade and Miller kept command of the regiment.
347. O'Toole was severely wounded at Sorauren and was replaced by Major John Lillie.
348. Campbell was superseded in the command when Michael McCreagh was promoted to colonel in the regiment at the end of July.
349. Barreto took command of the 3rd Brigade during September 1813 and was replaced by Major Archibald Campbell.
350. Hill was wounded at the storm of San Sebastian and at the beginning of October had permission to leave for Britain to recover. He was temporarily replaced in the command by Captain Joaquim António Duarte.
351. Douglas took command of the brigade at the end of August and was replaced by Lieutenant Colonel Ralph Ouseley. Ouseley was severely wounded on 31 August at Urdax and Major Francisco Eusébio Roxo took command. In September Roxo went on sick leave for three months, and the command was assumed by Captain António Venceslau Santa Clara. In November, on the eve of Nivelle, Beresford appointed Lieutenant Colonel Walter Birmingham, 21st Infantry, to command the regiment. However, he never returned to his regiment and remained commanding the 8th Infantry until he was killed at Toulouse.
352. Le Mesurier died on 30 July from wounds inflicted at Sorauren. He was temporarily replaced by Major Inácio Luís Madeira until Lieutenant Colonel João Pais de Sande e Castro took command in August after being transferred to the regiment. Lieutenant Colonel William Beatty, who had been absent from the

regiment since March 1813 while on leave in Britain, returned to the army in September. Castro was transferred to the 1st Infantry Regiment and Beatty took command.

353. Neil Campbell was the regiment's colonel but in January 1813 he left for Britain on sick leave. Colonel John Buchan, 22nd Regiment, was appointed to temporarily command in the Pyrenees. During the rest of the campaign Lieutenant Colonel Calheiros was in command.

354. Doyle took command of the 6th Brigade when Lecor was appointed to command the Portuguese Division in early December. He was replaced by Lieutenant Colonel Francisco José da Costa Amaral.

355. Algeo was killed at the passage of the Bidassoa. He was replaced by Major António Lobo Teixeira de Barros until Lieutenant Colonel Kenneth Snodgrass took command in November after being promoted to the battalion.

356. Hill was on leave from 14 September to the end of the year. He was temporarily replaced by Major Walter O'Hara and in October by Lieutenant Colonel João Pais de Sande e Castro who was appointed to the regiment.

357. Câmara was severely wounded at Tolosa on 25 June and was replaced by Major Kenneth Snodgrass until Lieutenant Colonel João Carlos de Saldanha was promoted to the regiment in September and took command.

358. Costa was in command because Colonel William McBean was on leave and returned only at the end of July.

359. McCreagh was promoted to colonel of the 3rd Infantry on 10 July. His promotion was not announced until it was published in the *Ordens do Dia* (Orders of the Day) of 31 July. He was replaced in August by Major John Hill, who commanded until the beginning of October, when Lieutenant Colonel Thomas St Clair took command.

360. Lieutenant Colonel Henry Watson returned to command in September.

361. Knight was superseded by Lieutenant Colonel Martinho Morais e Castro, promoted to the regiment in July.

362. When Barbacena assumed command of the brigade, he was replaced by Lieutenant Colonel António Carlos Cary.

363. Wellington, *Despatches*, vol. 10, pp. 451–2.

364. Ibid., p. 449.

365. Bayonne was the logistical centre and staging post for all troops entering Spain from France.

366. Oman, vol. 6, p. 757.

367. Fortescue, John, *A History of the British Army*, 13 vols. Naval and Military Press, 2004, vol. 9, p. 169.

368. AHM 1-14-243-18 ms 12–13.

369. Michell's Brigade.

370. Costa's Brigade.

371. Preto's Brigade.

372. AHM 1-14-243-18 ms 14–16.

373. Costa's Brigade.

374. Campbell's Brigade.

375. Brunton, Richard, 'A Narrative of the Services of Lieutenant Colonel Richard Brunton of the 13th Light Dragoons'. National Army Museum, File # 1968-07-461.

376. AHM 1-14-243-18 ms 20–1.

377. In fact, they were not ensigns but cadets, who were the flag bearers in the Portuguese Army.

378. Hennell, George, *A Gentleman Volunteer: The Letters of George Hennell from the Peninsular War 1812–1813*. Michael Glover (ed.). London: Heinemann, 1979, p. 90.

379. AHM 1-14-243-18 ms 57.

380. AHM 1-14-243-18 ms 65.

381. The return mentioned was sent blank. The battalion had no casualties.

382. AHM 1-14-256-5 ms 48.

383. Casualties were from artillery fire only.

384. John Rolt, 58th Foot.

385. Cole, Lowry, *Memoirs of Sir Lowry Cole*. Maud Cole (ed.). Cambridge: Ken Trotman, 2003, p. 97.

386. Nanclares de la Oca.

387. Close, Edward C., *The Diary of E.C. Close*. Mittagong: Highland House, 2015, p. 50.

388. Crowe, Charles, *An Eloquent Soldier: Peninsular War Journals of Lieutenant Charles Crowe of the Inniskillings 1812–1814*. Gareth Glover (ed.). London: Frontline, 2011, pp. 101–2.

389. A flag carried by the French infantry battalions instead of the national colours or an eagle.

390. Crowe, p. 102.

391. Oman, vol. 6, pp. 758, 760.

392. AHM 1-14-243-18 ms 61–3.

393. Alexander Anderson, 42nd Foot, was promoted to brevet major in the British Army for his conduct.

394. James Miller, 74th Foot, was promoted to brevet major in the British Army for his conduct.

395. Thomas Peacocke, 44th Foot.

396. George Phiffen, 3rd Foot, died from his wounds on 19 July 1813.
397. António Roque de Andrade.
398. Staff Surgeon David MacLagan.
399. The brigade's surgeon.
400. Stubbs was wounded.
401. Oman, vol. 6, p. 760.
402. AHM 1-14-243-18 ms 17–19.
403. Daniel Donahoe, 44th Foot, was slightly wounded and promoted to brevet lieutenant colonel in the Portuguese Army for his conduct.
404. Charles Waldron, 5th Foot.
405. Steevens, Charles, *With the 'Old & Bold' 1795 to 1818: the Reminiscences of an Officer of H.M. 20th Regiment During the Napoleonic Wars*. Leonaur, 2010, p. 76.
406. AHM 1-14-243-18 ms 3–5.
407. Promoted to brevet lieutenant colonel for his conduct.
408. George Crawfurd, 91st Foot.
409. Jerónimo Freire Corte Real.
410. Tomás António Rebocho.
411. He was listed as Rodolph Steiger, de Watteville's Regiment.
412. Pereira was punished by being put in the situation of *agregado* after being court-martialled accused of deferring his return to the regiment when he was recovering in Gouveia's hospital.
413. Cristovão de Sousa Abrunhosa.
414. Jerónimo Rogado de Oliveira.
415. Pedro António Rebocho.
416. João António Rebocho.
417. Manuel de Lemos.
418. *Porta Bandeira* literally means the flag bearer.
419. Promoted to ensign in the regiment for his conduct.
420. Miller claims that his regiment took two artillery batteries and wagons, yet Stubbs states that only the 11th Regiment captured some artillery brigades. Between the two regiments three French artillery companies were captured.
421. Marshal General was Wellington's rank in the Portuguese Army. Duke da Vitória, literally Duke of the Victory, was his Portuguese title since December 1812. It was awarded to him for the eviction of the French from Portugal.
422. AHM 1-14-243-18 ms 64.
423. Campbell, James, *A British Army, as It Was, – Is – and Ought to Be*. London: T&W Boone, 1840, p. 240. Campbell was Brisbane's brigade major and rode with the screen.
424. Ibid, p. 240.
425. Robinson, H.B., *Memoirs of Lieutenant General Sir Thomas Picton, G.B.C. &c Including His Correspondence, from Originals in Possession of His Family*, 2 vols. London: Richard Bentley, 1835, vol. 2, p. 190.
426. AHM 1-14-243-18 ms 37–40. The original is in English.
427. Francisco Joaquim Carreti, promoted to brevet lieutenant colonel for his conduct.
428. George Paty, 32nd Foot, promoted to brevet lieutenant colonel in the Portuguese Army for his conduct.
429. Matias José de Sousa was wounded and promoted to brevet major for his conduct.
430. John Graham, 88th Foot.
431. Archibald Ross, 91st Foot, was in the 9th Infantry. He was promoted to brevet lieutenant colonel in the Portuguese Army for his conduct.
432. William Cotter, 83rd Foot, was a captain in the 9th Infantry.
433. Samuel Jermyn, 57th Foot, was in the 21st Infantry.
434. Soares was in the 21st Infantry and was promoted to brevet major for his conduct.
435. Vilasboas was in the 9th Infantry and died the next day from his wounds.
436. James Johnston was promoted to major on 1 July but retained his position as Power's ADC.
437. AHM 1-14-243-18 ms 60. The original is in English.
438. AHM-1-14-243-18 ms 52–3. The original is in English.
439. António Rodrigues da Silva.
440. António Pinto Barbosa.
441. Sergeant major was not a rank or position in the Portuguese Army but was used by British officers when referring to an adjutant sergeant.
442. António Justiniano Vidal.
443. AHM-DIV-1-14-243-18 ms 79–81.
444. Oman vol. 6, p. 760.
445. AHM 1-14-243-18 ms 33–6.

446. Dudley Hill.
447. Gamarra Mayor.
448. Thomas Smith, 5th Foot.
449. Charles Fitzgerald, 82nd Foot, 15th Infantry.
450. AHM 1-14-243-18 ms 6-8. The original is in English.
451. Oswald commanded the 5th Division.
452. The Zadorra.
453. AHM 1-14-216-19 ms 4–5.
454. Edmund Williams was promoted to brevet lieutenant colonel in the British Army for his conduct.
455. William Queade, 77th Foot.
456. AHM 1-14-243-18 ms 84–6. The original is in English.
457. This provisional formation was formed with the brigade's four grenadier companies.
458. Kenneth Snodgrass, 52nd Foot.
459. AHM 1-14-243-18 ms 91–2. The original is in English.
460. Bitoriano.
461. Hueto Arriba.
462. Yurre.
463. Arriaga.
464. AHM 1-14-243-18 ms 9–10.
465. Georg Julius Hartman, KGA. In 1811 he temporarily commanded the Portuguese artillery stationed south of the Tagus in Dickson's absence. However, he was never commissioned into Portuguese service. In the 1813 campaign he commanded the Army's Reserve Artillery.
466. Brevet Major Sebastião José de Arriaga.
467. AHM 1-14-243-18 ms 55–6.
468. Charles Michell, Royal Artillery, was in the 3rd Artillery.
469. D'Urban, p. 307.
470. AHM 1-14-216-19 ms 1–3. The original is in French.
471. AHM 1-14-256-5 ms 45.
472. Preto's Brigade.
473. Michell's Brigade.
474. AHM 3-12-11-26 ms 1.
475. António Osório de Figueiredo.
476. AHM 1-14-256-5 ms 50.
477. AMH 3-12-11-28.
478. This column was left in blank in the original.
479. Joseph Palmer, 27th Foot.
480. William Galbraith, 51st Foot.
481. AHM 3-12-11-30.
482. José de Figueiredo Frazão.
483. Lieutenant Rodrigo António de Abreu, 16th Infantry.
484. AHM 1-14-256-5 ms 52.
485. AHM 1-14-243-18 ms 2.
486. Ordizia, Gipuzkoa, Spain.
487. Oman, vol. VI, p. 476.
488. Highway GI-2130.
489. Which battalion it was is not known.
490. AHM 1-143-243-14 ms 2.
491. José de Vasconcelos Bandeira.
492. AHM 3-12-11-44.
493. Bernardo Teles do Vale.
494. AHM 1-143-243-14 ms 3. The original is in English.
495. Promoted to brevet captain for his conduct during the combats of Villafranca and Tolosa.
496. AHM 3-12-11-31 ms 1.
497. Villafranca.
498. Benjamin Jones, 36th Foot.
499. AHM 3-12-11-31 ms 2.
500. Tolosa.
501. Luís Jerónimo Pinto.
502. Luís de Azevedo Pinto.
503. José Maria da Fonseca died later of his wounds.
504. João Baptista da Fonseca.

505. Joaquim Herculano Silva e Almeida.
506. José Manuel Correia.
507. Dom Francisco Xavier da Silva Lobo.
508. José Pais de Almeida.
509. Puerto de Velate.
510. Puerto Otsondo.
511. The 2nd Division was without Major General John Byng's Brigade, which had been detached to assist in the blockade of Pamplona.
512. AHM 1-14-243-29 ms 16–21.
513. Lieutenant Colonel John Cameron's Brigade, 2nd Division.
514. From Ashworth's Brigade, 2nd Division.
515. 14th British Light Dragoons.
516. The 2nd, 6th, and 14th Infantry.
517. John Forster Fitzgerald, 60th Foot.
518. Stewart was the commander of the 2nd Division.
519. Preto's Brigade.
520. João Teles de Meneses e Melo.
521. Lourenço Martins Pegado.
522. Domingos António Gil.
523. They were part of Campbell's Brigade.
524. AHM 1-14-243-29 ms 2–3.
525. AHM 1-14-256-5 ms 77.
526. AHM 1-14-256-5 ms 76.
527. On 17 July Brigadier General John Wilson took command of the brigade after Pack was promoted to major general in the British Army and assumed command of a British brigade in the 6th Division.
528. Jones, vol. 2, p. 14.
529. Unfortunately, the reports for the assault on 25 July could not be found.
530. Some sources state that the 5th Caçadores were also involved. It is possible, but we could not find any reports to support this claim.
531. AHM 1-14-243-12 ms 2. The original is in English.
532. Colonel Thomas Hill, 1st Infantry.
533. António Vicente de Queiróz.
534. António de Gouveia Cabral.
535. AHM 1-14-243-12 ms 1. The original is in English.
536. Joseph Barrallier, 71st Foot, was assigned to the 23rd Infantry. He was severely wounded at Salamanca.
537. Lieutenant José Teixeira de Melo died of his wounds on 15 July.
538. AHM 1-14-243-12 ms 24. The original is in English.
539. It was probably the 5th Caçadores.
540. AHM 1-14-243-12 ms 25. The original is in English.
541. Joaquim António Alvares.
542. Literally shooters.
543. Antonio Vicente de Queiróz.
544. AHM 1-14-243-12 ms 27.
545. Promoted to brevet captain for his conduct.
546. AHM 1-14-243-12 ms 29.
547. Major General Andrew Hay.
548. AHM 1-14-243-12 ms 30–1.
549. António Manuel Calheiros.
550. AHM 1-14-243-12 ms 12. The original is in English.
551. Kenneth Snodgrass, 52nd Foot, was a major in the 13th Infantry.
552. HMS *Surveillante* was a British frigate that provided artillery support during the siege.
553. A glacis is a gently rising slope before a fortification's walls. It was designed to prevent siege guns from hitting the walls.
554. AHM 1-14-243-12 ms 18–23. The original is in English.
555. Henry Craufurd.
556. Colin Campbell.
557. Lawrence Arguimbau.
558. 1st Foot.
559. John Cameron, 1st Foot.
560. James Taylor.
561. John Woodham, 9th Foot.

562. Badham Thornhill, 9th Foot.
563. John Cameron, 9th Foot.
564. George Berkeley, 35th Foot, was an AAG.
565. AHM 1-14-243-12 ms 9–10. The original is in English.
566. Joaquim António de Almeida.
567. Promoted to brevet lieutenant for his conduct.
568. Romão José Soares.
569. AHM 1-14-243-12 ms 6–8. The original is in English.
570. McCreagh was promoted to colonel and given command of the 3rd Infantry on 10 July 1813. Word of his promotion had not reached the army by the time of the assault.
571. AHM 1-14-243-13 ms 8–13. The original is in English.
572. António Inácio Caiola.
573. Dudley Hill, who was slightly wounded.
574. Luís do Rego Barreto.
575. Charles Stuart Campbell, 26th Foot, was promoted to brevet major in the British Army and brevet lieutenant colonel in the Portuguese Army, for his conduct. He also received the AGM for San Sebastian.
576. António Joaquim Rosado was promoted to brevet lieutenant colonel for his conduct.
577. Alexandre Marcelino Maio e Brito.
578. Walter Daniell was wounded.
579. Bento José Valente was promoted to brevet major for his conduct.
580. Charles Fitzgerald.
581. He became Spry's ADC on 27 August 1813.
582. AHM 1-14-243-13 ms 20–1. The original is in English.
583. Leith was the commander of the 5th Division.
584. Robinson's Brigade, 5th Division.
585. AHM 1-14-243-13 ms 22–3.
586. Thomas O'Neale, 32nd Foot.
587. Wounded and promoted to brevet lieutenant for his conduct.
588. Promoted to brevet lieutenant for his conduct.
589. Promoted to brevet lieutenant for his conduct, retaining his post of Adjutant.
590. Promoted to ensign in the regiment for his conduct.
591. Promoted to ensign in the 3rd Infantry for his conduct.
592. AHM 1-14-216-20 ms 1–4. The original is in English.
593. William MacBean, 6th Foot, commanded the 24th Infantry.
594. The Urumea river.
595. Promoted to brevet lieutenant colonel in the Portuguese Army and brevet major in the British Army for his conduct during the siege.
596. AHM 1-14-216-20 ms 12–13. The original is in English.
597. William Gordon, 1st Foot, received the AGM for San Sebastian. For an infantry officer to receive the medal, he had to be a commander of at least a battalion or have temporarily led a unit larger than a company. Gordon was probably temporarily in command of his battalion during the assault.
598. Romão José Soares.
599. José Azevedo Pinto was promoted to brevet captain for his conduct.
600. António de Pádua was promoted to brevet captain for his conduct.
601. Promoted to ensign in the regiment for his conduct.
602. João Pinto da Costa was promoted to ensign in the regiment for his conduct.
603. João Manuel de Abreu.
604. AHM 1-14-216-20 ms 14. The original is in English.
605. Ensign.
606. Ensign José Carrasco Guerra was promoted to brevet lieutenant for his conduct.
607. AHM 1-14-216-20 ms 1. The original is in English.
608. Promoted to brevet major for his conduct.
609. João António Pereira de Castro was promoted to brevet captain for his conduct.
610. Manuel Joaquim Ferreira da Cunha.
611. AHM 1-14-243-13 ms 48–50.
612. Brevet Major Sebastião José de Arriaga.
613. Promoted to brevet lieutenant colonel on 9 November 1813 for his services during the siege and in the following operations.
614. Promoted to brevet captain on 9 November 1813 for his services during the siege and in the following operations.
615. Promoted to brevet captain on 9 November 1813 for his services during the siege and in the following operations.

616. Promoted to brevet 1st lieutenant on 9 November 1813 for his services during the siege and in the following operations.
617. Manuel Caetano de Abreu Vasconcelos.
618. Dickson probably meant the main batteries on the right bank of the Urumea river.
619. Promoted to brevet colonel on 9 November 1813 for his services during the siege and in the following operations.
620. Both sergeants were promoted on 9 November 1813 to 2nd lieutenant in the 1st Artillery for their services during the siege and in the following operations.
621. AHM 3-12-11-39.
622. António da Silva Neves.
623. José Maria Maciel.
624. José Pedro de Abreu.
625. Manuel Joaquim Ferreira da Cunha.
626. Lourenço Justiniano de Lima.
627. José António Ferreira de Aragão.
628. José Manuel Correia died of his wounds.
629. Francisco Xavier Borges de Alpoim.
630. Napoleon prohibited Soult from calling them corps. Instead, they were named Lieutenancies of the Left, Right, and Centre. For the sake of simplicity, we refer to them as corps and use their commanders' names to identify them when necessary.
631. The heights are a kilometre north of the town of Huarte.
632. Olave.
633. Although there was no fighting there the subsequent battle was called Beunza.
634. Allan Campbell, 74th Foot.
635. AHM 1-14-243-6 ms 1.
636. AHM 1-14-243-6 ms 2–3.
637. Brunton.
638. This was also called the Ispegui Pass. It is about 10km southeast of the Maya Pass along the NA-2600 road.
639. AHM 1-14-243-29 ms 13–15.
640. Espegui Pass.
641. João Teles de Meneses e Melo.
642. Jorge de Avilez Juzarte.
643. Campbell's Brigade, which was detached on the right at Aldules, joined the forces defending the Roncesvalles Pass.
644. AHM 1-14-243-6 ms 4.
645. The heights are about a kilometre northeast of Oricain.
646. The heights are a kilometre north of Huarte.
647. Olave.
648. The battle was named after the village of Beunza, which was 3km to the west.
649. AHM 1-14-243-29 ms 24–7.
650. Promoted to brevet major for his conduct.
651. Armstrong was a brevet major in the British Army and was promoted to brevet lieutenant colonel in the British Army for his conduct.
652. Joshua Green, 4th Foot, was a major in the 10th Caçadores.
653. Promoted to brevet major for his conduct and continued to serve as the brigade major.
654. Promoted to brevet lieutenant for his conduct.
655. All this occurred on 27 July.
656. Allan Campbell.
657. Luís Maria de Sousa Vahia.
658. João Rodarte da Gama Lobo was promoted to brevet lieutenant for his conduct.
659. Archibald Campbell, 5th Foot, was promoted to brevet captain for his conduct. He was severely wounded on 27 July.
660. Wounded in the battle and promoted to ensign in the regiment for his conduct.
661. Promoted to ensign in the regiment for his conduct.
662. Lieutenant José Jorge Loureiro.
663. AHM 1-14-243-29 ms 22–3.
664. Campbell died of his wounds on 9 October 1813.
665. Angus MacDonald, 57th Foot.
666. Ralph Dudgeon, 71st Foot.
667. Donald McNeill, EOPS, was a lieutenant colonel in the 10th Infantry.
668. AHM 1-14-243-9 ms 59–61. The original is in English.

669. Thomas Dursbach.
670. Major Kilsha was baptised on 6 May 1782, which would mean he was about 31 years old. Power most likely meant he was an experienced officer.
671. AHM 1-14-243-9 ms 66–7.
672. Thomas Peacocke.
673. William O'Hara, 47th Foot, was promoted to brevet major for his conduct.
674. Stubbs' promotion to brigadier general was only published in the *Ordens do Dia* (Orders of the Day) dated 31 July 1813.When he wrote his report he was still the colonel of the 23rd Infantry. The government decree of the promotion was from 10 July 1813 where it was stated that his seniority in the rank was counted from 4 June 1813. This meant that in the Officers' Lists the date of rank would be 4 June. This decree promoted generals, colonels, and lieutenant colonels in the same way as Stubbs. Among them were Ashworth, Lecor, Bradford, Madden, Power, Elder, Sutton, and Le Mesurier. So, many of the officers who wrote reports at this point signed them with their previous rank.
675. AHM 1-14-243-9 ms 42.
676. AHM 1-14-243-9 ms 41.
677. Promoted to brevet captain for his conduct.
678. AHM 1-14-243-9 ms 65.
679. Lieutenant Colonel *agregado* João Paes de Sande e Castro was a supernumerary lieutenant colonel in the battalion.
680. Eusa.
681. The 8th Infantry had been detached to Olague, 12km to the north, to guard the left flank of the army.
682. AHM 1-14-243-9 ms 7–10. The original is in English.
683. Lieutenant Colonel Gustavus Brown, 60th Foot.
684. James Douglas, 45th Foot.
685. Inácio Luís Madeira de Melo.
686. Havilland Le Mesurier, 21st Foot.
687. Lawrence Arnot died of his wounds on 3 October 1813.
688. William Thornton, 32nd Foot.
689. João Borges Cerqueira de Alpoim.
690. Ensign Manuel José Correia.
691. João António Teixeira de Sampaio.
692. John Green.
693. Duarte Cardoso de Sá was promoted to brevet lieutenant for his conduct.
694. João José Barracho Correia de Abreu was promoted to brevet lieutenant for his conduct.
695. Sorauren.
696. At this point Madden was already a major general. See Note 674.
697. AHM 1-14-243-9 ms 4–6.
698. Eusa.
699. John Harrison, 38th Foot, was promoted to brevet major for his conduct.
700. Sorauren.
701. Promoted to brevet major for his distinguished conduct.
702. Promoted to brevet captain for his conduct.
703. Promoted to brevet lieutenant for his conduct.
704. Promoted to ensign in the battalion for his conduct.
705. Promoted to ensign in the battalion for his conduct.
706. Arraizko Bentak.
707. AHM 1-14-243-9 ms 19–21.
708. The Ulzama river.
709. George Zulke was promoted to brevet lieutenant colonel for his conduct.
710. Promoted to brevet major for his conduct. He died of his wound.
711. Vargas was punished in March 1811 because of a serious dispute with a fellow officer in the battalion. In April 1814 he was cashiered due to his generally bad behaviour.
712. Promoted to ensign in the battalion for his conduct.
713. Promoted to ensign in the battalion for his conduct.
714. Since February 1813, by Beresford's order, the cadets in the infantry and caçadores units were sent to the Infantry Depot at Mafra to receive instruction on their duties. Francisco José Pereira who was already with the battalion, being recently recognized as a cadet, asked to remain with the army instead of returning to Portugal.
715. Luís Diogo Pereira Forjaz was promoted to brevet lieutenant colonel for his conduct. He was the son of Lieutenant General Dom Miguel Pereira Forjaz, Secretary for War and Foreign Affairs in the Portuguese Government.

716. John Ross.
717. David A. Leslie, 50th Foot.
718. Unfortunately, Lecor did not mention which village, so it is not clear if this was on the 30 or 31 July. Leslie was wounded on 30 July, so it was likely that day.
719. Lieutenant Colonel Frederick de Hertzberg, Brunswick Oëls.
720. Charles Trapps, 72nd Foot, was promoted to lieutenant colonel for his conduct.
721. Francis Armstrong, 11th Foot.
722. Artze. The attacked occurred on 31 July.
723. Probably the Lizarrieta Pass near Echalar, on 1 August.
724. Thomas Shervinton, 11th Foot.
725. Also on 31 July.
726. Promoted to ensign in the regiment for his conduct.
727. John Buchan commanded the 7th Infantry. However, he was the colonel of the 22nd Infantry, which remained in Portugal and appears here commanding the 7th Infantry. This was a temporary appointment made by Beresford. His promotion to brigadier general was published in an *Orden do Dia* (Order of the Day) dated 31 July 1813.
728. John Doyle commanded the 19th Infantry.
729. Eguaras.
730. AHM 1-14-243-9 ms 32–8.
731. John MacDonald, 88th Foot.
732. Pegado had been a brevet lieutenant colonel since 1810.
733. Robert Ray, 50th Foot.
734. Dugald McGibbon, 57th Foot, was a captain in the 2nd Infantry and not in the 14th Infantry as mentioned.
735. Frederick Watson, 1st Royal Dragoons.
736. José Pinto Savedra.
737. Promoted to lieutenant for his conduct.
738. Captain Luís de Mendonça e Melo.
739. Manuel da Silveira Pinto da Fonseca Teixeira, the DAG, was the son of the Count de Amarante. He served as the acting ADC to his father during the time the Count commanded the Portuguese Division in 1813. He inherited his father's title as the 2nd Count de Amarante and was made the 1st Marquis de Chaves.
740. Promoted to lieutenant for his conduct.
741. Amarante meant since the beginning of the Portuguese uprising against the French rule that restored the Bragança Dynasty in Portugal.
742. Ashworth's Brigade.
743. Campbell's Brigade.
744. Azpilkueta.
745. AHM 1-14-243-9 ms 26–8.
746. Promoted to ensign in the regiment for his conduct.
747. Promoted to ensign in the regiment for his conduct.
748. Promoted to brevet major for his conduct.
749. AHM 1-14-243-9 ms 29–31.
750. David McPherson, 31st Foot.
751. AHM 1-14- 243-9 ms 11–13.
752. Buenza.
753. Venta de Urroz.
754. Manuel Pamplona Carneiro Rangel.
755. Henry Pynn, 82nd Foot.
756. Ralph Ouseley, 63rd Foot.
757. Promoted to brevet major for his conduct.
758. Hugh Lumley, 31st Foot.
759. Richard Brunton, 43rd Foot.
760. John Sutherland, 3rd Foot.
761. Promoted to brevet captain for his conduct.
762. Both were promoted to brevet captains in the respective regiments retaining their adjutant position, for their conduct.
763. Both sergeants were promoted to ensign in the regiment for their conduct.
764. At the time when Ashworth wrote his report, he was not aware of his promotion to brigadier general, which was published in the *Ordens do Dia* (Orders of the Day) dated 31 July 1813. See Note 674.
765. AHM 1-14-256-5 ms 84.
766. AHM 1-14-256-5 ms 87.
767. AHM 3-12-11-20 ms 3.

768. AHM 1-14-256-5 ms 43.
769. AHM 3-12-11-33 ms 1. This return is for the action of 28 July 1813.
770. Lieutenant Colonel Le Mesurier died on 30 July 1813.
771. William Thornton.
772. John Maher, 87th Foot, was a captain in the 8th Infantry.
773. AHM 3-12-11-33 ms 3.
774. AHM 3-12-11-37.
775. AHM 1-14-256-5 ms 69.
776. Combat of Venta de Urroz.
777. James Campbell.
778. AHM 1-14-256-5 ms 89.
779. Combat of Echalar.
780. AHM 3-12-11-47.
781. Robert Ray.
782. João Nepomuceno de Ataíde died of his wounds.
783. Arsénio Pompeu Correia de Freitas.
784. Luís Filipe Pereira de Vasconcelos.
785. AHM 3-12-11-32.
786. João Joaquim Pereira do Lago.
787. João Maria Pereira.
788. Manuel Pamplona Carneiro Rangel.
789. William Henry Temple, 52nd Foot.
790. Died of his wounds.
791. Ernest Barckhausen, 24th Foot.
792. AHM 3-12-11-26 ms 3.
793. Joaquim Maria de Vasconcelos.
794. Bera, Spain.
795. The citadel surrendered on 8 September 1813.
796. Oman, vol. 7, p. 531.
797. Zalain, Spain. The heights are about 3km downstream from Bera, Spain.
798. Wellington, *Supplementary Despatches*, vol. 8, p. 222.
799. AHM 1-14-256-5 ms 16–17.
800. The Bidassoa river.
801. John Lillie, 6th Foot.
802. This return was not found in the archives.
803. Oman, vol. 7, p. 531.
804. AHM 1-14-243-9 ms 21.
805. Dawn was 5:12 a.m.
806. Letter from Lord Dalhousie to Wellington, dated 2 September 1813. Wellington, *Supplementary Despatches*, vol. 8, p. 221.
807. AHM 1-14-243-19 ms 4–5.
808. Francisco Xavier Calheiros.
809. George Zulke.
810. AHM 3-12-8-43.
811. John Ross.
812. David Leslie.
813. António do Prado Fragoso, 2nd Caçadores.
814. Ensign Júlio César Augusto, 19th Infantry, died of his wounds.
815. AHM 3-12-11-48.
816. James Douglas.
817. William Connor, 7th Foot.
818. Jorge Alexandre de Miranda died of his wounds.
819. John Green was a captain in the 12th Infantry.
820. MacDonald was the commander of the 14th Infantry, 2nd Brigade.
821. McNeill was a battalion commander in the 10th Infantry, 4th Brigade.
822. AHM 1-14-243-3 ms 2.
823. AHM 1-14-243-2 ms 3–5.
824. Probably Arrolako Harria.
825. Hauza mountain.
826. Dugald Campbell, 91st Foot.
827. Saint-Étienne-de-Baïgorry, France.

828. Wellington, *Despatches*, vol. 11, p. 181.
829. AHM 1-14-243-3 ms 13–15.
830. Captain Duarte was the senior officer in the battalion at the time.
831. Archibald Campbell, 46th Foot.
832. Spry, the former commander of the brigade, had been absent in Britain since 7 September 1813.
833. Charles Fitzgerald was a captain in the 15th Infantry.
834. For this he was promoted to brevet major.
835. Dudley Hill.
836. Alexandre Marcelino Maio e Brito.
837. Colonel of the 15th Infantry.
838. AHM 1-14-256-5 ms 65.
839. Urrugne, France.
840. AHM 1-14-243-3 ms 19.
841. Robert MackIntosh, 4th Foot.
842. AHM 1-14-243-3 ms 21–2.
843. Tomás Teotónio de Carvalho.
844. AHM 1-14-243-15 ms 11.
845. AHM 1-14-243-15 ms 9–10.
846. William Dobbin, 27th Foot.
847. Daniel Kirk, 32nd Foot.
848. António Correia Leitão.
849. Manuel António Sobral.
850. Manuel Baptista Lisbon.
851. João Crisóstomo Guedes.
852. John Algeo.
853. Manuel Pinto da Silveira.
854. AHM 1-14-243-15 ms 4.
855. Manuel António Sobral was wounded.
856. Barros was slightly wounded.
857. AHM 1-14-243-15 ms 6–7.
858. He means the non-commissioned officers.
859. Promoted to captain for his conduct on this occasion.
860. Promoted to ensign in the battalion for his conduct.
861. António de Lemos Pereira de Lacerda was Beresford's Portuguese Military Secretary.
862. Commanded by Colonel James Douglas, 8th Infantry.
863. AHM 1-14-243-3 ms 17–18.
864. Plácido Joaquim Serra.
865. AHM 1-14-256-5 ms 64.
866. John Augustus Mathison, 77th Foot.
867. AHM 3-12-11-26 ms 2.
868. William G. Cummins, 83rd Foot.
869. William Murphy, 43rd Foot.
870. João José Baracho Correia de Abreu.
871. António Simplício de Morais.
872. Manuel Pereira Campos.
873. Died of his wounds.
874. Lieutenant Colonel Gustavus Brown.
875. Andrew Simpson was a sergeant major in the 95th Rifles when he was commissioned an ensign in the 2nd Foot in 1811. On 3 July 1811 he entered Portuguese service as a lieutenant and the adjutant of the 9th Caçadores.
876. Altxanger.
877. Now called Larrun (in Spanish) or La Rhune (in French).
878. Ainhoa.
879. Pont d'Amotz.
880. Graham had returned to England in October owing to medical problems.
881. All the brigade commanders were major generals and had the same date of rank of 4 June 1813. However, Lecor was senior because his date of rank to brigadier general was older than theirs.
882. The next night had a full moon.
883. Dawn was at 7:03 a.m. but nautical twilight was at 5:58 a.m.
884. AHM 1-14-243-5 ms 3–5.
885. General Hay.

886. AHM 1-14-243-8 ms 32–3.
887. Promoted to captain in the battalion for his conduct.
888. AHM 1-14-243-8 ms 38–9.
889. Both died from their wounds.
890. AHM 1-14-243-8 ms 14–16.
891. Promoted to brevet major for his conduct.
892. John King.
893. José de Vasconcelos e Sá was the colonel of the 23rd Infantry.
894. AHM 1-14-243-8 ms 36.
895. Promoted to brevet captain for his conduct.
896. Promoted to ensign in the regiment for his conduct.
897. AHM 1-14-243-8 ms 10–11.
898. Francisco de Paula Rosado.
899. Bartholomew Derenzy, 81st Foot.
900. Francisco Xavier da Silva Pereira.
901. Frederico César de Freitas.
902. Valentim Dufuret. This officer was appointed to the 7th Caçadores from the *Brigada Real da Marinha*, the Portuguese equivalent to the Royal Marines.
903. Promoted to ensign in the battalion for his conduct.
904. AHM 1-14-243-8 ms 4–5.
905. George Zulke.
906. Meaning France.
907. Colonel of the 19th Infantry.
908. Pont d'Amotz.
909. St Pée-sur-Nivelle.
910. AHM 1-14-243-8 ms 26–31. The original is in English.
911. The 11th Caçadores.
912. Promoted to brevet lieutenant colonel in the Portuguese Army for his conduct on this occasion.
913. Promoted to ensign in the battalion for his good conduct.
914. Power means adjutant sergeant.
915. Charles Sutton commanded the 9th Infantry.
916. Thomas Goodrick Peacocke, 55th Foot.
917. João Barbosa de Magalhães.
918. João Joaquim Pereira da Silva.
919. Promoted to ensign in the regiment for his conduct.
920. João Teles de Meneses e Melo.
921. Joaquim Teles Jordão.
922. William Galbraith.
923. Brigade Major Valadas was a captain in the 9th Infantry. He was promoted to brevet major for his conduct and retained his position as brigade major.
924. Cambo-les-Bains.
925. AHM 1-14-243-8 ms 42–3.
926. Inácio Luís Madeira.
927. John Maher, 87th Foot.
928. AHM 1-14-243-8 ms 45–8.
929. General Henry Clinton.
930. Espelette.
931. The 3rd Artillery Brigade had 6-pounder guns. The 4th Artillery Brigade had 9-pounder guns.
932. AHM 1-14-243-8 ms 1–2. The original is in English.
933. José Pinto Savedra.
934. AHM 1-14-243-8 ms 12–13.
935. Donald McNeill was slightly wounded.
936. Francis Armstrong.
937. Campbell was referring to the Battles of the Pyrenees. Captain Queiróz was wounded on 27 July 1813 at Sorauren.
938. He was wounded at Bussaco, the Pyrenees, and Nivelle.
939. There is some confusion here because Lieutenant Queiróz, 4th Caçadores, was severely wounded at the Siege of San Sebastian but did not die.
940. Promoted to ensign in the regiment for his conduct.
941. Promoted to ensign in the regiment for his conduct.
942. AHM 1-14-243-8 ms 37.

943. Died of his wounds.
944. Promoted to lieutenant in the regiment for his conduct.
945. Col de Pinodieta.
946. AHM 1-14-243-8 ms 44.
947. AHM 1-14-256-5 ms 5.
948. AHM 1-14-243-5 ms 6.
949. AHM 3-12-11-46 ms 3.
950. AHM 1-14-256-5 ms 7.
951. AHM 1-14-256-5 ms 2.
952. AHM 1-14-256-5 ms 1.
953. AHM 1-14-256-5 ms 4.
954. He was shot through the body.
955. AHM 1-14-256-5 ms 9.
956. AHM 1-14-256-5 ms 3.
957. Died of his wounds.
958. AHM 3-12-11-35.
959. João Rosendo de Mendonça.
960. Died of his wounds.
961. Pedro Pinto de Morais Sarmento.
962. João Rodarte da Gama Lobo.
963. AHM 1-14-256-5 ms 10.
964. AHM 1-14-256-5 ms 8.
965. AHM 1-14-256-5 ms 6.
966. The *Alveitar* was a person who treated animals' diseases and wounds. He was not a veterinarian but someone with practical knowledge.
967. The Mountain Brigade was commanded by Captain António da Costa e Silva.
968. The 1st Brigade was commanded by Brevet Lieutenant Colonel Sebastião José de Arriaga.
969. The 3rd and 4th Brigades were under Lieutenant Colonel Alexander Tulloh and were attached to the Portuguese Division.
970. Taupin's Division was disbanded owing to its poor performance during the Battle of the Nivelle. Those regiments which fought well were sent to other divisions, while those which did not were sent to Bayonne to strengthen its garrison. General Nicolas Conroux had been killed in the fighting on 10 November and Taupin took command of his division.
971. Sunrise was at 7:35 a.m.
972. Sunset was at 4:39 p.m.
973. AHM 1-14-243-7 ms 39. The original is in English.
974. He was colonel of the 8th Infantry.
975. AHM 1-14-144-27 ms 1. The original is in English.
976. Gustavus Brown.
977. Francisco Joaquim Pereira Valente.
978. AHM 1-14-243-7 ms 44. The original is in English.
979. Luís Maria Cerqueira.
980. Brown was severely wounded.
981. AHM 1-14-243-7 ms 35–6.
982. Promoted to brevet major for his conduct.
983. Simpson was promoted to brevet captain for his conduct but continued as the adjutant.
984. Promoted to brevet lieutenant for his conduct.
985. Brunton.
986. Severely wounded by a shot through the body.
987. AHM 1-14-243-7 ms 60–6.
988. He was slightly wounded.
989. William Temple.
990. Ensign Ernest Barckhausen was promoted to brevet lieutenant for his conduct.
991. Promoted to brevet lieutenant for his conduct.
992. Slightly wounded and promoted to brevet lieutenant for his conduct.
993. Promoted to brevet major for his conduct.
994. Lewis Appelius, 6th Garrison Battalion, was severely wounded and promoted to brevet captain for his conduct.
995. Promoted to brevet lieutenant for his conduct.
996. Promoted to ensign in the 7th Caçadores for his conduct.
997. Promoted to ensign in the corps for his conduct.

998. Phillip Ricketts, 62nd Foot.
999. Slightly wounded and promoted to brevet major for his conduct.
1000. AHM 1-14-243-7 ms 68–9.
1001. He was severely wounded.
1002. Promoted to brevet lieutenant colonel for his conduct.
1003. Promoted to brevet major for his conduct.
1004. Promoted to brevet lieutenant for his conduct.
1005. Promoted to brevet lieutenant for his conduct.
1006. Promoted to ensign in the corps for his conduct.
1007. AHM 1-14-243-07 ms 3–6.
1008. French light infantry.
1009. Luís Maria de Sousa Vahia.
1010. John Hill, 23rd Foot.
1011. Francisco António Pamplona Moniz.
1012. This list was not found in the archives.
1013. The former commander of the Portuguese Division.
1014. Lieutenant John Griffiths, 94th Foot, was a British DAQMG assigned to the division.
1015. Promoted to brevet lieutenant for his conduct.
1016. Jacinto Alexandre Travassos was promoted to brevet lieutenant colonel for his conduct but died of his wounds.
1017. AHM 1-14-243-7 ms 1–2.
1018. AHM 1-14-223-2 ms 1.
1019. AHM 1-14-320-22 ms 1.
1020. Lieutenant Colonel Tulloh.
1021. Promoted to brevet captain for his conduct.
1022. During the Battle of the Nivelle.
1023. Promoted to brevet captain for his conduct.
1024. Buys was promoted to brevet 1st lieutenant for his conduct.
1025. Oman wrongly claimed the Portuguese were surprised and had a dozen men captured. Oman, vol. 7, p. 241.
1026. AHM 1-14-243-7 ms 13–14.
1027. William McMahon, 96th Foot.
1028. He was wounded.
1029. Promoted to brevet captain for his conduct.
1030. AHM 1-14-243-7 ms 15.
1031. AHM 1-14-243-7 ms 19–20.
1032. George Murphy, 87th Foot.
1033. Promoted to brevet major for his conduct.
1034. Henrique José was promoted to ensign in the corps for his conduct.
1035. O'Hara was wounded and taken prisoner. He was later exchanged for a French engineer major.
1036. AHM 1-14-243-7 ms 21–2.
1037. Promoted to brevet lieutenant for his conduct.
1038. Promoted to ensign in the corps for his conduct.
1039. AHM 1-14-243-7 ms 49–52. The original is in English.
1040. Thomas Bunbury was promoted to brevet major for his conduct.
1041. Promoted to brevet captain for his conduct.
1042. Promoted to brevet lieutenant for his conduct.
1043. António Carlos de Mendonça Furtado.
1044. Promoted to brevet captain for his conduct.
1045. Luís Manuel de Lemos.
1046. Henry Rainey, 55th Foot, received a £200 pension for his wound.
1047. AHM 1-14-145-3 ms 1–6.
1048. Probably Arriaga's 9-pounder and Major Robert Lawson's 6-pounder artillery brigades.
1049. Charles Fitzgerald.
1050. Carvalho was adjutant in the regiment and was promoted to brevet lieutenant for his conduct. He retained his post as adjutant.
1051. McCreagh was the 3rd Infantry's commander.
1052. Promoted to brevet lieutenant colonel for his conduct.
1053. He was wounded.
1054. Promoted to brevet major for his conduct.
1055. Promoted to brevet captain for his conduct.
1056. Promoted to brevet lieutenant for his conduct.

1057. Promoted to ensign in the corps for his conduct.
1058. Promoted to brevet captain for his conduct.
1059. He was wounded and promoted to brevet captain for his conduct.
1060. AHM 3-12-11-42 ms 2.
1061. Combat of Villefranque.
1062. Brevet Major John Harrison.
1063. AHM 3-12-11-42 ms 4.
1064. Gustavus Brown.
1065. AHM 3-12-11-38.
1066. Lecor did not mention other officers in this return. It is likely that he sent the list of officers killed and wounded on another page which was not found.
1067. AHM 1-14-256-5 ms 13.
1068. AHM 1-14-256-5 ms 15.
1069. AHM 3-12-11.
1070. Died of his wounds on 14 December 1813.
1071. AHM 1-14-256-5 ms 14.
1072. AHM 1-14-256-5 ms 11.
1073. AHM 1-14-320-27 ms 11.
1074. AHM 3-12-11-46 ms 1.
1075. Luís de Vasconcelos Lemos Castelo Branco.
1076. AHM 3-12-11-45 ms 2.
1077. José Maria da Costa Freire.
1078. Sebastião Gustavo Pinto.
1079. Died the next day.
1080. Charles Lempriere, 58th Foot, died of his wounds on 12 December 1813.
1081. José Cardoso Sotomaior.
1082. Walter O'Hara.
1083. José Bruno Pereira.
1084. AHM 3-12-11-40 ms 2.
1085. AHM 3-12-11-40 ms 1.
1086. This return is missing a second ensign from the 5th Caçadores, Joaquim José Nogueira, who was also wounded.
1087. António Carlos de Mendonça Furtado.
1088. Died of his wounds.
1089. José Carrasco Guerra.
1090. Francisco Neri Caldeira.
1091. AHM 3-12-11-40 ms 3.
1092. Luís Pedro da Silva.
1093. Francisco Pinto de Almeida.
1094. António Caetano Aragão.
1095. AHM 1-14-256-5 ms 12.
1096. AHM 3-12-11-46 ms 2.
1097. António Carlos Pereira de Macedo.
1098. AHM 3-12-11-45 ms 1.
1099. António Bernardo da Cunha.
1100. Joaquim de Sousa Pinto Cardoso.
1101. Died of his wounds.
1102. AHM 3-12-11-45 ms 3.
1103. Alexander Campbell, 38th Foot.
1104. João António Correia de Castro e Sepúlveda.
1105. António Peito de Carvalho.
1106. Wellington, *Despatches*, vol. 7, p. 214.
1107. Bonloc.
1108. Osserain-Rivareyte.
1109. The Gave Réunis river is a 10km stretch of river created by the joining of the Saison and Gave d'Oloron rivers.
1110. Aire-sur-l'Adour.
1111. Vic-en-Bigorre.
1112. About £45,000.
1113. When Avilez assumed command of the 2nd Brigade he was replaced by Major Bernardo António Zagalo.
1114. In March Lieutenant Colonel Richard Armstrong took command of the regiment. He was transferred to the regiment in September 1813 but had been on leave to recover from a severe wound received at the Pyrenees.

1115. Hardinge was an AQMG on the Portuguese staff.
1116. Lieutenant Colonel Maxwell Grant, wounded at Nive, returned to command the regiment in March.
1117. Lieutenant Colonel Henry Pynn, wounded at the Pyrenees, returned to command in January.
1118. Fearon was killed at Garris. The command devolved to Captain Manuel Vaz Pinto Guedes until Brevet Major Thomas Bunbury was appointed in April.
1119. Sutton was ill during February and was replaced by Major António Joaquim Rosado.
1120. Kilsha was killed at Orthez and was replaced by Major Francisco de Paula Rosado.
1121. Colonel of the 23rd Infantry.
1122. Miller left Portuguese service at the end of January. He was replaced by Lieutenant Colonel José Correia de Melo who was severely wounded at Orthez and Major George Murphy from the staff was temporarily appointed to the command.
1123. Colonel of the 15th Infantry.
1124. At the end of December 1813 Rosado replaced Colonel Michael McCreagh, who returned to Britain owing to poor health.
1125. At the end of January Lieutenant Colonel Campbell, who was wounded at Nive, left for Britain for six weeks' leave. Lieutenant Colonel Francisco Joaquim Carreti, who was promoted to the regiment, took command.
1126. Lieutenant Colonel Dudley Hill returned to the battalion at the beginning of February.
1127. Colonel of the 8th Infantry.
1128. Killed at Toulouse.
1129. Cerqueira replaced Lieutenant Colonel Gustavus Brown, who was severely wounded at Nive. In March he was promoted to the 3rd Caçadores and Major Luís Evaristo de Figueiredo took command.
1130. Colonel of the 19th Infantry.
1131. On 8 March Colonel George Elder took command. He was severely wounded at the storming of Badajoz in 1812 and only rejoined the army in November 1813, but as a convalescent unfit for command. He accompanied the army without a command until he was appointed colonel of the 7th Infantry.
1132. Snodgrass was severely wounded at Orthez and was replaced by Major Manuel Jorge Rodrigues.
1133. Figueiredo replaced Brevet Lieutenant Colonel Manuel Pinto da Silveira, who went on sick leave in December 1813 and did not return. Major Manuel Caetano Teixeira Pinto, the battalion major, was severely wounded at Nive and only returned in February. He held the command briefly because on 11 March Lieutenant Colonel Luís Maria Cerqueira was promoted to the battalion.
1134. When Hill took command of the 1st Brigade Major Walter O'Hara replaced him.
1135. Vidigal replaced Colonel Francisco Homem de Magalhães Pizarro who was captured at Nive. In mid-February he was promoted to colonel and returned to Portugal, being replaced by Major António Pedro de Brito.
1136. At the end of January Williams returned to Britain for two months to recover his health. During this leave he was replaced by Major Peter Adamson.
1137. MacBean was severely wounded at Bayonne on 27 February and was replaced by Lieutenant Colonel Inácio Emídio Aires da Costa.
1138. Ashworth was severely wounded at the Nive.
1139. Amado was in temporary command due to Captain Charles Michell's absence.
1140. AHM 1-14-243-26 ms 7–9. The original is in English.
1141. Bon Loc.
1142. AHM 1-14-243-26 ms 2–4.
1143. AHM 3-12-12-31 ms 1.
1144. Both were from the 10th Caçadores.
1145. AHM 1-14-243-20 ms 1.
1146. Anthony Philip, Baron de Borgh, 60th Foot.
1147. AHM 1-14-256-6 ms 12.
1148. AHM 1-14-256-6 ms 20.
1149. Hélette.
1150. Osserain-Rivareyte.
1151. AHM 1-14-243-23 ms 1–2.
1152. Maxwell Grant.
1153. AHM 1-14-243-21 ms 4–5.
1154. António do Prado Fragoso.
1155. Francisco Félix do Prado.
1156. Francisco António Pamplona Moniz.
1157. Baigts-de-Béarn.
1158. Some sources state that there were four assaults.
1159. AHM 1-14-243-22 ms 18.

1160. He died a few days later.
1161. Promoted to brevet major for his conduct.
1162. Promoted to brevet captain for his conduct.
1163. Promoted to brevet captain for his conduct.
1164. Promoted to ensign in the corps for his conduct.
1165. AHM 1-14-243-22 ms 13.
1166. José Correia de Melo.
1167. John King, brigade major, was promoted to brevet major for his conduct, but retained his post of brigade major.
1168. Promoted to brevet captain for his conduct.
1169. Promoted to brevet captain for his conduct.
1170. Promoted to ensign in the corps for his conduct.
1171. Promoted to brevet major for his conduct.
1172. AHM 1-14-243-22 ms 15–16.
1173. Smith, Harry, *The Autobiography of Sir Harry Smith 1787–1819*. London: Constable, 1999, p. 165.
1174. AHM 1-14-243-22 ms 36–7.
1175. Andrew Barnard, 95th Rifles.
1176. Kenneth Snodgrass.
1177. Avilez was the former commander of the battalion.
1178. AHM 1-14-243-22 ms 35.
1179. AHM 1-14-243-22 ms 12.
1180. AHM 1-14-243-22 ms 21–6. The original is in English.
1181. Promoted to brevet captain for his conduct.
1182. Promoted to ensign in his battalion for his conduct.
1183. António Rodrigues da Silva.
1184. José Bento de Magalhães Fontoura.
1185. Power mis-wrote this and meant regiments not battalions.
1186. William Galbraith.
1187. Thomas Goodrick Peacocke.
1188. Promoted to brevet lieutenant for his conduct.
1189. João Leandro de Macedo Valadas.
1190. Alexander Lesassier.
1191. AHM 1-14-243-22 ms 19.
1192. 21st Chasseurs.
1193. Walter Birmingham, 29th Foot, was a lieutenant colonel in the 21st Infantry but had commanded the 8th Infantry since Nivelle.
1194. Captain John Maher.
1195. Although he was only an ensign in the Portuguese Army, Holman had been promoted to lieutenant in the 52nd Foot on 11 November 1813. This is one of the few examples where a British officer's rank was lower in the Portuguese Army than in the British Army.
1196. José Marques.
1197. AHM 1-14-256-6 ms 14.
1198. AHM 1-14-256-6 ms 15.
1199. AHM 3-12-12-32.
1200. AHM 3-12-12-34.
1201. António de Gouveia Vasconcelos.
1202. Joaquim Maria Lucena de Beltrão.
1203. AHM 1-14-256-6 ms 6.
1204. AHM 1-14-256-6 ms 10.
1205. AHM 3-12-12-31 ms 2.
1206. AHM 3-12-12-35 ms 1.
1207. AHM 1-14-256-6 ms 7.
1208. Aire-sur-l'Adour.
1209. Vic-en-Bigorre.
1210. This river has since been dammed in many places and does not show up on some maps.
1211. Barcelonne-du-Gers.
1212. AHM 1-14-33-3 ms 59–60. The original is in English.
1213. This was an unofficial designation of the 2nd Brigade because the regiments were recruited in Algarve, the southernmost region of Portugal.
1214. General António Hipólito da Costa.
1215. Portuguese Division.

1216. 2nd Regiment commander.
1217. James Hamilton, 2nd Regiment.
1218. Manuel de Brito Mozinho.
1219. Leés river.
1220. Contemporaries referred to this as the Lesser Leéz river.
1221. The 10th Chasseurs was one of the strongest cavalry regiments in Soult's Army with a strength of about 400 men. Despite having so many men, the regiment was without its 3rd and 4th Squadrons, which had been sent to Germany. At Viella it had its 1st and 2nd Squadrons, plus the 9th Company.
1222. Gellemalle.
1223. AHM 1-14-243-26 ms 25. The original is in English.
1224. John Campbell.
1225. AHM 1-14-243-26 ms 11. The original is in English.
1226. Conchez-de-Béarn.
1227. Promoted to brevet captain while retaining his post as adjutant for his conduct.
1228. Pedro Raimundo Franco de Oliveira.
1229. AHM 1-14-243-26 ms 10.
1230. AHM 1-14-243-25 ms 1–4. The original is in English.
1231. João Barbosa de Magalhães.
1232. Leopoldo António Ferreira.
1233. Promoted to brevet lieutenant colonel for his conduct.
1234. António de Azevedo e Cunha.
1235. Thomas Goodrick Peacocke, 9th Infantry.
1236. AHM 3-12-12-28 ms 1.
1237. Major Rodrigo Vito Pereira da Silva.
1238. Thomas Potter, 28th Foot.
1239. Pedro Alexandrino Pereira.
1240. William Hardcastle, 31st Foot.
1241. AHM 3-12-12-29.
1242. AHM 1-14-243-26 ms 10.
1243. AHM 3-12-12-33 ms 2.
1244. Canal du Midi.
1245. L'Hers river.
1246. Oman claims that Captain Michell's Brigade of 9-pounders was with Hill. It was not. Michell had been detached to support Espoletta's 4th Spanish Division in its attack on the other side of the Garonne.
1247. Legend has it that Lillie was not reinstated until the morning of the Battle of Toulouse.
1248. Oman, vol. 7, pp. 556, 560.
1249. According to the British National Army Museum, Lillie was left for dead on the battlefield for 48 hours before he was recovered.
1250. AHM 1-14-243-24 ms 34.
1251. Bartholomew Derenzy, 81st Foot, was promoted to brevet major for his conduct.
1252. Promoted to brevet captain for his conduct.
1253. Promoted to lieutenant in the regiment for his conduct and continued to serve as the adjutant.
1254. AHM 1-14-243-24 ms 12–13.
1255. John Lillie.
1256. Francisco Xavier da Silva Pereira.
1257. Promoted to brevet lieutenant in the battalion for his conduct.
1258. Pack's and Brisbane's Brigades had more casualties.
1259. AHM 1-14-243-24 ms 24–5.
1260. Lieutenant Colonel Beatty, 12th Infantry, took command of the brigade after Douglas was wounded.
1261. Douglas lost his leg and was awarded a £350 pension by the British Government.
1262. Promoted to brevet lieutenant colonel for his conduct.
1263. The 12th Infantry.
1264. Captain John Maher, 8th Infantry, was promoted to brevet major for his conduct and continued to serve as the brigade major.
1265. Ensign Guedes, 12th Infantry, was promoted to brevet lieutenant for his conduct.
1266. Adjutant Sergeant Varejão, also from the 12th Infantry, was promoted to ensign in the 8th Infantry.
1267. AHM 1-14-243-24 ms 21–2. The original is in English.
1268. This is one of the few surviving examples of a report sent to the division commander. It is different from the one sent to the AG.
1269. Varejão's rank was adjutant sergeant.
1270. Benjamin Sullivan, 33rd Foot.
1271. AHM 1-14-243-24 ms 14.

1272. AHM 1-14-243-24 ms 17–18.
1273. AHM 1-14-243-24 ms 19–20.
1274. When providing a screen, a battalion deployed half its troop in open order and kept the other half in formation to reinforce the screen or to protect it when it withdrew.
1275. AHM 1-14-243-24 ms 11.
1276. He probably means the redoubts on Mont Rave, which Oman refers to as the Great Redoubt.
1277. AHM 1-14-243-24 ms 10.
1278. This is probably an overstatement. Only in the final stages of the battle did the Allied troops occupy the redoubts on the northern part of Mont Rave, after the French retired. It is likely that the battalion attacked some redoubts near the canal in the first stages of the battle and remained there.
1279. AHM 1-14-243-24 ms 53.
1280. AHM 1-14-243-24 ms 35.
1281. Arentschild was a lieutenant colonel in the 1st Artillery and an officer in the King's German Artillery.
1282. AHM 1-14-243-24 ms 39–40.
1283. AHM 1-14-243-24 ms 43–5.
1284. José de Ezpeleta, Brigadier Count de Ezpeleta, Spanish Army.
1285. Promoted to brevet captain for his conduct.
1286. Promoted to brevet 1st lieutenant for his conduct.
1287. AHM 3-12-12-26.
1288. James Douglas.
1289. Luís Pinto de Sousa.
1290. Died of his wounds.
1291. AHM 1-14-256-6 ms 4.
1292. AHM 1-14-256-6 ms 2.
1293. AHM 1-14-256-6 ms 3.
1294. Dobbs, John, *Recollections of an Old 52nd Man. Staplehurst: Spellmount, 2000,* pp. 45–6.
1295. AHM 1-14-243-22 ms 6–8. The original is in English.
1296. Thomas St Clair.
1297. Inácio Emidio Aires da Costa.
1298. Manuel Caetano Almada.
1299. Promoted to brevet major for his conduct.
1300. Promoted to brevet lieutenant for his conduct.
1301. Promoted to ensign in the corps for his conduct.
1302. AHM 1-14-243-22 ms 11.
1303. Died from his wounds.
1304. Loustau.
1305. Dobbs, p. 46.
1306. AHM 1-14-256-6 ms 35–6. The original is in English.
1307. AHM 1-14-256-6 ms 32.
1308. The colonel of the 1st Infantry.
1309. AHM 3-12-12-27 ms 2.
1310. Sebastião Luís Soares Barbosa died of his wounds.
1311. AHM 3-12-12-27 ms 1.
1312. John Dobbs, 52nd Foot.
1313. Richard Clearey, 76th Foot.
1314. AHM 1-14-256-6 ms 33.
1315. Commonly known as Francisco da Silveira.
1316. Volunteer irregular troops, serving as light infantry.
1317. Commonly known as Luís do Rego.
1318. His full name was Joaquim da Câmara e Saldanha. Being a nobleman, he was commonly called Dom Joaquim da Câmara.
1319. Ensign in the cavalry was the equivalent to cornet in the British Army.
1320. The Lisbon Police.
1321. The Prince's Royal Volunteers Division.
1322. Light Troops Legion.
1323. His full name was João Teles de Meneses e Melo.
1324. The Army between the Tagus and Mondego.
1325. AHM 1-14-345-2 ms 1.
1326. AHM 1-14-218-1 ms 5.
1327. Equivalent to midshipman.
1328. In this case as a supernumerary colonel because the regiment had already a colonel, James Douglas.
1329. His full name was João Carlos Gregório Domingos Vicente Francisco de Saldanha Oliveira e Daun.
1330. Commonly known as António de Lacerda.

Bibliography

Arquivo Histórico Militar (AHM) (Portuguese Military Archives)

PT- AHM 1-14-174 folders 16 and 17
PT-AHM 1-14-216 folders 19 and 20
PT- AHM 1-14-219 folder 46
PT-AHM 1-14-243 folders 1 to 29
PT-AHM 1-14-256 folders 2 to 6
PT-AHM 3-12-8
PT-AHM 3-12-9
PT-AHM 3-12-11
PT-AHM 3-12-12

British Archives

Brunton, Richard, 'A Narrative of the Services of Lieutenant Colonel Richard Brunton of the 13th Light Dragoons'. National Army Museum, File # 1968-07-461.

Print and Internet Sources

Almanach do ano de 1807. Lisbon: 1807.
Almanach para o ano de 1800. Lisbon: 1800.
Almanach para o ano de MDCCCXX. Lisbon: 1820.
Almanak Militar ou Lista Geral dos Officiaes do Exercito de Portugal. 1813, 1814, 1817, 1818.
Almanak Militar Parte I. Lisbon: 1809.
Amaral, Manuel, *A Luta Política em Portugal nos Finais do Antigo Regime. A Aplicação da Reforma do Exército de 1803 (1805–1823)*, 3 vols. Lisbon: Tribuna da História, 1811.
Amaral, Manuel. 'O Exército Português em Finais do Antigo Regime'. *O Portal da História Online*, 2020.
Anonymous. *Historia da Legião Portugueza em França*. London: Hansard, 1814. (The author was Manuel de Castro Pereira de Mesquita, a former officer of the *Legion Portugaise*.)
Annual Biography and Obituary, vol. XVIII. London: Longman, Rees, Orme, Brown, Green & Longman, 1833.
Barralier, Joseph, 'Adventure at the Battle of Salamanca'. *United Services Magazine*, October, 1851, 274–7.
Beatson, F.C., *Wellington: the Crossing of the Gaves and the Battle of Orthez*. London: Tom Donovan, 1994.
Beresford, Marcus de la Poer, *Marshal William Carr Beresford: The Ablest Man I Have Yet Seen With the Army*. Newbridge: Irish Academic Press, 2017.
Borrego, Nuno Pereira, *As Ordenanças e as Mílicias em Portugal. Subsídios para o seu Estudo*, vol. I. Lisbon: Guarda-Mor, 2006.
Brito, Pedro de, 'British officers in the Portuguese service 1809–1820'. Academia.edu. 2020.
Bromley, Janet and David, *Wellington's Men Remembered: A Register of Memorials to Soldiers who Fought in the Peninsular War and at Waterloo*, 2 vols. Barnsley: Praetorian Press, 2012.
Brown, Steve, *Wellington's Redjackets: the 45th (Nottinghamshire) Regiment on Campaign in South America and the Peninsula, 1805–1814*. Barnsley: Frontline, 2015.
Bunbury, Thomas, *Reminiscences of a Veteran*, 3 vols. Uckfield: Naval & Military Press, 2009.
Burnham, Robert, *Charging against Wellington: Napoleon's Cavalry in the Peninsular War 1807–1814*. Barnsley: Frontline, 2011.
Burnham, Robert and Ron McGuigan, *The British Army against Napoleon: Facts, Lists, and Trivia, 1805–1815*. Barnsley: Frontline, 2010.
Cameron, Sir John, *The Memoirs and Letters of Colonel Sir John Cameron 9th Foot 1809–13*. Godmanchester: Ken Trotman, 2013.

Campbell, James, *A British Army, as It Was, – Is – and Ought to Be*. London: T&W Boone, 1840.

Centeno, João Torres, 'Portuguese Army Ranks and their British Equivalents'. *The Napoleon Series Online*, 2020.

Centeno, João Torres, *O Exército Português na Guerra Peninsular. Do Rossilhão ao fim da Segunda Invasão Francesa*. Lisbon: Prefácio, 2008.

Centeno, João Torres, *O Exército Aliado Anglo-Português na Guerra Peninsular – As Divisões do Exército Anglo-Português e as Brigadas Independentes Portuguesas*. Lisbon: Tribuna da História, 2011.

Chaby, Cláudio de, *Excerptos Historicos e Collecção de Documentos relativos à Guerra denominada da Peninsula e às anteriores de 1801, e do Rossillon e Cataluña*, 6 vols. Lisbon: Imprensa Nacional, 1863–1882.

Challis, Lionel, 'British Officers Serving in the Portuguese Army, 1809–1814'. *Journal of the Society for Army Historical Research*, vol. 27, No. 110 (Summer, 1949), 50–60.

Challis, Lionel, 'The Peninsular Roll Call'. *The Napoleon Series Online*, 2020.

Chartrand, René, *The Portuguese Army of the Napoleonic Wars*, 3 vols. Oxford: Osprey, 2000–2001.

Close, Edward C., *The Diary of E.C. Close*. Mittagong: Highland House, 2015.

Cobbett's Political Register. Various dates.

Coelho, Sergio Veludo, *Os Arsenais Reais de Lisboa e Porto, 1800–1814*. PhD thesis submitted to the department of Ciencias da Educação e Património of the Universidade Portucalense, 2009.

Cole, Lowry, *Memoirs of Sir Lowry Cole*, Maud Cole (ed.). Cambridge: Ken Trotman, 2003.

Collecção das Ordens do Dia, 1809–1828.

Collecção de Papeis Oficiaes da Junta Provisional do Governo Supremo (...). Oporto: 1808.

Collins, Bruce, *Wellington and The Siege of San Sebastian 1813*. Barnsley: Pen & Sword, 2017.

Colville, John, *The Portrait of a General: a Chronicle of the Napoleonic Wars*. Salisbury: Michael Russell, 1980.

Cook, John, *A True Soldier Gentleman: the Memoirs of Lt. John Cooke 1791–1813*. Swanage: Shinglepicker, 2000.

Costa, António José Pereira da (ed.), *Generais do Exército Português – Quatro Séculos de História*. Vol. 2: *Das Invasões Francesas à queda da Monarquia (1807–1910)*, Book 1 (1807–1864). Lisbon: Biblioteca do Exército, 2004.

Costa, Dom Antonio da, *Historia do Marechal Saldanha*, 2 vols. Lisbon: Imprensa Nacional. 1879.

Costa, Fernando Dores, 'Army Size, Military Recruitment and Financing in Portugal during the Period of the Peninsular War 1808–1811'. *e-Journal of Portuguese History*, vol. 6, no. 2. Oporto: 2008.

Crowe, Charles, *An Eloquent Soldier: the Peninsular War Journals of Lieutenant Charles Crowe of the Inniskillings 1812–1814*, Gareth Glover (ed.). London: Frontline, 2011.

De La Fuente, Francisco, *Dom Miguel Pereira Forjaz; His Early Career and Role in the Mobilization of the Portuguese Army and Defense of Portugal during the Peninsular War, 1807–1814*. Lisbon: Tribuna da História, 2011.

Divall, Carole, *Wellington's Worst Scrap. The Burgos Campaign 1812*. Barnsley: Pen & Sword, 2012.

Doyle, Arthur, *A Hundred Years of Conflict: Being some Records of the Services of Six Generals of the Doyle Family 1756–1856*. London: Longmans & Green, 1911.

D'Urban, Maj.-Gen. Sir Benjamin, *The Peninsular Journal, 1808–1817*, ed. I.J. Rousseau. London: Greenhill Books, 1988.

Esdaile, Charles, *The Peninsular War. A New History*. Basingstoke: Palgrave MacMillan, 2003.

Estrela, Paulo J., *Ordens e Condecorações Portuguesas: 1793–1824*. Lisbon: Tribuna da História, 2009.

'Field Officer's Gold Medal Awarded to Colonel G.H. Zulke'. *Catalog of Orders, Decorations, Medals and Militaria*. London: Nimrod Dix, 2012.

Fortescue, John, *A History of the British Army*, 13 vols. Naval & Military Press, 2004.

Gazeta de Lisboa, 1808–1824.

General Regulations and Orders for the Army. London: Adjutant General's Office, 1811.

Gil, Coronel Ferreira, *A Infantaria Portuguêsa na Guerra da Peninsula*, 2 vols. Lisbon: Tipografia da Cooperativa Militar, 1912.

Glover, Michael, *The Peninsular War 1807–1814. A Concise Military History*. London: David & Charles, 1974.

Gray, Anthony, *The French Invasions of Portugal 1807–1811: Rebellion, Reaction and Resistance*. MA by Research submitted to the Department of History of the University of York, 2011.

Griffith, Robert, *Riflemen: the History of the 5th Battalion 60th (Royal American) Regiment 1797–1818*. Warwick: Helion, 2019.

Halliday, Andrew, *The Present State of Portugal and the Portuguese Army*. Edinburgh: 1812.

Hayes, Richard, 'Biographical Dictionary of Irishmen in France'. *Studies: Irish Quarterly Review*. Publishers Studies, 1946, p. 252.

Haythornthwaite, Philip J., *The Armies of Wellington*. Brockhampton Press, 1998.

Hennell, George, *A Gentleman Volunteer: The Letters of George Hennell from the Peninsular War 1812–1813*, ed. Michael Glover. London: Heinemann, 1979.

Henriques, Mendo Castro. Salamanca - 1812. Companheiros de Honra. Lisbon: Prefácio. 2002.

Henriques, Mendo Castro, *Vitória e Pirinéus, 1813. O Exército Português na Libertação de Espanha*. Lisbon: Tribuna da História, 2008.

Henriques, Mendo Castro, *A Invasão de França, 1813–1815. O Exército Anglo-Português na Derrota de Napoleão. O Congresso de Viena e Waterloo ou Montevideu*. Lisbon: Príncipia Editora, 2018.

Jones, John, *Journal of the Sieges Carried on by the Army under the Duke of Wellington in Spain, between the Years 1811 & 1814*, 3 vols. Cambridge: Ken Trotman, 1998 (3rd edn).

Jourdain, H.F.N., *The Connaught Rangers*, 3 vols. London: Royal United Service Institution, 1924.

Lipscome, Nick, 'Wellington's Gunner in the Peninsula: Lieutenant Colonel Alexander Dickson'. *Nick Lipscombe: Historian, Author & Tour Guide*. Online, 2 September 2020.

Lista dos Officiaes de Exercito em 1811 de Ordem da Sua Alteza Real o Principe Regente. Lisbon: Impressao Regia, 1811.

London Gazette. Various dates.

MacArthur, Roderick, 'British Army Establishment during the Napoleonic Wars'. *Journal of the Society for Army Historical Research*, vol. 87, no. 350 (Summer 2009), 150–72.

MacArthur, Roderick, 'British Army Establishment during the Napoleonic Wars (Part 2): Cavalry, Artillery, Engineers and Supporting Units'. *Journal of the Society for Army Historical Research, vol. 87, no. 352* (Winter 2009), 331–56.

Mainer, George, 'O'Hara, Walter'. *Dictionary of Canadian Biography*. Online, November 2020.

'Major Benjamin Sullivan'. *Free Settler or Felon*. Online, 2 September 2020.

Marques, Fernando Pereira, *Exército e Sociedade em Portugal no Declínio do Antigo Regime e Advento do Liberalismo*. Lisbon: Publicações Alfa, 1989.

Martelo, David, *Os Caçadores. Os galos de combate do exército de Wellington*. Lisbon: Tribuna da História, 2007.

McGuigan, Ron, 'EOPS Officers in the Portuguese Army'. Unpublished paper.

McGuigan, Ron and Burnham, Robert, *Wellington's Brigade Commanders. Peninsula and Waterloo*. Barnsley: Pen & Sword, 2017.

Military History of Perthshire: 1660–1902, ed. Marchioness of Tullibardine. Edinburgh: William Brown, 1908.

Muir, Rory, *Salamanca 1812*. New Haven: Yale, 2001.

Muir, Rory et al., *Inside Wellington's Peninsular Army: 1808–1814*. Barnsley: Pen & Sword, 2006.

Myatt, Frederick, *British Sieges of the Peninsular War*. Staplehurst: Spellmount, 1995.

Naval and Military Magazine. Various dates.

Neves, José Acúrsio das, *Historia Geral da Invasão dos Franceses em Portugal e da Restauração deste Reino*. 5 vols. Lisbon: 1810–1811.

Noticias biographicas de Francisco Homem de Magalhães Pizarro (...) pelos seus Ajudantes de Ordens. Rio de Janeiro: Impressão Régia, 1819.

Nogueira, Ricardo Raimundo, *Memórias Políticas. Memória das Coisas Mais Notáveis Que Se Trataram nas Conferências do Governo (1810–1820)* , ed. Ana Cristina Araújo. Coimbra: Imprensa da Universidade de Coimbra, 2012.

Nunes, J. Lucio, 'As Brigadas da Cavalaria Portuguesa na Guerra Peninsular'. *Revista Ocidente*, 1954.

O Exército Português e as Comemorações dos 200 Anos da Guerra Peninsular, coord. Adelino Matos Coelho and Carlos Alberto Fonseca, 3 vols. Lisbon: Tribuna da História, 2008–2011.

Oman, Charles, *History of the Peninsular War*, 7 vols. New York: AMS, 1980.

Oman, Charles, *Wellington's Army, 1809–1814*. London: Greenhill, 1986.

O Porto e As Invasões Francesas 1809–2009, coord. Prof. Valente de Oliveira, 4 vols. Porto: Público e Câmara Municipal do Porto, 2009.

Pedreira, Jorge and Costa, Fernando Dores, *D. João VI*. Lisbon: Círculo dos Leitores, 2006.

Pereira, José Rodrigues, *Campanhas Navais 1793–1807. Vol. I: A Armada e a Europa. A Marinha Portuguesa na Época de Napoleão*. Lisbon: Tribuna da História, 2005.

Pringle, William, 'Unpublished letter from Major General William Pringle to Major General John Oswald dated 27 October 1812'. *The Waterloo Association Online*, 26 July 2020.

Quinta-Nova, Jorge, 'No Real Serviço'. *Blog about the 18th and 19th Century Portuguese Army*. Available at: https://aorealservico.blogspot.com/. 2020.

Quinta-Nova, Jorge, 'Os Voluntários Reaes'. *Blog about the Prince's and after King's Royal Volunteers Division*. Available at: https://dvr18151823.blogspot.com/ . 2020.

Quinta-Nova, Jorge, 'The Life and Times of Carlos Frederico Lecor' *Blog about General Lecor*. Available at: http://lecor.blogspot.com/ . 2020.

Regulamento Provisional do Real Corpo de Engenheiros. Lisbon: 1812.

Robinson, H.B., *Memoirs of Lieutenant General Sir Thomas Picton, G.B.C. &c Including His Correspondence, from Originals in Possession of His Family*, 2 vols. London: Richard Bentley, 1835.

Rose, George Maclean (ed.). *A Cyclopedia of Canadian Biography: being Chiefly Men of the Time*. Toronto: Rose Publishing, 1886.

The Royal Military Calendar, 5 vols. London: 1820,

Sepúlveda, Cristóvão Aires de Magalhães, *Historia da Cavallaria Portugueza*, 4 vols. Lisbon: Imprensa Nacional, 1889–1894.

Sepúlveda, Cristóvão Aires de Magalhães, *Historia Organica e Politica do Exercito Portuguez*, 17 vols. Lisbon and Coimbra: Imprensa Nacional and Imprensa da Universidade, 1896–1932.

Silva, António Delgado, *Collecção da Legislação Portugueza (...) 1763 a 1774*. Lisbon: 1826.

Silva, António Delgado, *Collecção da Legislação Portugueza (...) 1802 a 1810*. Lisbon: 1826.

Silva, António Delgado, *Collecção da Legislação Portugueza (...) 1811 a 1820*. Lisbon: 1826.

Smith, Harry, *The Autobiography of Sir Harry Smith 1787–1819*. London: Constable, 1999.

Soriano, Simão José da Luz, *Historia da Guerra Civil e do Estabelecimento do Governo Parlamentar em Portugal comprehendendo a historia diplomatica, militar e politica deste reino desde 1777 até 1834*, 19 vols. Lisbon: Imprensa Nacional, 1866–1809.

Steevens, Charles, *With the 'Old & Bold' 1795 to 1818: the Reminiscences of an Officer of H.M. 20th Regiment During the Napoleonic Wars*. Leonaur, 2010.

Stephen, Leslie and Sidney Lee, *Dictionary of National Biography*, 23 vols. Oxford: Oxford University, 1958–1960.

Teixeira Botelho, José, *Novos Subsídios para a História da Artilharia Portuguesa*. Lisbon: Publicações da Comissão de História Militar, 1944.

Tottenham, F.St.L., 'Captain Synge's Experiences at Salamanca'. *The Nineteenth Century and After*, vol. LXXII, July–December 1912, 54–68.

Vichness, Samuel E., *Marshal of Portugal: The Military Career of William Carr Beresford, 1785–1814*. A dissertation submitted to the Department of History of the Florida State University, 1976.

Warre, William, *Letters from the Peninsula 1808–1812*, ed. Revd Edmond Warre. London: John Murray, 1909.

Wellington, Duke of, *The Dispatches of Field Marshal the Duke of Wellington, During his Various Campaigns in India, Denmark, Portugal, Spain, the Low Countries, and France, from 1799 to 1818*, ed. Lt-Col. John Gurwood. London: John Murray, 1834–9. [Referenced as 'Wellington, *Despatches*']

—. *Despatches, Correspondence, and Memoranda of Field Marshal Arthur, Duke of Wellington, K.G*, edited by his son, the Duke of Wellington, 'in continuation of the former series'. London: J. Murray, 1857–1880.

—. *Dispatches of Field Marshal the Duke of Wellington, During his Various Campaigns in India, Denmark, Portugal, Spain, the Low Countries, and France*, ed. Lt-Col. John Gurwood. London: Parker, Furnivall & Parker, 1844–1847.

—. *Supplementary Dispatches, Correspondence, and Memoranda of Field Marshal Arthur Duke of Wellington, KG*, ed. the 2nd Duke of Wellington. London: John Murray, 1860–1871. [Referenced as 'Wellington, *Supplementary Despatches*']

—. *Selections From the General Orders of Field Marshal Arthur Duke of Wellington, During his Various Campaigns. Compiled by Colonel Gurwood*. London: Parker, Furnivall & Parker/Military Library, Whitehall, 1847.

Index

The index is divided into three sections: Battles and Campaigns, Units, and People

Portuguese Unit Index

Names

Note: Due to the large number of times that their names appear throughout the book, we have not included Wellington, Marshal Beresford or Manuel de Brito Mozinho in the index. Likewise, we have not included the Portuguese names mentioned in the reports and casualty returns unless they were also a report writer.